THE ENCYCLOPEDIA OF
WARFARE

THE ENCYCLOPEDIA OF
WARFARE

General Editor: Robin Cross

GREENWICH
EDITIONS

A QUANTUM BOOK

This edition printed in 2005 by
GREENWICH EDITIONS
The Chrysalis Building
Bramley Road, London W10 6SP

An imprint of Chrysalis Books Group plc

ISBN 0-86288-799-2

QUMWAR

This book was produced by
Quantum Books Ltd
6 Blundell Street
London N7 9BH

Printed in Singapore by
Star Standard Industries (Pte) Ltd

CONTENTS

INTRODUCTION

LOOKING BACK at the story of warfare from the vantage point of the 21st century, it is all too easy for even the most conscientious military historian to draw obvious conclusions and slip into generalities. Today, for instance, the popular view is that both Napoleon and Hitler made the same fatal error of embarking on all-out campaigns to defeat Russia. Napoleon was defeated as much by a primitive and over-extended communication and supply system as by the military muscle of the Tsarist armies. Hitler's failure was due to a mixture of military amateurishness, exemplified by his own confused orders, and a grotesque over-estimation of the power of the German armed forces to defeat their Soviet opponents.

Yet at the time, many well-informed observers did not share these views. Russia, after all, had made peace with Napoleon before, and the impressionable young Tsar Alexander I had dangled before him the prospect of a grand alliance in which French and Russian troops would march side by side to carve out an eastern empire at the expense of the British in India. As far as Hitler's invasion of the USSR was concerned, the informed view of the British War Office at the start of the campaign was that Soviet resistance would last for a matter of weeks, or at the most a few months. The power of hindsight is a potent one, but the duty of the modern chronicler is – or should be – to see "how it really was", as the German historian Ranke put it.

If historians can be misled, how much more difficult must it have been for the men on the battlefield to gain a distinct, comprehensive view of what they were fighting for and what they were actually achieving. Frequently it is only the civilian observers, tucked up safely at home or well behind the lines, who claim to have a clear vision. It is they who can visualize a grand strategy, and see war in terms of glorious victories or gallant defeats.

Thomas Hardy, in *The Dynasts,* wrote that war makes "rattling good history", but the Duke of Wellington, one of the greatest commanders of all time, grimly commented that "next to a battle lost, there is nothing so melancholy as a battle won". Most military men would agree with Napoleon's reply to a question about how he went about planning a battle: "Well, you engage your opponent and then you see!"

What is clear, as this book demonstrates, is that man is on the whole a pugnacious animal and certainly has never been a pacifist by nature. Throughout human history there has rarely been a moment of total peace. Somewhere, somehow, and at some time or other, some form of conflict is taking place, whether on a small or a large scale. Political philosophers, sociologists and psychologists have long debated whether war is a weakness of human nature or an inevitable consequence of the emergence of organized societies and civilizations.

If the first premise is true – if, in common with Thomas Hobbes, we take the grim view that man's life is inevitably "nasty, brutish and short" – then it follows that the art and practice of war, however sophisticated it has become, is merely camouflage for an innate barbarism. According to the military historian David Chandler, it is only by "an intensive and long process of education for peace" that this might be eradicated. He suggests that if the second theory is correct, war can be eventually eliminated, just like a disease.

What such arguments ignore is the clear link between war and historical change and evolution. Though some would claim that economic considerations are equally important, it is undeniable that the rise and the fall of the world's great empires have always been linked to military success and failure. Without falling into the trap of slavishly following the "Cleopatra's nose" theory of history (the French philosopher Blaise Pascal seriously argued that the entire history of the world would have been changed, if Cleopatra's nose had been half an inch shorter), the fact remains that it is possible to identify battles, sometimes fought in the space of a few brief hours, as true historical turning-points. What would the future of America have been, for instance, had the Confederacy triumphed at Gettysburg? What if the Japanese had won the battle of Midway? What would have been the consequences, not just for medieval Britain but for Europe as a whole, had Harold and his Saxons driven Duke William and his invading Normans into the sea at Hastings? It is this type of speculation that instantly appeals to the romantic in all of us, young and old.

Of course, it goes without saying that war is basically wrong. There is no such thing as a totally "just" war; whatever the justifications produced for embarking on war it is always as much motivated by national self-interest as by ideals. Britain did not go to war in 1914 solely to honour its treaty obligations to "gallant little Belgium"; an equal consideration was that of preserving the European balance of power and Britain's own world position. The same might be said of the USA in 1917. Though the *causus belli* was undoubtedly Germany's decision to resume unrestricted submarine warfare, the injudicious telegram sent by the German Foreign Minister Artur Zimmermann, with its offer of military support to Mexico. was obviously an additional factor, as were the billions tied up in the financing of the Allied war effort.

When Clausewitz wrote that "war is the continuation of politics by other means", he was emphasizing a truism that is as accurate today as it ever was. Bismarck put it even more brutally and succinctly, saying that most states at some stage or another will almost inevitably adopt a policy of "blood and iron" if they feel their national interests or ambitions are at stake.

What must be remembered also is that for much of human history – in fact up to the present century – wars have on the whole been fought by relatively small numbers, though obviously – particularly in the ancient world – defeat could bring about political consequences that affected whole nations or states.

The actual battles were fought by levies of peasants who had no voice or choice in the matter, officered by professionals largely drawn from the aristocracy. Even though in 1792 Revolutionary France raised a citizen-army of over 600,000 men when faced with a hostile Europe, the long years of war that followed left national ways of life relatively untouched, even with the later introduction of the levee-en-masse and conscription. Napoleon might have sought to impose his Continental System on his European allies and vassals, but it was still possible for, say, a Beethoven or a young Schubert to live in Hapsburg Vienna relatively unscathed.

The American Civil War saw the beginning of a wholesale change, and the siege of Paris in 1870–1 also pointed the way to the future. It was not until the advent of airpower, however, that civilians as well as soldiers found themselves well and truly in the firing line. In both world wars, modern technology was married to national ambitions to broaden the scope and cost of conflict to a point where whole populations were involved.

Even so, developments in warfare can be seen as having a positive side. The rate of technological advance witnessed in the last 100 years would have been much slower without the stimulus of the two world conflicts. For example, the Allied blockade of imperial Germany between 1914 and 1918 led German chemists to pioneer the development of a whole range of synthetics, which have gone on to alter our entire way of life and many key inventions ranging from radar to penicillin and other antibiotics were also the children of war. War has its uses, though such benefits as it has indirectly conferred can certainly never make up for its destructive cost.

1

THE FIRST MILITARY EMPIRES

BELLICOSITY IS AS OLD as mankind, but the origins of warfare are shrouded in the darkness of prehistory. Nevertheless, the colossal circular tower at the Neolithic settlement of Jericho demonstrates that warfare in the ancient Near East is virtually as old as urban life and the practice of agriculture. Indeed, it was the material wealth of such settlements – Jericho itself dominated an oasis – which helped promote human strife.

The first kingdoms of the ancient Near East flourished early in the third millenium BC in southern Mesopotamia or Sumer. Politically, Sumer was divided into several petty, warring temple-states, consisting of a capital city ringed by outlying towns and villages and surrounded by rich, irrigated, agricultural land and uncultivated pasturage. Endemic squabbles over watercourses and hinterland were the norm.

The turning point came with the rise of Sargon of Akkad, the foremost figure of his age. One-time cupbearer of Ur-Zababa, king of Kish, Sargon survived his master's overthrow by his rival, the king of Uruk and overlord of southern Sumer, Lugalzaggisi, and eventually (c.2316BC) liberated Kish and went on to bring the whole of Sumer under his sole rule.

In order to suppress the fiercely independent traditions of the conquered temple-states, Sargon replaced their rulers with his own governors, invariably Akkadians and members of his own clan. But his imperialistic designs did not terminate at Sumer's frontiers. Following Sumer's conquest, he campaigned in Iran against a confederation of four kings headed by the ruler of Awan, a powerful state centred on the southern Zagros mountains, and established his own governors in the subjugated territories. Campaigns to the north-west resulted in the crushing of the Syrian states of Mari, Iarmuti, Ibla and Tutul, and, more importantly, the control of the cedar forests and silver mines of the Lebanon. Akkad became an empire that recognized no boundaries of language, religion or geography, for Sargon's writ ran, according to one inscription, "from the Lower Sea [the Gulf] to the Upper Sea [the Mediterranean]".

1481 BC

CAMPAIGN OF THUTMOSE III

DATE c.1481BC

OBJECT Campaign to crush revolt in Syria and northern Palestine, led by Qadesh, a city commanding upper Orontes.

DESCRIPTION The king of Qadesh, leading a coalition of Canaanite and Syrian princes, moved south to bar Thutmose's advance at Megiddo, between Palestine's coastal plain and the Jezreel valley. Thutmose's response was dynamic: in nine days, averaging 16 miles a day, his army reached Gaza; three days later he held a council of war in Yehen. Three routes offered access to the coalition's position: a direct route via the Aruna defile, a northern alternative through Djefti and a southern alternative to Ta'anach. Although Egyptian commanders cautiously urged avoidance of the first option since it meant moving in column-of-march against an enemy in line of battle, Thutmose decided on the first option, establishing a camp along Qina brook.

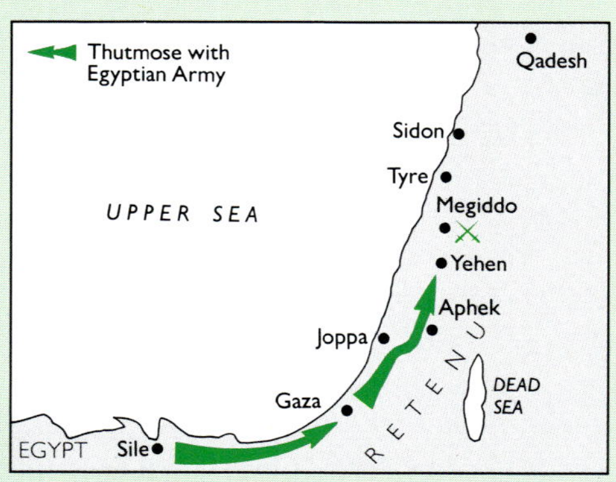

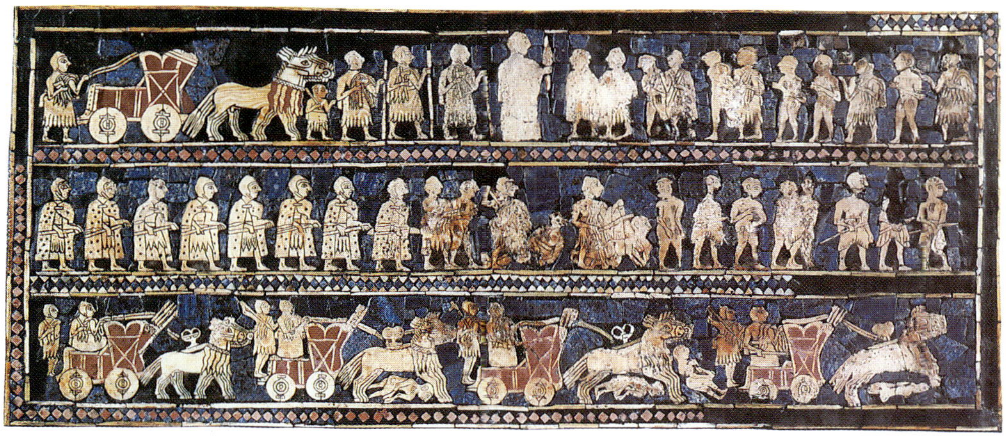

"The Standard of Ur" c.2500BC, depicting Sumerian battle-cars and spearmen. Note the quiver and javelins on the battle-cars, and their draught consisting of four asses. The spearmen wear copper helmets and long ox-hide capes studded with copper discs.

Sargon's instrument for controlling this polyglot empire was a large standing army. In one inscription he boasts that no less than 5,400 soldiers ate daily in his palace, and these household retainers undoubtedly formed the professional core of his army. During times of war the king would levy both royal and temporal feoffees for military service and this feudatory militia provided the main battle-line of close-order spearmen and shield-bearers. Alongside these were ranged the four-wheeled "battle-cars", two-man vehicles whose primary function was to charge, frighten the enemy and engage him at medium range with javelins, then close in with the spear.

But it is the nature of empires to rise and fall and Akkad was no exception. The far-flung empire of Sargon jolted through a multitude of internal revolts, finally to collapse with the sacking of Kish (c.2154BC).

THE EGYPTIAN NEW KINGDOM

"I will take over the chariotry," trumpets the early 16th-century BC document recording the boast of the Theban pharaoh, Kamose, as he set out to reunite Egypt and break the rule of the Hyksos king, Apophis, though it was left to his brother and founder of the 18th Dynasty, Ahmose, to complete the expulsion of the Hyksos and thus launch the Egyptian New Kingdom. Nevertheless, Kamose was shrewd enough to see the potential advantages of incorporating the chariot into the Egyptian armoury. Introduced into Egypt by the Hyksos, it had played an important part in their conquest of the country by the mid-17th century BC. Now, as a result of the successful struggle against the Hyksos, Ahmose and his successors, particularly Thutmose III and Rameses II, were able to forge a "New Model Army" which was to spearhead an imperial expansion into Palestine, Syria and Nubia.

1481 BC

MEGIDDO

DATE c.1481BC

DESCRIPTION The king of Qadesh had been wrong-footed by Thutmose's boldness. The coalition's forces lay north-west of Megiddo and to the southeast near Ta'anach. At dawn Thutmose unleashed his attack. He had divided his army into three "battles", one to attack defenders in the north, another in the south, and the main "battle", under himself, to strike at Canaanite and Syrian chariotry outside Megiddo. In the ensuing engagement, Egyptians swept away the coalition's forces, pursuing them to the city walls. Fugitives abandoned their chariots in order to be hauled up the walls. 924 chariots were captured, but Thutmose failed to storm Megiddo since his troops had stopped to loot the enemy camp.

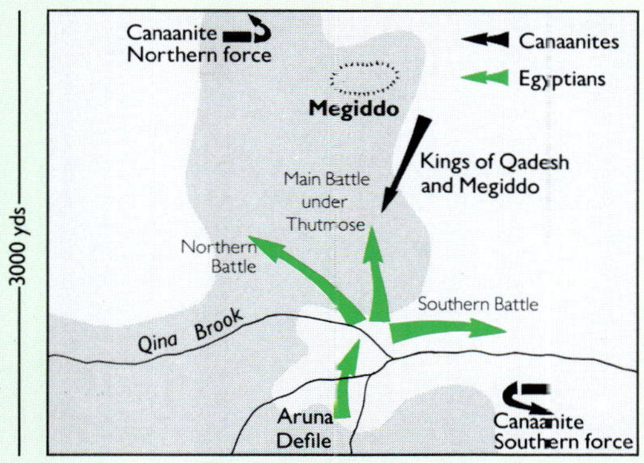

RESULT Megiddo eventually fell after seven months.

Early New Kingdom close-combat infantry, XVIII Dynasty, c. early 15th century BC. The spearmen carry wooden shields covered in hide, but do not appear to benefit from armour at this date – apart from the "striped headcloth" which in truth was a quilted textile helmet suited for a hot climate.

Thutmose III (c.1504–1450BC) was a compulsive imperialist who extended the Egyptian empire to its furthest limits. For 20 years he led campaigns into Asia, some involving bitter fighting, others mere parades of strength, against the Mitanni – Indo-European warriors who had subjugated northern Syria – and their Canaanite vassals who ruled the mercantile city-states of Syria-Palestine. His martial endeavours netted him the strongholds of Megiddo (see page 9), Qadesh (see below) and Carchemish, thus setting the Taurus mountains and the River Euphrates as the northern boundary of his empire, while his generals extended the conquest of Nubia up to the 5th Cataract of the Nile. Eventually his empire stretched 1,500 miles from north to south.

The northern domains did not long remain quiescent. The Hittites, a more formidable race of Indo-Europeans, descended from their Anatolian fastness and rapidly devoured the decaying Mitannian empire. By the mid 14th century BC, Hittite and Egyptian were in head-on conflict, and it was left to the self-assertive Rameses II (c.1304–1237BC) to bring this to a climax. After a series of hard-fought campaigns across Syria, which seriously weakened both sides, a pact was signed (c.1283BC) defining the common border as the Orontes, south of Qadesh.

The pharaonic army at this time consisted of the royal guard or "Pharoah's Braves" and four autonomous divisions which marched under the divine protection of the patron-deity of the town where the unit was quartered: Amon of Thebes, Re of Heliopolis, Ptah of Memphis and Seth of Pi-Rameses. Egyptians were conscripted as either "shooters" or "strong-arm boys". Archers drew up in close-order and supported the close-combat troops who advanced at a rapid pace, shields slung over backs, both hands free to wield side-arm and spear. If compromised by missiles, shields would be swung round and the pace slackened. Chariotry was employed to support and protect the infantry as well as adding long-range mobility to operations.

In contrast, Hittite tactics were based on the offensive use of chariots with infantry in support. A feudal military aristocracy formed the chariotry, fiefs being held from the king with an obligation to serve. Infantry included native Hittites and imperial levies, predominantly armed with spear, dagger and shield, though Syrians were best suited for skirmishing, being equipped with javelins, hurling-sticks and bows.

About 1200BC the ancient Near East was turned topsy-turvy. Egypt was suffering from repeated Libyan incursions and with these came the first wave of "Sea Peoples", a rag-bag of predatory wanderers. Egyptian records are blunt: "all at once nations were moving and scattered by war. No land stood before their arms ... they were wasted." The Hittites attempted to stem the onslaught but were overrun, as were the Levantine city-states. But Egypt itself survived, thanks to the efforts of Rameses III, though its empire was extinct.

1296 BC

QADESH CAMPAIGN

DATE c.1296BC

OBJECT The question at issue between the Hittites and Egypt was who was to dominate Syria.

NUMBERS Muwatallis, the king of the Hittites, moved south from Asia Minor with his imperial army numbering 17,000. Rameses II commanded 20,000, divided into four divisions, each composed of sub-units of archers, spearmen and chariots.

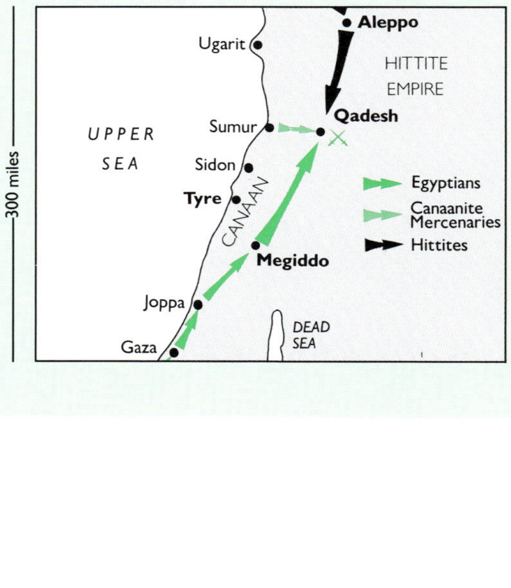

DESCRIPTION Rameses marched northward via a coastal route for 30 days – covering an average of 32 miles a day – to arrive 38 miles south of Qadesh at Shabtuna, where there was a ford across the Orontes. After spending the night encamped at Shabtuna, Rameses crossed the ford, leading his Amon division. Here he was met by Hittite agents, pretending to be deserting Shessu-bedouin, who misled him into believing Muwatallis was at Aleppo, whereas the Hittite army really lay outside

RISE AND FALL OF THE ASSYRIAN EMPIRE

On his death-bed, Shalmaneser III of Assyria (859–824BC) left behind a kingdom in decline. Despite their military prowess, the Assyrians had not been able to forge a viable empire out of their conquests, only a sphere of influence within which they ruled supreme, and their far-flung obligations had begun to stretch their empire's limited capabilities – in his 35-year reign Shalmaneser had to levy his "feudal" army at least 31 times. Civil war and rebellion took hold as a succession of weak kings followed, each unable to maintain stability and thus preserve Assyria's suzerainty over the Fertile Crescent.

Out of chaos came order, and Assyria's fortunes rose like a phoenix from the ashes when, in 745BC, a revolt in Nimrud elevated a certain general Pulu to the throne. Pulu, assuming the name of Tiglath-Pileser III (745–727BC), proceeded to remodel the government of Assyria in order to strengthen the central authority and weld its conquests into an empire. Assyria itself was reorganized into smaller provinces, while vassal states were annexed and transformed into further provinces. Each was governed by a state-appointed governor and an efficient courier system was established, enabling the king to maintain an iron grip throughout his realm.

"Sea People", XX Dynasty, c. early 12th century BC. At the land battle on Egypt's eastern frontier c. 1189BC, these warriors were to be found both arrayed against and in the ranks of Rameses III's army. They have the characteristic horned helmet, round buckles and long two-edged sword of the Shardana.

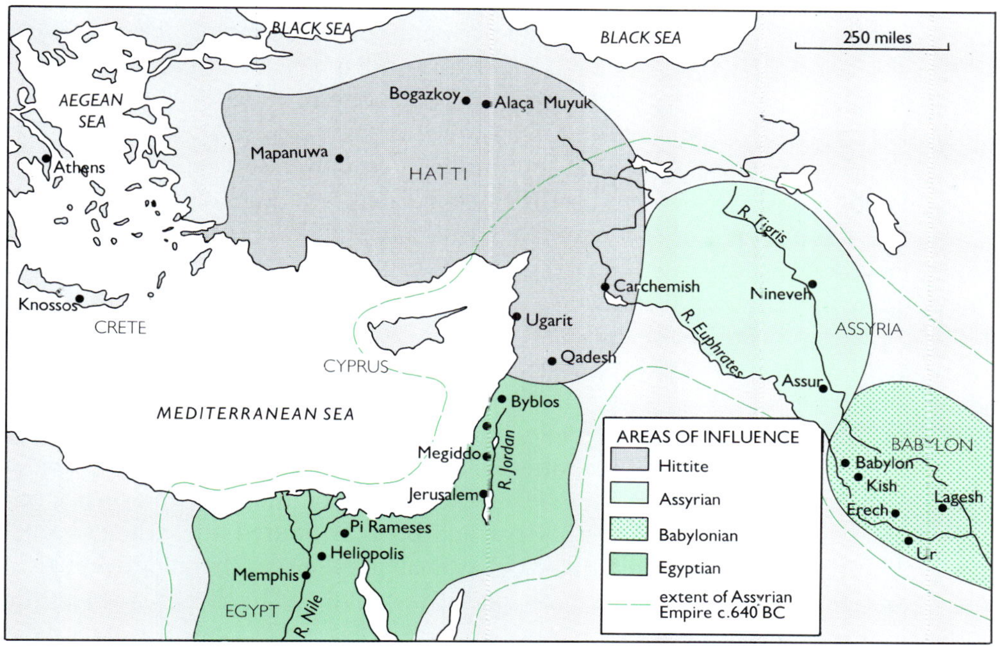

Map showing areas of influence in the Ancient Near East, c. 13th century BC.

1296 BC

Qadesh. Deceived, Rameses rushed ahead with his retinue to establish a camp north-west of Qadesh, hoping to invest the city before the Hittites arrived, while his army followed in a column of march several miles long. The Battle of Qadesh followed.

BATTLE OF QADESH

DATE C.1296BC

DESCRIPTION While Rameses awaited his army, two prisoners revealed that the enemy army was nearby; Rameses was trapped. As Re division marched northwards, Muwatallis launched 2,500 chariots into its flank; that division broke in panic, followed by Amon. Hittites encircled the camp but, leading his retinue, Rameses counter-atttacked, checking the ▸

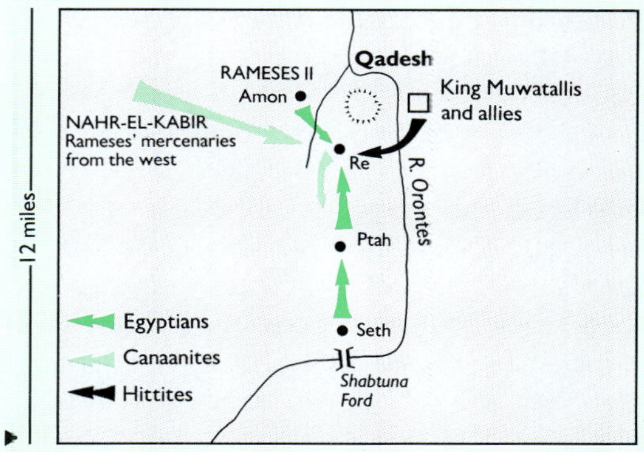

(Above) Assyrian slingers at the siege of Lachish, part of Sennacherib's campaign in Palestine. Lachish fell to the Assyrians in 701 BC; this depiction is taken from Sennacherib's palace at Nineveh. (Above centre) Assyrian archers, Ashurnasirpal II's army, early 9th century BC. They wear plain woollen tunics with wrap-around kilts and are armed with composite bows. Assyrians also levied archers from the subject Aramaean states. (Above right) Assyrian unarmoured spearmen, Ashurbanipal's army, mid-7th century BC. Helmets are of iron inlaid with bronze and have integral cheek-pieces and crest-holders. The shields are reed-work versions of the new large body-shield armoured spearmen were equipped with.

A full-time army was also created, reinforced in times of war by a well-organized call-up of men obliged to render military service. This imperial war machine was made up of four components: the "household troops" who protected the royal family – they could include mercenaries; the "king's standing army", a large force composed of regular professional soldiers – chariotry, cavalry, spearmen, shield-bearers, archers and slingers – maintained by the state and including the better soldiery from subjugated nations (elements of this force garrisoned the empire); the "king's men", holders of land-grants from the king and thus duty-bound to serve in times of war; and the "general levy", a levy *en masse* of imperial subjects in times of national crisis.

The paramount arm of the Assyrian army was the chariotry. The large four-horsed chariot was primarily employed in a "shock-charge" capacity to break the enemy line either through fear or collision. Initially, the crew had consisted of three, but by the seventh century BC the standard crew comprised four heavily-armoured men – a driver, archer and two spearmen-cum-shield-bearers. Chariotry would be closely supported by cavalry, which the Assyrians used as mounted warriors as opposed to scouts or messengers. Originally cavalry had operated in pairs consisting of an archer and a shield-bearer, the latter holding the reins of the former's horse and screening him with the shield while he shot. However, by the seventh century BC, horsemen were equipped with both spear and bow, armoured and riding barded mounts (horses wearing textile armour), thus enabling them to charge into contact. This equestrian revolution hastened the redundancy of the war-chariot, being more economical and tactically flexible.

1296 BC

enemy and rallying his troops. The tide of the battle had turned. Sensing victory, Hittite charioteers began to plunder, but Rameses reorganized the remnants of Re and Amon and took the offensive, aided by the fortuitous arrival of Canaanite mercenaries. Muwatallis now committed a further 1,000 chariots, but Rameses drove them in rout back across the Orontes, pursued by the newly-arrived Ptah division. At dusk Seth division was also deployed. Alone with his infantry, King Muwatallis was powerless. He withdrew into Qadesh.

RESULT Since both sides were badly mauled, a non-aggression pact was signed, Rameses being too weak to besiege Qadesh, and Muwatallis happy to sit inside.

SENNACHERIB'S CAMPAIGN IN PALESTINE

DATE 701 BC

OBJECT The Assyrian king, Sennacherib, marched west to crush a rebellion of Assyrian vassals in Palestine, headed by the Judaean king, Hezekiah.

DESCRIPTION Advancing along the Levantine coast, Sennacherib dethroned the king of Tyre and received surrenders of petty kingdoms of Ashkelon and Ekron. With

Assyrian campaigns were swift and ruthless. Tiglath-Pileser systematically reduced the Urartian kingdom, Babylonia, the Aramaean states and Israel. Subject peoples were deported *en masse* and re-settled in other parts of the empire. Imperial expansion reached its zenith in the first half of the seventh century BC. In 671 Esarhaddon (681–668BC) marched into Lower Egypt, toppled Pharaoh Taharqa and installed his own governors. Two years later, however, he was forced to mount another Egyptian campaign, Taharqa having overthrown the Assyrian governors, but en route he fell ill and died. His son, Ashurbanipal (668–627BC) resolved the issue. Mobilizing the forces of 22 vassal kings along the Levantine coast, he crushed Egypt. The empire now extended over the entire Fertile Crescent.

Assyria's end came with surprising rapidity. Already, under Ashurbanipal, Egypt had freed itself from the Assyrian yoke. His successors found themselves between two emerging rivals, Babylonia and the Medes, both of whom abetted the Assyrian imperial disintegration. In 612BC Nineveh fell to a Babylonian-Median coalition.

BABYLONIAN EXPLOITS

Under Nebuchadnezzar II (604–562BC) the Babylonians created an empire that encompassed virtually all the previous Assyrian domains. A resurgent Egypt under the Saite Pharaohs attempted to prevent this but, after Babylonian successes around Harran and Carchemish, was pushed back from the Euphrates to its own borders. Babylonian efforts to conquer Egypt were unsuccessful – both sides, according to the Babylonian Chronicle, "smote the breast of each other and inflicted great havoc on each other" in bloody conflict near the Egyptian frontier fortress of Migdol – but they did find success in Judah when, in 598, Nebuchadnezzar led his army against Jerusalem, after the Judaeans had risen in arms. The city was stormed and its king, Jehoiachim, exiled along with a host of Judaean notables. A puppet ruler was installed. Ten years later, Judah revolted once more. This time the Babylonians destroyed the strongholds of Judah and Jerusalem was razed to the ground.

Nebuchadnezzar was succeeded by three kings who ruled amid internal disorder, until Nabonidus was placed on the throne by a *coup d'état*. In 550BC the Persian prince, Cyrus, conquered Achmetha (Ecbatana) and inherited the vast kingdom of the Medes, the rivals of Babylonia. Four years later he defeated Croesus, king of Lydia. In 539BC, according to the Babylonian Chronicle, "the army of Cyrus entered Babylon without battle". Thus was inaugurated the Persian empire, the largest the Near East had ever seen. Under Cambyses (530–522BC) and Darius (522–486BC), the Persian empire was to stretch from the Indus to Macedonia and from the Caucasus to Egypt. However, Xerxes' failure to conquer Greece halted the empire's expansion, and it was eventually destroyed by Alexander the Great.

THE "GOLDEN AGE" OF THE CHARIOT

Under the Rameside pharaohs the Egyptian chariot was a formidable weapon, light, manoeuvrable and stable, drawn by two horses, each around 12.5 hands. The crew comprised a charioteer-cum-shield bearer and an armoured warrior wielding a composite bow, javelins and sidearm. The Hittite chariot was more robust. The crew consisted of a shieldless charioteer and spearman and a shield-bearer, all armoured. The sturdier, less-manoeuvrable Hittite chariots would try to interpenetrate the opposing lines, where their heavier weaponry and extra crewmen would tell against the lighter, more agile Egyptians.

Amenhotep III (1417–1379BC) demonstrates his martial prowess.

701 BC

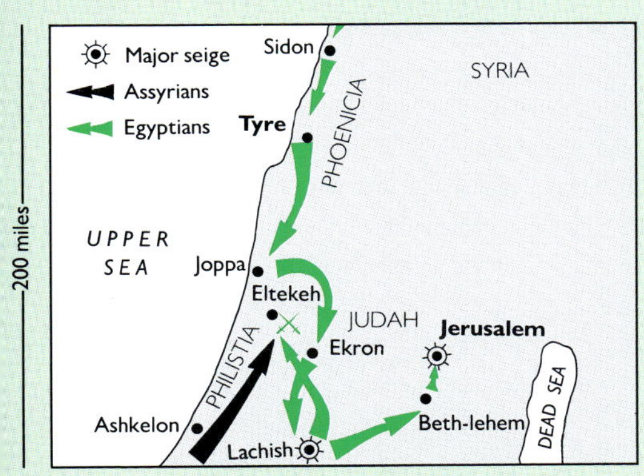

Philistia secured, the Assyrian king turned towards Judah. Hezekiah was prepared: he had strengthened the defences of Jerusalem, taken steps to deny any besiegers access to water, and fortified and provisioned the central towns of Judaea; he had also sought aid of the Kushite ruler of Egypt, Taharqa. Sennacherib, however, still took 46 Judaean walled towns and countless villages, besieging Lachish and Jerusalem in turn. Judah was wasted, though Jerusalem itself was not taken. Sennacherib was then forced to tackle the Egyptian army which threatened his retreat northward. The armies clashed in the plain of Eltekeh.

RESULT Though Sennacherib claimed victory, the Assyrians mysteriously withdrew.

2

HOPLITES TO HANNIBAL

AT FIRST SIGHT it may seem surprising that when Greek warfare emerges into the light of history, it not only soon comes to be dominated by the close-packed, heavy infantry known as "hoplites", but continues to be so for some three centuries (c.650–350BC). Greece is a mountainous country, whereas, as a Persian general is supposed to have remarked, hoplites required flat land to be effective and even there the necessity to maintain formation meant that a hoplite army was unwieldy and inflexible. Moreover, since hoplites were normally expected to provide their own equipment, the majority of the population in any given state was necessarily excluded.

WHY HOPLITES?

There were, however, good geographical, socio-political and military reasons for this situation. First, the relatively small areas of flat land were vital to the very existence of the city states, since it was there that most of their food was grown and, sooner or later, an invading army could be compelled to confront the defending hoplites. Secondly, in many states the full rights of citizenship were only accorded to those who could afford to take their place in the hoplite line-of-battle, so that the hoplites effectively *were* the "nation in arms", and it would have been unthinkable to arm the poor majority. It was only in a state like Athens, where the navy became important, that the poor, who rowed the ships, came to have a significant military role – hence Athenian democracy. Horses, on the other hand, were too expensive for all but the richest citizens, so that cavalry forces, south of Boeotia, were necessarily small. Finally, as events were to show, hoplites were extremely formidable. Anyone who doubts this should, above all, read Xenophon's account of the experiences of himself and his fellow-mercenaries in their march, first, to confront the Persian king at Cunaxa, near Baghdad, where their employer, the rebel prince Cyrus, was killed, and then home again via Armenia and the Black Sea coast.

490 BC

MARATHON

DATE August or September 490BC
CAMPAIGN Graeco-Persian Wars
OBJECT Persians were seeking to punish Athens for aiding rebel Greeks in Asia Minor, and to reinstate the Athenian "tyrant", Hippias.
NUMBERS c.24,000 Persian infantry (1,000 cavalry), under Datis and Artaphernes; c.10,000 Athenian and Plataean infantry, under Callimachus and Miltiades.

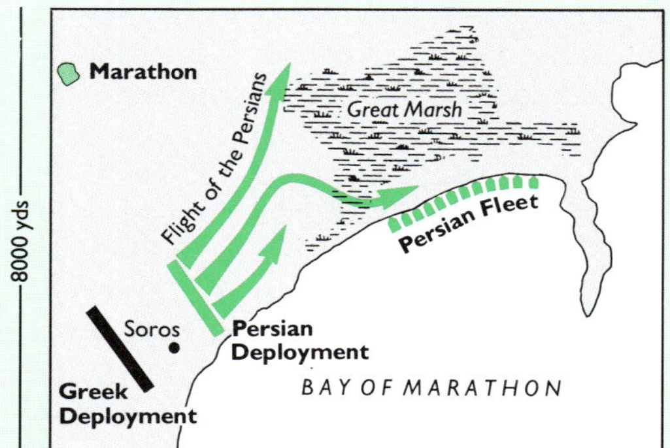

DESCRIPTION The Athenians marched to confront the enemy near Marathon, probably taking up position in the southeast corner of the plain, covering the road to Athens, where they were joined by the Plataeans. After several days' delay, the Persians advanced. The Greeks lengthened their line by thinning their centre to avoid being outflanked, and charged at the double to cut losses by arrow-fire. They won easily on both wings but, instead of pursuing, they wheeled inwards to take the

Map of the Eastern Mediterranean in Early Classical times. The city-states of Classical Greece united in the face of invasion by the mighty Persian empire, first defeating Darius at Marathon and then routing the fleet of his successor, Xerxes, at Salamis. The victors fell out, however, and in the Peloponnesian Wars, Athens and Sparta battled for supremacy, Sparta eventually triumphing with its victory over the Athenian fleet at Aegospotami and the surrender of Athens the following spring. Spartan domination came to an end in its turn at Leuctra in 371 BC.

EQUIPMENT

Hoplites began to appear when the spread of Greek colonies around the shores of the Mediterranean and into the Black Sea brought about a more general prosperity in the homeland and increasing numbers of men could afford to arm themselves in the latest gear. At first this included bronze helmets covering the back and sides of the head, with a nose-piece, which left only the eyes and lower face exposed. Chest and back were protected by solid bronze plates, and the lower legs by bronze greaves. For offence, the throwing-spear was soon abandoned in favour of the stabbing-spear, with a sword for use if the spear was broken. Later on metal armour probably gave way to jerkins of laminated linen strips or of leather, and some hoplites may have discarded armour altogether. Helmets, too, were modified in various ways.

But, with the stabbing-spear, their shield remained characteristic of hoplites throughout their existence. Thus Spartan hoplites were allegedly exhorted to 'come back with their shields or on them", and when in the 220s BC they finally abandoned the hoplite shield for a smaller, Macedonian-style buckler, they effectively ceased to be hoplites. However, the double-grip with which the hoplite shield was fitted meant that, if carried comfortably, it only covered the left side and hence a man depended on the shield of the man on his right for the protection of the other half of his body. Thus the phalanx was born, with ranks of warriors standing shoulder to shoulder, with interlocked or overlapping shields, and to leave the line became the worst offence a soldier could commit, since it might cause the death of his comrades.

480 BC

victorious Persian centre in both flanks, then pursued the enemy to its ships, driving many into the marshes in the northern half of the plain.

CASUALTIES 6,400 Persian dead (and 7 ships lost) for 192 Athenians; no figures for Plataeans or prisoners.

RESULT Defeat of the first Persian expeditionary force to Greece.

SALAMIS

DATE c.24 September, 480 BC

CAMPAIGN Graeco-Persian Wars

OBJECT The Persians wanted to destroy the Greek fleet before completing the conquest of Greece by invading the Peloponnese.

NUMBERS 310 or 368 Greek triremes under Eurybiadas of Sparta, including 110 or 180 Athenian ships under Themistocles, against c.600–700 Persian ships under various admirals.

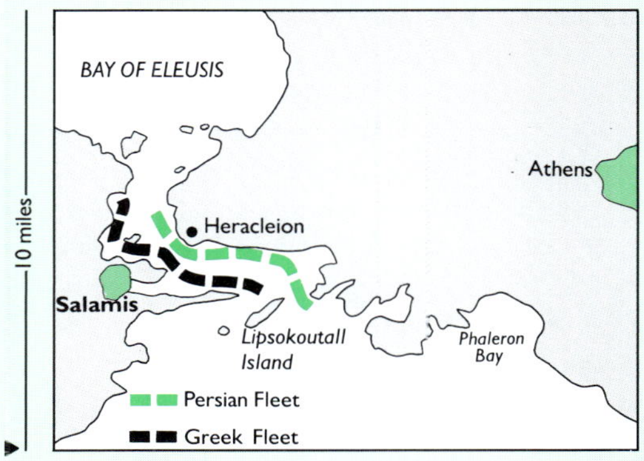

HOPLITE SHIELDS

Possibly invented in Caria and introduced to the mainland via Argos between 700 and 650BC, the shield *(aspis)* was 2½–3 ft in diameter, with a wooden core, offset rim and facing of bronze, and lining of leather. It was held by inserting the left arm through the central armband *(porpax)*, gripping the hand-grip of bronze or cord *(antilabê)* near the rim. Thus half the shield projected to the left. Shields usually carried blazons, either individualized – gorgon-heads, cocks, etc. – or referring to the hoplite's city (e.g. "A" for "Athenians", or a club for the Thebans). The shield was a hoplite's essential piece of equipment and to throw it away was a sign of cowardice.

A 5th century BC relief.

HOPLITE WARFARE

The first real test of the effectiveness of hoplites against different types of troops came with the two Persian invasions of Greece in 490 and 480–479BC. In the first the Athenians and their Plataean allies shattered a Persian army at Marathon (see page 14); in the second, a tiny force of some 7,000 hoplites, with a hard core of only 300 Spartans, successfully defended the pass of Thermopylae for two days before being taken in the rear, and then, in 479, the Persian army was almost totally destroyed at Plataea in Boeotia. Herodotus, our main source for these wars, leaves no doubt that, at Plataea, the Persians, largely depending as they did on missile-armed troops, had no answer to the impact of hoplites fighting *en masse*, like a huge, armoured rugger-scrum, even though the Greek army had split into three parts, and the crucial encounter involved only 11,500 of the 38,700 hoplites present.

Hoplites could, of course, be beaten by other troops in particular circumstances. Caught on terrain which did not suit them, they could, for example, be destroyed by javelins thrown from a distance. This happened to a small Athenian force in the Aetolian hills in 426BC. Cavalry could occasionally ride them down if they were caught in the open and not properly formed, as happened to part of the Greek army at Plataea. But an earlier stage in the Plataea campaign demonstrated that cavalry could not defeat hoplites by frontal assault, and light troops armed with missiles had to be very skilfully handled and, above all, had to be backed up by hoplites of their own, if they were to stand any chance. The cutting to pieces of a *mora* (regiment) of the Spartan army by Athenian *peltasts* (light troops) under Iphicrates, in 390BC, was an almost unique occurrence, and here there were certainly Athenian hoplites present, though they played no part in the actual fighting until the very end.

Morale was supremely important, and many a hoplite battle ended almost as soon as it had begun, with one side breaking and running. If this did not happen, the two phalanxes would close to within a few feet, whereupon those in the front two or three of the eight or more ranks would try to stab their opposite numbers, aiming for the face, neck or shoulders over the rim of the shield. But the pressure of those behind inevitably, sooner or later, brought the two formations crashing together, and then it is quite clear that it was literally a question of trying to "shove" the enemy back. Finally one side or the other would have to give way and the rout would begin, with men trampling each other underfoot as they tried to run. But the pursuit was not usually carried far, mainly because it would cause the pursuers to break formation and so expose themselves to the danger of a counter-attack. Thus losses were comparatively slight in most hoplite battles, ranging from about 2 per cent for the winners to about 15 per cent for the losers.

Obviously there was a limit to the tactical skills that could be employed in this

480 BC

DESCRIPTION Either because they were tricked into believing the Greeks were about to flee, or because they hoped to achieve surprise and so finish the naval war before winter, the Persians infiltrated the straits between Salamis and the mainland during the night. But the Greeks, warned by a deserter, were ready at dawn. The course of battle is uncertain, but the fleets were almost certainly aligned east-west, and the Phoenicians on the Persian right, opposite the Athenians, may have got ahead of the rest and been outnumbered and cut off; in the later stages, Aeginetans from the Greek right also cut the enemy line. The Greeks evidently relied on ramming – no enemy ship is recorded as being captured in the fighting – so the heavier Greek ships possibly stood up to collisions in confined space better than the faster and more manoeuvrable enemy ships.

RESULT Defeat of the Persian fleet and so the end of its naval threat.

FIRST MANTINEA

DATE Summer 418BC

CAMPAIGN Peloponnesian Wars

OBJECT Spartans, seeking to recover control of Mantinea, started to flood its territory by diverting streams, compelling confrontation.

NUMBERS 10,000–11,000 Spartans, Tegeates, etc, under King Agis, against 8,000–9,000 Mantineans, Argives, Athenians, etc, commander unknown.

kind of fighting, and it is important to realize that nearly all hoplites, from the generals downwards, were almost entirely untrained. This is made clear by the constant references in ancient literature to the uniqueness of the Spartan training-system, and even in Sparta generals were picked for their social standing rather than their ability – indeed, the commander-in-chief of a Spartan army was usually a king or another member of one of the two royal families. All generals could do was to get their men into formation and then lead them into battle, and many a hoplite general fell as a result.

THE SPARTANS

The Spartans, however, demonstrated that highly trained hoplites, articulated into units as small as 30–40 men and with a proper chain of command – things that were unique in Greece until at least the 4th century BC – could be manoeuvred on the battlefield. In particular, they could exploit the tendency of hoplite armies to edge to the right, described by Thucydides, as each man sought the protection of the shield of the man to his right. Often this led to stalemate, as each side won on its right and set off in pursuit of the enemy left. But by ignoring the fleeing enemy left, the Spartans learned to wheel to take the victorious enemy right in flank, as it returned across the battlefield. At Mantinea in 418BC (see below) this seems to have been almost accidental, but at the Nemea in 394 there is not much doubt that the Spartans deliberately sacrificed their left in order to be in a position to outflank the enemy's left and roll up their line. Most strikingly of all, at the second battle of Coronea just after the Nemea, they even managed to countermarch their phalanx when the Thebans got in their rear by breaking through their left.

In the end, however, even the Spartans met their match in the genius of the one hoplite general who seems to have thought in anything but the simplest tactical terms – Epaminondas of Thebes. At Leuctra (see page 19) he deliberately massed his left 50-deep, and refused his centre and right, thus negating the usual Spartan tactics and overwhelming their 12-deep line; at the second battle of Mantinea, he added to these tactics the charge of a mixed formation of cavalry and light troops, trained perhaps to run into battle holding the horses' tails. But even this battle, which foreshadows in some ways the tactics of the Macedonians, Philip and Alexander, ended in typically hoplite fashion with Epaminondas falling mortally wounded as the phalanx he was leading crashed into the enemy.

MACEDONIA AND THE COMING OF ROME

Greek warfare was transformed by Philip II of Macedon (359–336BC). His kingdom had long had fine cavalry, the king's "Companions" *(hetairoi)*, armed with lances, not

Gravestone of Aristion of Athens. This relief (c.510BC), and the late 5th-century relief (opposite), illustrate hoplite armour. Note the composite corslets, Aristion's greaves and long spear, and the "Corinthian" helmet and rim shield-grip of the central figure (opposite). Aristion's helmet is peculiar, but damage to the stone may have concealed a "Corinthian" helmet.

418 BC

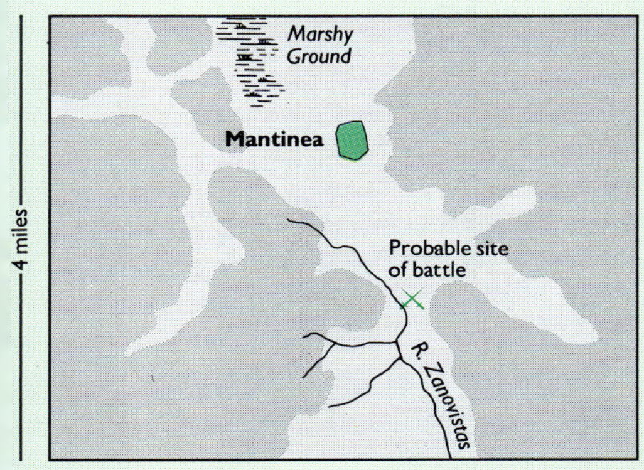

DESCRIPTION As each army edged to the right in advance, Agis ordered his left to shift left, and two units from the right to plug the resulting gap. When the two unit commanders refused to obey orders, the enemy charged into the gap and routed the Spartan left, pursuing it to camp. But the Spartan right outflanked the allied left, and when the Athenians there retreated, covered by cavalry, Agis wheeled his right to the left and took the enemy right in its shieldless flank as it streamed back across the battlefield. Thus the Spartans, under perfect control, exploited their advantage on the right, whereas the enemy failed to do so.

CASUALTIES c.300–400 killed on Spartan side, 1,100 enemy losses.

RESULT Defeat of the Athenian attempt to build up an anti-Spartan coalition in the Peloponnese.

A typical, though elaborate, "Corinthian" helmet, which probably dates from the 5th century BC. Made of bronze, it is of the type worn by the hoplites.

the missile-weapons of Persian and other Greek cavalry but, lacking a "middle class", had never developed hoplites. Philip was a hostage in Thebes in the 360s, and may there have become convinced of the necessity of complementing his cavalry with solid infantry. It was almost certainly he who created the "Foot Companions" *(pezhetairoi)*. Their 18-foot pike, the *"sarisa"*, required two hands, so they could not carry a hoplite shield, but the hedge of *sarisai* itself afforded protection, so they only needed a small buckler, probably hung from the neck to cover the left shoulder, and little or no body armour. Thus the equipment was cheap and large numbers of troops could be recruited.

Macedonian "phalangites", however, although similar to hoplites, were not intended to be battle-winners. Their job was to hold the enemy infantry long enough for the cavalry to exploit any opportunity, and these were the tactics used by Philip in his first battle, against the Illyrians, and at Chaeronea (see page 22). On both occasions, significantly, the king appears to have commanded the infantry, not the cavalry, perhaps to show his confidence in his new soldiers. It was this *combination* of different types of troops that was Philip's chief contribution to the art of war.

Alexander, Philip's son, inherited both his army and his plans for the invasion of the Persian empire, but any skills he learned from his father can hardly have prepared him for the far more wide-ranging and complex campaigns he was to fight. In any case, he was a different kind of general: Philip's great strength lay in his grasp of grand strategy, Alexander's in his tactical sense of timing. Nevertheless, it is interesting that the two greatest ancient generals – Alexander and Hannibal – should both have been sons of fine generals.

Integration of all types of troops reached fruition in Alexander's army. The heavy infantry – the Foot Companions and "Shield-bearers" (*hypaspistai*, derived from the old royal bodyguard) – were probably all armed with the *sarisa* for the set-piece, but a shorter spear for other purposes, and were articulated into even smaller units than the Spartan army, with greater potential for manoeuvre. Light infantry armed with missile weapons screened the phalanx and performed specialized tasks, while allied and mercenary hoplites were used in minor roles. The shock troops were the Macedonian cavalry, but there was also other cavalry, the Thessalians, in particular, being of high calibre.

In siege warfare Alexander also followed his father. Philip had perhaps been the first mainlander to use the recently invented catapult, and Alexander used not only the conventional mounds, towers and rams, but also both arrow-firing and stone-throwing catapults, above all in his siege of Tyre (332BC). Philip had also, finally, developed an efficient commissariat, enabling him to move fast from one end of Greece to the other, and to campaign all year round, to the consternation of his

406 BC

ARGINUSAE

DATE 406BC
CAMPAIGN Peloponnesian War
OBJECT An attempt to relieve the Athenian fleet blockaded at Mytilene.
NUMBERS 143 Athenian and allied triremes in a hastily assembled scratch fleet, partly rowed by freed slaves, under eight admirals, against 120 Spartan and allied vessels under Callicratidas.
DESCRIPTION Callicratidas, having to cover Mytilene, had fewer but faster ships in a single line abeam, ready for *diekplous* or *periplous*. Athenians, as counter, were in double line abeam, possibly on either side of the western island. The course of battle is uncertain: Callicratidas, on the right, was lost overboard when his ship rammed another, possibly after cutting the first Athenian line, and the Athenian right got the better of the Spartan left. After the battle, bad weather prevented the Athenians from picking up survivors who were

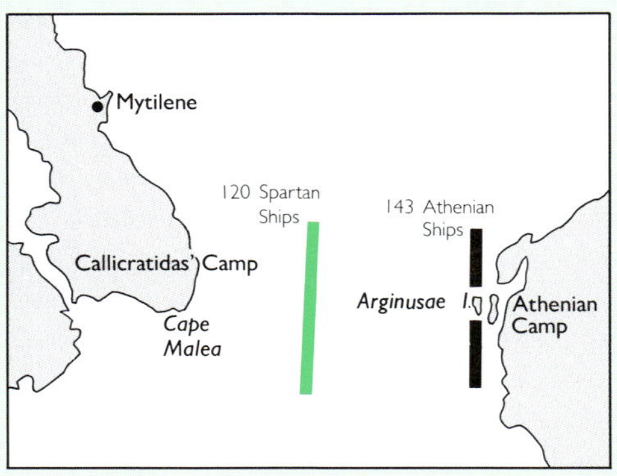

enemies, and modern studies have illuminated the sound logistical back-up behind Alexander's campaigns.

Alexander is said to have bequeathed his empire "to the strongest", and it soon broke up into separate kingdoms under his marshals. They added little that was innovatory in warfare, though they continued the process, begun by Alexander, of introducing native elements, with specialized equipment, into their armies. But there was also a tendency for cavalry to become less important and infantry more inflexible and unwieldy, and this was to be of crucial significance when their successors had to face Rome. At both Cynoscephalae in 197BC and Pydna in 168, cavalry was unimportant, and the phalanxes, though initially carrying all before them in parts of the field, were eventually routed by the more flexible Roman legions.

Alexander the Great, from the sarcophagus made for the contemporary king of Sidon, now in the Istanbul Museum. In battle Alexander would certainly have worn armour, but the fact that he is on horseback emphasizes the new importance of cavalry.

PYRRHUS AND HANNIBAL

The first of the successors to fight Rome was Pyrrhus, who came to Italy in 280BC to fight on behalf of some of the Greek cities of the south, with 25,000 soldiers trained in Macedonian methods, and 20 war-elephants. With these forces he won two victories, at Heraclea in 280 and Asculum in 279, in the first using his phalanx to hold the Roman infantry while his cavalry and elephants – which untrained horses will not face – broke the Roman cavalry and attacked their flanks; in the second eventually breaking the Roman infantry with his elephants. But on both occasions he lost heavily – hence the term "Pyrrhic victories" – and he displayed astonishing strategic frivolity by departing for Sicily on a new adventure. When he returned to Italy, he was fought to a standstill at Beneventum in 275, and went back to Greece.

The true heir to Alexander, and the last great threat to Rome, was the Carthaginian, Hannibal. The story goes that when asked by Scipio to list the world's greatest generals, he put Alexander first, Pyrrhus second, and himself third, adding that, had he won Zama, he would have put himself first. He was certainly too modest: he was not only a better tactician than Pyrrhus, but a far greater strategist, and it is even arguable that he surpassed Alexander. He never enjoyed the immense superiority in quality of troops which enabled the latter to fight his way out of difficulties, and at Zama, the only battle he lost, had to depend on inferior mercenaries and raw levies for two thirds of his infantry, while his cavalry was weaker both in number and in quality. Hannibal's holding back of his third line here was possibly the first example of a true reserve, and he might still have won the battle if the Roman cavalry, perhaps deliberately lured from the field, had not returned in the nick of time.

Unfortunately we know little about Hannibal's army. The Spaniards and north Italian Celts who fought in the line were certainly swordsmen and the Africans

Continued on page 22

371 BC

clinging to wrecks, and six admirals who returned to Athens were executed.
CASUALTIES Spartans lost 9 of their 10 ships, and more than 60 of their allies', the Athenians 25.
RESULT The last Athenian victory of the war.

LEUCTRA

DATE July 371BC
NUMBERS c.10,000 Spartan and allied infantry and 1,000 cavalry, under King Cleombrotus, against c.7,000 Boeotian infantry and 700 cavalry, under seven 'Boeotarchs', of whom Epaminondas was the most influential.
DESCRIPTION Epaminondas massed c.4,000 Thebans on the left 50 deep, with the crack "Sacred Band" probably forming ▶

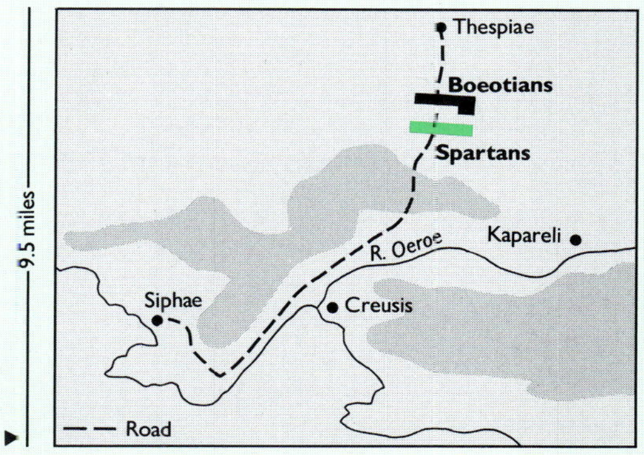

THE SPARTAN ARMY

THE SPARTAN ARMY evolved from a primitive, tribal force, based on kinship groups, probably through an organization based on locality, to one in which men from different families and localities fought in the same unit. Eventually it was articulated into units of 40 men or fewer *(enômotiai)*, and had a command structure, unlike other Greek armies, enabling it to carry out manoeuvres beyond their capacity.

All Spartans from 20 to 60 were liable for military service, and were grouped in age-classes, probably in such a way that there were five men from each group of five age-classes in each full-strength *enômotia*. By varying the number of age-classes called up, different numbers of men could be simply and swiftly mobilized. Thus, before the battle of Leuctra, the first 35 age-classes in four *morai* (regiments) were called up, and after it the remaining five age-classes and two *morai*.

In battle men were also ranged by age, with the youngest in front, so that the first five, ten or fifteen age-classes, as the case might be, could be ordered out, e.g. to drive off missile-armed troops. On at least one occasion young Spartan hoplites managed to catch light troops armed with javelins, who had not yet even come within range, and they could also attack up hill and co-operate with cavalry, though Spartan cavalry was neither numerous nor efficient. It, too, was divided into *morai*, but we do not know how many men each of these contained.

In addition to the six infantry *morai*, there were 300 *hippeis* ("horsemen" or "knights"), who, despite their name, fought on foot and acted as the king's guard. They were probably recruited from the 10 youngest age-classes and drawn from noble families.

Spartan boys began their training at latest by the age of 14, though they did not join the army until they were 20. Originally the entire army consisted of full citizens, called *Spartiatai* or *homoioi* ("equals"), who were elected to a military mess *(phidition* or *sussition)* at the age of 20, and were expected to dine there each evening, and to sleep there until they were 30. This gave the army a magnificent *esprit de corps*.

From about 460BC onwards, however, the number of full citizens declined, and the deficit was then made up either from the *perioikoi* ("neighbours", i.e. men from the small, semi-independent communities in the southern Peloponnese, allied to Sparta), or more probably from *hypomeiones* ("inferiors", i.e. Spartans who had lost their full status). At Leuctra there were only 700 *Spartiatai* present, of whom 400 were killed.

(Above) Bronze statuette of an early Greek hoplite – note the helmet and double-grip shield.
(Below) Spartan hoplites were organized into units called enômotiai. *Each had a maximum strength of 40 men, but usually contained 30–35 men on campaign, the oldest age-classes being left to defend Sparta. The number and depth of files varied. Probably four* enômotiai *made up a* pentekostys *(bottom), four* pentekostyes *a* lochos *and two* lochoi *a* mora. *This system enabled Spartans to carry out manoeuvres such as the anastrophe and counter-march shown on the opposite page, and gave their generals a much greater degree of control in battle.*

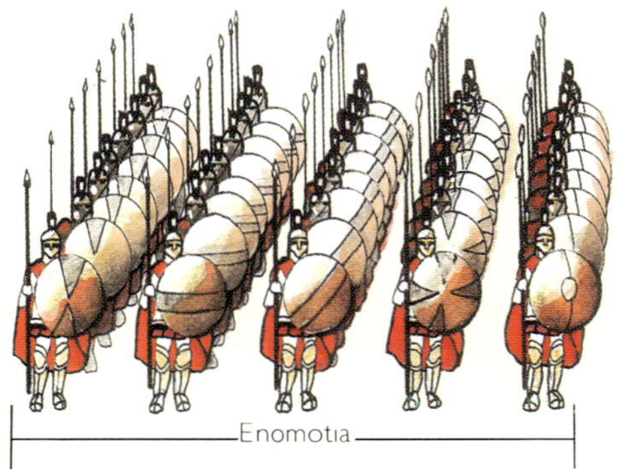

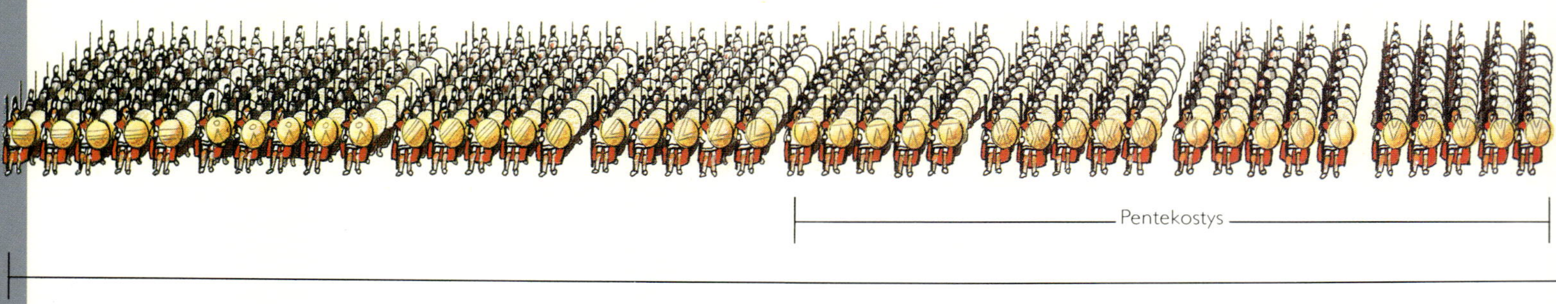

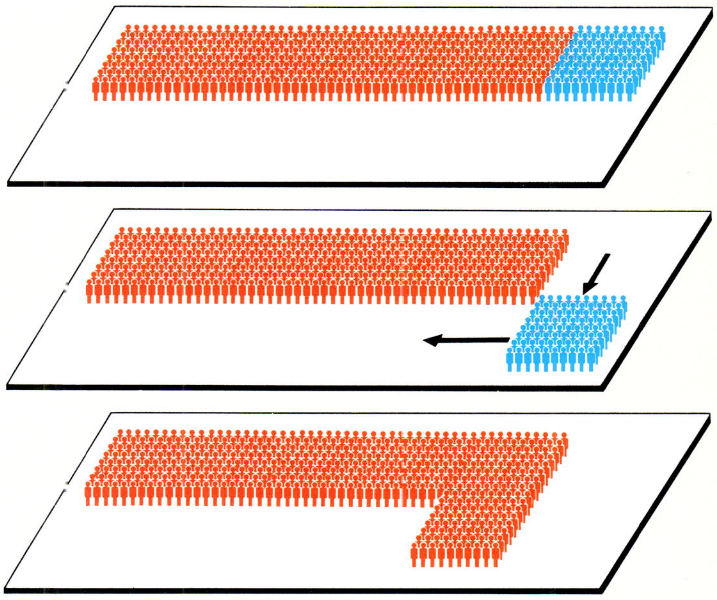

(Above) Anastrophe*: the manoeuvre used by the Spartan army to double the depth of the phalanx. A number of files about-turned, marched to the rear, and wheeled left or right to come up behind the files in front. This was dangerous if the enemy attacked during the manoeuvre, as may have happened at Leuctra in 371*BC.

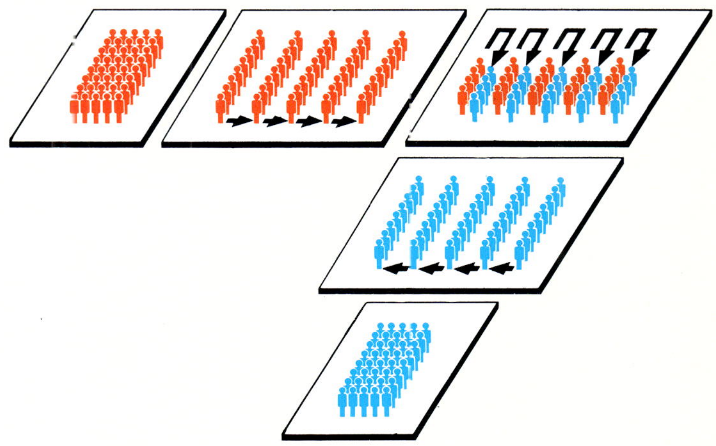

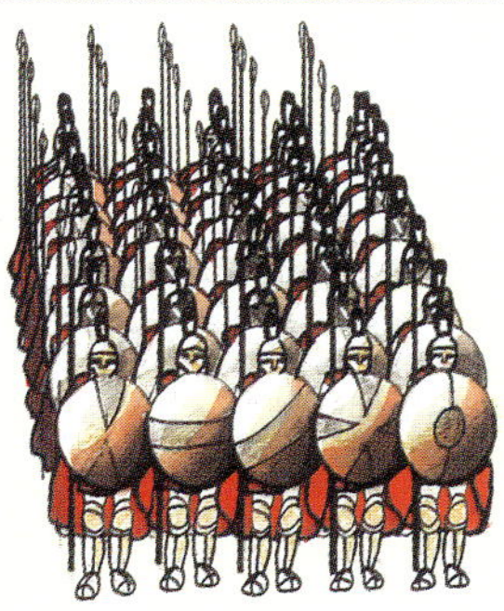

(Left) In battle, hoplites formed up shoulder to shoulder, shields touching or even overlapping, but for some manoeuvres the more open order illustrated far left would have been used.

(Above) An early 5th-century BC *bust of a Spartan warrior. The elaborately decorated helmet, and the date, suggest that it is an idealized portrait of King Leonidas, killed at Thermopylae in 480*BC.

*(Above) Counter-march: the manoeuvre used to reverse the phalanx, if the enemy appeared in the rear. The phalanx adopted open order, then each file about-turned, the rear man stood fast, and the front man led the rest of the file to take post in front of him. The ranks thus remained in the same order and gave an impression of the phalanx advancing. Used at Coronea in 394*BC.

Lochos

Climax of the battle of Gaugamela as depicted on 1st century AD mosaic from Pompeii, possibly based on a contemporary painting.

possibly were too, since Hannibal later armed them with captured Roman equipment. The light infantry probably included some troops armed with stabbing-spears and slingers from the Balearic islands. The Numidians, from what is now Algeria, were mostly light cavalry, superb for scouting, raiding and screening in battle or on the march, but certainly not capable of riding down unbroken infantry, and the Spanish and Celtic cavalry, although in some sense clearly regarded as "heavy", equally certainly did not consist of shock troops like Alexander's Macedonians.

Out of these heterogeneous elements, only the higher-ranking officers being Carthaginians, Hannibal succeeded in forging a precision instrument, and one of his great qualities was that he never asked his men to do something that was beyond them. He never won a "Pyrrhic" victory and one cannot imagine his being faced with mutinous troops refusing to go any further, as Alexander finally was.

Since we know more about Alexander's army, his victories seem more sophisticated, but his tactics were, in essence, simple, and Hannibal's three great victories were more subtle. The battle of Trebbia was a trap which depended on the Roman belief that no trap was possible in such apparently open terrain; the terrain at

the front four ranks, and advanced obliquely to the left, refusing his right and centre, and screening his advance with cavalry. The Spartan cavalry, also unusually in front of the phalanx, were pushed back into their own infantry. The latter were perhaps both trying to deepen their 12-deep formation and to extend to the right in the usual way. Into this confusion, the Sacred Band crashed at the double. Cleombrotus fell, mortally wounded, and although the Spartans held long enough to recover his body, perhaps all 80 files directly in front of the massed Thebans were annihilated, including the 300 *hippeis* of the royal guard ; the Spartan left fled on seeing their right defeated.

CASUALTIES c.1000 Spartans and c.300 Boeotians killed.

RESULT Victory for the Boeotians and the end of the myth of Spartan invincibility.

CHAERONEA

DATE c.2 August 338 BC

OBJECT Philip of Macedon, determined to assert authority in central Greece, confronted a coalition mainly of Athenians and Boeotians on the main route into Boeotia from the north.

NUMBERS Philip had c.30,000 infantry and 2,000 cavalry, the enemy a total of 30,000–35,000.

DESCRIPTION The course of the battle is

Trasimene, by contrast, was "made by nature for an ambush", as a Roman historian said, but what general in command of 25,000 men could really have imagined that he could be *ambushed*? Cannae (see page 28) was the masterpiece. The terrain was open again, and no part of Hannibal's army concealed. But his dispositions themselves constituted a trap, inviting the Romans to attack the projecting centre and hinting that the cavalry could have little part to play, since most of it was on the left, apparently confined by the river, and only the Numidians were out on the open flank. Yet, by the end of the day, outnumbered 2:1 in infantry, and for the loss of at most 16 per cent of his own men, Hannibal had inflicted on the Romans the greatest losses ever suffered by a European army in a single day, and over 78 per cent of their soldiers were either dead or in his hands.

Even more remarkable was Hannibal's strategic genius. Rome was a "super-power", able ultimately to call on three-quarters of a million men, and so to absorb defeats like Cannae which would have crushed almost all other ancient states. Lesser generals might have been able to realize that the way to defeat her was to invade Italy and break her hold on the allies who furnished over half her manpower. But few other generals would have believed it possible, particularly without command of the sea. Alexander, in contrast, merely had to contend with the vastness of the Persian empire, and although, for example, his strategy of nullifying Persia's naval superiority by capturing her naval bases, was brilliant, his invasion of Egypt allowed the king of Persia time to assemble another and more numerous army.

In the end, too, what was the point of it all? Alexander evidently saw himself as some kind of "hero" and conquest as an end in itself. Hannibal fought for a purpose, and when he finally lost at Zama, insisted that Carthage make peace. Alexander seems the more brilliant and charismatic, but there was something feverish about his genius. Hannibal's was perfectly tuned.

NAVAL WARFARE

Strategy and tactics in ancient naval warfare were dependent on the warships used, which were oar-powered galleys. Sails were used for moving from place to place, and a galley could probably move faster under sail than under oar, but they could really only sail before the wind and it was too dangerous to rely on the wind in combat. Masts and sails were invariably lowered before battle, sometimes left ashore, and to hoist sail was a sign of flight. Warships were designed to pack as many men as possible into a given length, to provide maximum motive power, and hence had little living or storage space. They were not designed to remain at sea for any length of time, and this limited their strategic capabilities.

Apart from the armed men on board, the only weapon was the ram. From the 4th

Continued on page 26

WAR-ELEPHANTS

Elephants were first encountered by Alexander at Gaugamela, (see page 26), and later at the Hydaspes in India. These would have been Indian elephants large enough to carry a number of armed men. Such elephants were used by Alexander's successors. Carthaginian elephants were the smaller, "forest" variety, found in west Africa. Ridden by a single mahout, the elephant itself was the weapon. Hannibal made effective use of them at the Trebbia, but all but one died during the winter of 218–217BC. The last, possibly called "Surus" ("the Syrian"), may have been an Indian. A few were landed at Locri, in 215, and took part in Hannibal's attempt to relieve Capua in 211. At Zama, they proved useless.

War-elephant on a Carthaginian coin.

338 BC

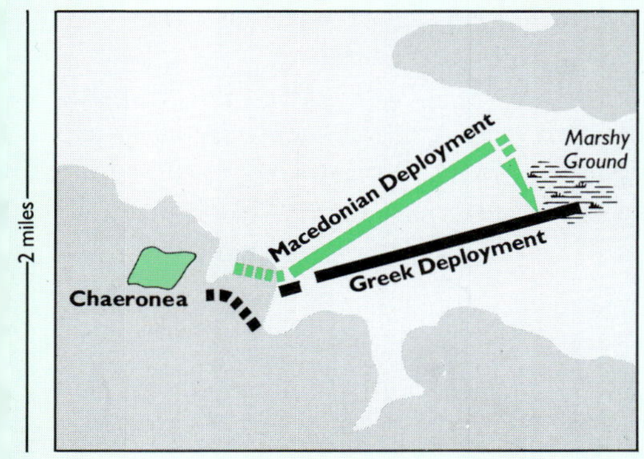

uncertain: it is usually thought that Philip, commanding the right, deliberately withdrew, drawing Athenians on the allied left after him, thereupon stretching the allied line and creating a gap on the right into which his son, Alexander, charged at the head of the cavalry, while Philip launched a counter-attack.

CASUALTIES Losses on the allied side were severe: half the Athenians were either killed or taken prisoner, and the Boeotians probably suffered even more heavily, the "Sacred Band" being annihilated – the "Lion of Chaeronea" perhaps marks their burial-place; a mound by the river Cephisus, 2 miles to the east, is probably where the Macedonian dead were cremated.

RESULT A decisive battle, Chaeronea effectively ended the hoplite era and the independence of the Greek city states.

THE EVOLUTION OF THE FIGHTING GALLEY

THE EARLIEST GREEK WARSHIPS were *pentekonters* (i.e. ships with 50 oars, probably rowed at one level, 25 each side), but as early as the eighth century BC there is evidence of ships rowed at two levels, and at about 650BC comes the first reference in surviving literature to a trireme (in Greek *triêrês*, i.e. "three-rower"). Such ships were possibly invented at Corinth, and first used in battle against her recalcitrant colony Corcyra (Corfu) in about 610. But they were expensive, above all because their large numbers of rowers had to be paid: slaves were only used in an emergency and were then freed. Thus it was probably not until the sixth century that triremes came into general use. A lucky strike in the Laureum silver-mines enabled the Athenians to build the first really large fleet of triremes – up to 200 vessels – just in time to face Xerxes' invasion in 480BC.

By this time triremes had become the standard warships used by the maritime powers of the eastern Mediterranean, though some old-fashioned pentekonters were still to be seen. By then, too, the normal complement of a trireme seems to have been 200 men, and later evidence suggests that these would have been made up of 170 oarsmen, 85 a-side (31 in the upper row, 27 each in the middle and bottom rows), 16 officers and deck-crew and 14 marines. But the number of marines could be varied. At Lade the Chiot ships carried 40, and each ship in Xerxes' fleet had 30 extra, perhaps because of Persian experiences with the Chiots at Lade.

Unfortunately, we do not know how many marines the Greek triremes carried in 480, but one doubts whether it was less than the Persians, and the best evidence suggests that the Phoenician triremes in Xerxes' fleet, and particularly those of Sidon, were the fastest vessels on either side. Hence the significance of the narrow waters at Salamis, where the Persian advantages in speed and numbers were nullified. Earlier in the campaign, off Artemisium in Euboea, in waters nowhere narrower than five miles, the Greeks had barely managed to hold their own.

Later warships carried more men – at Ecnomus, for example, the Roman quinqueremes had crews of 300 and 120 marines – but it is not certain how they were rowed. Probably no warship ever had more than three *banks* of oars, and the larger numbers were accommodated by doubling up on some of the oars. The largest warship ever built was the *tesserakontêrês* ("40-rower") of Ptolemy IV of Egypt (221–204BC), and it is inconceivable that it had 40 banks of oars – in any case, it apparently never sailed.

(Above) Relief from the Acropolis at Athens (c.400BC), showing the central section of ship rowed at three levels, presumably a trireme. This was important in modern reconstruction.

(Below) The evolution of oarage systems, from a single "bank" rowed across gunwales, via three "banks" of trireme, to a doubling up on one or more "banks" to produce quinqueremes, etc.

(Left) A rather fanciful depiction of Salamis, giving some idea of the chaos of ancient sea-battles. War-galleys of 480BC would not have carried masts and sails in battle and would have been longer and slimmer.

(Above) How a trireme may have looked with side-screens in position. Sails were carried for cruising, and triremes could probably move faster under sail than under oar, with a favourable wind. But such a rig made tacking virtually impossible and thus fighting under sail too risky, it being essential to avoid presenting vulnerable sides or sterns to the enemy. Hence both masts and sails were lowered before battle, or even left ashore.

THE TRIREME RECONSTRUCTED

(Right) The reconstructed trireme *Olympias.* Trials have shown that such a ship is very manoeuvrable, can exceed seven knots and cruise for more than seven hours at four or five knots, though so far no attempt at ramming has been possible! The picture of the interior (below) gives a good idea of how cramped conditions aboard would have been, but at least it was light and airy, unlike the "ships-of-the-line" of Nelson's day.

Late Geometric Attic spouted-bowl (735–710BC), now in the British Museum, possibly depicting the departure of Theseus and Ariadne from Crete, possibly the abduction of Helen. The ship is apparently one rowed at two levels, and if this is the case, it is among the earliest evidence for such ships. However, the impracticability of having two rows of men apparently rowing through the open side of a ship suggests the artist may have been trying to show both sides of the ship, within the conventions of Geometric art.

century BC onwards there are references to the mounting of catapults on warships, but these were "man-killers" rather than "ship-killers", and there seems to be no reference to the sinking of a ship by catapult fire. The ram could smash a hole in an enemy galley and so cripple her, but probably could not literally sink her: ancient sources use words meaning "sink", but it is evident that ships so "sunk" could still be towed away. But whether boarding or ramming, ships had to collide, and this also limited their tactical capabilities.

Seapower was a factor in strategic thinking by the 6th century BC, and c.499 the Greeks of Asia Minor, about to rebel against Persian rule, are said to have been advised to win command of the sea. It was certainly their defeat off Lade in 495(?) which ensured that their revolt failed. The Persians also sent the expeditionary force to Marathon by sea, and a large navy accompanied Xerxes' invasion in 480. Its job was to protect communications, and to by-pass Greek positions, but not to convoy supplies, as is often said: it would have needed all the supplies it could carry or convoy itself. The Persian army continued the struggle after the navy's defeat at Salamis (see page 15) and clearly either had its own supplies or lived off the land.

THE RISE AND FALL OF ATHENS: THE LIMITATIONS OF SEA POWER

After Xerxes' defeat, Athens used sea power to liberate the Greeks under Persian rule and to create the first great maritime empire, mainly around the Aegean and the Sea of Marmara, though her navy enabled her to strike as far as Cyprus and Egypt, the latter about 1,000 miles away by sea. Inevitably sea power formed the basis for her strategy in the Peloponnesian War with Sparta and her allies (431–404BC). Basically the strategy was to avoid confrontation with the Spartan army by withdrawing the population inside the fortified complex formed by Athens and the Piraeus, linked by the "long walls", and to supply it by sea.

This war perfectly illustrates the advantages and limitations of sea power. The latter is vital to the defence of an island or archipelago, or any state which depends on imports, but cannot be effective against a continental enemy which is self-sufficient. Athens could hit any of her enemies within reach of the sea, and even transport an expeditionary force to Sicily. But she could not prevent the enemy sending help to Sicily, let alone effectively blockade the Peloponnese, because her warships could not remain permanently at sea, and her raiding had a limited effect. Even when, from 425, she established permanent bases on or off the enemy coasts, they were too easy to confine. In any case, the enemy did not depend upon imports and so was not vulnerable to sea power. The only time Athens could have won the war was in 418 when, backed by a temporary coalition of Peloponnesian states, she forced the Spartans to stake their all at Mantinea.

331 BC

GAUGAMELA

DATE c.1 October 331BC
OBJECT Conquest of Persia by Alexander the Great of Macedon.
NUMBERS Alexander had c.40,000 infantry and 7,000 cavalry, while Darius III of Persia had more numerous forces, including Greek mercenary hoplites, cavalry of good quality, scythed chariots and elephants, precise numbers unknown.
DESCRIPTION The course of the battle is uncertain: Alexander formed his army in a rough oblong, with allied cavalry, Foot Companions, Hypaspists and Companions in front, allied infantry behind, mixed cavalry and light infantry at the sides, and advanced obliquely to the right. As the Persian left moved left to forestall outflanking, a gap appeared between it and the centre, into which Alexander led the Companions, wheeling left. The enemy centre crumpled before this attack and a frontal assault by Foot Companions and

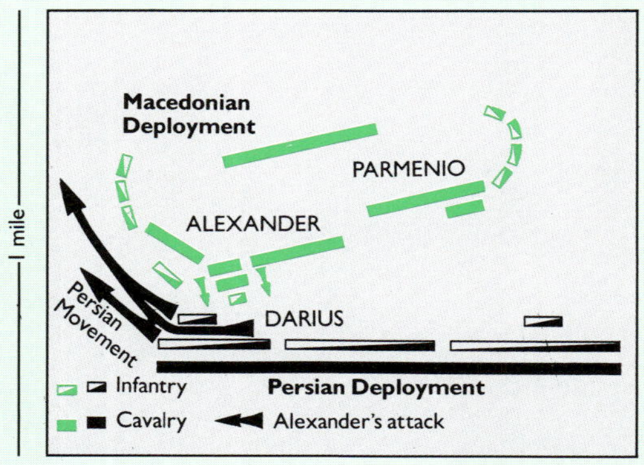

But Athens herself *was* vulnerable to sea power. She depended upon it not only to protect her sea-borne supplies, but also to maintain her hold on her empire, from which she derived revenue and manpower, and in the end it was sea power which brought her down. Her Sicilian expeditionary force was destroyed in 413, and this gave Sparta the chance to match her at sea, encouraged her allies to revolt and induced the Persians to throw their financial weight behind her enemies. Once the Spartans had found a competent admiral in Lysander, and Persian gold had started to flow, it was only a question of time. When the Athenian fleet was annihilated at Aegospotami in the Hellespont, in 405, Athens was forced to surrender.

THE PUNIC WARS

The first two wars between Rome and Carthage (264–241 and 218–201BC) also illustrate these points. The first was essentially a struggle for control of an island – Sicily – and the decisive battle was fought at sea, off western Sicily. But before Rome acquired a navy, the limitations of sea power were shown up again by the Carthaginian failure to prevent her from transporting an army to Sicily in 264, and the Carthaginians themselves later demonstrated the impossibility of an effective blockade, when Hannibal "the Rhodian" repeatedly managed to run supplies into the besieged Carthaginian base at Lilybaeum (Marsala).

Rome, however, not only won the war, but showed how sea power should be exploited, when she sent an army to Africa in 256. Though this was defeated, Scipio was to show in the second war that this was the way to inflict a decisive defeat on Carthage. It was when, in 256, the first expeditionary force was on its way to Africa that there occurred the greatest naval battle of ancient history – indeed, in terms of numbers of men, probably the greatest ever fought before Leyte Gulf in the Second World War – when 330 Roman quinqueremes, each carrying 420 men, defeated 350 Carthaginian quinqueremes off Ecnomus in southern Sicily (see below).

The Second Punic War was not a great naval war like the First, but Roman sea power was one factor in her victory. It prevented Hannibal from transporting his army to Italy by sea, which would have been quicker and less costly, and effectively starved him of reinforcements from home. It checkmated his ally, Philip V of Macedonia, and enabled Rome to transport armies to Spain, Greece, Sardinia, Sicily and Africa, and to supply and reinforce them. Indeed, Roman sea power is often forgotten in attempts to explain her rise to dominance in the Mediterranean world.

TACTICS AND COUNTER-TACTICS

Because ancient warships had no means of eliminating enemy vessels without colliding with them, naval tactics were necessarily limited. Once the ram had been

Rhyton in the shape of a trireme's bow, dating from the 3rd or 2nd century BC. Actual examples of such rams have been found (for instance off Athlit, near Haifa), and a ram like this was capable of smashing a hole in a ship's side. But a ship holed in this way, though crippled, would not sink until its timbers became completely waterlogged. Ramming also put great strain on the hull of the successful vessel, and there was always a danger of the ram's being caught in the enemy vessel's side, thus allowing a crippled vessel's marines to board.

256 BC

Hypaspists, and Darius fled. Meanwhile the outflanked Macedonian left stood its ground, though hard pressed, until the rout elsewhere caused the enemy right to retreat.

CASUALTIES c.500 Macedonians killed, Persian losses unknown.

RESULT Victory for the Macedonians meant the end of the Persian Empire and gave Alexander mastery of southwest Asia.

ECNOMUS

DATE 256BC

CAMPAIGN First Punic War

OBJECT A Roman attempt to invade Africa.

NUMBERS 330 Roman quinqueremes under Atilius Regulus and Manlius Vulso, against 350 Carthaginian quinqueremes under Hanno and Hamilcar.

DESCRIPTION The Roman fleet was in four squadrons, 1st, 2nd and 3rd forming a triangle, with the 3rd at its base, towing ▸

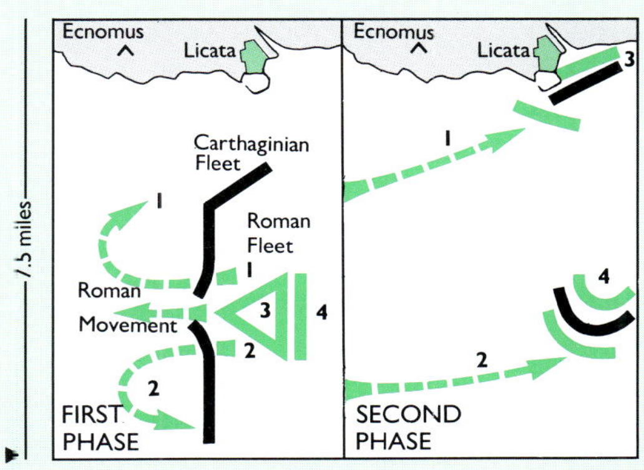

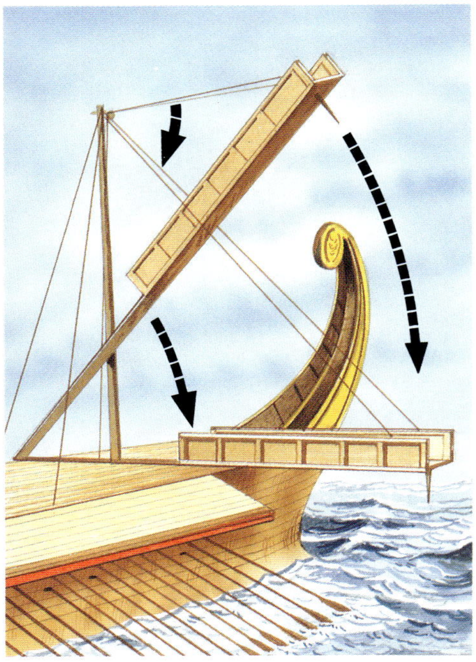

The corvus*, a device invented by the Romans in the early years of the First Punic War to counteract the speed and manoeuvrability of Carthaginian warships. First used at the battle of Mylae in 260*BC*, it led to a number of Roman successes, down to the battle of Cape Hermaeum in 255, but was apparently thereafter abandoned.*

invented, the ship itself could be used as a weapon, but the problem was to avoid damaging one's own ship or becoming so entangled with the enemy vessel that boarding became inevitable. Speed and manoeuvrability could make it possible to attack vulnerable sides and sterns, and during the 5th century the manoeuvres known as the *diekplous* and *periplous* were developed, particularly by the Athenians. The difference this could make was shown at the battle of Sybota, in 432, when a mere 10 Athenian triremes prevented the Corinthians from completely defeating Athens' Corcyran allies, and by the exploits of the Athenian admiral, Phormio, in the Gulf of Corinth, in 429, when, in command of only 20 ships, he first defeated 44 Peloponnesian ships, then 77.

But such tactics were too easily countered to be decisive in normal circumstances. Slower and less manoeuvrable ships could contrive to fight in a confined space, as the Greeks did at Salamis (see page 15), or the Syracusans in the Grand Harbour of Syracuse in 413. They could adopt a defensive formation, such as the "circle" adopted by Phormio's opponents in the first of his victories, and allegedly by the Greeks off Artemisium in 480, though one doubts whether 271 triremes could literally have formed a circle – it would have been about three miles in circumference! A larger fleet could form up in two lines abeam, instead of the usual one, as the Athenians did at Arginusae in 406, (see page 18), thus making the *diekplous*, if not impossible, at any rate very risky, since ships trying it would have to cut through two lines instead of through one.

Most famous of all the methods for nullifying faster and more manoeuvrable enemy vessels was the *corvus* (crow), invented by the Romans in the First Punic War. This was a boarding plank, rotating round a spar in the bows of their ships, with a spike at the other end, which could be let down on to an approaching enemy, thus both joining the two ships together and providing a means of boarding for the Roman marines. It was this device which enabled the Romans to win most of the early battles of the war, including Ecnomus, though the device was apparently abandoned after c.255. Perhaps it rendered Roman ships liable to capsize in heavy seas, and was responsible for their devastating losses in a storm off southern Sicily in that year.

It is clear from ancient accounts that sea battles rapidly degenerated into chaos, and it is doubtful whether any, except minor skirmishes like Phormio's, were won by tactics. As was the case with hoplite battles, an admiral could really do no more than arrange his ships, and it is worth remembering that the same men commanded on both land and sea: Lysander, for example, perished in a land-battle, and even Epaminondas once led a fleet to sea. Fleet tactics had to wait for a means whereby one fleet could damage the other, without its ships literally coming into contact with the enemy, and so risking equal damage.

256 BC

transports, covered by the 4th at the rear. The Carthaginians had 263 ships in the centre and on the right, in a single line abeam extending out to sea and 87 more on the left at an angle along the shore. The Carthaginian centre feinted retreat and was pursued by the first two Roman squadrons. Meanwhile, the right attacked the 4th and the left drove the 3rd, which had cast off the transports, towards shore. Having defeated the Carthaginian centre, the 2nd Roman squadron returned to help the 4th, driving the Carthaginian right out to sea, and finally the 1st, 2nd and 4th Roman squadrons joined the 3rd in defeating the Carthaginian left.

CASUALTIES Romans lost 24 "sunk", Carthaginians 30 "sunk" and 64 captured; *corvus* still much in evidence on Roman side.

RESULT The Romans were able to get their army to Africa, though it was defeated in the following year.

CANNAE

DATE 2 August 216BC

CAMPAIGN Second Punic War

OBJECT Carthaginian attempt to destroy the Roman army and compel Rome to negotiate.

NUMBERS 40,000 infantry, 10,000 cavalry, under Hannibal, against 80,000 infantry, 6,000 cavalry under Varro and Paullus.

DESCRIPTION The Roman infantry was drawn up in three lines, behind a screen of

TRIREME BATTLE TACTICS

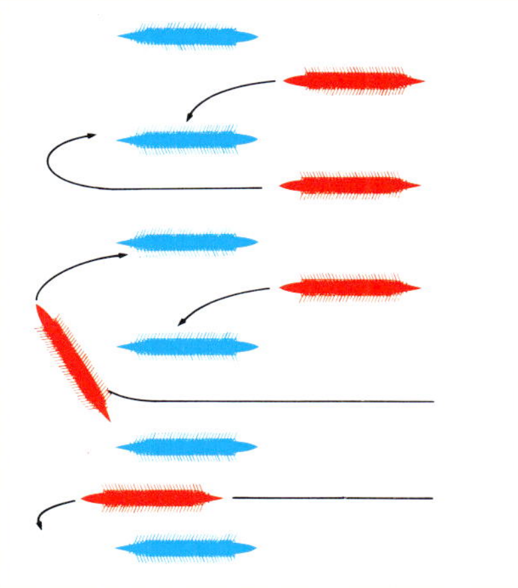

Diekplous

The most famous manoeuvre was the *diekplous*, almost certainly involving single ships in line abeam – the normal battle formation – trying to cut through the enemy line. Each helmsman would try to steer for a gap between enemy ships, and either turn suddenly to port or starboard to ram one in the side, or row clean through the line, swing round and attack from the stern. Sheering away enemy oars as a ship cut through the line might have been possible, but only if one's own oars could be shipped in time, which seems unlikely. The *periplous* was either a variation involving outflanking the enemy line, or the final stage of a *diekplous*, when the manoeuvring vessel, having cut through the line, swung round to attack from the stern.

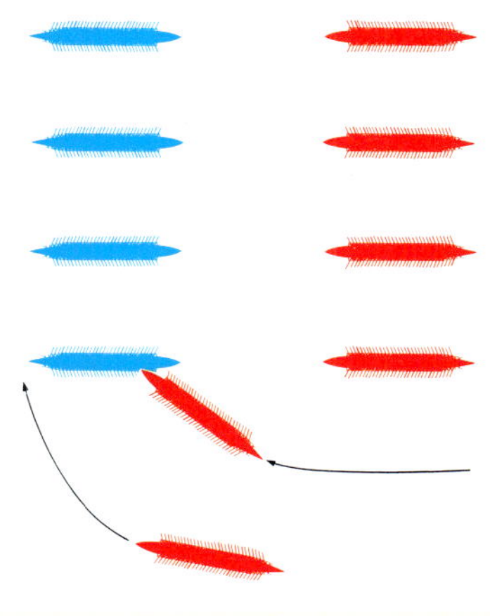

Periplous

Scene on Attic black-figure cup (540–500BC) showing war-galley rowed at two levels, apparently about to ram a merchantman head-on. Since the other vessel is not a warship, the scene possibly represents an attack by pirates. In battle, the galley would not have carried mast or sails, and would probably have tried to avoid a head-on collision.

216 BC

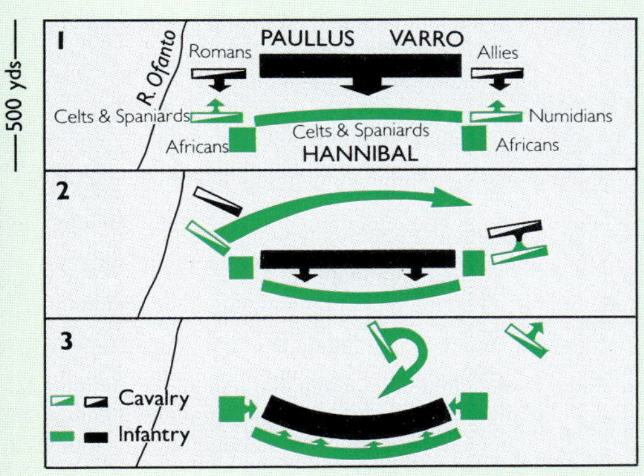

skirmishers, the Carthaginian in a single, convex line, screened by skirmishers, with Celts and Spaniards in the centre, Africans on the wings; Celtic and Spanish horse were on the left, Numidians on the right. The Celtic and Spanish cavalry routed the Roman cavalry, then rode round behind the advancing Roman infantry to fall on the rear of the Italian cavalry, opposite the Numidians. The Roman infantry pushed back the Celtic and Spanish foot, but avoided the Africans, who swung inwards to attack the flanks. The Celtic and Spanish cavalry left the Numidians to pursue the Italian cavalry, and attacked the rear of the Roman infantry, drawing pressure off the Celtic and Spanish infantry and effectively surrounding the Roman infantry.

CASUALTIES 48,200 Romans killed, 4,500 captured on the field, 14,800 elsewhere; up to c.8000 Carthaginians killed.

RESULT Cannae is regarded by military historians as a classic example of victorious double envelopment.

3

THE MIGHT OF ROME

BEFORE THE SECOND PUNIC WAR (218–201BC), Rome's influence extended no further than the Alps; within a century, the seeds of empire had been sown in Spain, Africa and the Greek east.

THE MIDDLE REPUBLIC (c. 200–100BC)

In 211BC, Rome had become embroiled in war against Philip V of Macedon, when he made common cause with Hannibal; an uneasy peace had ensued in 205, but no sooner had Rome humbled Carthage than her troops were again taking the field against Philip.

After a false start, the command passed to T. Quinctius Flamininus in 198BC; his peace terms were rejected by Philip and, in the fighting which followed, he pushed the Macedonians back into Thessaly. In 197, the Romans met Philip's army near Pherae: the Macedonians numbered around 26,000, against a Roman force of 30,000. However, both sides disengaged, preferring to seek a more suitable battlefield. Two days later, after torrential rain and in the midst of a thick mist, they met again in a chance encounter at Cynoscephalae (see below); the battle ended in victory for Flamininus, and delivered Greece into the hands of the Romans.

It was here that the legion first proved its superiority over the phalanx: the great hedge of pikes was only effective as long as it remained together, with its flanks guarded; lack of flexibility meant that rough ground was enough to break the line and disorganize its formation. Antiochus III of Syria tried to remedy the problem when he met the Romans in battle at Magnesia.

Antiochus had crossed to Europe late in 192BC, attracted by the power vacuum which Philip's defeat had created. The Romans crushed his army at Thermopylae (191) by emulating the tactics which the Persians had used in 480BC. The Romans carried the conflict over to Asia Minor and met Antiochus on ground of his own choosing at Magnesia (winter 190–189). Antiochus' grand army numbered over

198 BC

CYNOSCEPHALAE

DATE 198BC
CAMPAIGN Second Macedonian War
DESCRIPTION The armies of Philip V of Macedon and Flamininus were encamped on either side of a ridge, each ignorant of the other's whereabouts. It was misty, and the advance forces which both commanders had sent to occupy the heights met unexpectedly. Reinforcements arrived on both sides, and Flamininus led out his whole army – two legions at full strength with allied troops. A large part of the Macedonian army was absent foraging, so Philip deployed only half of his phalanx (c.8,000 men) on the ridge and charged down on to the Roman left, driving all before him. Flamininus took command of the Roman right, positioning his elephants in front, and charged uphill against Philip's left, where the rest of his forces were arriving in disorder; the Romans quickly routed them.

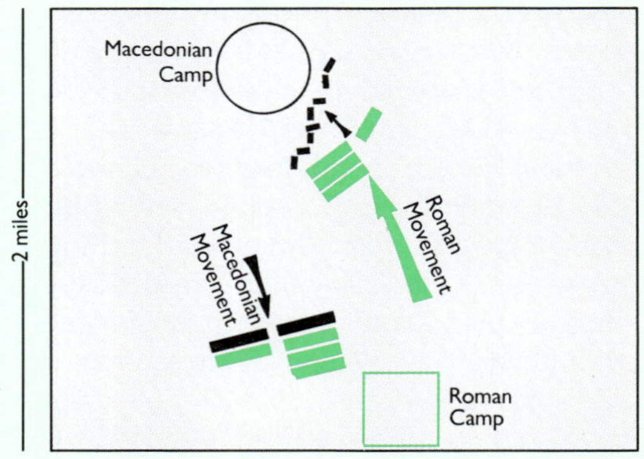

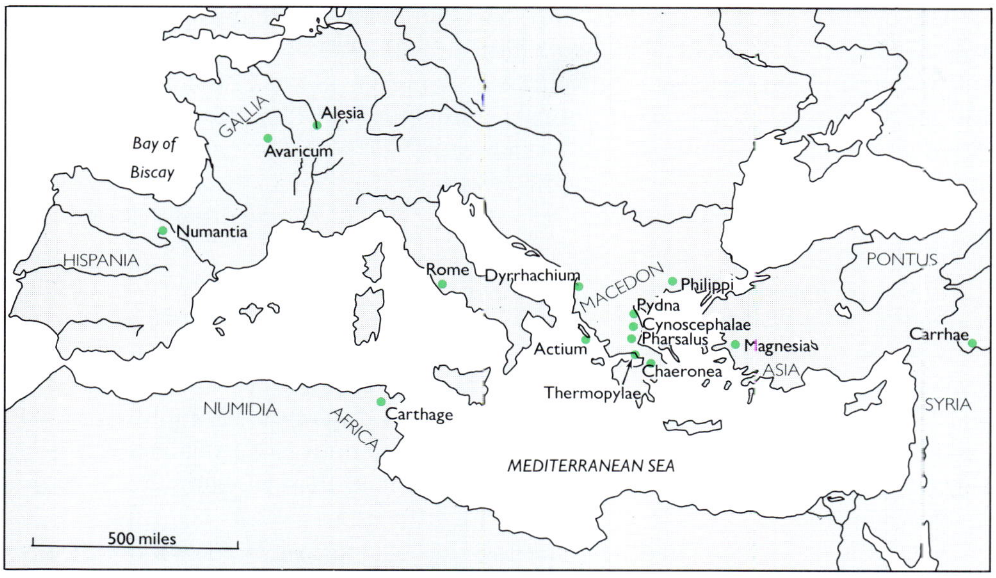

(Above left) Map of the Mediterranean c. 100 BC.

70,000 men and comprised several discrete elements with little cohesion: central to the whole force was a 16,000-strong phalanx; unusually, it was articulated – that is to say, the 10 blocks of pike-men were separated, one from another, by elephants. However, Antiochus and his cavalry abandoned the phalanx in their pursuit of the Roman left wing, and it was a simple matter for the Roman centre to stampede the elephants and breach the line.

Rome again became embroiled in conflict with Macedon in the late 170s, this time against Perseus, eldest son of Philip V, who had acceded on his father's death (179BC). Roman incompetence prolonged the war to 168, when the veteran L. Aemilius Paullus took command and brought Perseus to battle at Pydna (see below). Yet again, the flexibility of the legion proved superior to the massive weight of the phalanx. From now on, Macedon's days of independence were numbered: in 149, Rome finally, and reluctantly, annexed the country. Three years later, Carthage was razed to the ground by Scipio Aemilianus, a son of Aemilius Paullus and a grandson (by adoption) of the great Scipio Africanus.

Meanwhile, the Romans faced a rather different situation in Spain. Roman troops had first set foot in the peninsula in 218BC, during the war with Hannibal, but sporadic fighting in the interior kept two legions (and later, four) busy for another 85 years; indeed, Spain was not formally annexed until the time of Augustus.

THE MIDDLE REPUBLIC ARMY

In a typical year, the two consuls raised four Roman legions, each requiring 4,200–5,000 infantry and 300 cavalry.

The legion was divided into 30 maniples, ten each of *hastati, principes* and *triarii*; each was accompanied by 40 light-armed skirmishers *(velites)*. The maniples of *hastati* and *principes* comprised 120 heavy infantrymen who were required to arm themselves with a short, thrusting sword *(gladius)*, a long, oval shield *(scutum)*, and two heavy throwing javelins *(pila)*. The *triarii* were similarly equipped, except that they carried a thrusting spear *(hasta)*. The legionary cavalry were divided into 10 *turmae*, and armed with long spears and circular shields.

168 BC

RESULT The initiative of one of Flamininus' officers won the day: he wheeled 20 maniples (c.2,000 men) around from the victorious Roman right, and fell upon the rear of the Macedonian right. Philip was completely defeated.

PYDNA

DATE 168BC
CAMPAIGN Third Macedonian War
NUMBERS Perseus commanded a Macedonian army of 4,000 cavalry and around 40,000 infantry, including a 20,000-strong phalanx.
DESCRIPTION Aemilius Paullus and the Roman forces, perhaps four legions with allied troops, came upon the Macedonians unexpectedly, and withdrew on to rising ▸

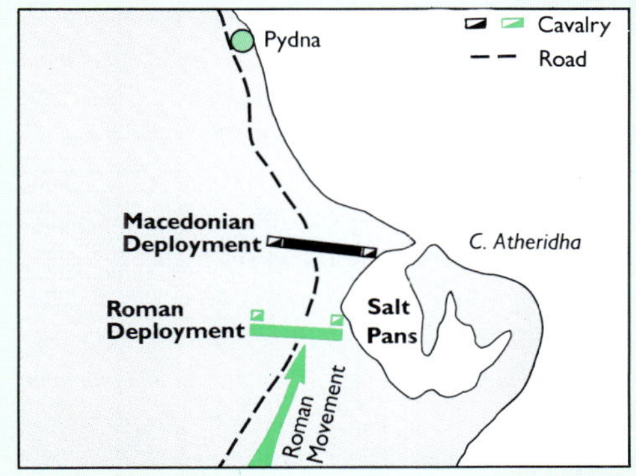

MARIUS' MULES

The two major reforms attributed to the genius of Marius required arms and armour to be mass-produced, resulting in some standardization. Every legionary was now uniformly equipped with the *gladius*, the *scutum*, two *pila* and a mail shirt. One *pilum* was heavy, the other light: the iron point of the heavy one was joined to the wooden shaft by a rivet and a wooden peg which was intended to splinter on impact, thus denying the enemy use of the weapon. Full armour, including helmet, must have weighed around 30 kg (66 lb). Besides all this, the legionaries were now obliged to carry much of their own luggage: this amounted to entrenching equipment, cooking utensils, emergency rations and personal baggage, all strapped onto a forked pole. It was as a result of this that the soldiers gained the nickname of "Marius' mules".

The Lusitanians of the far west and the Celtiberians of the north gave constant trouble down to the late 140s, by which time only the hilltop town of Numantia still held out against Rome. A series of camps at Renieblas, 8 km (5 miles) to the east, housed the troops of successive Roman commanders in their attempts to reduce the town. Finally, in 134BC, the task was entrusted to Scipio Aemilianus. He was something of a siegecraft expert, having reduced Carthage in 146, and his blockade of Numantia, reportedly the first operation of its kind, eventually forced the capitulation of the inhabitants (133).

One man who had served as a Roman ally at Numantia was Jugurtha, a prince (and later, king) of Numidia. Many years later, affairs arising out of the murder of some Italian merchants in his country escalated into war with Rome. A succession of commanders sent to restore the situation culminated in the appointment of Gaius Marius (107BC), another veteran of Numantia. Jugurtha was finally captured in 105, having been betrayed to one of Marius' officers, a certain L. Cornelius Sulla. Both Marius and Sulla were destined to play major parts in the unfolding drama of the next decade.

Marius is usually credited with the institution of a professional Roman army; in fact, the two major changes ascribed to him were probably the result of a gradual process which had been gathering momentum for many years. First, Rome's amateur militia of conscripted men serving for six years was replaced by a professional long-service army of volunteers. The crucial factor was the lowering of

168 BC

ground where they built a camp. Almost a week passed, during which the Macedonians' positions turned through 90 degrees, before a minor clash of light-armed troops finally precipitated the battle. Perseus' line stretched for some 2 miles, with the phalanx in the centre and cavalry on either wing; he himself commanded on the right. He succeeded in wrong-footing the Romans – Aemilius later recalled his terror in the face of the advancing phalanx – and destroyed their front ranks. But the Macedonian line became disorganized in the process, and the legionaries rushed into the resulting gaps, where they wreaked havoc amongst the encumbered phalangites.

RESULT The Macedonian left was routed by Aemilius' elephants, Perseus and his cavalry fled the field, and the phalanx was exterminated.

CHAERONEA

DATE 86BC

CAMPAIGN First Mithridatic War.

NUMBERS Sulla's forces amounted to some 15,000 infantry and 1,500 cavalry; Archelaus, Mithridates' general, commanded an army at least three times as large.

DESCRIPTION Sulla and Archelaus met in the Boeotian plain north of the town of Chaeronea. As Sulla crossed the plain, he was obliged to turn his column left into the

(Above and opposite left) *Scenes from the "Altar of Domitius Ahenobarbus" depicting five legionaries, one of them a cavalryman, dating from the time of Marius. All wear mail shirts, belted at the waist to take some of the weight off the shoulders, and the infantrymen carry the characteristic oblong* scutum *with central spine and iron boss. Their helmets have horsehair plumes.*

the prescribed property qualification for service in order to draw upon the vast pool of *capite censi*, those citizens who owned no property and were thus normally excused military service. This in turn necessitated the equipping of soldiers at the state's expense.

The second major change was a tactical reform, discarding the maniple as the chief sub-unit in favour of the cohort. Each cohort resulted from the fusion of three maniples, one from each of the old divisions of *hastati, principes* and *triarii* (or *pilani*). The six centuries probably comprised 80 men, as the centuries of the Imperial army did, though pre-Marian centurions had commanded 60 men or fewer. The six centurions of the cohort preserved the old manipular terminology in their titles (e.g. *hastatus*).

The later 90s BC saw civil war erupt in Italy, with consequent repercussions on the army. Rome's Italian allies (the *socii*) were discontented with their military obligations and, in 91BC, rose in rebellion. Marius (now almost 70) was active in putting down the revolt in northern Italy, Sulla in the south. The war was over by 88BC, and Sulla was fêted as consul and promised the command against Mithridates VI of Pontus, who was threatening war in the east by invading Greece. As a result of

86 BC

line of battle to meet Archelaus' approach. His left wing was seriously outflanked, but reserve cohorts were posted on the foot-hills to the rear. Archelaus' army comprised a phalanx of 15,000 liberated slaves, protected by scythed chariots, and strong contingents of cavalry and light troops on the wings. As he engaged with his right wing, the Roman reserve advanced to protect its outflanked comrades, but was driven back. Therefore, Sulla himself came across with his cavalry from the right and

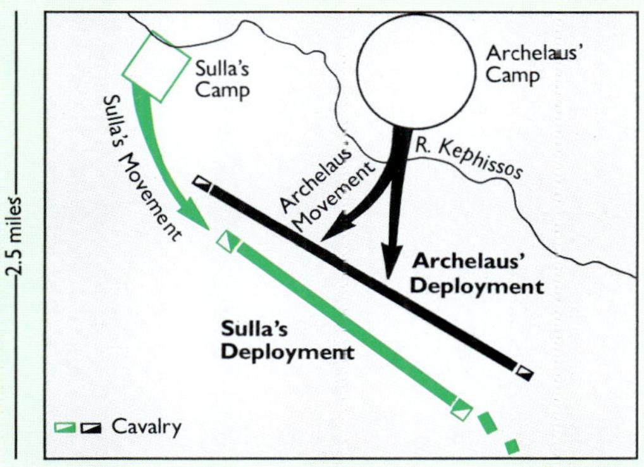

flung Archelaus back. The Roman left was again reinforced by the reserve and Sulla returned to the right wing, where Archelaus was now pressing the attack. Here, the Romans prevailed again, breaking through the enemy line.

RESULT Archelaus' army fled in confusion.

THE LATER REPUBLIC LEGIONS

Roman legions each bore a numeral reflecting the sequence of their creation; the numbers I to IV were traditionally reserved for the consuls each year. At the time of Marius, the legions appear to have been reconstructed every year, but during the later Republic they began to retain their identity. Service was, in the first instance, for six years, though the total period of liability to service was 16 years.

During the 70s BC, there were around 14 legions in the field in any one year. Throughout the 50s, Caesar steadily increased his Gallic army, and by 49BC he controlled some 30 legions. During the Civil War, there were almost 50 legions under arms. The rank and file had to be rewarded: Caesar doubled his soldiers' pay to 225 *denarii* a year to secure their loyalty, and time-served veterans were entitled to a plot of land.

the Social War, the allied contingents which used to accompany the legions on campaign ceased to exist: all Italian recruits were now entitled to become legionaries. The number of legions consequently multiplied, particularly in preparation for major campaigns.

THE LATER REPUBLIC (c.100–44BC)

Sulla's war with Mithridates was inconclusive, despite two victories in the field (one at Chaeronea – see page 32) and he was forced to seek a diplomatic agreement. He had left Rome under a cloud – his army had marched on the city after the Senate tried to deprive him of his eastern command – and he returned to renewed civil unrest. By the end of 80BC, as dictator, he was master of the Roman world. His death in 78BC ushered in a new round of civil war in which the main players were the late dictator's legates. One, Gnaeus Pompey, was active against rebel forces in Spain. Another, M. Licinius Crassus, crushed Spartacus and his army of renegade slaves: he employed an elaborate system of earthworks to confine his quarry to the toe of Italy, a device perhaps inspired by Scipio Aemilianus' blockade of Numantia. A third, L. Licinius Lucullus, enjoyed initial success against a renascent Mithridates, until a mutiny paralysed his army (67BC); the command was given to Pompey, who finally consolidated Roman authority in the east.

At around this time, a young nobleman named C. Julius Caesar rose to prominence. By 60BC, he had joined Pompey and Crassus in an informal alliance known to us as the First Triumvirate; until the death of Crassus in 53BC, this trio successfully imposed their collective will on the State.

In 58BC, Caesar embarked upon a five-year command in Gaul (later extended to ten years). He was immediately called upon to deal with the Helvetii, who were in the process of migrating west from the area of modern Switzerland. In order to deny them access to Roman territory, Caesar had the only legion available to him construct a barrier along the Rhône for a distance of some 17½ miles; the whole thing, comprising rampart, ditch and guard posts, was completed in around a fortnight, testifying to the engineering skills of the legionaries. Caesar later brought up three more legions and raised two for the final confrontation, which saw the utter defeat of the Helvetii.

From now on, Caesar intervened directly in Gallic affairs, raising a further two legions in 57 and campaigning as far afield as Brittany. Disaffection smouldered on as the Gauls gradually realized that Caesar planned to occupy their territories: a legion was destroyed in the winter of 54–53, but Caesar increased his complement to 10 in the following year (borrowing a legion from Pompey in the process). In the summer of 52, the great Gallic revolt flared up under the leadership of Vercingetorix. By this

52 BC

ALESIA

DATE 52BC
CAMPAIGN Gallic Wars
DESCRIPTION Caesar encamped his forces at key points around the hilltop town of Alesia and enclosed Vercingetorix and his 80,000-strong army within siegeworks. Caesar's scheme was rather more elaborate than a simple blockade: one line of fortifications confined Vercingetorix within Alesia; another faced outwards against the

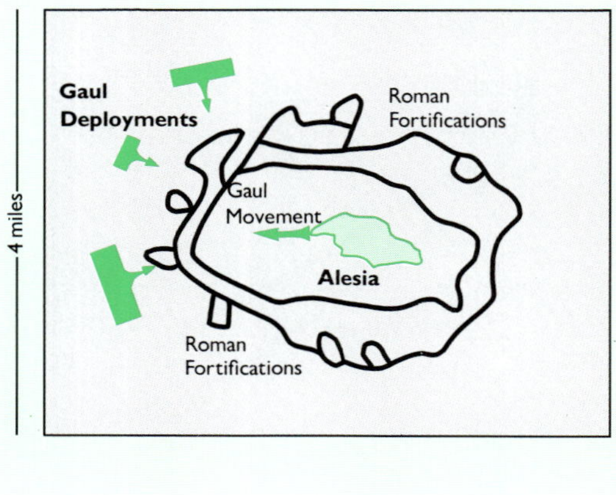

inevitable Gallic relieving force. Each line comprised several different elements. First, there was the rampart itself, crowned with a palisade and fortified with towers every 27 yards; forked branches (*cervi*) projected horizontally from the top. Next, there was a pair of ditches, each 5½ yards wide, the inner of which was filled with water. Beyond these lay various booby-traps: sharpened branches (*cippi*) set in trenches and interwoven to form a hedge of spikes; eight rows of pointed stakes (*lilia*)

time, Caesar's army probably consisted of 12 legions. His first move was to attack the town of Avaricum, which the inhabitants had chosen to defend, rather than retreat with Vercingetorix; such was the Roman engineering expertise that the town was reduced by siege in under a month. His attempt to storm Gergovia, however, ended in failure, but he was able to trap Vercingetorix in the hilltop town of Alesia (see page 34), where the Gauls were starved into submission. One or two actions in the following year (51) effectively finished off the Gallic war.

When Caesar's command in Gaul was renewed (55BC), his fellow Triumvirs, Pompey and Crassus, were granted respectively as their provinces Spain and Syria. Crassus unwisely provoked the sleeping giant of Parthia, a loosely organized confederation of states under the authority of a central monarchy. In 53, he crossed the Euphrates with an army of seven legions accompanied by light troops, and ran into a force of Parthian cavalry and horse archers in the vicinity of Carrhae. The legionaries presented a sitting target for the enemy missiles and were unable to retaliate: the Romans reportedly lost 20,000 killed (Crassus amongst them) and 10,000 prisoners.

Meanwhile, a breach had opened between Caesar and Pompey. The Senate put their trust in Pompey, whereupon Caesar swept down into Italy (49BC). Pompey rapidly retreated before Caesar's advance and embarked for the east; Caesar pursued him across the Adriatic, after quickly neutralizing his forces in Spain. Pinning Pompey on the coast south of his base at Dyrrhachium, Caesar hemmed him in with a circumvallation, but Pompey simply built a line of counter-works in reply. After fierce skirmishing, Caesar withdrew. Pompey followed and the two forces met at Pharsalus, where the Pompeians were soundly beaten; Pompey himself fled to meet his death in Egypt, and his troops were reorganized into four more legions for Caesar's huge army. After the war with Pompey, Caesar released his veteran legions from service and, as dictator, made plans for a Parthian campaign; these were foiled by his assassination in 44BC.

THE FOUNDATION OF THE EMPIRE

By late 43BC, the major players in the next phase of fighting had resolved themselves into two camps: Caesar's murderers, the self-styled "Liberators" (principally Brutus and Cassius) in exile east of the Adriatic; and the coalition known to us as the Second Triumvirate, comprising the Caesarian partisans Mark Antony and Aemilius Lepidus, and Caesar's great-nephew and heir, Octavian. There were still some 37 legions under arms; several of Caesar's veteran legions had been reformed into the bargain. Leaving Lepidus in charge of Rome, Antony and Octavian transported 20 or so legions across the Adriatic to meet the 19 legions of the Liberators. The two armies

Continued on page 38

SERVICE IN THE AUGUSTAN ARMY

The conditions of service under the Principate differed significantly from those under the Republic. Augustus abolished the hitherto standard six-year stint, and by AD5 new regulations required each soldier to serve for 20 years, with a further five years as a reservist. This last distinction faded with time, and as discharges were made only every second year, some men served a total of 26 years.

The rewards of service were regularized as well. Augustus founded the military treasury to meet the costs of the armed forces: besides an annual salary, varying according to rank and pay-grade, the legionary could look forward to a substantial gratuity on discharge. Furthermore, the custom arose whereby each new emperor paid the soldiers a bonus on his accession.

Gem portrait of Augustus, who brought the Republic to an end in 27BC.

42 BC

embedded vertically in pits and concealed with brushwood; and a scattering of barbed spikes (*stimuli*) anchored in blocks of wood. The inner line ran for some 10 miles; the outer was over 17 miles long.

RESULT Gallic attempts to co-ordinate attacks on the Roman lines from within and without were unsuccessful, and Vercingetorix surrendered.

PHILIPPI

DATE 42BC

CAMPAIGN Civil war, between the Liberators (Brutus and Cassius), and the Triumvirs (Antony, Octavian and Lepidus).

DESCRIPTION The Liberators were encamped on either side of the Via Egnatia, Brutus to the north with his right flank resting on the mountains, Cassius to the south with his left flank against a large marsh. The camp of the Triumvirs sat ▸

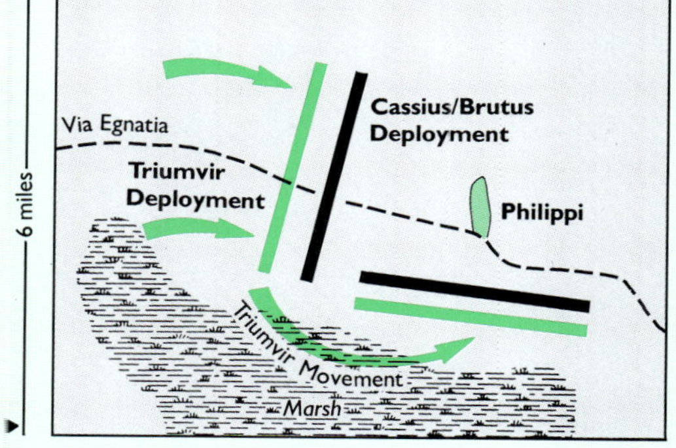

ROMAN NAVAL WARFARE

ROME'S FIRST FLEET was built during the First Punic War (264–241BC) to counter the Carthaginian mastery of the sea. Rome had the financial strength and the stocks of timber to maintain a large fleet, but after the defeat of Carthage and the crushing of the naval power of Syria and Rhodes (mid-2nd century BC) there was a general naval disarmament. In the absence of adequate maritime policing, pirates terrorized the seas unmolested. At last, Pompey was given command over the whole Mediterranean (67BC) and, in a lightning campaign, eradicated piracy. Roman naval power was never again allowed to fall into abeyance.

During the civil wars, fleets proliferated just as the legions did; they were necessary for controlling trade routes and transporting armies. Ironically, it was a son of Pompey, Sextus Pompeius, who emerged as scourge of the Mediterranean in 43BC; Octavian and his lieutenant, Agrippa, finally defeated him in two battles off the Sicilian coast (36BC). Antony, too, relied on naval power in the eastern Mediterranean, and the contest for control of the empire was, finally, settled by a naval encounter.

As part of his reorganization of the Roman Imperial Navy after Actium, Augustus concentrated his ships at Misenum on the Bay of Naples and Ravenna on the Adriatic. The *classis Misenensis* was the largest fleet: it has been calculated that, in the mid-1st century, its manpower exceeded 10,000. The *classis Ravennas* was perhaps half as large. Both were commanded by high-ranking equestrian (i.e. non-senatorial) officers *(praefecti classis)* responsible only to the emperor. Independent squadrons were soon established on all the major waterways: the Black Sea, the English Channel, the Rhine and Danube, and off the coasts of Syria, Egypt and Mauretania. These provincial fleets were commanded by more junior *praefecti*, responsible to their respective provincial governors.

The standard warship of the republic had been the quinquereme, though galleys could be much larger in size. In the imperial fleet,

(Above) Marines on the deck of a cataphract trireme.

(Top) Roman relief showing a trireme, c.100 BC-AD100. In earlier times, the topmost bank of oars was accommodated in the outrigger; here, all three banks clearly emerge from beneath the outrigger, which was perhaps retained as a bumper, protecting the rowers from buffeting and the oars from any attempts to shear them.

(Below) The Romans built two sorts of trireme: the cataphract (or armoured) and the lighter aphract (unarmoured). The vessel shown here is the former, as it might have appeared during the early Empire. There is a massive forecastle in the bows, and a cabin for the captain in the stern. The ram is single-pointed, as opposed to the triple rams of earlier galleys.

however, the most prevalent warship was the trireme and, in the provincial fleets, the *liburnian* (a swift, two-banked galley); one *hexeres* (a double-banked galley with three men per oar) was retained in the Misenum fleet as the flagship, and there were a few quadriremes and quinqueremes.

The captain of each ship *(trierarch)* had a staff of petty officers and ratings; superimposed on this naval organization was a military one, whereby the entire crew, regardless of size, was organized as a *centuria* under the command of a centurion. On a trireme, for instance, the crew numbered about 200 and on a quinquereme, 300. The individual sailors were not slaves, as is often thought, but provincials who were granted Roman citizenship after 26 years' service. In peacetime, the galleys patrolled their own areas and despatched letters and orders; the riverine fleets escorted supply convoys and kept a watch on the frontiers. The personnel often acted as an onshore militia and, at sea, kept piracy at bay.

(Above) Warship of the Late Republic, usually linked with Antony at Actium because of the Egyptian crocodile emblem on the prow. The ship is a two-banked cataphract, probably a quadrireme or a quinquereme. The outrigger appears to be furnished with louvres providing ventilation for the rowers. Towards the bow, there is a rectangular box housing a bust of the ship's patron deity, perhaps a gorgon.

(Left) Auxiliaries stow equipment on a cargo boat, while legionaries man a two-banked liburnian, the most common craft in the provincial fleets. The scene is the River Danube c. AD100.

Silver coin issued in 44-43 BC by one of Sextus Pompeius' admirals, Q. Nasidius. The galley is perhaps a two-banked quinquereme, the standard ship-of-the-line.

ROMAN MILITARY EQUIPMENT

At some time in the early 1st century, a new type of armour was introduced: the so-called *lorica segmentata*. It is usually thought to have been restricted to legionaries. Many soldiers continued to wear mail shirts, and armour must have varied from unit to unit. Other equipment remained substantially the same. However, auxiliaries appear to have used flat oval or hexagonal shields, as opposed to the legionary *scutum*, and cavalry troopers, who required a longer reach than infantry, were armed with a long sword *(spatha)*. Cavalry helmets were often elaborately decorated, and covered most of the head, leaving only the eyes, nose and mouth exposed. Extraordinary circumstances necessitated special equipment: the legions engaged in Trajan's Dacian wars were issued with greaves and armguards, and the cross-bracing of helmets became common.

met at Philippi in Macedonia (see page 35), where the Triumvirs eventually prevailed. After the battle, the time-served veterans were released and sent to Italy with Octavian; the remainder were regrouped into 11 legions, three of whom accompanied Octavian. The eight remaining to Antony included his favourite legion, V *Alaudae*, raised by Caesar in 52BC.

The Triumvirate was due to expire in 33BC. Relations between its prime movers had, in any case, deteriorated, chiefly it would seem as a result of Antony's liaison with Cleopatra, Queen of Egypt. The Senate declared war on her in 32, thus providing Octavian's excuse for a showdown with Antony.

By then, both men had substantially increased their armies. Antony assembled a force of 23 legions on the west coast of Greece at Actium; others of his legions were absent in Cyrenaica. Octavian fielded about 24 of his 30 or so legions: while he harassed Antony by land, his lieutenant Agrippa hemmed in Antony's fleet and cut his communications. At last, Antony staked all on a naval engagement (31BC), but he and Cleopatra simply broke free of the blockade and fled to Egypt, where they later took their own lives. Antony's army surrendered, all time-served veterans were discharged and the remainder were incorporated into Octavian's new order of battle.

Octavian was now effectively the ruler of the Roman world. He ensured his primacy by assuming all the key Republican offices himself, and in 27BC he took the new name of Augustus. His long reign (he died in AD14) consolidated the position of emperor in the Roman world and the Republic was never restored. His position, and that of his successors, was guaranteed by a strong and loyal military. After Actium, the swollen ranks of the army were reduced, perhaps over several years: by 25BC, there were 28 legions under arms, though quite how Augustus arrived at that number, by what stages of reorganization, is not known. The incorporation of five or six complete Antonian legions (all, significantly, old Caesarian units) led to the duplication of numerals which persisted throughout the imperial period. (In fact, Augustus retained *three* legions with the numeral III.) Other legions, bearing the title *Gemina* ("Twin"), were clearly formed by the amalgamation of two existing units.

Augustus set about forging the far-flung conquests of the later Republic into an empire. Rome now controlled territories from Portugal in the west to the Euphrates in the east, from Belgium in the north to the Sahara in the south, but the interior was not wholly Romanized. Augustus secured the Alpine lands to the north of Italy, completed the long-overdue conquest of Spain, and annexed the regions south of the Danube, but his attempts to conquer Germany east of the Rhine were frustrated; three legions were lost in the process. Claudius (AD41–54) was the next emperor to initiate a war of conquest by invading Britain, and Nero's reign (AD54–68) saw warfare on the eastern frontier. In AD66, a revolt flared up in Judaea and quickly

astride the road itself, with a rampart and ditch running southwards. Antony attempted to outflank Cassius by cutting a path through the marsh and, though thwarted, brought on the general engagement. Brutus' forces overran the opposing lines and captured the main camp; Antony in turn broke through Cassius' defences, routed his soldiers and took his camp, whereupon Cassius killed himself. Both sides then retired to their original positions and settled down for nearly three weeks. Octavian, meanwhile, shifted the axis of battle through 90 degrees by constructing three camps on the northern fringes of the marsh, thus threatening Brutus' flank. To avoid encirclement, Brutus extended his lines east, but morale in his army was low. Finally, he bowed to pressure from his general staff and offered battle.

RESULT The Triumvirs won and the beaten forces fled.

SECOND CREMONA

DATE 24 October AD69

CAMPAIGN Civil war of AD69

NUMBERS Flavians – five legions plus auxiliaries; Vitellians – four complete legions, detachments of seven legions, and a selection of auxiliary troops.

DESCRIPTION In the evening of 24 October, a Flavian army arrived in the vicinity of Cremona to do battle with the Vitellian army. The Flavians took up their position

After the death of the emperor Titus in AD81, a marble arch was built to commemorate his capture of Jerusalem in AD70. This sculptural scene portrays the triumph celebrated by him and his father, Vespasian. Legionaries carrying the spoils of the Temple are depicted in undress uniform and wearing olive wreaths. Their treasure includes the Table of Shew-bread with incense-cups, two silver trumpets and the seven-branched candelabrum (the menorah). The objects would have been described on the placards which the soldiers carry.

assumed major proportions: this was the so-called Jewish War, lasting until AD73 or 74, when a pocket of resistance on the rock of Masada was finally crushed.

The power struggle following the death of Nero initiated a new round of civil war. First Galba, then Otho became emperor; then Vitellius, with the backing of the seven legions on the Rhine, decisively defeated Otho's army at Cremona. Meanwhile, the armies of the east had declared for T. Flavius Vespasian, the general conducting the Jewish War. His deputies won the empire for him: Antonius Primus stripped the Danube of troops and defeated Vitellius' army, again at Cremona (see below). The subsequent revolt of Batavian auxiliaries on the Rhine had wider repercussions in the order of battle: whole legions were cashiered in the aftermath and new ones raised (or created by amalgamation). Legion V *Alaudae* probably disappeared at this time, but the overall complement was brought up to 28 once again.

AD 69

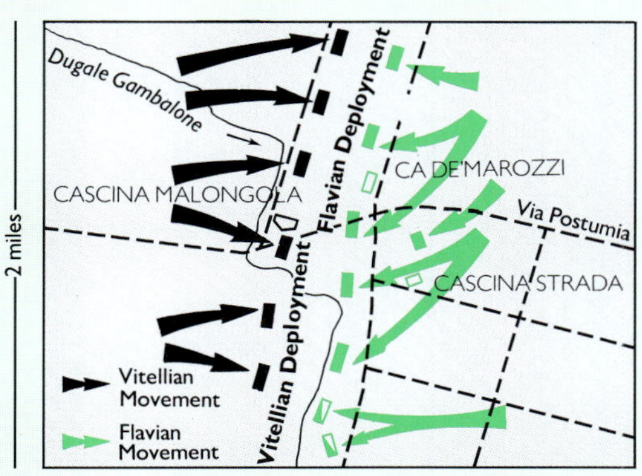

astride the road, with a screen of German horse ranged in front. The Vitellians attacked in the gathering darkness and set up their artillery on the roadway; the ensuing battle continued through the night. One stone-throwing *ballista* in particular wreaked havoc in the Flavian ranks until two soldiers infiltrated the Vitellian lines and sabotaged it. At sunrise, the Flavian Third legion turned and raised a cheer, at which the Vitellians lost heart and fled, thinking that the soldiers were greeting reinforcements. (In fact, legion III *Gallica* had been stationed in Syria for the past century, and most of the men were of sun-worshipping eastern origin.) The Vitellians took shelter in nearby Cremona which, despite a show of surrender, was ferociously sacked by the Flavians.

RESULT Victory for the Flavians.

(Above) Bronze head of the emperor Hadrian.

(Right) Hadrian's wall. The frontiers of the Roman Empire gradually became permanent, as further conquest ceased. Artificial barriers were only required where no natural boundaries existed. Mainland Europe had the rivers Rhine and Danube; much of north Africa and the East had great tracts of desert. In Britain, however, the emperor Hadrian decided to build a frontier wall stretching 75 miles from Tyne to Solway, with forts every six miles or so. The sheer scale of construction must have been intended to overawe Rome's northern neighbours.

AD 69

DANUBIAN WARS

DATE AD69–178

DESCRIPTION North of the Danube lay the lands of the Suebic Germans (Marcomanni and Quadi) and, further east, on either side of the Dacian kingdom, the Sarmatians (Jazyges and Roxolani). Diplomacy kept these peoples quiescent until AD69, when serious raiding by the Roxolani prompted firmer fortification of the Danube. However, it was not until AD85 that crisis point was reached: the Dacians invaded Moesia and defeated two Roman armies; they were themselves defeated at Tapae in AD88 and accepted peace terms. Meanwhile, the Suebic tribes were becoming restive and, in AD92, enlisted the aid of the Jazyges in an invasion of Pannonia. The Danube had now become the key frontier, with nine legions stationed along its length. Domitian's treaty with the Dacians was rejected, some years

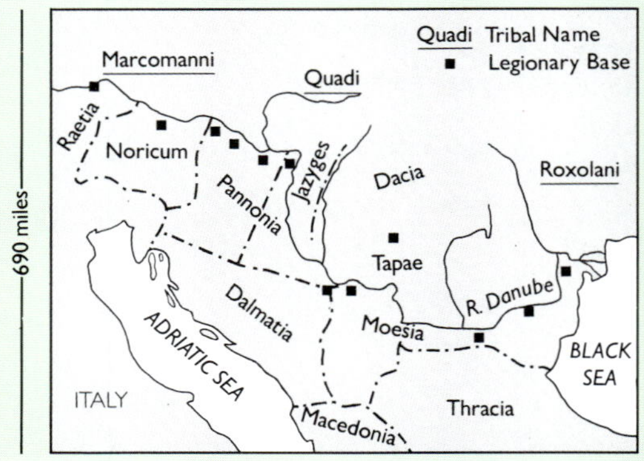

Camp at Masada. The clavicula *forced the invader to expose his unshielded side when entering.*

THE ARMY ON THE MARCH

A marching army comprised three main sections: the vanguard of light-armed troops, for screening and scouting; the main body of heavy infantry, including the baggage train; and the rearguard. Cavalry provided cover in advance and on the flanks. Behind the vanguard, pioneers cleared the route for the marching column, and a detachment of legionaries carried the tools for laying out the temporary camp, the army's overnight accommodation. Camps could range widely in size and form, but most were roughly rectangular with rounded corners. The perimeter was normally defined by a ditch and rampart, crowned with a palisade of stakes. Gates were often provided with earthwork defences – the camp at Masada shown left demonstrates the *clavicula*, a curving length of rampart and ditch projecting inwards from the right.

Under the three Flavian emperors, Vespasian, Titus and Domitian (AD69–96), there were no great wars of conquest, though Roman forces continued to advance in Britain, and the German frontier was extensively remodelled. The accession of Trajan (AD98–117) brought fresh annexations on the Danube (see below) and in the east, though there are few details of the warfare which must have accompanied them. His successor, Hadrian, was more concerned with consolidating the frontiers, and the Golden Age of Antoninus Pius (AD138–161) saw little major warfare. The unfortunate Marcus Aurelius (AD161–180), however, was faced with a Parthian war (see page 42), a plague and a full-scale invasion of northern barbarians; it seems that he intended to conquer territory north of the Danube, but failed. The Roman world was soon again convulsed in civil war, and the victor was Septimius Severus, who ruled from AD193 to 211.

Throughout this period, the army comprised a number of different elements. In the later Republic, generals had enlisted the aid of irregular troops provided by friendly tribes and kings. These were usually cavalry and archers, making good the

AD 178

later, by Trajan. In the course of two campaigns (AD101–2 and AD105–6) he defeated them and annexed their kingdom as a Roman province. The details of warfare remain unknown; the first campaign at least ended in a major battle, but tactics and strategy are lost to us. The Sarmatians continued to give trouble, though after Hadrian negotiated new peace treaties in AD118, the frontier lay dormant for 50 years. This was the lull before the storm which broke during the reign of Marcus Aurelius. First, German tribes invaded Pannonia in AD166; then, the Romans retaliated with a massive offensive across the Danube in AD170, but were unsuccessful: all along the frontier there were barbarian incursions, and the Marcomanni and Quadi even invaded northern Italy. Around 174, the focus shifted east to the Jazyges, who eventually sued for peace and provided 8,000 cavalry to serve in the Roman army. Marcus himself remained on the frontier until AD175, but returned to take command in AD178. He allegedly wished to annex the territories west of Dacia as the provinces of Marcomannia and Sarmatia; indeed, there were some 20,000 Roman troops wintering there. But Marcus fell ill and died in AD180; his son and successor, Commodus, withdrew the garrisons.

RESULT Diplomacy ensured a peaceful frontier for over 50 years.

THE PARTHIANS

The armies of the Parthian empire consisted largely of super-heavy cavalry and horse archers. At Carrhae in 53BC, the ratio was probably about one to 10, with the proportion of super-heavy cavalry generally increasing thereafter. The super-heavy cavalry were "cataphract" lancers: their panoply comprised full armour, including arm- and thigh-guards; the horse, too, was often armoured, or half-armoured. The chief materials were laminated iron, mail, scale and *lamellae* (horn plates overlapped and laced, vertically and horizontally), often worn in combination. The main weapon was the lance *(kontos)*.

The horse archers wore no armour, relying on speed as their defence, and used the composite bow. In battle, they generally operated in concert with the lancers, harassing the enemy and breaking up their formations in preparation for a lancer attack.

(Above right) Beyond the modern road, the ruins of Hatra's city wall can be seen, dotted with towers and bastions. Traces of a circumvallation cross the road in the foreground.

(Right) Copy of graffiti from Dura Europos on the Euphrates, depicting the two types of Parthian horsemen. The lancer and his horse are armoured in mail and laminated plates; the archer is probably equipped with the gorytos, *a combination bowcase and quiver.*

deficiencies of the legion. Augustus appears to have regularized such auxiliary troops into infantry cohorts (modelled on the legionary cohort) and cavalry *alae* ("wings"). Each *ala* comprised sixteen *turmae* of 30-odd men, including three officers. A third type of unit, perhaps inspired by Caesar's German mixed cavalry, was the *cohors equitata*, an infantry battalion with a cavalry element attached; in battle, the two were separated and each was brigaded with its fellows, rather than fighting as a mixed unit. All auxiliaries were normally non-citizens, in contrast to the citizen legions but, on discharge, they would receive citizenship.

There was considerable variation within the *auxilia*. At some time in the late 60s,

AD 114

PARTHIAN WARS

DATE AD114–97

DESCRIPTION The Euphrates was the *de facto* boundary between Rome and the east. The only disputed territory was the kingdom of Armenia, sitting like a buffer between Rome's north-eastern frontier and the Parthian vassals in Mesopotamia. Since the days of Augustus, the king of Armenia had been a Roman nominee; during the reign of Nero, however, the Parthians captured Armenia, but magnanimously allowed Rome to crown the Parthian-nominated king. Trajan decided to rectify the situation by annexing Armenia. In AD114, he embarked on an invasion of Parthia and, by AD116, Ctesiphon (the Parthian capital) had fallen without resistance, but revolts and a Parthian resurgence led to the rapid abandonment of all territories beyond the Euphrates. An uneasy peace lasted until AD162, when the Parthians suddenly invaded Armenia (where

Map of the Roman Empire c. AD 100. Six legions were distributed along the Eastern frontier and two were based in the Nile delta area, but the whole of North Africa lay under the control of a single legion. Another was based in Spain, and Britain's garrison numbered four, but the bulk of Rome's legions lay in fortresses along the Rhine and Danube. This imbalance became more pronounced throughout the 2nd century.

double-sized units (so-called *milliaria*) were introduced, and some units were composed entirely of archers *(sagittarii)*. From the time of Hadrian, there were units of heavily-armoured lancers *(cataphracti)* while, at the other end of the spectrum, there were units of completely unarmoured North African bareback riders. Many of the ethnic peculiarities of the specialized troops were gradually lost as the *auxilia* settled down to their role of frontier defence.

Of course, warfare was by no means the only occupation of the army. The daily routine demanded all sorts of tradesmen and specialists: in return for exemption from fatigues and, in many cases, extra pay, soldiers performed any one of over a 100 duties, from carpenters to medics. Promotions and transfers could carry a man from one branch of the service to another, and from one end of the empire to the other, in a military career often lasting a lifetime.

Legions and *auxilia* were not the only troops: irregular units of ethnic origin were later introduced, perhaps to recapture the élan that had been lost with the standardization of the *auxilia*. There were also military and para-military forces in Rome, such as the imperial bodyguards (the Praetorian Guard and their cavalry equivalent, the *equites singulares Augusti*), and naval squadrons patrolled the major waterways. In time of crisis, the whole military machine worked in concert. But, from the time of Septimius Severus, fundamental changes were in store.

AD 197

they installed a Parthian prince on the throne) and Syria. Marcus Aurelius sent large forces and capable commanders: Armenia was subjugated (AD163–4), Edessa and Nisibis seized (AD165) and Ctesiphon destroyed (AD166). Unfortunately, the returning armies brought plague to the west, but the eastern frontier was secured and substantially remodelled, taking in an area beyond the Euphrates. The fortress-city of Dura Europos received a Roman garrison now. In AD197, Septimius Severus launched an invasion of Parthia, the so-called Second Parthian War. (The First, in AD195, was simply aimed at the Arab peoples of the north who had taken the opportunity of the civil war in the west to turn on the local Roman garrisons.) The Romans sacked Ctesiphon yet again, but Severus failed (as had Trajan before him) to capture the independent desert city of Hatra. It seems that he spent only 20 days besieging the city, during which the defenders managed to destroy his siege-machinery; a mutiny amongst his troops finally forced Severus to withdraw.

RESULT The net result of the eastern campaigns was the establishment of a new Roman province called Mesopotamia, but covering only the northern area around Nisibis.

ROMAN SIEGECRAFT

ONE OF THE EARLIEST Roman siege-operations was mounted at Agrigentum in Sicily in 262BC. A twin line of fortifications, linking two camps, was constructed around the town, the inner line to confine the enemy, and the outer to repel any relieving force. After seven months, it was lack of vigilance which finally cost the Romans victory. Nevertheless, the technique of bicircumvallation was basically sound, and was used again and again: the most celebrated example is Caesar's siege of Alesia. Of course, it was only necessary when there was danger of attack from the rear. Besieging an isolated enemy required nothing more elaborate than a single circumvallation. These sieges were essentially blockades; that is to say, they depended upon the surrender of the enemy. More commonly, the Roman commander would mount an assault, with or without a blockade. This generally involved the construction of a ramp, providing the siege-machines with a gentle gradient and a smooth approach to the town walls.

The besieger's arsenal included a battering-ram – a long, iron-tipped wooden beam suspended by ropes from a sturdy mobile housing called a "tortoise"; this was the classic means of breaching a wall. The Romans also used siege-towers, which provided an elevated platform for missile attacks, either by archers or artillery; they often incorporated a battering-ram at ground level. These machines had to be proof against fire and bombardment, so they were often iron-clad or covered with layers of wicker and hides.

Each legion had a complement of artillery, useful in siege-warfare, particularly for providing covering fire. Ancient artillery fell into two constructionally distinct groups – arrow-shooting *catapultae* and stone-throwing *ballistae* – though, around AD100, a revolution in artillery design meant that both types were technically *ballistae*. By far the most common arrow-shooter was the 3-span variant (a machine about 5ft high, firing arrows some 25 in long), but stone-throwers could range up to monstrous machines 15 ft high, capable of throwing stones weighing 110 lb.

During siege operations, personnel were protected by sheds and wicker screens. Legionaries moving up to the wall would adopt the *testudo* (or "tortoise") formation, with shields locked over their heads, though at Jotapata in AD67 the defenders broke up a *testudo* by pouring boiling oil over it.

The engineering skill and dogged determination of the Romans seldom failed. One conspicuous exception was at Hatra, the desert city which repulsed both Trajan and, on two occasions, Septimius Severus. The remains of Roman siegeworks are preserved at several sites, but none is more spectacular than at Masada in the Judaean desert. Here, rather than filling a ravine, the Romans were obliged to build a ramp up the side of a mountain, and haul an iron-clad tower with battering-ram up the 1:20 incline. The ramp, circumvallation and camps are still clearly visible today, a monument to the siegecraft of the Romans.

(Above) One of the classic manoeuvres of the Roman legionaries was the testudo, *or tortoise. This is described by many ancient authors with minor variations in size and form, but the end result was the same.*

(Right) After investing Masada with a circumvallation, the Romans constructed a ramp up the side to carry an iron-plated mobile tower and battering-ram. Remains of the ramp can be seen on the left of the photograph shown here.

(Above) The basic weapon in the besieger's arsenal was the battering-ram, housed within a mobile tortoise. The Roman model had a distinctively triangular cross-section, with the ram suspended from the ridge-piece by long ropes. The tortoise itself was protected by boards and layers of clay or hide mattressing.

(Left) Caesar's siegeworks at Alesia presented a formidable system of obstacles facing both inwards and outwards. Here we see a section of the inner line comprising rampart and two ditches, the inner of which was filled with water. Various booby-traps inside the circumvallation ensured the security of the whole scheme.

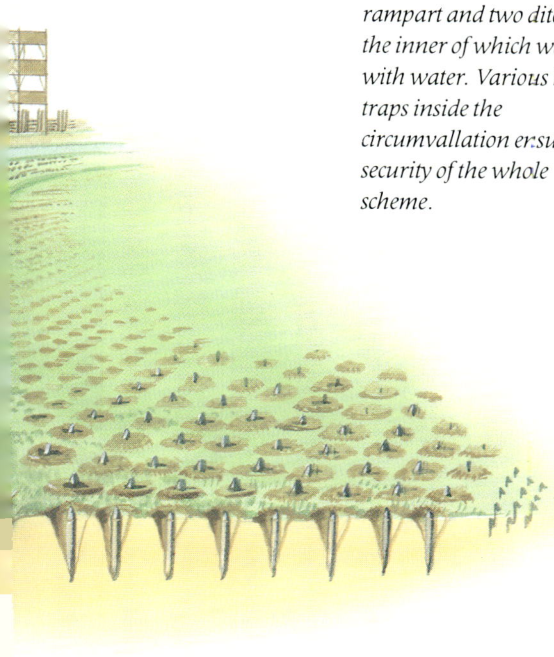

(Below) The stone-throwing engine of the Romans was the ballista. *The machine shown here dates from around* AD*230, and is of medium to small calibre, firing stones of only 6 lbs.*

(Above) Up until around AD*100, the Romans employed the arrow-firing* catapulta *of the Greeks. The model shown here is a 3-span (i.e. medium calibre) catapult, which fired a 25-in arrow.*

4

ROME'S DECLINE AND FALL

WHEN THE EMPEROR Marcus Aurelius (161–80) died, the Roman empire declined, it was said, from a realm of gold to one of rust and iron. Military corrosion had already begun. Marcus' predecessors, by choosing to consolidate existing frontiers, risked losing the initiative. He inherited a prospect of war on two fronts: the Parthians destroyed a legion in Armenia, and the northern tribes threatened to cross the Danube. In the event, however, the eastern armies defeated the Parthians with the help of three legions from the Rhine and Danube, before the storm broke in the north. Here at first a Roman counter-offensive, spearheaded by the release of two lions across the Danube, as suggested by a quack oracle, ended in disaster; the German Quadi and Marcomanni seized the chance to cross the river from what is now Czechoslovakia and penetrated to the gates of Italy. One of Marcus' generals, Claudius Fronto, the man who raised two new legions, was honoured posthumously with a statue "because he fell fighting bravely for his country after victories against the Germans". Then in a series of painful counter-attacks in the 170s, Marcus carried the war into the enemy's homeland, murderous untidy episodes depicted in the carved reliefs of his stone column: his glum bearded face can still be seen, surveying not the tidy warfare of Trajan's Column, but what his modern biographer calls the "grim and sordid necessity" of it all. He was a devout philosopher who equated military operations with a spider catching flies, forced by the logic of the military crisis to assume personal command. This would be true of his successors for the next two centuries; and they would die if they lost the army's confidence.

Marcus' unworthy son Commodus (180–92), by abandoning his father's conquests, threw away the chance of dominating central Europe. Instead he sought distinction as a gladiator, and he was lucky that the only major crisis of his reign was in northern Britain. Here the tribes were defeated by Ulpius Marcellus, an eccentric disciplinarian who lived on (very stale) bread sent out from Rome, and ingeniously convinced his men that he never slept, by writing out his orders before he went to bed

AD 193

SIEGE OF BYZANTIUM

DATE AD193–5
CAMPAIGN Civil war between Septimius Severus and Pescennius Niger
OBJECT To eliminate resistance to Severus.
DESCRIPTION Byzantium was impregnably sited on the promontory defined by the Golden Horn, the Bosphorus and the Sea of Marmara. It had massive walls with enfilading salients and towers, well equipped with artillery. In AD193 it supported Severus' rival, the governor of Syria, and continued to resist a year after he was dead. Only when reduced to cannibalism did the garrison surrender to a force from the legions of the lower Danube. (In AD324, Constantine refounded it as his New Rome. Constantinople, as it was soon called, was enlarged in the early 5th century, and given the elaborate walls which survive in Istanbul.)
RESULT An end of the resistance to Severus in the east.

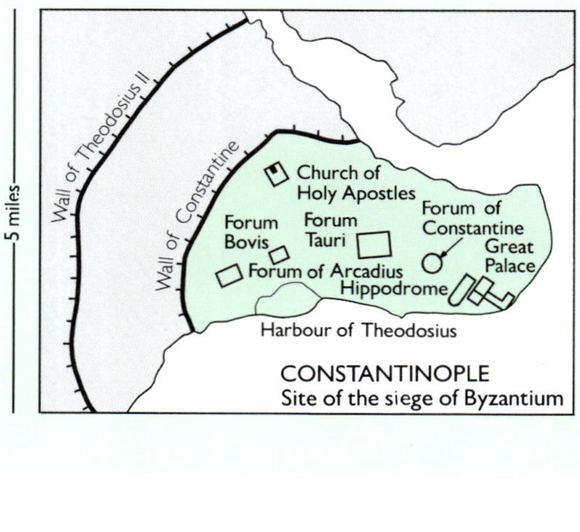

CONSTANTINOPLE
Site of the siege of Byzantium

and having them issued at intervals during the night. His successor Pertinax, a former schoolmaster whom Marcus had promoted for his military ability like Maximianus, actually became emperor when Commodus lost the confidence even of his intimates and was murdered. But within a few weeks he too was dead, at the hands of the Praetorian Guard. The civil wars that followed proved once more what was said of the Year of the Four Emperors (69): "the secret of Empire was out: emperors could be made outside Rome". The emperor was explicitly commander-in-chief, and once again the Danubian legions, now much the largest army group, imposed their nominee.

SEPTIMIUS SEVERUS

Because Septimius Severus (193–211) lacked military experience, he delegated at first to his generals, their armies consisting of legionary detachments, a sign that it was no longer feasible to move whole legions. Significantly too, the battles which overthrew the armies of Syria (193) and Britain (197) were both decided by the intervention of cavalry operating independently; it thus foreshadowed the cavalry corps of the later third century.

Severus trusted the dreams which told him he would become emperor, but he remained emperor by paying attention to the army and its needs. "Enrich the troops, and despise everyone else," he is supposed to have told his sons. He personally directed a successful invasion of the Parthian empire, in which northern Mesopotamia was annexed, the Roman Empire's last significant conquest. Its garrison was two more new legions, commanded not by the usual senatorial legates, but by experienced officers who had twice been the senior centurions of a legion. A third new legion, II *Parthica*, was not committed to frontier defence, but was based just south of Rome. Here the old Praetorian Guard was disbanded and replaced by 10 cohorts at least 1,000-strong, recruited from experienced legionaries. These élite forces of heavy infantry, equivalent to at least three legions (when the largest provincial army was only two legions), with the addition of cavalry guards seconded from the provincial armies, were the forerunners of the 4th-century "mobile army". They offered a determined emperor the solution to the military and political problems of war on two fronts: he retained a strategic reserve, first to protect himself from a rebellious general in the provinces, and then to reinforce the provinces against outside attack.

WAR ON TWO FRONTS

Severus, like Vespasian, believed that an emperor should die on his feet: despite failing health, he directed a last campaign in Britain (see below), where he died at

THE RAIN MIRACLE, AD 173–4

The Column of Marcus Aurelius depicts Roman soldiers victorious under the wings of the god responsible for the Rain Miracle (AD173–4). A Roman army had been cut off in the land of the Quadi and was suffering from heat and thirst, when suddenly there was a thunderstorm and they were drenched in drinking water, while the Quadi were struck by lightning. Various people claimed the credit, including the Christians, who were being persecuted for refusing to worship the old gods: to prove they were patriotic, they retailed the legend of a Christian legion, the Twelfth *Fulminata* (Thundering) Legion. The miracle suggests a loss of confidence and hysterical relief: there would be stories of divine intervention in the civil wars of the fourth century; and in our own century, the Angels of Mons.

Column of Marcus Aurelius, Rome: the Rain God saves the Roman army.

AD 208

SEVERUS IN BRITAIN

DATE AD208–11
OBJECT To complete the conquest of Britain.
NUMBERS 40,000 men
DESCRIPTION Septimius Severus was 63 and almost unable to walk when he tried to complete the conquest of Britain. The fleet in Britain was reinforced from the Rhine and Danube, legionaries marched through Amiens "on their way to the British expedition", grain was stockpiled at Corbridge on the road to Scotland, and at South Shields twenty granaries were built, enough to feed 40,000 men for three months. Severus began to build a permanent base at Carpow, and was preparing another campaign when he died, aged 66, at his headquarters in York. It was the end of the last Roman attempt to conquer new territory in the west.
RESULT The northern frontier reverted to Hadrian's Wall and its outposts.

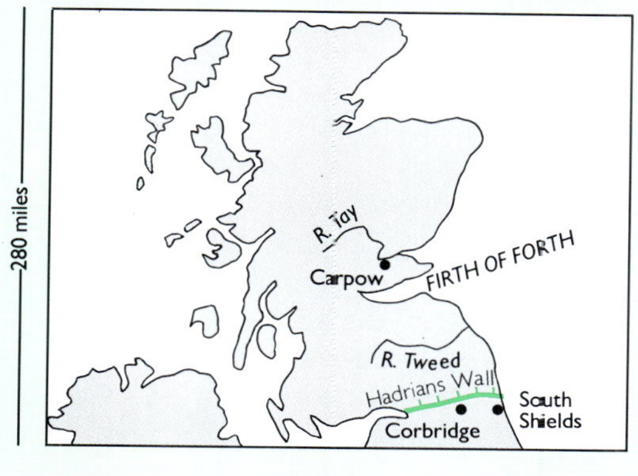

York. His conquests in the north were abandoned by his son Caracalla (211–17), who turned his attention to a new enemy, the Alamanni. They were a coalition of tribes (the name means "All men") pressing against the linear defences that linked the middle Rhine to the upper Danube. Their counterpart on the lower Rhine was another new coalition, the Franks. It was ominous for the future that in Europe the imperial armies, although they retained their qualitative superiority for another two centuries, were now being opposed by larger, better-organized tribal groups. The major threat was still on the Danube, where the Goths and Vandals were migrating southwards, first pressing other peoples against the frontier and then breaching it themselves; in the mid-3rd century the Goths even took to boats and ravaged the coasts of Asia Minor. Further east, the strategic balance tilted in the mid-220s when the loose-knit Parthian empire was overthrown by an aggressive Persian revival. The ensuing struggle lasted four centuries.

Caracalla's successors Alexander Severus (222–35) and Gordian III (238–44) both campaigned against the Persians with limited success. The Second *Parthica* accompanied them to Syria, as it had Caracalla: we know this from recent excavations at Apamea, where the walls incorporate its tombstones. The legionaries were mostly Thracians, Romans only by courtesy, recruited from the hinterland of the lower Danube frontier. This was the milieu of Maximinus (235–8) "the Thracian", one of Alexander's most senior officers; when the army returned to Europe, and Alexander tried to negotiate with Alamanni invaders, it proclaimed Maximinus instead: he was the first emperor to rise from the ranks, the first of the soldier emperors who saved the Empire. Ruthlessly he taxed the civil population to pay for the army, provoking an uprising which spread from Africa to Italy; while attempting to crush it, he was murdered in his turn by mutineers from II *Parthica*, anxious for the families they had left behind.

The history of the next half century, until the accession of the great Diocletian (284–305), has been likened to "a dark tunnel, illuminated from either end, and by rare and exiguous light wells in the interval". We can only glimpse how Severus' army evolved into that of Diocletian and Constantine (306–37), a miracle of improvization on the cliff edge. In these years (235–84) there were at least 20 emperors recognized at Rome and many more usurpers, most of them generals proclaimed by armies asserting the priority of their own front. This was the consequence of the long process that anchored the legions to the frontiers where they recruited, where the legionaries raised their families and retired. Moreover, if the legion were withdrawn, an invasion would follow. This surrender of the initiative has been vividly compared to a failed *Blitzkrieg*: the advancing spearhead halts and becomes a defended position, which is finally overrun.

VALERIUS MAXIMIANUS

Marcus Aurelius in the winter of AD 179–80 stationed 20,000 troops in the homeland of the Quadi and Marcomanni (modern Czechoslavakia) to force them to submit. One detachment, 855 men from the legion based in Aquincum, was posted to Laugaricio (Trenčin) 80 miles north of the Danube, where it cut an inscription on the rock-face above the river Váh (Waag). Its commanding officer was Valerius Maximianus, a former cavalry officer whom Marcus had decorated for killing a German chieftain with his own hands. Maximianus came from what is now Yugoslavia, and had also proved himself in administrative posts before being given the senatorial rank that qualified him to command a legion. He was a professional soldier, like the great "Illyrian" emperors of the 3rd century from the Danubian provinces, whom he foreshadows.

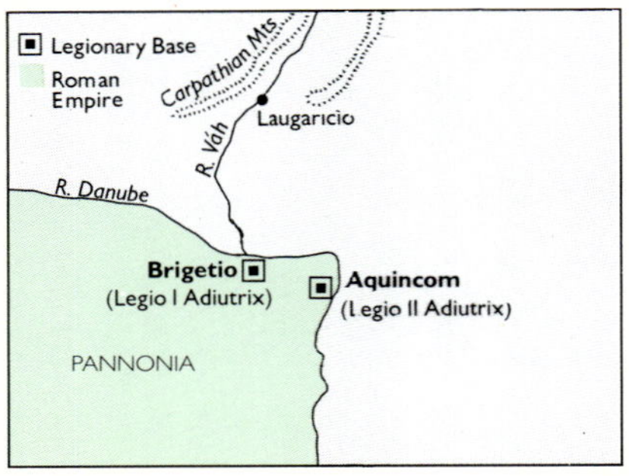

AD 241

KING SHAPUR OF PERSIA

DATES AD241–4 and 250s
CAMPAIGN Persian invasions of the eastern Roman empire and Roman counter-attack
OBJECT Rome and Persia competed for prestige in the Syriac-speaking world; Persia sought booty, prisoners and Roman territories once part of the old Persian empire.
DESCRIPTION Shapur commemorated his triumph over three Roman emperors in a rock-cut relief: he holds Valerian with his hand, receives the submission of Philip (in 244) and tramples Gordian III. He also left a written account of his wars. Gordian was killed in a great battle, and Philip sued for peace and paid tribute. In a second war Shapur destroyed an army of 60,000 men and captured 37 Roman cities including the capital Antioch. In the third war he invaded Roman Mesopotamia, and was attacked by Valerian with an army 70,000 strong: "There was a great battle, and we

The Romans surrender to King Shapur.

A THIRD-CENTURY BRIGADE

This bronze disc, 6.6in in diameter, belonged to Aurelius Cervianus, an officer in a third-century brigade formed by detachments from the two legions in southern Britain, the XX *Valeria Victrix* and the II *Augusta*; each parades under its own flag and legionary symbol. Instead of moving whole legions, expeditionary forces were assembled from such detachments, like "the British and German legions with their auxiliaries" recorded near Belgrade in the reign of Gallienus. Gallienus honoured the Rhine and Danube legions by name on his coinage in 259–60, which is found in northern Italy where his "élite army" was based. These detachments operated independently and were the forerunners of the fourth-century mobile units.

During this dark age almost every emperor died a violent death, Decius (249–51) in battle against the Goths, the others by assassination or in civil war. The only exceptions are themselves significant: Valerian (253–60) captured by the Persians, Claudius (268–70) dead of the plague after his crushing defeat of the Goths, Carus (282–3) allegedly struck by lightning after his capture of the Persian capital Ctesiphon. This was in reprisal for the spectacular campaigns of the Persian king Shapur (241–72) (see page 48), whose conquests were halted only by a Roman protectorate, the caravan city of Palmyra. In the 260s she usurped Rome's control of the eastern provinces, while in Italy Valerian's son Gallienus (254–68) lost the

AD 278

took Valerian prisoner with our own hands; and we captured his generals, and led them away prisoner into Persia; and we burnt Syria, Cilicia and Cappadocia" (there follows a list of 36 cities). This account, inscribed on the wall of a Persian fire temple, is a unique glimpse of the 3rd-century crisis from the other side of the hill.
RESULT A stalemate costly to both sides.

SIEGE OF CREMNA

DATE AD278
OBJECT Reduction of rebel-seized city
DESCRIPTION Even in Asia Minor cities were being refortified in the 3rd century against the threat of Gothic or Persian raids, including Cremna, whose name means "cliff": a reference to its inaccessible site. It was seized by a brigand called Lydius, who withstood a prolonged siege, the ancient account of which has been ▸

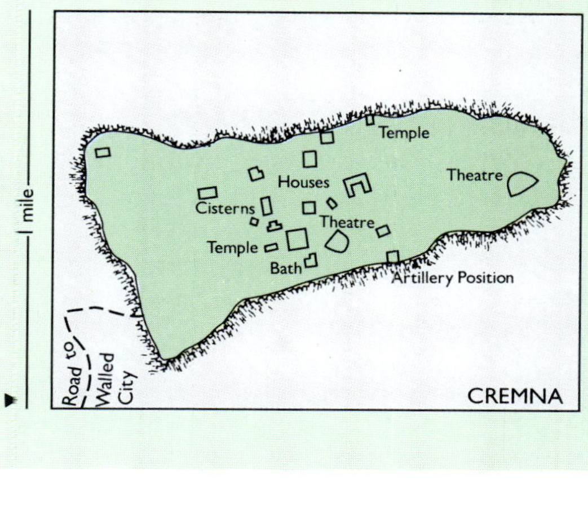

LOGISTICS

Ancient authors like Ammianus Marcellinus (and other surviving documents) tell us a great deal about Diocletian's reforms and how late-Roman units were fed, equipped, and moved to where they were needed. St Ambrose, for example, describes the route march: food stockpiles, a day's rest every four days, with longer rests in cities with markets and good supplies of water (here they would be billeted on civilians). Papyrus fragments survive from the files of an Egyptian deputy governor, writing to local officials "so that by all means the most noble soldiers may receive their supplies without complaint".

western provinces to a separatist "Gallic" empire, retaining only Africa and intermittently the Danubian provinces. Yet this cultured emperor not only patronized Plotinus, the philosopher who made Platonism a rival to Christianity, he also developed the weapon with which his "Illyrian" successors fought off Persians and Germans alike. This was what a contemporary calls the "élite army", a mobile force not committed to frontier defence, in effect the Roman army as it once had been. A medieval writer credits Gallienus with being the first to form cavalry units, "the Roman army having previously been largely infantry". This is an exaggeration, but we do now hear of *the* cavalry under its own general: it included Moorish light cavalry, mounted archers from the east, the legions' cavalry component *(promoti)*, mounted legionaries *(stablesiani)* and detachments from frontier units. Mobile infantry Gallienus found in the usual way: like Septimius Severus he supplemented the Praetorian Guard and the II *Parthica* with detachments from the frontier legions, in Britain and on the Rhine and Danube. He was doing what modern armies have often done, forming units for special purposes by drawing on existing units.

Gallienus was later blamed for the disasters of his reign: "The memory of his vices will endure while there are cities to bear the mark"; but this libel came from the aristocrats whom he barred from a military career. Valerius Maximianus, had he lived now, would not have needed senatorial rank to qualify. Gallienus promoted professional soldiers like the Thracian Traianus Mucianus, who enlisted in an auxiliary unit, transferred to II *Parthica* and then the cavalry component of the Guard, before rising to command a series of cavalry units and legionary detachments. Like other officers in the "élite army" he bore the title *protector* used by Gallienus to distinguish his officer corps, not that he retained their loyalty: the defection of his cavalry general Aureolus was followed by a conspiracy involving Mucianus' patron, the commander of the Guard, and the future emperors Claudius and Aurelian (270–5). They were the leaders of a virtual junta of "Illyrian" officers born in the Danubian provinces where so much of the Roman army was now recruited. In a relentless series of campaigns, Claudius defeated the Goths, Aurelian overthrew Palmyra and ended the "Gallic" empire, and Probus (276–82) cleared Gaul of the German invaders who poured in when Aurelian was assassinated. But although imperial unity was precariously restored, the Alamanni retained the territory they had seized in southern Germany, and the province of Dacia beyond the Danube was surrended to the Goths. Insecurity was felt in the heart of Asia Minor, and even Rome itself was given walls by Aurelian after he had defeated a German invasion of northern Italy.

DIOCLETIAN

These were the birth-pangs of the Late Empire: the midwife was Diocletian (284–305), the genius who reduced fifty years of improvization to a system. He shared

AD 278

confirmed by a recent survey. The Romans battered the walls with artillery, whose effect can still be seen; the defenders fired back stone balls carved out of public buildings. When food ran short, Lydius ruthlessly pitched non-combatants over the cliffs. Resistance only collapsed when he was shot by a Roman bolt-firing catapult, aimed at him by his own chief of artillery, who had deserted.

RESULT Capture of Cremna.

THE MILVIAN BRIDGE

DATE 28 October AD312

CAMPAIGN Constantine's invasion of Italy

OBJECT Overthrow of Maxentius

DESCRIPTION This famous battle confirmed Constantine's new faith in the Christian god, whose initials he had painted on his men's shields in consequence of a dream; in later years he claimed to have seen a cross of light in the sky. His rival Maxentius at first intended to defend the impregnable walls of Rome, and cut the Milvian Bridge on its northern approaches; then he changed his mind, crossed the Tiber on a pontoon bridge, and advanced. But Constantine's army was battle-hardened and confident; Maxentius' army was thrown back in confusion and, as it retreated across the river, the bridge collapsed under its weight.

RESULT Maxentius and his armoured

power first with his fellow-officer Maximian (285–305) and then with two more "Illyrians", Constantius (293–306) and Galerius (293–311). Four emperors now watched each other's back, in civil wars and on the frontiers. Thus in 287 Maximian ravaged Germany, while Diocletian reasserted Roman authority in Armenia by a treaty with the Persians. Maximian made the mistake, however, of creating a naval command in the North Sea and Channel for a Belgian officer called Carausius; he rebelled and could not be dislodged from Britain and northern Gaul. It was only 10 years later, after several failures, that Constantius was able to mount the seaborne expedition that reconquered Britain. Meanwhile (in 297) Diocletian was suppressing a revolt in Egypt, and Galerius was recovering from a humiliating defeat by the Persians in Armenia; next year he achieved the regime's greatest success when he caught the Persian army off guard: King Narseh, son of the great Shapur, barely escaped with his life, and his harem fell into Roman hands. "By the kindly favour of the gods we have crushed the seething greed of barbarian peoples by slaughter of the same," proclaimed Diocletian in his Edict on Maximum Prices (301), which unsuccessfully applied the tactics of intimidation to the Roman economy. The energy which had reasserted Roman authority from Britain to Egypt, from Africa (where Maximian campaigned) to Armenia, is echoed in the record of his travels inscribed by one of Diocletian's veterans on his wife's tombstone: Aurelius Gaius, a legionary cavalryman who rose to be a lieutenant *(optio)* in the imperial entourage, crossed the Rhine and Danube repeatedly, served in upper Egypt and almost every province from Mesopotamia to Mauretania, but never visited Italy or Rome.

Soldiers now speak of serving in the *comitatus*, the Imperial entourage, from which comes the term for the mobile army, the *comitatenses*. Diocletian's was small by later standards: to the Guard he added the famous *Ioviani* and *Herculiani*, legions formed from Danubian legionaries armed with the late-Roman weighted dart instead of the old javelin, and the *lanciarii* like Aurelius Gaius, legionaries armed with the lance; in cavalry we find the first *scholae* (mounted guards) and the crack *Comites* and *Promoti*, brigaded from detachments of the Guards cavalry and the old cavalry guards. But expeditionary forces still consisted of temporary detachments from the frontier armies: thus Galerius drew on the Danubian garrisons for his defeat of the Persians, and in Egypt a papyrus of 295 records the issue of fodder not only to the *Comites* in Diocletian's field force but also to as many as ten pairs ("brigades") of legionary detachments. Gallienus' cavalry corps was actually broken up into detachments, which were drafted into the frontier armies. Here there is abundant archaeological evidence – new forts and extensive rebuilding – of Diocletian's emphasis on fixed defences; an ancient writer says, with exaggeration: "By the foresight of Diocletian the frontiers everywhere were fortified with cities, forts and

Colossal head of the Emperor Constantine, Rome. Constantine was one of the most dynamic of the later Roman emperors, rising to supreme power by defeating his rival, Maxentius, at the battle of the Milvian Bridge just north of Rome in 312. Among his military innovations was the formation of a new style of shock infantry unit, called the auxilium. The crack troops the auxilia contained were largely recruited from along the Rhine.

AD 357

The battle of the Milvian Bridge.

cavalry were drowned, a scene depicted on the Arch erected at Rome to commemorate Constantine's victory "by divine inspiration". At Maxentius' death, Constantine was accepted as emperor of the Western Empire.

STRASBOURG

DATE AD357
CAMPAIGN Roman counter-attack against Alamanni invasion and occupation of the Rhineland
OBJECT To defeat the Alamanni and expel them from Roman territory.
NUMBERS Roman – 13,000, Alamanni – 35,000.
DESCRIPTION On a hot summer's day Julian and his men advanced 21 miles ▸

(Above) Diocletian (reigned 284–305). Marble portrait head from his capital city Nicomedia (now Izmit in Turkey) of the founding genius of the Late Roman Empire. He reorganized the Empire's logistic base and directed the military revival achieved by able colleagues like Galerius.

(Right) Detail of the arch erected by Galerius (reigned 293–311) at his capital city Thessalonica (now Salonika in Greece) to celebrate his defeat of the Persians in 298. In successive scenes Galerius leaves his headquarters (top), defeats the Persians (centre), and is enthroned in triumph with his colleagues (bottom).

AD 357

from Saverne to the western approaches of Strasbourg, where the Roman road descended into the Rhine valley. Here he was confronted by the Alamanni, mostly infantry, whose right flank was protected by a marshy water-course; there was cavalry mixed with light infantry on their left wing, opposing the armoured cavalry and horse archers at the head of the Roman column (and thus on the right wing). The Roman cavalry was driven back in disorder, but the decisive fighting was in the

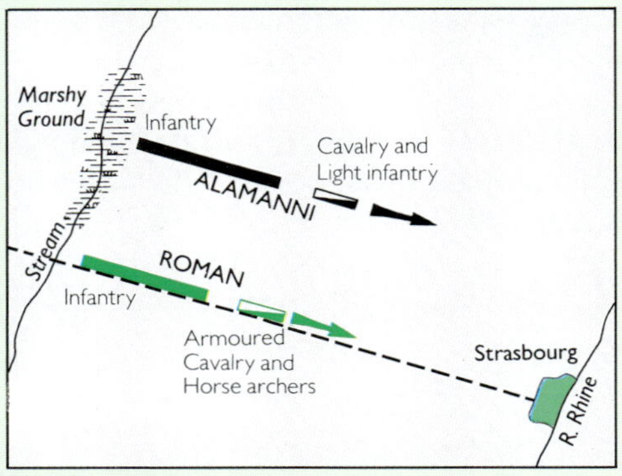

centre, where the disciplined Roman infantry and especially the *Primani* legion withstood a series of Alamannic charges. Finally the Alamanni faltered and gave way, leaving 6,000 dead on the field and in their retreat to the Rhine, where many more were drowned.

RESULT The defeat of the Alamanni, and their expulsion from the Rhineland.

towers, and the whole army was stationed there." Many new units were formed – the 33 legions of Septimius Severus were increased to about 60 – and the army's numbers may have doubled to more than half a million men. Food, clothing, horses, raw materials, even recruits, were levied from the civil population like taxation, under the supervision of an expanding bureaucracy. Diocletian's reforms gave the Empire the means of survival, but at heavy cost.

CONSTANTINE

Diocletian abdicated in 305 and retired, appropriately, to a fortified palace on the Dalmatian coast near his birthplace. He had secured unity of command in a war on two fronts, but without lasting success, since Galerius was unable to dominate his colleagues as Diocletian had done. The disturbing influence was a general of genius, Constantius' son Constantine (306–37), who was proclaimed at York when his father died there. "Beginning in Britain by the sea where the sun sets", he told the people of Palestine in 324, "by the Almighty's power I abolished all existing evils, and finally reached the east." He is referring to the series of civil wars in which, supported by his new god, he eliminated first Maximian's son Maxentius (306–12) and then Galerius' lieutenant and successor Licinius (308–24). The campaign against Maxentius which culminated in the battle of the Milvian Bridge (see page 50) emphasizes the new strategy of mobility. Constantine used only a quarter of his available forces to surprise and overwhelm a numerically superior opponent. By the same logic he enlarged the "élite army", by recruiting new units especially from German volunteers and prisoners-of-war, and by withdrawing legionary detachments and cavalry from the provincial armies. The historian who praises Diocletian contrasts him with Constantine: the latter fatally weakened the frontiers by drafting most of the army to cities that did not need a garrison. (*Comitatenses* had no fixed stations, in fact, but were quartered where convenient.) Constantine's critic wilfully misunderstands his strategy, which is that of Frederick the Great: "He who defends everything, defends nothing." While its neighbours retained the initiative, the empire could not hold every frontier against all attack. Instead, it could hope the reduced garrisons would control minor raiding, and would even contain invaders passively by guarding stocks of food. In the time thus gained, the emperor would concentrate his mobile army, his insurance policy incidentally against rivals, and would counter-attack. His troops were better fed and equipped than their adversaries, better organized, trained and disciplined, and could expect to win against numerical odds.

Constantine's last campaigns were on the lower Danube, where he briefly recovered part of Dacia, but he was planning war with Persia. This was inherited by his son Constantius II (337–61), a conscientious but ungifted general, who is said to

Egyptian wood carving, c. AD 400, perhaps the biblical Siege of Gibeon. Roman infantry are driving off mounted barbarians who have assaulted a city under divine protection. The garrison watches from the walls, in front of which the barbarians' leaders have now been gibbeted.

AD 359

AMIDA

DATE AD359

CAMPAIGN Persian invasion of eastern Roman Empire

OBJECT To cross the Euphrates and penetrate Syria.

NUMBERS Ammianus states that Amida was defended by 20,000 Romans, greatly outnumbered by the Persians.

DESCRIPTION The magnificently preserved 6th-century walls of Amida (Diyarbakır), founded on cliffs above the Tigris in south-east Turkey, give an impression of its strength in 359 when it was defended by seven Roman units and inflicted 74 days' delay and 30,000 dead upon the Persian invaders. The Persians raised siege mounds and iron-plated towers to command the walls, to which the Romans responded with stone-lobbing "scorpions" (mangonels). A band of Persian archers seized a tower by means of a secret passage (exploited once more in the siege of 502), ▸

Amida: basalt cliff and tower.

(Right) Map showing the extent of the Roman Empire, c. AD300.

(Far right) Theodosius, in the imperial box at the Hippodrome, Constantinople, receives submissive barbarians bearing gifts.

(Below) The adversaries. Gold medallion portraits of (top) the Persian king Shapur II (reigned 309–79) and (bottom) the Roman emperor Constantius II (reigned 337-61). In 359 Shapur personally directed the siege of Amida as part of his mission to recover territory lost to the Romans. The defenders heard the Persians acclaiming him "King of Kings" and responded by acclaiming Constantius, who was then directing operations on the middle Danube, as "Lord of this World".

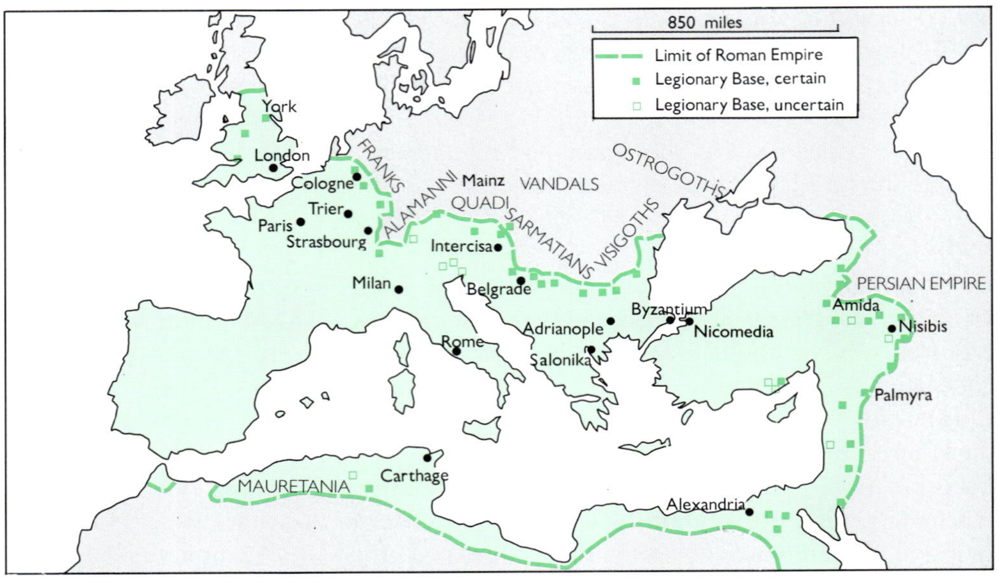

have fought the Persians nine times without success. The war, which lasted until the mid-380s, was one of sieges and inconclusive field operations. Thus the Persians besieged the Roman fortress of Nisibis three times in twelve years without capturing it: its massive defences, in the words of a Syriac chronicle, made it as safe as "a rose behind thorns". In 359 Shapur II (309–79) changed his strategy at the suggestion of a well-informed Roman defector: instead of crossing the Mesopotamian plain, where the Romans burnt off the available fodder, he struck northwards up the Tigris valley, intending to invade Syria from the north-east. But even this initiative failed, when he halted to besiege the Roman fortress of Amida (see page 53): the two months' siege is brilliantly described by a participant, the historian Ammianus Marcellinus, who tells us most of what we know about the late-Roman army in action.

Constantius could never concentrate on the eastern front. In the west, his brother Constans (337–50) was overthrown by the general commanding the *Ioviani* and *Herculiani*, and Constantius was forced to fight a civil war. His victory was remembered for its appalling losses: 30,000 dead, it was alleged, from an army of 80,000. Moreover the Alamanni seized the chance to establish themselves in the Rhineland. Constantius was unlucky in appointing his cousin Julian (355–63) to titular command in Gaul. Julian, a philosophy student, quoted Plato while he learnt to drill ("If an ox can carry a knapsack, then so can I"), but his energy and enthusiasm

AD 359

but were dislodged by bolt-firing catapults. The city fell when a Roman counter-mound collapsed, bridging the gap between the wall and a Persian mound, and the Persians surged across. Ammianus Marcellinus, an officer in the garrison, fortunately escaped; his superb history of the years 353–78 was published at Rome in the 390s.

RESULT Amida fell, but the Persians were unable to invade Syria.

JULIAN'S PERSIAN EXPEDITION

DATE AD363

OBJECT To restore Roman prestige after Persian invasions in the 340s and 350s, ideally by capturing the Persian capital of Ctesiphon, defeating the Persian field army, and deposing King Shapur II.

NUMBERS Roman armies of 18,000 (and Armenian allies) and 47,000; Persian numbers not known, but greater.

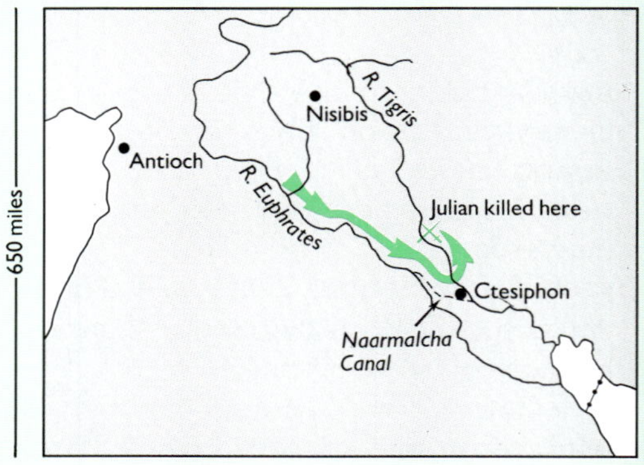

appealed to the army; it did not know, and would not have cared, that he had secretly renounced the Christianity forced upon him by Constantius. A surprising victory over the Alamanni gave him the initiative, which he exploited in campaigns of reprisal against their homeland, but when Constantius demanded reinforcements instead for the eastern front, where whole legions had been lost, the Gallic army mutinied and proclaimed Julian emperor. Another civil war was impending, when Constantius died of natural causes. Julian had thus seen the difficulty of balancing the demands of two fronts, but as sole emperor, convinced that the gods had chosen him to restore paganism, he could decide priorities. He bungled the decision. Instead

Continued on page 58

A ROMAN GENERAL'S AUTOGRAPH (344)

The Roman army generated documents of all kinds written on papyrus. This is a handsome example, the letter of dismissal received by Abinnaeus, commandant of a fort in Egypt, from his superior Count Valacius, the general commanding the frontier of Lower Egypt. The text is written by a secretary, but Valacius has added as his signature (a unique survival), the words "fare well" in his own hand. Abinnaeus kept the letter, even though he secured his reinstatement from the emperor himself. Valacius, however, met a macabre fate. The hermit St Antony cursed him for persecuting Catholic nuns and monks; five days later, out riding near Alexandria with the civil governor of Egypt, Valacius was savaged to death by his own horse.

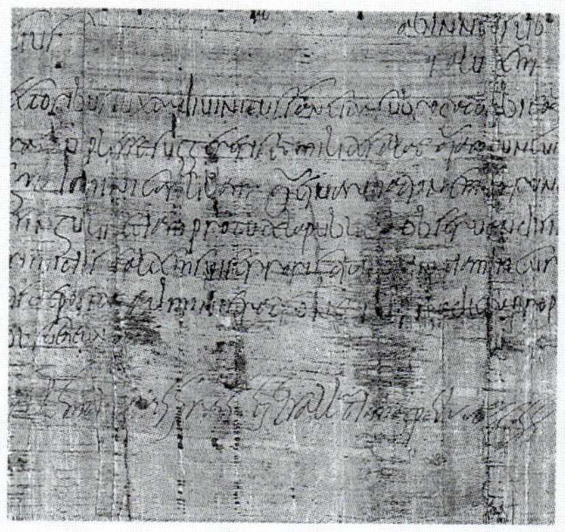

AD 378

DESCRIPTION Julian assembled 65,000 men and a fleet of at least 1,000 boats to carry supplies down the Euphrates. After detaching 18,000 men to make a feint towards the Tigris, he met only light resistance at first, bypassing fortresses or reducing them with siege artillery. The Persians flooded the approaches to Ctesiphon, but Julian reached it after a pitched battle. However, he felt unable to assault it; after hesitation, he burnt his boats instead and retreated up the Tigris. This was fatal, for the main Persian army confronted him, and all available fodder was burnt in his path. The Romans retreated in good order but were desperately short of food and harassed by Persian attacks, in one of which Julian was killed. They only extricated themselves by accepting Persian terms of peace which included the surrender of Nisibis.

RESULT The forced retreat of the Romans, with the death of Julian and heavy losses of men, material and prestige.

ADRIANOPLE

DATE 9 August AD378

CAMPAIGN A Roman attempt to contain and defeat Gothic invasion.

OBJECT To impose terms upon the Goths, with or without defeating them in a pitched battle.

DESCRIPTION It was a very hot day, and the Gothic wagon laager was eight hours' march from the Roman base at Adrianople. The Roman army advanced in column and ▸

NOTITIA DIGNITATUM AND THE LATE-ROMAN ORDER OF BATTLE

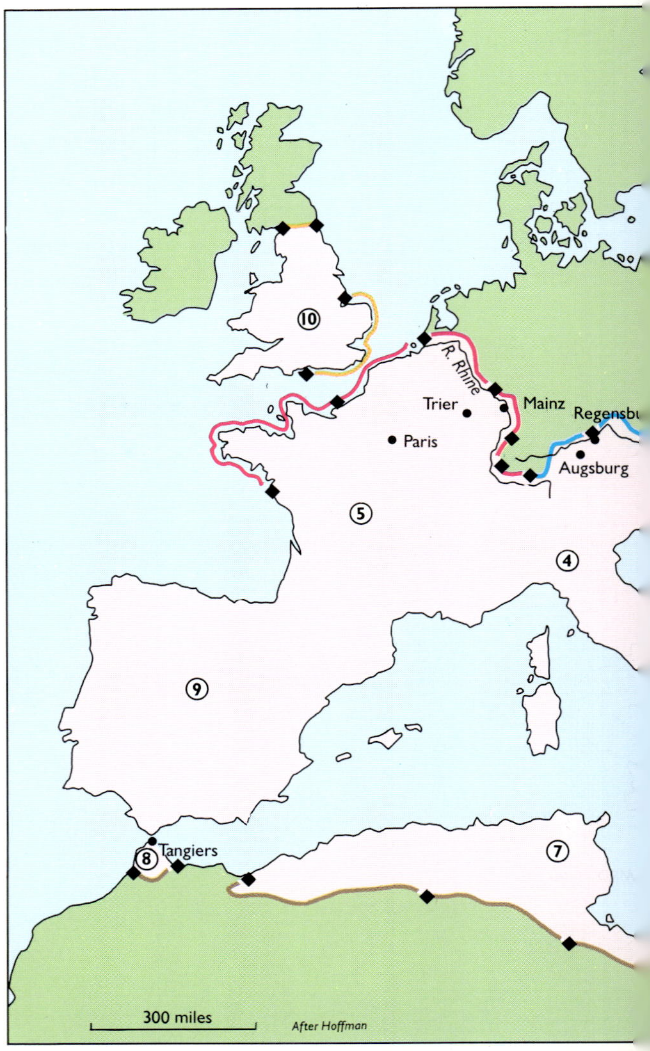

THE *NOTITIA*, to translate its full title, was the late-Roman "List of all high offices, civil and military" in the east and west, dating from the division of the empire in 395. Several indirect copies survive, made in the 15th and 16th centuries from a unique Carolingian copy preserved at Speyer, but long since disappeared. One of these copies, now in Munich, includes a second set of illustrations traced from the Speyer manuscript which are the closest to the late-Roman originals; some of these are reproduced here. The purpose of the *Notitia* is unclear, but it is possible that it was used as an *aide-mémoire* by the office staff of the western commander-in-chief, whose incomes derived from issuing letters of appointment; the western list was certainly updated for a few years, perhaps until the fall of Stilicho in 408. The *Notitia*, whatever its purpose, is divided into chapters, each one devoted to a high official or army commander, with a schematic picture of his duties and a detailed list of his subordinates and other responsibilities. Generals commanding mobile armies are thus represented by the shield devices of their units listed by unit type and seniority, frontier generals by a picture of their sector and a list of garrison units with their stations.

The *Notitia*, although it is a civil document as well, pays most attention to military matters; in theory at least, it lists every military unit in the empire, and thus embodies the order of battle of the

(1)

(2)

(3)

Illustrations from the Munich copy of the Notitia Dignitatum. *(1) The Count of the Saxon Shore, whose sector consisted of nine coastal forts in Britain from the Wash to the Solent. (2) The Count of the Sacred largesses, responsible for money taxes and the storage and processing of gold and silver. (3) The master of the offices, responsible for the imperial secretariat, the regiments of bodyguards,*

Late Roman Order of Battle

Mobile Armies	Cavalry Units	Infantry Units (+up-graded Frontier Units)	
(1) Emperor (2 armies)	31	47 (+1)	EASTERN
(2) East	10	11 (+10)	EASTERN
(3) Danube, Thrace (2 armies)	9	36 (+9)	EASTERN
(4) Italy	12	35 (+2)	WESTERN
(5) Gaul	12	24 (+27)	WESTERN
(6) Danube		18 (+6)	WESTERN
(7) Africa	20	12	WESTERN
(8) Tangiers	3	4	WESTERN
(9) Spain		16	WESTERN
(10) Britain	5	3	WESTERN

Frontier Armies	Number of Sector Commands	
◆ Limit of Sector Command		
Egypt – Black Sea	10	EASTERN
Lower Danube	4	EASTERN
Upper Danube	4	WESTERN
Rhine and Gaul	6	WESTERN
Britain	2	WESTERN
Africa	4	WESTERN

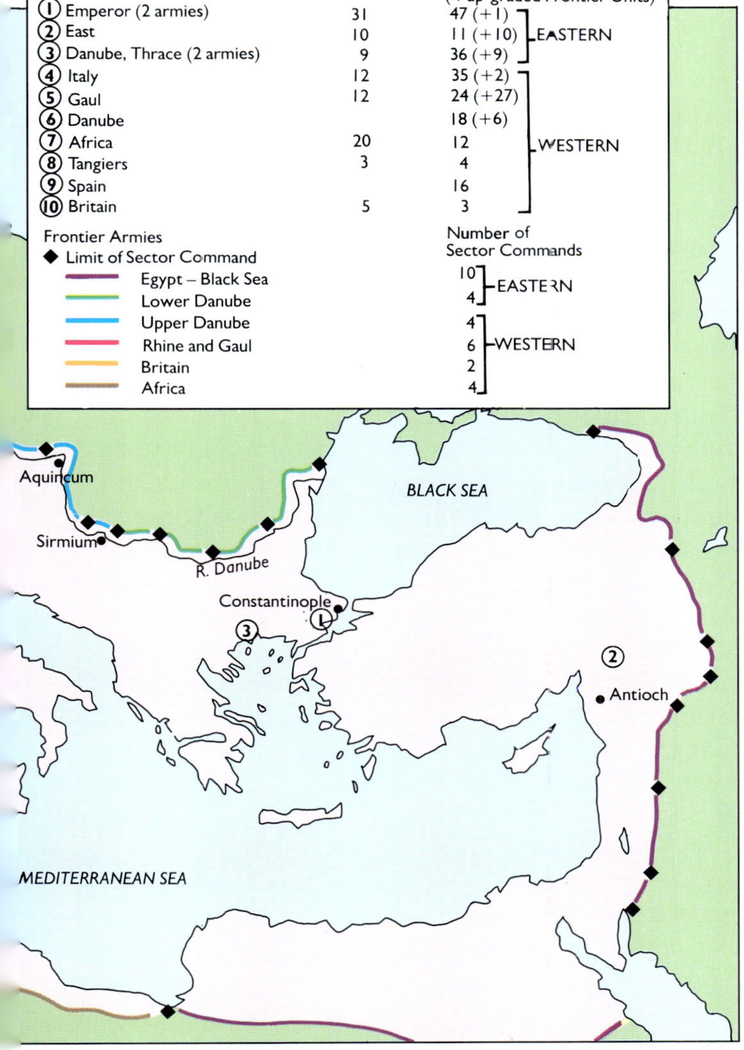

Roman armies at the end of the fourth century. Many details are corroborated by literary sources like Ammianus Marcellinus (names of units, for example, and "brigades"), or by other documents such as laws, inscriptions and papyri, but there are some puzzling discrepancies. Thus the garrison of Hadrian's Wall seems to have remained unchanged for more than 150 years, there was no sign of the *Notitia*'s alleged 16 mobile units when the Germans overran Spain in 409, and Stilicho when Italy was invaded in 405 mustered only 30 units, although the *Notitia* credits him with almost 50, not to mention many more in Gaul. Moreover, the *Notitia* says nothing about a unit's establishment, one of the outstanding problems in late-Roman army studies, although it lists four types of cavalry unit and at least six different types of infantry. In any case, we do not know whether units were up to strength. (Other evidence suggests they were rather small by earlier standards and not up to strength.) The *Notitia* has its theoretical and schematic aspects, such as the charming illustrations, but there is no doubt it preserves the broad features and many details of late-Roman strategy and military organization.

Many units in the *Notitia's* order of battle (left) can be dated, and since mobile units are listed by seniority, it is possible to unpeel "layers" in the *Notitia*; to see the effects of invasions, of Adrianople, the military reforms of Constantine and Diocletian, even the history of Gallienus' cavalry corps, and the survival of units from the army of Septimius Severus and Marcus. The enhanced importance of cavalry is obvious, both in the high proportion of units and the practice of listing them before infantry in the frontier armies and in the eastern mobile armies. This is part of the premium set on mobility, seen most of all in the distinction between mobile armies held in reserve and the armies of the frontiers. This is the strategy of Constantine and his successors, but its origins can be seen in the 3rd-century crisis, indeed as early as the 2nd century.

(4) (5)

and arms factories. (4) The western commander-in-chief, the Master of the Infantry, a post held by Stilicho from 394 to 408. In front of his letter of appointment are ranged the shields of the mobile units under his command. (5) The Count of the Egyptian Frontier, a post held by Valacius in the 340s. His letter of appointment makes him responsible for forts in Lower Egypt.

of campaigning against the Goths, as his staff advised, or of securing the Rhine, likewise the scene of major fighting after his death, he chose to invade the Persian Empire. It was a disaster of logistics (see page 54) for which Julian atoned by his characteristically reckless death in a skirmish.

Julian was succeeded by the last great "Illyrian" emperor, Valentinian (364–75), who divided the empire with his submissive brother Valens (364–78) and reasserted the priority of the west, for the last time, by campaigning with fair success against the resurgent Alamanni; a brutal but efficient Spanish general called Theodosius restored order in Britain and Africa with small mobile forces. Valentinian also directed the last reconstruction of the fixed defences of the west, and his death was dramatically appropriate: he suffered a stroke when the Quadi alleged that one of his new forts had provoked them into invading his native province of Pannonia. Within less than a year, Valens was confronted with a major crisis. The Goths had been dislodged by the sudden onset of the Huns from central Asia, and begged for permission to resettle south of the Danube. Valens agreed, not out of compassion, but to recruit them for the army and to reduce the burden of taxes on Roman civilians. It was a reasonable decision: Germans had been serving loyally in Roman units since the time of Constantine, if not before, and immigrant tribes under supervision had been absorbed in the empire for centuries. However, in 376 the operation was bungled: food ran short, Roman officials exploited the starving Goths, and they rebelled. Valens' generals made vain attempts to contain them; finally Valens mobilized his whole army and attacked the Gothic encampment near Adrianople (see page 55). By sunset on 9 August 378, the Black Day of the late-Roman army, Valens and two-thirds of the eastern mobile army were dead.

THE COLLAPSE OF THE WESTERN EMPIRE

The western empire never recovered from the blow. The surviving western emperor, Valentinian's son Gratian (375–83), made Theodosius' son Theodosius eastern emperor (379–95), and between them they tried to limit the damage. The desperate shortage of trained soldiers, however, made it impossible to defeat the Goths; instead they were allowed to settle south of the lower Danube, their social structure intact, in return for providing contingents for service *with* the Roman army. The preposition is important: these contingents were commanded by their own chieftains, they were co-belligerents who had little cause to like or trust the Romans. They marched with Theodosius, to the embarrassment of his apologists, in both the civil wars he fought against western usurpers. The defeat of Magnus Maximus (383–8) enabled Theodosius to draft mobile units to the east. In 394 he overcame the second usurper in a two-day battle; the first day ended in defeat, the brunt of it borne by his Gothic

AD 378

deployed awkwardly to assault the laager, infantry in a crescent, cavalry on the wings, by which time men and horses were tired, thirsty and hungry. The Goths were waiting for their cavalry to return from foraging. Roman cavalry units, apparently part of the left wing, attacked prematurely and were forced to retreat. At this moment the Gothic cavalry appeared "like a thunderbolt", fell upon the Roman left wing and drove into the unprotected flank of the advancing infantry. The infantry was trapped between the Gothic cavalry and the Gothic infantry in the wagons, and fought crammed together until it broke. The fugitives were pursued until darkness fell. The emperor Valens and two-thirds of his army were killed.

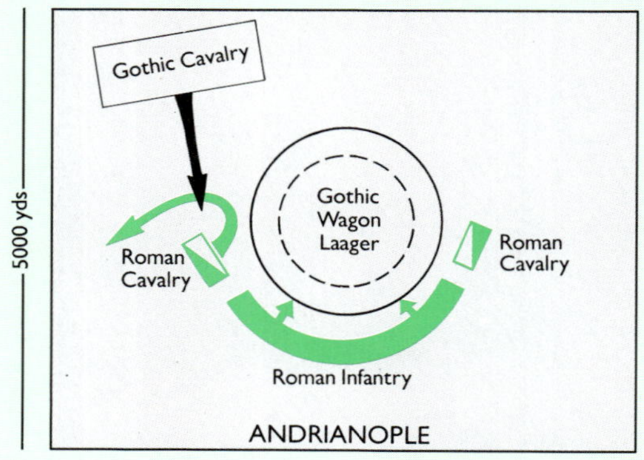

RESULT A major defeat of the Roman army, with heavy losses of infantry units and consequent inability to coerce the Goths.

allies, 10,000 of whom are said to have been killed. "To lose *them*", commented a Christian admirer, "was a victory in itself."

The western empire was thus weakened by civil war and by replacing eastern losses. It was outflanked by the collapse of the Danube frontier; by contrast the eastern empire in Asia Minor, Syria and Egypt had much stronger natural defences, the sea, mountains and desert; it was much richer than the west, and its logistical base was almost intact. It shared the same internal weaknesses, the "idle mouths" of army, bureaucracy and Church, for example, and the aspects of its social structure loosely called "corruption", but externally it was under far less pressure. It was unfortunate that Theodosius died five months after his victory, and that the empire was divided once more, between his incapable sons Honorius (395–423) and Arcadius (395–408). In north Italy Honorius' court was dominated by his father's general Stilicho, the son of a Vandal-born officer as it happens, who bravely tried to make economical use of the shrinking western army. The *Notitia* (see pages 56–7) credits him with almost 50 mobile units in Italy alone, but in the crisis of 405 when Italy was invaded, he mustered only 30, which seems to be a more realistic index of his resources. The Goths were on the move once more, many of them under a dynamic new leader, Alaric; Stilicho was unable or unwilling to defeat him decisively, yet he might have controlled him, but for a new disaster. On 31 December 406 the Vandals and other German peoples crossed the frozen Rhine, and in their wake came the Franks and Alamanni.

An iron helmet from Intercisa, Hungary. Helmets of this kind were mass-produced in factories.

These tribes were never expelled. In a kaleidoscope of wars and alliances they entrenched themselves in the western provinces, the Roman government finding itself cast in the role of the moujik pursued by wolves: whom next to throw off the sledge? In Britain the garrison proclaimed emperor a common soldier, Constantine III (407–11), who invaded Gaul and briefly controlled Spain, but Britain rebelled from him and Roman rule was never restored. In Italy Stilicho fell from power (408), but his successors were even less able to control the Goths; after inconclusive negotiations, Alaric carried out his threat to sack Rome (see below). Next year (411) he died, and the Goths remained dangerous nomads, devastating the tribes in Spain on Roman orders, before they were allowed to settle by treaty (418) in south-west Gaul. The survivors of this devastation in Spain, the Vandals, succeeded where other invaders had failed: in 429 they crossed the Strait of Gibraltar. When the western empire's last intact provinces were replaced by an aggressive Vandal kingdom, its decline was irreversible. In 444 the western emperor, Theodosius' grandson Valentinian III (425–55), admitted economic and military bankruptcy: the taxpayers were exhausted, the soldiers were cold and hungry. The eastern empire would survive for centuries, but the western empire was bleeding to death.

AD 410

SACK OF ROME

DATE AD 410
CAMPAIGN Gothic invasion of Italy
OBJECT To force the west Roman government to negotiate.
DESCRIPTION The picture (right) is the Porta Salaria, the gate by which the Goths entered Rome on 24 August 410. Three days of pillage followed. The walls of Rome were a massive obstacle, 11 miles of brick-faced concrete nearly 13 feet thick and 67 feet high, with 381 enfilading towers and 18 gates. Alaric blockaded Rome twice, in the winter of 408–9 and again in 409, to force the government of Honorius in Ravenna to give his people land. When negotiations failed once more in 410, Alaric returned to Rome and soon broke in.
RESULT The "fall" of Rome; some material damage, a great loss of prestige, and shock; no immediate political settlement between Romans and Goths.

The Porta Salaria, Rome, as it looked in 1747.

5

THE DARK AGES

This splendid helmet was found in the ship burial at Sutton Hoo in East Anglia, possibly the tomb of King Redwald (died between 616–27). The workmanship is Swedish, but this is a Germanic version of a late Roman parade helmet – a symbol of authority rather than practical armour.

THE PHRASE "DARK AGES" is applied to a period in European history stretching from about 400 to around 1000AD, a time otherwise known as the Early Middle Ages. The era is "dark" in that there is a shortage of historical evidence. Central and eastern Europe are only emerging for the first time into the historical light by 1000, but for western Europe the years after the end of Roman rule are in fact better served by documentary evidence than those before. Where evidence is sufficiently detailed it reveals that the conduct of war in barbarian Europe often reached a sophisticated level even if the literary evidence frequently obscures it with its emphasis on heroic deeds and individual actions.

RECRUITMENT AND ORGANIZATION OF ARMIES

The military system of the Roman Empire was in decline long before the western empire ceased to exist. By the fifth century, western Roman armies consisted of barbarian war bands serving under their own leaders, paid from taxation. The East too relied heavily on such mercenaries. Long before 500 in the West the central administration responsible for collecting taxation and allocating resources to armies had withered away in Gaul and Spain; only in Italy did it continue to function under barbarian rulers until the devastating wars and invasions of the next century.

The central feature in the military organization of the barbarian kingdoms was the war band or retinue of kings, princes and aristocrats (including ecclesiastics), made up of adolescents and young men of noble birth who lived in permanent attendance upon their lords in return for their sustenance, gifts of treasure, and ultimately in the expectation of land. Among the Franks they were called *antrustions*, in Lombard Italy *gasindii*, and *thegns* in Anglo-Saxon England. The nucleus of a royal army was the king's household, supplemented by nobles' retinues.

These were not the only sources of soldiers. Where town life survived, south of the Loire in Gaul, in Italy and in Spain, levies from the cities and their districts were

535

BYZANTINE CONQUEST OF ITALY

DATE 535–554

OBJECT Part of Emperor Justinian's opportunistic scheme to conquer the western Mediterranean coast.

NUMBERS Gothic military manpower was some 20,000, plus escaped slaves. The first Byzantine army was less than 10,000 strong; in the early 550s more than 20,000 men were sent to Italy.

DESCRIPTION The 20-year Gothic war shows the strengths and limitations of the 6th-century Byzantine military system.

After rapid success in Vandal Africa, Count Belisarius took Ostrogothic Sicily, then Naples and Rome, by exploiting naval superiority. Outside Rome, Gothic spear-armed cavalry were defeated by Belisarius' mounted archers. After successfully defending Rome, he fought his way up the peninsula and occupied the former imperial capital at Ravenna.

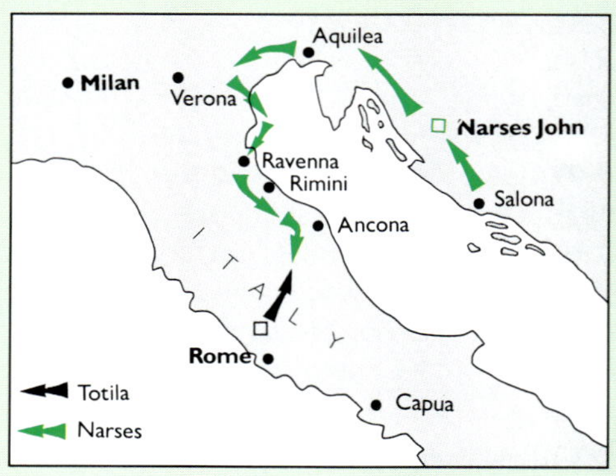

available at least for defence and local wars. In Gaul, Spain and Italy military service was initially limited to the barbarians, but it was a fiction that the Roman population was entirely demilitarized. Roman aristocrats soon began to behave like barbarians, recruiting their own retinues and participating in warfare. In exceptional circumstances in Visigothic Spain and Ostrogothic Italy, slaves were armed in the 6th century, and they may have formed a significant source of military manpower.

In theory, all free men, or at least those who possessed sufficient property to equip themselves, were subject to military service. The numbers of such men should not be overestimated, for the majority of the population was unfree. Moreover, the costs of campaigning made such soldiers of limited military value. By the 8th century in some areas steps were taken to reduce the number of men performing service by requiring poor free men to club together to equip one of their number. The most famous example of this comes from the reign of Charlemagne (768–814), but at some time a similar system was introduced into England where it was still in force in the 11th century.

Weapons from pagan graves are a major source of evidence for Dark Age equipment. This warrior from 10th-century Norway had (clockwise from top) arrows, knives, sword, spear and axe. In the centre are the shield boss and belt buckle. Either he did not possess helmet and body armour, or his relatives could not afford to bury them with him.

THE GROWTH OF FEUDALISM

Limiting the amount of service owed by free men was one reason why military service increasingly (but never exclusively) became the preserve of the aristocracy. Another was that kings granted to their nobles estates, in part to reinforce their loyalty, in part so that they could the better equip themselves and their military followers. Such grants of benefices or fiefs were conditional on the performance of military service. In 8th-century Francia the ties between king and follower were reinforced by oaths of vassalage. In this lies the origin of the military feudalism of the Middle Ages. So long as the king was active and successful he could keep control over his nobles, but by the late 9th century Frankish monarchs were losing control over many counts and their lands.

In this way military and political power became fragmented in much of Francia and Italy, and this fragmentation continued in many areas as lesser nobles who controlled castles established their independence. This process did not occur everywhere, however. In Normandy, Flanders and Anjou, for example, counts successfully retained control over their vassals and built powerful states, while the kings of West Francia (which would become France) found their power increasingly restricted and localized around Paris. In England and Germany the 10th-century kings kept control over their nobles, helped by the prestige of military success against Viking and Magyar (Hungarian) invaders.

Paid standing armies were unknown in the West during most of the Middle Ages. In the surviving East Roman (Byzantine) empire a standing army financed from

554

The rapid conquest was only superficial. From the main Gothic settlements north of the Po, King Totila reconquered Italy and Sicily, except for a few coastal cities. A disastrous plague and crisis on the Empire's eastern frontier meant the armies in Italy were starved of men and money.

Not until 550 were sufficient resources available for Italy. The eunuch general Narses' demands for sole command and full financial backing were met, and the Gothic fleet was defeated off Ancona (551). Narses' army was the greatest Justinian sent westwards, 20,000-plus, with a high proportion of Huns and Germans. He outflanked the Gothic positions on river lines using his fleet and pontoon bridges. In 552 Totila fought at Taginae to cover Rome. He attempted a surprise attack but was enveloped by Narses' horse-archers. Totila was killed and his army dispersed.

Ostrogoth resistance continued north of the Po. At Casilinum (554) a supporting Frankish-Alemanni army was destroyed by Narses, using the same enveloping tactics. A strong infantry centre absorbed the ferocious Frankish charge, then the mounted wings closed the trap. Not until 561, however, did Narses reduce the last Gothic garrisons in northern Italy.

The Aberlemno stone no 2, from Scotland, celebrates the defeat and death of the Northumbrian King Ecgfrith at Nechtansmere (Dunnichen Moss). The Picts (on horseback) have helmets, shields, swords and spears; the English (on foot) are similarly equipped. The helmets here and on the Anglo-Saxon Franks Casket parallel the recently found Coppergate (York) helmet.

taxation continued to exist. However, the armies with which Justinian's generals conquered Africa and Italy (530s–50s) depended heavily on the recruitment of bands of barbarians and prisoners of war. The disastrous losses of territory suffered in the 7th century forced the Byzantine rulers to settle many military units on the land and to recruit from the resulting military districts *(themes)*. It was in the Muslim world that the only true standing armies were to be found. The vast Arab expansion in the 7th and 8th centuries led to the recruitment of armies of slaves *(mamelukes)*, consisting largely of Turks in the east, and of Christian and Slavonic captives, many purchased from the Vikings, in Spain.

The *housecarls*, who appear in England after the Danish conquest by Cnut (1016), have been interpreted as a paid standing army, perhaps of a few thousand men. The evidence shows the housecarls to have been the military household of Cnut, similar to those maintained by kings and aristocrats throughout the early Middle Ages. From 1012–50 English rulers did maintain a permanent, mercenary *fleet*. Such household bands continued to form the nuclei of armies in the 11th century, as well as serving as castle garrisons, especially in frontier regions.

WEAPONS AND MILITARY EQUIPMENT

In the early Middle Ages iron weapons and armour were almost prohibitively expensive. Full sets of military equipment were the prized possessions of kings and aristocrats, who gave them as gifts to their followers. Military success depended to a great degree on a plentiful supply of these costly and frequently beautiful weapons. The main sources of information for weapons in the 5th to 7th centuries are pagan graves in which they were deposited. Conversion to Christianity caused this practice to end and information comes instead from chance finds, manuscript illustrations and sculptures.

Defensive weaponry consisted of helmets, shields and shirts of mail, or metal or horn scales sewn to leather jerkins and shields. The 7th-century royal burial at Sutton Hoo in East Anglia contained a highly decorated helmet, round shield and the remains of mail. The helmet was based on a Roman parade model, but is too impracticable to have been worn in action. Greaves have been found in Frankish burials and formed part of the best-armed warriors' equipment. The 8th-century helmet found at York has nose and cheek-guards, and a mail curtain protecting the neck. Its style is parallelled on a sculpted stone at Aberlemno in Scotland, probably erected to commemorate the Pictish victory over a Northumbrian host at Nechtansmere in 685.

The Bayeux Tapestry depicts the armour current in England and northern France in the 11th century. English infantry and Norman cavalry both wear conical helmets

768

THE CAMPAIGNS OF CHARLEMAGNE

DATE 768–812

CAMPAIGN The campaigns of Charles (Charlemagne) demonstrate his abilities and Frankish military effectiveness.

OBJECT Charles' campaigns were waged opportunistically, to eliminate threats, win lands and treasures with which to reward his followers, gain renown, and to please God (as he saw it).

DESCRIPTION His first task was to finish the subjugation of Aquitaine in 769. The campaign reveals the hallmarks of his generalship: swiftness, concentration of force, building of strongholds and use of terror. The conquest of Saxony, begun in 772, occupied much of the next 33 years. Charles' biographer Einhard described it thus: "no war ever undertaken by the Frankish people was more prolonged, more full of atrocities or more demanding of effort". All the methods of colonial warfare were employed – ravaging, hostage-taking, massacre, construction of strongholds, plantation of Frankish settlers and conversion to Christianity. But geography and the Saxons' primitive political organization made them resilient, and there were many revolts.

Charlemagne's second great feat was the destruction of the Avars (Huns), after gaining control of Bavaria in 787. Due to Saxon revolts he led only one campaign in person (791) in eight years, and it was left

with noseguards, hauberks which reached to the knees and elbows and carry round, and oblong or kite-shaped shields. This equipment provided a high degree of protection.

Offensive weapons consisted of long swords, short swords *(scramaseaxes)*, throwing axes *(franciscas*, a characteristic weapon of the Franks), spears (for example, the Frankish barbed *ango*, and the English *aetgar*), and the Viking battleaxe, whose use by the English is depicted on the Bayeux Tapestry. Bows and arrows were also used in war, but their penetrative power is not known.

This equipment was extremely expensive and only very rich men could afford all of it. In the early part of this period the most complete sets of arms and armour were restricted to the wealthy, to kings, aristocrats and their followers. Successful warfare led to the acquisition of such military equipment, and no race was so successful at war from the 5th to the early 9th centuries as the Franks under their Merovingian and Carolingian rulers.

From the late 8th-century on some rulers took steps to improve the military equipment of their soldiers. Around 800, Charlemagne laid down that the infantry were to equip themselves with spear, shield and bow. The traditional armament of the cavalry was lance, shield and long sword *(spata)*, to which was added the bow. But some of the Carolingian cavalry were much more completely equipped: the armoured knights, the striking force of Frankish armies of the time, included among their armament mail-shirts, helmets and even metal leg-guards. Charlemagne laid specific emphasis on the possession of this equipment by his most important subjects. The war-horse was a major cost, having a value equivalent to 18–20 cows. Thus this equipment was limited to the wealthiest free men and royal vassals, and such of their companions as they chose to arm with it. Export of such weaponry was prohibited at the end of the 8th century.

In the 10th century both the rulers of Wessex and the Ottonian kings of Germany, soon to be emperors, increased the quality and quantity of military equipment. The success that these kings enjoyed over internal rivals and neighbours was due in large measure to this increase. Their conquests were achieved by men who, to their victims, were "made of iron", and who practised a form of *blitzkrieg*. By the middle of the 10th century the West Saxon descendants of Alfred succeeded in creating a single kingdom of England. The armament of their warriors is indicated by the death duties which nobles paid, consisting of horses, coats of mail, helmets, swords, spears and shields. The greatest landowners occasionally added warships to their bequests. In 1008 King Æthelred II (975–1016) collected a tax in the form of helmets, and an indication of how much war-gear he amassed is the belief of a contemporary German writer, Thietmar of Merseburg, that Æthelred had 24,000 coats of mail in London.

Continued on page 66

Designed by a Norman, the Bayeux Tapestry was made by English nuns at Canterbury. The English dismounted to fight, and used the fearsome two-handed battle-axe, which could shear through armour and man. By 1066 the Norman cavalry was starting to hold the spear firmly underarm – the beginning of the standard knightly technique of the Middle Ages.

812

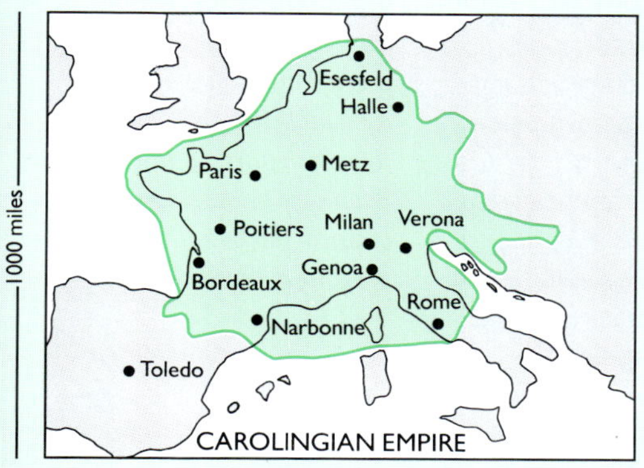

to lieutenants to break into the Avar "ring" and carry off immense plunder.

Nor was this all. In 773-4 Charles conquered Lombard Italy, confounding his opponent by campaigning over winter. He led armies into Spain, against the Slavs across the Elbe, and into Italy beyond Rome. Up to 800 he led in person – it was a matter of note that he did *not* campaign in 790 – and after retiring from active campaigning he directed armies to all frontiers. In 810, aged nearly 70, he led his last host against an expected Danish invasion.

Charles and his subordinates created an empire which stretched from the Atlantic to Hungary, from Denmark to the Ebro in Spain and south of Rome in Italy. This was the achievement of a master of strategy and logistics, yet he fought only two pitched battles, both in 783. Although Charlemagne's empire did not long survive him as a political entity, he shaped the future of Europe.

THE RISE OF HEAVY CAVALRY

THE CHARACTERISTIC figure in medieval warfare is the knight, a heavily armed cavalry soldier who fought with lance and sword. As the Middle Ages progressed, his armour became increasingly heavy and effective, and correspondingly expensive. This more than anything else led to the domination of warfare by heavy cavalry. How it came about is not easy to establish.

The defeat of a Roman army and the death of the emperor Valens at the hands of a Gothic-Hun army has been seen as a turning point, after which the Imperial government abandoned its traditional reliance on infantry and turned instead to heavy cavalry. But the role of barbarian cavalry at Adrianople has been over estimated, and it was largely an infantry battle. Anyway, the Romans had been increasing their armoured cavalry units since the third century. Among the barbarian invaders heavy cavalry did not predominate either. The expense of armour, warhorse and weapons meant this style of fighting was restricted to kings and nobles.

Another turning point in the rise of heavy cavalry has been placed in the 8th century. It has been argued that the Frank, Charles Martel, used church lands to build up a heavy cavalry force after his clash with the Arabs at Poitiers in 732 convinced him of the need for one. Although this theory was discredited, another was substituted for it. This was that the introduction of the stirrup in western Europe in the early 8th century made possible "mounted shock combat" by giving the rider a firmer seat. It was this which made cavalry the master of the battlefield.

The benefits conferred by the stirrup are indisputable, but there is no evidence that knowledge of it reached the West precisely in the first half of the 8th century. Cavalry was certainly not unknown in Frankish armies before this time, but it did not become the dominant element before the end of the century. The reasons for the Carolingian dynasty's successful wars of conquest, which continued for almost a century, lay in its methods. Its armies operated with a destructiveness and sheer savagery that destroyed the ability and desire of opponents to resist.

This is not to deny the significance of heavy cavalry in the armies of Charlemagne. Estimates of the total numbers available around 800 vary from 5,000 to 35,000, but it is certain that the Franks possessed a formidable heavy cavalry. The explanation for this lies in their ability to equip significant numbers of warriors with expensive armour and equipment. Charlemagne paid careful attention to the equipment of his armies – light cavalry and infantry, as well as heavy cavalry – and to logistics on campaign. The great men of the realm were given estates from which they were required to provide well-equipped horsemen. The incentive was participation in profitable and glorious campaigns of conquest.

Although pitched battles were rare in these wars, when they did occur the Frankish armoured cavalry had a great advantage over their more lightly armed opponents. Their tactic was a disciplined

(Above) The backbone of Roman armies was the heavy legionary infantry, but from the later 3rd century the use of cavalry of all types was increased, especially after the reforms of Constantine (AD324–37), in response to new threats.

(Right) Cavalry came to play a greater role in the Byzantine empire during the Dark Ages. Many of its enemies – like the Bulgars shown here – were Asiatic cavalry.

(Above) This 11th-century Greek illustration purports to show 9th-century Byzantine and Muslim cavalry, both shown using the stirrup. Stirrups enabled the cavalry man to have much greater control over his horse, and much greater stability in the saddle. It is no longer accepted that the Arabs introduced it to Western Europe in the first half of the 8th century.

(Right) Frankish cavalry from the late 9th century. The mix of classical and contemporary features in this manuscript make it difficult to use as a guide; the helmet in particular looks as if it might be based on a classical model rather than a real one of the 9th century.

close-order charge, and they relied on swords in the mêlée. Nor were the Franks incapable of dismounting when the occasion required it. Superior equipment made them irresistible – so long as they remembered their discipline. At the battle of the Süntel Mountains against the Saxons in 782, and in 891 at the battle of the Dyle against the Danes, the Frankish cavalry were over-confident and forgot their discipline. In consequence they were defeated.

The 9th-century divisions of the Carolingian empire left the East Frankish (German) kingdom short of well-equipped Franks to draw on. When the Saxon Duke Henry the Fowler became king (918–36) he converted the Saxon nobility, hitherto used to fighting as light cavalry, into a force of armoured horsemen. This amounted to a military revolution. He turned them into disciplined, professional "men of iron", who gave his dynasty (the Ottonians) the edge over its enemies in Germany, the Magyars (Huns), Slavs and opponents in Italy. Like the Franks, they relied on a close-order charge. Before the battle of Riade (933) against the Magyar horse archers, Henry reminded his men of the need to maintain their line, to use their shields to deflect the first discharge of arrows, and only then to spur their horses to close contact. Ottonian success in the 10th and 11th centuries was founded on King Henry's foresight.

The emergence of armoured horsemen as a significant force had already occurred by the year 1000. It was due to a gradual evolution not a revolution. The major development in the 11th century, and the conclusion to the trend, would be the effective deployment of the lance through the technique of "couching" it firmly under the arm, which can be seen on the Bayeux Tapestry (c. 1080). By the 11th century, among Western Europeans only the English did not fight on horseback. Although their military equipment closely resembled that of, for example, the Normans, they rode to battle but dismounted to fight. Yet it is important not to exaggerate the dominance of heavy cavalry. Medieval armies contained infantry, spearmen and archers, whose role was well appreciated and significant – this is clear whenever detailed evidence is plentiful, as for example it is for the battle of Hastings (1066) and the First Crusade.

(Above) Viking ships were technologically advanced. The combination of oars and sails gave them the mobility to terrorize the coastal regions of western Europe. (Below) Viking coastal raiding was succeeded by the establishment of winter bases and the requisitioning of horses to spread their activities farther inland.

SIZE OF ARMIES

It is impossible to calculate the size of early medieval armies, indeed the historian is frequently unable to say anything on this matter. Dark Age and medieval writers do sometimes give figures for armies, of the order of tens or even hundreds of thousands. But historians are unanimous in agreeing that these are gross exaggerations and of no use. There is also general agreement that armies were normally no more than a few thousand strong, and often only a few hundred. The contrast with the notion that in barbarian society all free men were liable to military service is striking, but can be explained. The cost of equipment limited swords and armour to only a few warriors, but their military effectiveness was out of all proportion to their numbers. A few hundred well-equipped men were capable of great deeds.

A prominent example of this is the activities of the Vikings in Western Europe during the 9th century. These pagan raiders from Denmark and Norway (the Swedes tended to operate in Russia) demoralized and terrorized their enemies, and subsequently made substantial conquests and settlements in England and Francia. Not surprisingly, it was been assumed that large hosts were needed to achieve this. However, an examination of the chronicle evidence led the historian Peter Sawyer to conclude that even the "Great Danish army" (*magnus exercitus* in Latin, *micel here* in Anglo-Saxon) which conquered and settled three of the four ninth-century Anglo-Saxon kingdoms was less than 1,000 strong at any one time. Nicholas Brooks has subsequently made a convincing case for numbering the great army of 865, and its successor, which came to England in 892, in thousands, while accepting that no precision is possible. These two forces were led by Danish kings, and were the focus of Viking activities in the West. In short, they were coalitions of the small personal warbands of hundreds which normally launched hit-and-run raids.

There is similar difficulty in establishing the size of the forces which invaded the Roman Empire, or the armies of Charlemagne. From his vast empire he might have been able to field 5–35,000 armoured cavalry (depending on whose calculation is used) supplemented by hordes of lighter cavalry and infantry. But only a fraction of these would have been assembled at one time, and the most significant factor in Carolingian military successes was not quantity but quality and organization.

COMMAND

In the Dark Ages and long after, one of the chief attributes of kingship and of nobility was leadership in war. To a great extent this was the justification for monarchy and success in war was also vital for successful rule. Only in the Muslim world did military and political leadership become separated, but in outlying areas like Spain military governors were able to establish their independence from the centre.

865

VIKING GREAT ARMY IN ENGLAND

DATE 865–79

OBJECT To plunder and reduce defeated Anglo-Saxon kingdoms to tributary status; then to settle conquered areas.

NUMBERS Numbers on both sides are impossible to calculate. The Anglo-Saxon kingdoms probably fielded a few thousand warriors each. The great army, led by several kings, included most Danish bands hitherto raiding in the West, and so probably numbered a few thousand. Elements settled in 875 and in 877, but the remainder was able to overrun part of Wessex and settle East Anglia (878–80). Wastage due to casualties and retirement was offset by the arrival of new bands.

DESCRIPTION When West Frankish resistance became too stiff, the Viking bands operating in the West joined up to operate in England. The Vikings of the great army adopted a new strategy. Each

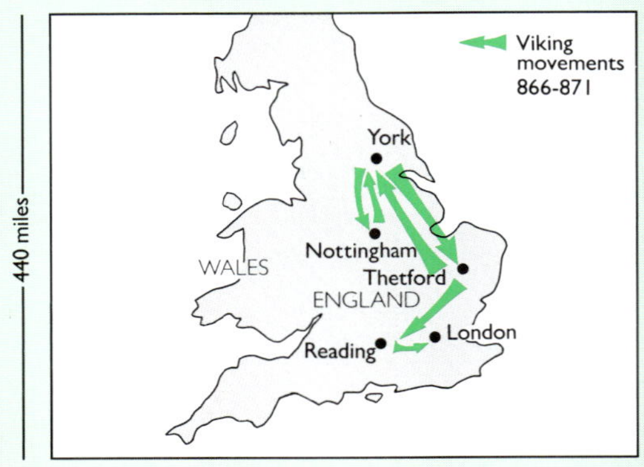

The largest armies were led by kings in person, although it made sense for them to avoid actual combat. Indeed, the death of a king in battle, as at Hastings in 1066, brought resistance to an end. At a lower level, members of the nobility led hosts, either on their own account or at the command of their king. In England *ealdormen*, often of royal blood themselves, led the warriors from their shires, while in Francia this was performed by counts and, in border districts, dukes who had responsibility for several counties. Similar noble officers are met with in Italy and Spain. But the delegation of military power was not without its dangers for, if central authority weakened, these noble office-holders were likely to become independent, which is what happened in the Carolingian empire in the 10th century.

Bishops and abbots were also prominent as army commanders in the Carolingian empire, by virtue of their noble birth and the great landed wealth of the Church. This is found too in late Anglo-Saxon England and in Germany. In theory powerful ecclesiastics could not establish their own dynasties and so the military power of their estates was at the disposal of the Crown. This does not mean that the ecclesiastics fought in person. In the arts of war as in peace their experience, literacy and lands made them indispensable royal servants.

Below these prominent levels of command little is known. Beneath the county or shire the most important unit was the following of an individual lord, commanded by a noble or his delegate. The military household reinforced by a lord's leading tenants was the chief tactical unit of medieval armies.

Charles the Great (Charlemagne) was the most successful ruler of Dark Age Europe: his dominance was founded on an appreciation of the importance of logistics and of bringing overwhelming force to bear. He was far more than a mere barbarian warlord, but it was on his consistent triumph in war that all his other achievements rested.

STRATEGY

War in the Middle Ages was almost constant in many regions, whether it was public war between states, or private war between neighbours or rivals. Much of it was small-scale raiding. Grand strategy is frequently difficult to distinguish, but this does not mean medieval generals were incapable of executing operations on the grand scale. As in so much else the clear example is Charlemagne (Charles "the Great"). On several occasions we meet the use of multiple invasions which would split the defenders' strength as well as easing problems of movement: two columns invading Italy (773) and crossing the Pyrenees (778), and three hosts sent into Bavaria from three points of the compass (787).

In 791 two armies advanced into Hungary, one on each bank of the Danube, with a supply fleet linking them. This arrangement made possible the outflanking of the Avar (Hun) defence lines on the south bank of the river. For the next campaign Charles ordered the construction of a pontoon bridge, but it was never put to use as rebellions caused the king to be called away.

The Viking great armies certainly followed a coherent strategy, consisting of

879

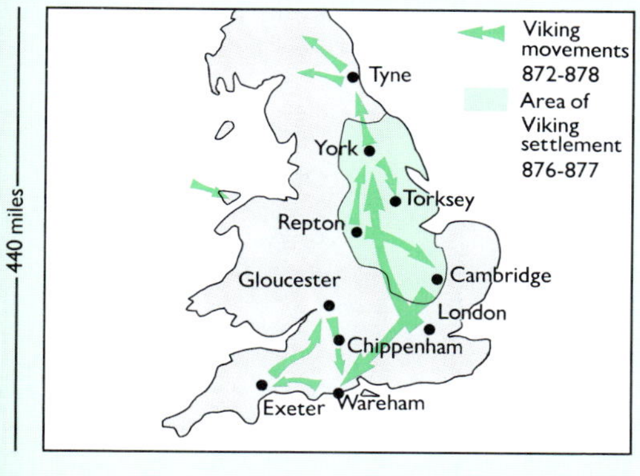

autumn they moved to a new district and seized a royal centre, usually with existing fortifications, to serve as winter quarters and a secure base while the bulk of the host was plundering.

Initially there was little the Anglo-Saxon kingdoms could do other than pay tribute in order to ward off further plundering. Alfred fought eight battles in 871, but he too came to terms. He was more successful in 875–7 when he kept a close watch on the invaders, making it difficult for them to forage or plunder. But in January 878 he was taken by surprise at Chippenham and driven into the Somerset marshes until he could raise another army, blockade the Danes in Chippenham and enforce surrender on terms.

RESULT In 879 the leaders of the great army accepted that West Saxon resistance would not be overcome; the army split again, part settling East Anglia, the remainder returning to the Continent.

A grandson of Charles the Great, Charles the Bald inherited the western part of the Frankish empire. He is shown here, on the winning side at Fontenoy in 842. In the 860s his defence works in northern France forced the Viking "great army" to migrate to England. But by his death in 877 royal authority in "France" had been seriously weakened.

seizing a fortified base on a major river and exploiting the region around it before moving to another region. The first great army followed this strategy in Britain from 865 until 879 (see page 66), by which time many of its surviving members had become settlers. It was reinforced and left England, where West Saxon resistance had become too stiff, for Francia where this second great army campaigned until 892. Again the West Franks organized effective resistance and so the whole army migrated to England. But Alfred had prepared for this and in 896 the great army broke up.

Indeed, the strategy adopted against the Viking great armies in West Francia and Wessex was noteworthy. Its main feature was the mobilization of labour to reconstruct Roman walls or build new fortresses to be held against the Vikings, and fortified bridges to impede the movement of their fleets inland. Both Charles the Bald (West Frankish king, 840–77) and Alfred (Wessex king, 871–99) employed this strategy with success. In England the fortress strategy was adapted by Edward the Elder (Wessex, 899–924) for the conquest of the Danish settlements in the Midlands and East Anglia. Now his control was extended by the building of one or more fortresses each campaign from which to bring more land under military domination. This process of "nibbling" away resulted in the conquest of the land between the Thames and Humber in only a decade. At about the same time the German king Henry the Fowler (911–36) was establishing a similar network of fortresses with permanent garrisons in Saxony to defend and extend the frontiers against Slavs and Magyars.

The most widely employed and most effective medieval strategy was "ravaging". It was a form of economic warfare which was generally more productive than a battle-seeking strategy. Pitched battles carried too many risks when strategic objectives could usually be achieved by organized raiding. This operated at all levels of warfare and fulfilled several functions. At the highest level the systematic destruction of the means of production, as practised by the Carolingians in Aquitaine in the middle decades of the 8th century, destroyed the material base and will to resist. Conquest could thus follow on the heels of ravaging. Raids could also be immensely profitable, both in material and prestige. At the operational level pillaging supplied armies (although commanders did not ignore the need for large armies to carry supplies with them) and enriched the participants and so provided a major incentive to fight. The standard counter to a raiding strategy was to assemble a field army in the vicinity of an invading force. Then it could either be forced to desist from pillaging or defeated in detail. This method of active defence was used with success by, for example, Alfred against the Viking great army in the late 870s and again in the 890s. In regions of strong fortified sites, that is where Roman town walls remained defensible (in southern France and Italy for example), a passive defensive strategy

991

MALDON

DATE 10 or 11 August 991
OBJECT Olaf Tryggvason's fleet came to Folkestone to raid the coast of south-east England, moving north to Sandwich and Ipswich, before establishing a base on Northey Island in the Blackwater estuary.
NUMBERS The English numbers are unknown. Their commander was Ealdorman Brihtnoth, whose army included his own household and retainers and the Essex militia (*fyrd*). Olaf's fleet was put at 93 ships, a possible maximum of 7,000 warriors, but probably considerably less.
DESCRIPTION Viking raids on England were renewed in 980 ("the second Viking Age"), and Maldon was the first serious English setback. The significance of Maldon lies in its description in a contemporary poem. If the poet was not an eyewitness, his account is nevertheless the only detailed record of an Anglo-Saxon army in battle. Beneath the heroic formulae

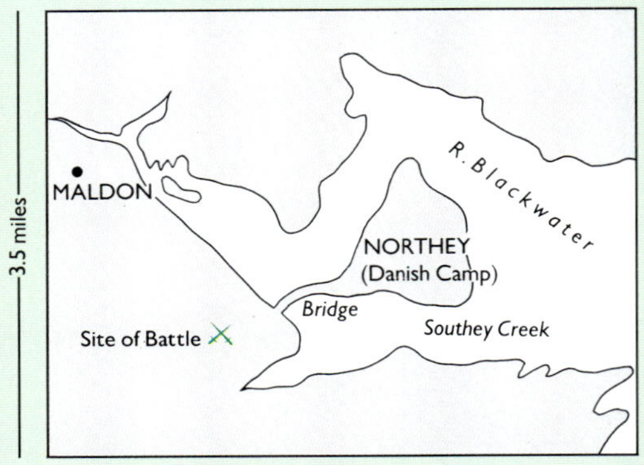

involved taking refuge until the invader withdrew. The disadvantage of this strategy was that it did not prevent considerable damage being caused to economic resources, nor would it work against determined and well equipped invaders like the 8th-century Carolingians.

TACTICS

Pitched battles were rare throughout the Middle Ages, except where fortified sites were few. In this case the defender was constrained to give battle or suffer dangerous loss of resources and prestige. However, it is difficult to describe tactics used when battles did occur due to the inadequacy of narrative sources. Descriptions of battles are few, and they give fewer details of tactics, being largely concerned with the heroic deeds of individuals. But this is not the same thing as saying that Dark Age battles were undisciplined The discipline required for the Frankish cavalry charge from the late 8th century onwards is described in the feature on heavy cavalry (see pages 64–65). For an indication of the degree of tactical sophistication which early medieval armies were capable of, the historian has to wait until the battle of Hastings in 1066. This reveals the co-ordination of infantry and cavalry, and a high degree of discipline. This is true not only of Duke William's army, which was recruited widely in France, but to a lesser extent of the English shield-wall. Although this formation seems to have been incapable of more than rudimentary manoeuvres, it was a tough nut to crack as long as it maintained its formation. One counter-measure against cavalry not employed by the English in 1066 was the digging of traps; their use is, however, recorded from the early 6th century, when the Thuringians broke up a Frankish cavalry charge in this way. Nevertheless, in general it seems to be true that early medieval battles tended to be brief and relatively unsophisticated, and that for much of this period the most elaborate tactics were those of the Byzantine armies. This did not, it should be noted, protect the Byzantine empire from severe setbacks and losses of territory at the hands of Persians, Muslims, Asiatic and Slav invaders in the Balkans and Germanic enemies in Italy. The Byzantine empire survived, and in the 6th and 10th centuries it expanded again, but it would be unsafe to attribute this to a permanently superior military system.

A brief survey such as this can not do justice to the multiplicity of military systems and methods of the Dark Ages. There have always been inadequate military systems and incompetent commanders. Moreover, the nature of the evidence for warfare in the Early Middle Ages often defeats analysis. There is sufficient evidence, however, to show that this period was not barren of military innovation, discipline and application of the science of war.

A HANDBOOK FOR GENERALS?

The most popular military handbook of the Middle Ages was *On War (De re militari)* by the late-Roman Flavius Vegetius Renatus. Vegetius commented on all aspects of war. Some principles could not be applied to medieval armies, but two were relevant. One concerned supply: the army which was not carefully provisioned courted disaster. The second concerned laying waste enemy territory, which enriched the soldiers, making them enthusiastic to fight, and reduced enemy resources. Over 300 copies survive, the large number testimony to its relevance throughout the Middle Ages.

Illustration from a medieval version of De re militari.

991

lies an important insight.

Ealdorman Brihtnoth drew up his host opposite Northey, where a causeway joins the island to the mainland. After heroic preliminaries he permitted the Vikings to cross the causeway and form battle order. Why did he take this risk? If he had not, the raiders would have sailed away to plunder elsewhere. A century of successes had probably made the English confident of the outcome of battle.

The English dismounted, sending their horses to the rear, and formed the traditional shieldwall. The Vikings were in a similar formation. Battle opened with an exchange of spears and archery before the two shieldwalls engaged in close combat with spears and swords. The turning point of the encounter came when Brihtnoth himself was wounded and then cut down. Panic set in and many of the English ran to the horses and fled. The surviving portion of the poem concludes with the heroic resistance of some of Brihtnoth's retainers, whose names are celebrated in the epic. As portrayed in the poem, the conflict had been a simple one – indeed it is likely that the shieldwall was not capable of more than rudimentary manoeuvre.

RESULT This battle looks like the turning point in the reign of Æthelred II ("the Unready"), although it took 20 years before the Danish king Swein could aim at conquest, and another five years before it was achieved by his son Cnut.

6

MEDIEVAL WARFARE

THE MEDIEVAL PERIOD was one of technological innovation. Fortifications grew from simple towers, to great concentric castles and eventually became artillery-proof bastion forts. Siege weapons both led and responded to these developments: the 12th century produced the trebuchet and the 14th century gunpowder artillery. Ships grew from low-lying galleys to towering galleons. Protection improved from ring-mail coats to complete suits of plate armour. Missile weapons, in the hands of English bowmen or French arquebusiers, eventually transformed the "hosts" of horsemen into armies of footsoldiers.

CAVALRY AND CASTLES

It is a myth that warfare in the Middle Ages was dominated by the mounted warrior, the knight. This is no more true than to say that the tank is the sole battle-winner today. Their tactical roles are not dissimilar, but we should not translate one into the other too literally. Cavalry is the spiritual ancestor of the armoured fighting vehicle, but the mounted arm has always played a part in co-operation with, rather than in isolation from the rest.

In contrast, fortification, expressed in the form of the castle, was central to the conduct of war c.1000–1400. The link between the mounted warrior and the castle was a social one; lords and their retinues lived in and around their fortress. This conjunction was a product of a social and political change seen in continental Europe and West Francia (France) in the two centuries following the reign of the Emperor Charlemagne c.800–1000. A combination of factors including the attacks of the Vikings, Muslims and Magyars and the decline of central, monarchical authority, led to power descending to local level in western Christian Europe. Any lord with a castle and following of knights was a force to be reckoned with and to be wooed by princes.

The result was a military development which proved to be an efficient vehicle for expansion and conquest under the leadership of Frankish rulers. The knight, a mail-

1053

CIVITATE

DATE 17 June 1053
CAMPAIGN War between Pope Leo IX and Norman lords
OBJECT To prevent Leo from joining up with his Byzantine allies
NUMBERS Papal – several thousand men, including a strong force of Swabian infantry; Norman – reckoned at 3,000 cavalry by the later chronicler Geoffrey Malaterra, but probably less than 1,000 knights.
DESCRIPTION Robert Guiscard commanded the Norman left wing, Humphrey the centre and Richard of Aversa the right. Spying disorganization in the Italo-Lombard forces, Richard charged and dispersed them. In the centre the Norman horsemen could make no headway against the Swabian foot. With Guiscard's force in reserve and the return of Richard's wing the Pope's forces were eventually overcome.
RESULT The Papal army was destroyed and Leo taken prisoner.

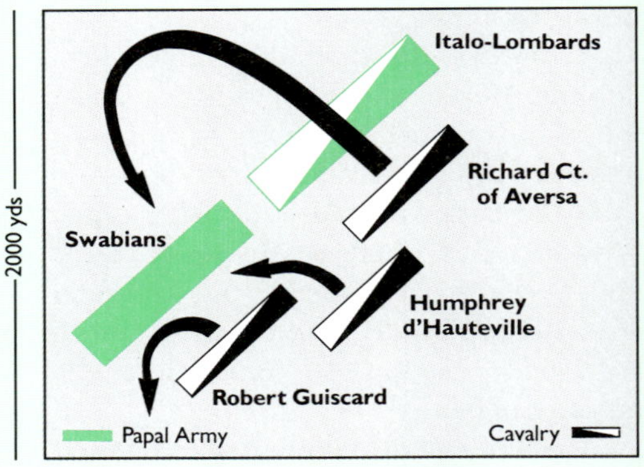

clad and shielded cavalryman carrying sword and lance, proved more than a match tactically for most opponents. The Westerners' competence at the related arts of fortress building and siege techniques meant that they could take and hold fortresses, so riveting their rule on the land.

This military success is usually associated with the Normans. William the Conqueror won a decisive victory at Hastings in 1066, and consolidated his hold over England and much of northern France in the next two decades. A little earlier, the Norman Hauteville family had begun to carve out an empire in southern and central Italy. Robert Guiscard even led forces against Byzantium following his conquest of Bari in 1071. Ten years later he defeated the Emperor Alexius at Durazzo (in modern Albania). The emperor's daughter described the charge of the Frankish knights as "able to pierce the walls of Babylon", whose thickness was legendary.

This might seem to support the idea of the invincible knight, but in fact the victory was due to co-operation with missilemen. At Hastings, the Norman archers wore down axe-wielding foot soldiers until the knights could charge in. At Durazzo it was Italian crossbowmen who performed the same role. When the Varangian Guard seemed about to win the battle, the bowmen pinned them down and broke up their formation until the retreating knights could regroup and counter-attack. Significantly the campaign was won through the capture of the fortress port of Durazzo and a naval victory by the Venetians, rather than the battle alone. Western technological advantages and all-arms co-operation was the winning combination. It is no coincidence that sons of both William the Conqueror and Robert Guiscard, respectively Robert Curthose and Bohemond, were leading figures on the great military expedition known as the First Crusade. But it was not just the Normans who employed knight and castle as a weapon for conquest. It was a technique employed by all the Frankish rulers in Anjou, Flanders and Aquitaine.

The German emperors also relied upon the military service of knights by the end of the 11th century. Pope Gregory VII, in his dispute with Emperor Henry IV, declared his enemy excommunicate and dissolved his vassals' obedience to him. The result was civil war and the destruction of the emperor's military forces. The only way successive emperors could assert themselves over the popes was to campaign in Italy. This involved taking armies of knights south over the Alps from Germany, but little could be achieved by even such a powerful ruler as Frederick Barbarossa (1154–90) without the siege equipment to overwhelm the cities of northern Italy.

This is often seen as an example of something "new" – the defeat of an army of knights by foot soldiers. But once again the true reason was the combination of Italian cavalry with the stolid holding power of infantry found throughout the Middle Ages. The Anglo-Norman rulers had already expressed their awareness of

Continued on page 74

1061

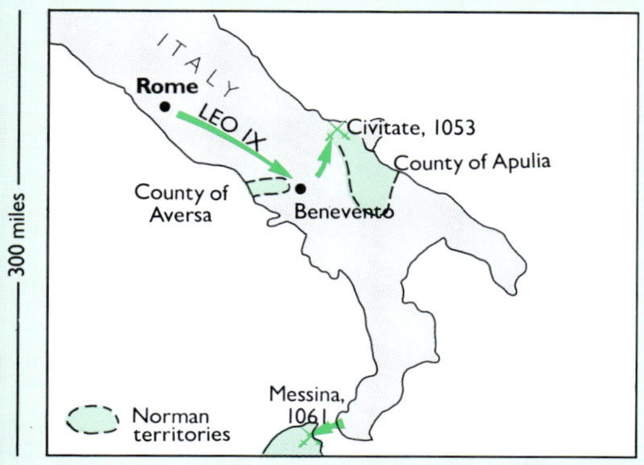

SICILY

DATE February/May 1061
OBJECT Norman invasion of Sicily
NUMBERS 470 knights on Norman side.
DESCRIPTION Five years before the Norman conquest of England, Roger de Hauteville crossed the straits of Messina to attack Sicily, then under Muslim control. After an unsuccessful raid in February, he returned in force in May. Roger used the daring innovation of carrying the knights' horses across with them. There were not enough vessels so they had to make two trips, first carrying 270 knights and their mounts, then 200 more.
RESULT With the Normans marching on Messina before dawn, the city fell without a fight. It is possible that some of the Normans involved in this operation advised William the Conqueror on his much larger invasion force in 1066.

THE BATTLE OF HASTINGS

THE BAYEUX TAPESTRY, the Anglo-Saxon Chronicle and Duke William's biography by the soldier turned chaplain, William of Poitiers, provide unusually detailed evidence for the campaigns of 1066. Harold (crowned 6 January 1066) faced threats from his brother Tostig, King Harald Hardrada of Norway and Duke William of Normandy. Tostig, first off the mark in the spring, was easily driven off. Harold defended the south against the Normans, leaving the northern earls Edwin and Morcar to face the Norwegians. The responses of the three leaders to the problems of seaborne invasion and defence demonstrates the high degree of military organization of 11th-century states. The greatest task faced William, who had to build a fleet. The depiction of this on the Bayeux Tapestry shows the justified Norman pride in this achievement.

During the summer of 1066 Harold's men guarded the south coast, his fleet at the Isle of Wight, until 8 September. After four months he dispersed them, their service expired and money exhausted. William, meanwhile, assembled a polyglot army which he held together for six weeks until ready to sail in late September. The delay may well have been intentional. If so, it worked. What both commanders achieved during the summer was to keep their armies supplied, avoiding the danger of epidemics inherent in static warfare. In one sense Harold's achievement was greater: his men had no prospect of plunder to motivate them.

The main fighting was crammed into one hectic month. When Harold reached London he learned that the Norwegians were in the Humber. His decision to march north, assembling an army on the way, was justified when the northern earls were defeated at Gate Fulford (20 September). Harold took the Norwegians by complete surprise at Stamford Bridge (25 September). He was completely victorious in a great battle of which no reliable details survive. Both King Harald of Norway and his ally Tostig were among the dead. This was Harold's first pitched battle.

Meanwhile the winds in the Channel changed, allowing the Norman fleet to sail on the night of 27 September. William made his first base at Pevensey, moving thence to Hastings, from where he plundered for supplies and to provoke Harold.

(Above) The church at Bosham, Sussex. Harold departed from here in 1064 on his mission to Normandy. He campaigned with William in Brittany, but in 1066 was out-generalled by him.

(Below) The site of the battle of 14 October 1066. The ridge on which the English position was formed gave them a considerable advantage – Harold fell on the right of the picture.

(Left) Bayeux Tapestry: the start of battle. The Norman assault was opened by infantry, followed by cavalry. Neither could make any impression on the English shieldwall, but the combination of archers and cavalry, decisive in winning the battle, can already be seen here.

Harold reacted decisively: in a fortnight he was within ten miles of Hastings (the night of 13 October). His actions have been criticized as reckless and impulsive, and he probably did fight before all his strength was mustered. The Vegetian maxim "courage is worth more than numbers, and speed is worth more than courage" may explain his strategy. A surprise attack was made possible and his proximity would restrict Norman foraging and invoke starvation. The Normans were out foraging when the English advance was learned of, and stood to during the night of 13–14 October fearing a surprise attack. But William's scouting enabled him to seize the initiative. He marched to confront the English on the morning of 14 October. The risk he took was great: the English were in a strong position, and William had to attack.

The English fought on foot in the customary shieldwall. Battle opened about 9am. Two lines of Norman infantry failed to break the English position, as did the Norman heavy cavalry. The rumour spread that William was dead, the Bretons on the left fell back, and rout threatened. In this crisis William rallied his men. Now William altered his tactics. The cavalry used the feigned flight to lure some of the English to destruction. Combined attacks by infantry, especially archers, and cavalry reduced English numbers. Towards the end of the day Harold was struck in the face (clearly shown on the Bayeux Tapestry), and as the English at last began to crumble he was cut down by a party of knights. With his death, English resistance ceased. It took William most of the day to crack the English position, but his generalship, and the discipline of his army were of the highest order. The battle was won, but not yet the war – English rebellions continued until 1070.

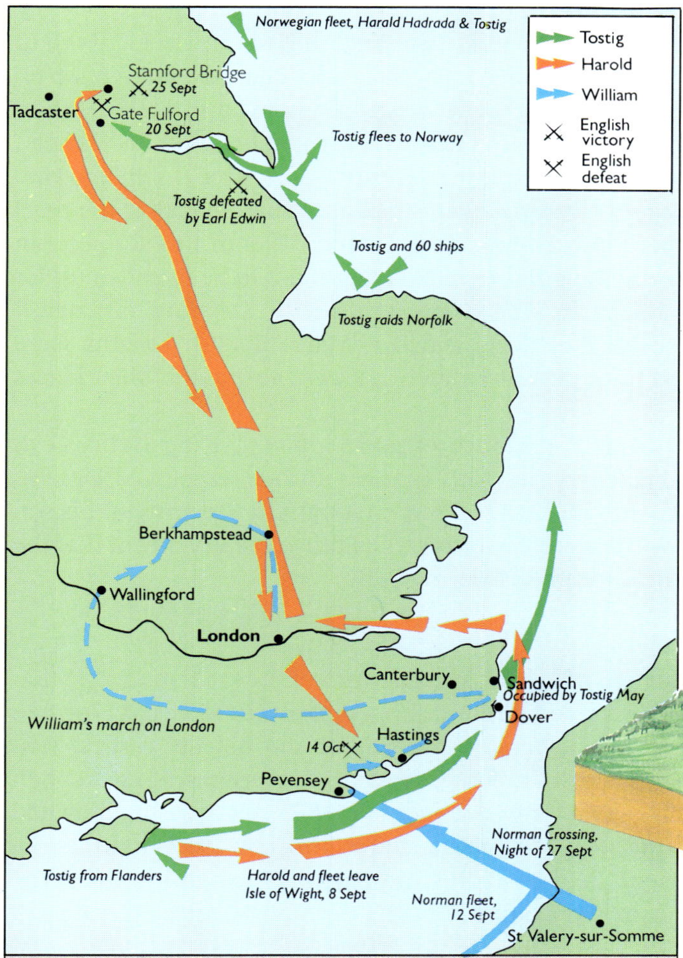

(Above) Harold of England was caught between two fires. His march north took the Norwegians by surprise, and the return to the south was even more impressive. He led the core of his army 250 miles southwards, assembling a new host and sending a fleet into the Channel. But William was equal to this and turned the tables on Harold.

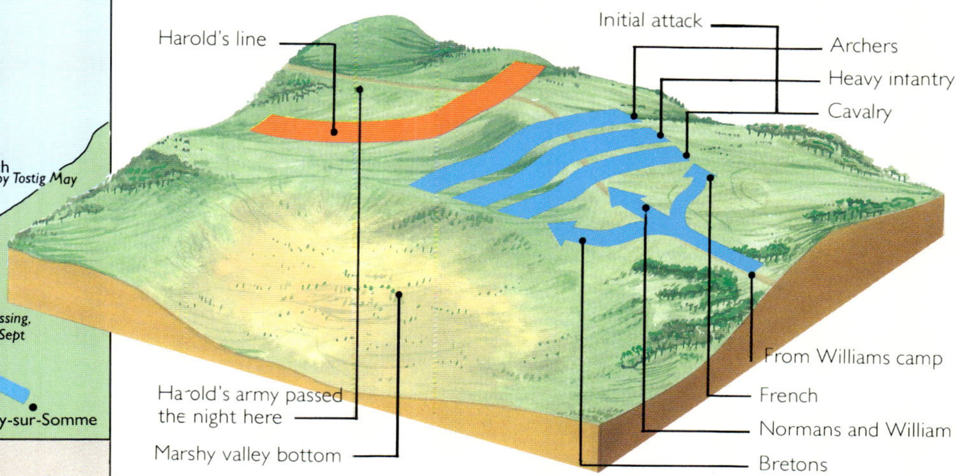

(Right) Harold was forced to give battle, but it was in a superb defensive position – on a sharp ridge with well-protected flanks. Moreover, William had to attack if he was to win England. The slope negated the effect of the Norman cavalry, and English axes inflicted fear-some wounds. William's tactics reveal a high order of generalship.

(Left) Bayeux Tapestry: Norman cavalry attack English shieldwall, early in the battle. The disciplined English shieldwall drove off the first Norman cavalry attacks, using spears, axes and clubs. The Normans are using their lances in various ways – the couched lance was best used against a mounted enemy.

Chainmail – so called because it was composed of thousands of tiny interlocking rings – was the most consistently popular form of protection in the Middle Ages. The torso was protected by the hauberk and the head by a coif, the two parts often being made in one piece.

this. In a series of battles in the first half of the 12th century commanders had actually *dismounted* their knights in order to win battles. The English king, Henry I, did this at Tinchebrai (1106) against his brother Robert, whose cavalry charges could make no headway against them, and then won the battle with a mounted flank attack. He also defeated the French king at Brémule in 1119, with a combination of archery, dismounted knights and cavalry. In 1124, one of Henry's professional soldiers, Odo Berleng, led a tiny garrison force of archers and dismounted knights against the rebel Waleran of Meulan. An impetuous cavalry charge by the Waleran was simply shot down by the archers, unhorsing the knights and leaving them to be rounded up for ransom by the royalist foot. Finally, in 1138, at the Battle of the Standard, an English army defeated the Scots led by their king David I. Many English knights were dismounted and placed in the front rank alternately with archers, so that their lances protected the missilemen.

All rulers were aware of the importance of good infantry. King Henry II of England, the most powerful ruler in mid-12th century Europe, employed Flemish and Brabançon foot. At Bouvines in 1214, such men fought in the army of his son John's ally, the emperor Otto. Their success against the French cavalry meant that the eventual victory of Philip II of France was long in doubt.

CASTLE WARFARE

Battles were in any case often secondary to fortress warfare. It was remarkable that the conquest of England was achieved without long, drawn-out sieges. A Norman chronicler pointed out that this was because the English did not use castles. Two generations later, after sustained castle-building, the civil war between King Stephen and the Empress Matilda dragged on for two decades (1138–53). Castle-building had long been known on the Continent. Fulk Nerra, count of Anjou (987–1040) and a "pioneer in feudal government" had based his campaigns of expansion upon the construction of stone castles in the Loire valley. In Germany, Duke Frederick of Bueren did the same along the Rhine.

How did castles control the land? They could not interdict the passage of an enemy (except in the narrowest passes) before the development of gunpowder artillery. Essentially they were bases for supplies, refuges in case of defeat and jumping-off points for raids and sallies. The building of such a fortification in, or on the borders of, enemy territory, was a declaration of hostile intent. Further, the garrison, though not the castle itself, could threaten lines of communication. Only if it was taken did it cease to become a threat. It could then be removed (razed) or turned against its previous owner.

The conquest of England provides a most instructive example of castle strategy.

1189

SEIGE OF ACRE

DATE August 1189–11 July 1191
CAMPAIGN Third Crusade of western rulers against the Muslim forces of Saladin
OBJECT Crusaders besieging the city to capture it were in turn surrounded by Muslims looking to relieve it.
DESCRIPTION Guy, King of Jerusalem, set out to capture the most important port in the Holy Land with a few hundred men. He dug in on a nearby hill. Reinforcements

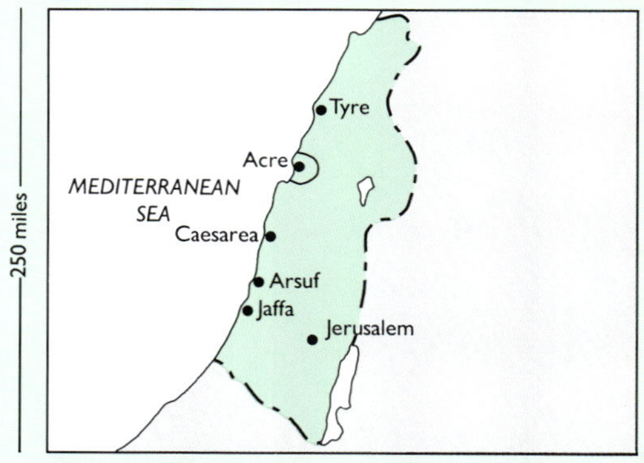

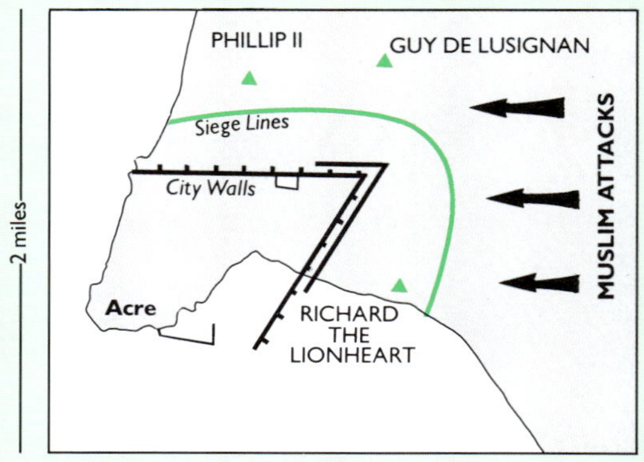

The capture of a French town during the Hundred Years War. Fortification was an important element in medieval warfare, the majority of battles being concerned with the siege of a castle or of a town. Until the advent of gunpowder and cannon, the defenders normally had the advantage over the attackers; it often took starvation or the outbreak of plague to force a surrender.

The first thing William did on landing was to raise a castle at Hastings, made from timber and earth as the Bayeux Tapestry shows. He did the same at Dover on a magnificent natural site. Once in control of London he ordered to be built a tall, square stone building still known as the Tower. This he matched at the strategically important site of Colchester. When faced with rebellion at Exeter and York in the following year he built new castles as strongpoints after capturing the cities. As the king did, so did his barons, staking claims to the English countryside with hastily raised "motte-and-bailey" constructions. On the dangerous Welsh border there are literally hundreds of these sites still visible.

In the 12th century many sites were rebuilt in stone, some abandoned. The Anglo-Norman realm produced some of the best stone castles: Dover (Kent), Castle Rising (Norfolk) and Durham in England; Falaise and Château Gaillard in Normandy.

Sir Geoffrey Luttrell sits proudly on his warhorse. He wears the armour of the mid-14th century and his wife is handing him the great helm which he wears over a close-fitting bascinet. Every piece of his equipment bears the Luttrell arms, expressing pride in his family name and knighthood.

THE CRUSADES

In November 1095 at Clermont in central France, pope Urban II, himself a Frenchman from the knightly class, preached that it was necessary for military men to march east to recover Jerusalem from the Turks. Or, at least that is what many understood him to mean. The result, the Crusades, entailed 500 years of conflict between the Christian and non-Christian world. It was not just Muslims, or Saracens

1191

allowed a Christian blockade of the city by April 1190. In April and June of 1191 respectively, Philip II of France and Richard I of England led their forces into the besiegers' camp. There followed a period of intensive assaults on the city and attacks by Saladin's forces on the Crusader camp. The armies had risen to number tens of thousands on both sides; this was the climax of the war, but Saladin was unable to drive off the besiegers.

RESULT Fall of Acre to the Christians.

ARSUF

DATE 7 September 1191
CAMPAIGN Third Crusade of western rulers against the Muslim forces of Saladin
OBJECT Saladin was trying to prevent Richard I of England (the Lionheart) from reaching Jerusalem.
DESCRIPTION Richard led his army south along the coast from Acre towards Jaffa, in defensive formation. His knightly cavalry were kept covered up behind the infantry ▶

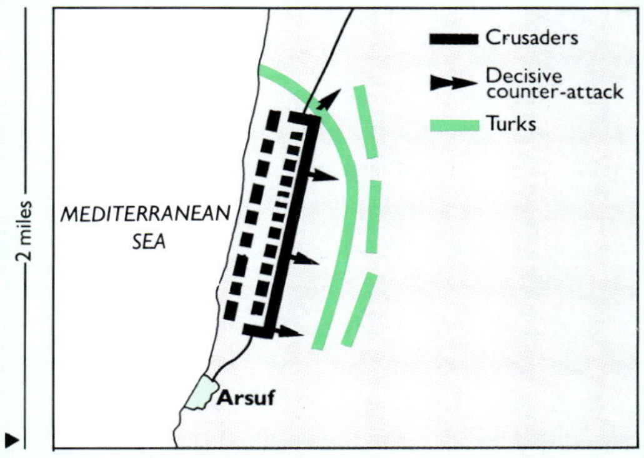

When Pope Urban II preached the recovery of Jerusalem in 1095, as depicted here in a 15th-century manuscript, he initiated 500 years of warfare between Christians and those designated as their enemies: Muslims, heathens and heretics. The Crusades inspired armies of knights, foot-soldiers, women and simple pilgrims to cross thousands of miles of seas, mountains and deserts in pursuit of an ideal. The Crusader states in the East, founded in 1099, were largely recaptured for Islam by Saladin (d. 1192), but Crusades continued.

as the Crusaders called them, who were the enemy, the pagan tribes of Lithuania and Prussia were also legitimate opponents. As it turned out, the conquest of the Holy Land, although brilliantly achieved with the capture of Jerusalem in 1099, was the shortest-lived. The *Reconquista* in Spain and the "Drive to the East" from Germany brought new lands permanently under Christian rule.

The First Crusade took perhaps 20,000 knights and 100,000 others (not all combatants) from all parts of Western Europe to Asia Minor and Syria. To the Byzantines they resembled hordes of locusts and they were happy to let them pass on to do battle with the Turks who had terrorized their empire for half a century. In 1097, the Crusaders captured Nicaea and then marched across waterless Asia Minor. It was here they first encountered the Eastern way of war. Instead of charging hand-to-hand the Turks skirmished at a distance with their powerful bows in the classic nomad manner. This was to be the model for countless battles of the Crusader era. In the battle fought at Dorylaeum under a burning June sun the westerners hit on the tactical response. Almost beaten by the heat, dust and arrows which dropped the knights' horses, they fell back on their camp where bows and crossbows held the Turks at bay. Then a second Crusader column arrived and took the enemy in the rear.

ANTIOCH AND JERUSALEM

The next test was the great city of Antioch, fortified by six miles of tall walls. Storming it was impossible and it took 10 months, including the harsh Syrian winter which almost destroyed the besieging army, before the city fell by treachery. A Turkish relieving force arrived too late and was fought and beaten only a few days later. At Jerusalem, which was reached in the summer of 1099, Western siege technology was employed to the full. The Crusaders constructed three great siege-towers and from one of them gained the foothold that caused the city's fall.

Victory in battle against the forces of the Egyptian caliphate at Ascalon in southern Syria consolidated the Crusaders' position. Four states were established based on the cities of Edessa, Antioch, Tripoli and Jerusalem. The first generation following 1099 was one of expansion at the expense of the Muslim powers, but a series of great commanders reconquered the lands for Islam. At the battle of the 'Bloody Field' in 1119, Roger, Duke of Antioch, carelessly led his men into an ambush, pursuing a feigned flight by Turkish troops. In 1140, the Atabeg Zengi recaptured Edessa and pressure was increased on the other states. A series of counter-attacks into Egypt led by the energetic King Almaric was eventually frustrated by the Turkish general Shirkuh. But it was his protégé, a Kurd known as Saladin, who proved the ablest commander. He led the Christian army under its impetuous commander King Guy into a trap at the Horns of Hattin, near Lake Galilee in 1187.

1191

to protect their precious horses from archery. The infantry was divided in half and alternated in position between the landward and seaward side, to rest them. Muslim harassing attacks meant that the Crusaders' march was very slow, but their morale held. They continued to march even while their padded *gambesons*, or protective tunics, bristled with the shafts of Muslim arrows. Eventually Saladin was forced to deliver an all-out assault on the Crusader army. Richard kept his men well in hand despite the frustrations of thirst and constant archery attack. His counter-thrust with his knights was well-timed, and in three successive charges the Muslims were thrown back and fled.

RESULT Although Saladin's casualties were not heavy the blow to his prestige was, and Richard was able to develop his strategy unhindered.

CHÂTEAU GAILLARD

DATE 27 August 1203–4 March 1204

CAMPAIGN War between Philip II of France and King John of England, for Normandy

OBJECT Capture of the most important fortification of the river Seine.

DESCRIPTION Château Gaillard was part of a system of fortification involving the island and town of Les Andelys and a river barrage. It both blocked a French advance down the Seine and was a bulwark for

These lavish illustrations from late medieval manuscripts show two sides of siege warfare. (Above) The armies of the First Crusaders sally forth from Antioch, which they had just captured, to defeat the vastly superior forces of the Caliph of Baghdad. (Left) Antioch is taken by surprise, Bohemond, a Norman leader, having bribed a tower commander to let the besiegers in.

1204

invasion. King John's attempt to raise the siege failed owing to the river currents. The French then broke the stockade, enabling them to receive supplies by water and to surround the castle. Advancing from the south, their siege engines slowly battered into the barbican, outer bailey, inner bailey and keep. No castle could stand without support from friendly forces.

RESULT The capture of a key fortification contributed to the fall of Normandy to Philip in 1204.

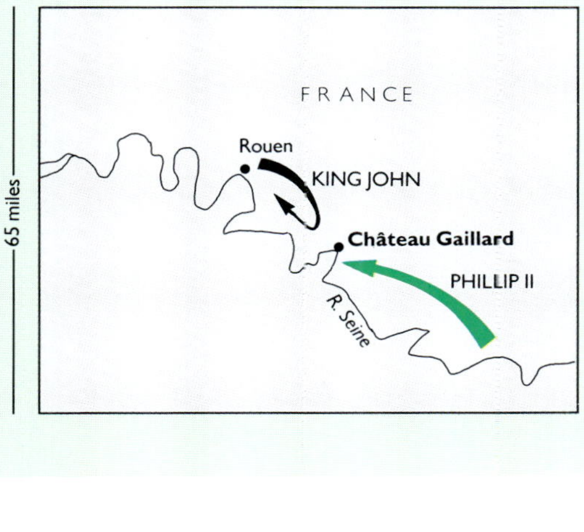

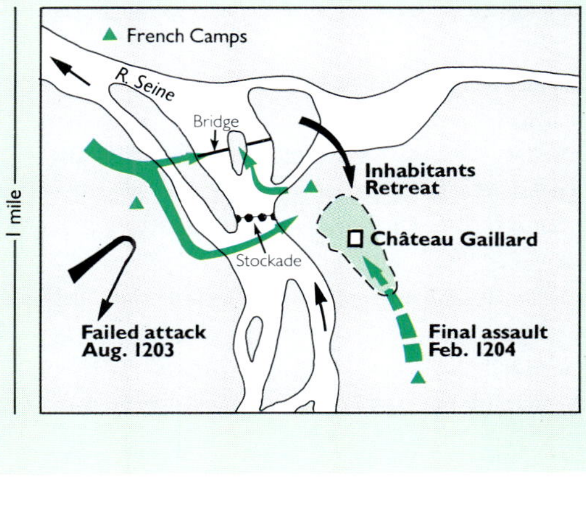

RICHARD "THE LIONHEART"

King Richard I, King of England 1189–99, has become a legend and his military talents quite justify this. He was the embodiment of the perfect knight. He was physically brave and robust and a fine fighter. He also had a charisma and determination which made men follow him. Even when critically ill during the siege of Acre (1189–90 – see page 74) and when the Crusaders were themselves besieged by Saladin's vast army, he held his motley force together. He knew the importance of fortifications and how necessary it was to both build and capture them – he died of a crossbow wound at a siege.

Richard was also a tactician of genius. Under his command he inflicted two decisive defeats on the Muslims, at Arsuf (see page 75) and Ascalon. His control and discipline enabled the knights and crossbowmen to work in unison.

The Crusader states were always short of manpower and now their king, barons and almost all their knights fell into enemy hands. There was no one to defend the castles or cities and they all fell under Muslim control except for strongly fortified Tyre.

The loss of Jerusalem had a profound effect in the West and the three most powerful monarchs, Richard of England, Philip of France and Emperor Frederick Barbarossa all took the cross. The Third Crusade (1189–92) achieved little apart from the capture of the important port of Acre, because Frederick died on route, Philip defected and Richard had to leave before he could exploit his victories over Saladin. The Crusade movement never again achieved such heights. The Fourth Crusade was diverted to and conquered Christian Constantinople in 1204. Successive Crusades to Egypt in 1219–21 and 1248–50, while initially successful, eventually floundered in the swamps of the Delta. King Louis of France was actually captured with all his army on the latter expedition. A combination of the use of fleets and siege weapons achieved more than battle, in which the Christians ran the risk of being defeated. In fact it was not military action but diplomacy which won back Jerusalem for a short period from 1228–40.

LEGACY OF THE CRUSADES

The Crusader states left a remarkable architectural heritage. Their castles were the largest and most sophisticated of the time. In northern Syria, Saône stands just inland from Lattikiah, between two gorges, a 98 ft rock-cut ditch further protecting it from

This splendidly imaginative Victorian rendering of a duel between Richard the Lionheart and Saladin never took place in reality. But it shows how long lasting was the image of these two great commanders as representing the conflict between the Christian and Islamic worlds.

1260

AYN JALUT

DATE 3 September 1260
CAMPAIGN Invasion of Syria by Mongols under Kitbugha against Mameluke Sultan Qutuz.
OBJECT The Mongols were attempting to conquer Syria and Egypt.
NUMBERS Mongols – two "tumans" at half strength, 10,000 horsemen and a large proportion of non-Mongol subject troops; Mamelukes – 12,000 cavalry, including élite guard troops and an unknown number of infantry.

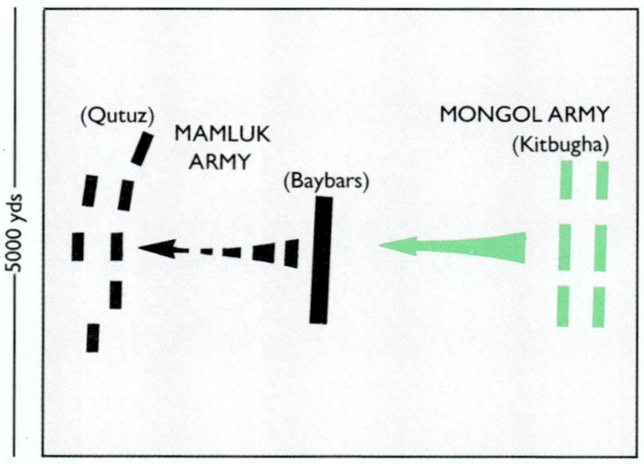

DESCRIPTION Sultan Qutuz's dispositions concealed his greater strength. Baibar's feigned flight drew the Mongols into contact. Mongol allies fled on their left wing, while their right was overwhelmed by greater Mameluke numbers. As Qutuz and Kitbugha clashed the Mamelukes achieved a double-envelopment.
RESULT The Mongol force was destroyed and Kitbugha captured and executed.

attack. Further south, standing against Muslim Homs is Krak des Chevaliers, the most perfect example of concentric fortification in the East. The "Knights" from which it takes its name were the Templars, an order of military monks founded in 1128. Along with the Hospitallers, or Knights of St John, they provided a large proportion of the knightly cavalry for Crusader armies. They were so feared by the enemy that Saladin had all captured brothers executed after Hattin. Their orders also became immensely wealthy owing to donations of property in Europe and, in the case of the Templars, through banking. Only they had the resources to take on the expense of the vast stone castles necessary to defend the Holy Land. This they did successfully until in there were no more men to man the walls. This was the fate of Krak, which finally surrendered in 1271.

Other Orders were instrumental in the religious wars elsewhere. They played a part in the Spanish *Reconquista*, although this was carried out by the Christian kings of the Peninsula rather than by crusade. In central and northern Europe the Teutonic Knights carved out an empire for themselves after they transferred their headquarters to Prussia in 1229. Their huge castle complex at Marienburg represented their military might. Although checked by the Russians at Lake Peipus in 1242, the Teutonic Knights were an important power, rivalling kingdoms, until they were finally humbled by defeat at Tannenberg in 1410 by a coalition of states.

MAMELUKE AND OTTOMAN WARFARE

Eastward from the Hungarian plains into central Asia and from Egypt to Persia the main weapon was the bow. Unlike in the Western world, it was wielded from horseback. The main protagonists of this style of warfare were nomadic steppe-dwellers, travelling peoples who roamed over great areas of grassland in order to feed their flocks and herds. The primary exponents of nomadic warfare were the Turks and Mongols of Central Asia, and it was from here that waves of invasion rolled west into the Christian and Arab world and east into China.

In the mid-11th century nomadic Turks invaded the Middle East. They established a dynasty, known as the Seljuks, in Asia Minor, in old Byzantine lands, and other groups established themselves in Iran, Iraq and Syria. Their disruption of the Muslim world was one reason for the success of the First Crusade. However they came not only as conquerors but also as mercenaries, selling their skills to established regimes. The Byzantine emperor and the Baghdad caliph alike took them into their service. In fact, states living on the edge of the nomadic world had long experience of absorbing such military peoples. It was normal practice to form regiments of invading tribes and use them to keep others out. In the 11th and 12th centuries the Byzantines employed Normans, Varangians (Viking and English) and Turks, whilst the Cairo

Continued on page 82

SALADIN

Salah al-Din, Sultan of Egypt 1169–93, served his military apprenticeship under Nur-ed Din, a leader who strove to unite the Muslims against the Crusaders. Saladin was thus able to base his power on Egypt, but it still needed his great strength of character to keep the forces of the disparate emirs in the field. He showed both strategic vision and tactical ability in handling his armies. If not quite the chivalrous opponent of Western legend, he was a shrewd politician, devoted to Islam and more merciful in his reconquest of Jerusalem than his Christian opponents. Although he suffered setbacks at the end of his life, he lived just long enough to thwart the objectives of Richard I's Crusade.

1415

AGINCOURT

DATE 26 October 1415
CAMPAIGN Invasion of France by Henry V of England against the armies of Charles VI
OBJECT To show that an English army could march unhindered to Calais across French territory
NUMBERS English – 1,000 men-at-arms and 5,000 archers led by King Henry; French – 20,000–25,000 men-at-arms plus large numbers of unengaged foot under joint and confused command by French nobles.
DESCRIPTION Forced to fight vastly superior French forces, Henry was able to get them at a disadvantage on a cramped battlefield between two woods where the superiority of the enemy numbers was nullified. As the French chose not to attack, Henry seized the initiative and advanced into bowshot. Now his deadly archers, protected by stakes, shot down a cavalry charge and threw the dismounted knights' attack into confusion. The tiny English ▸

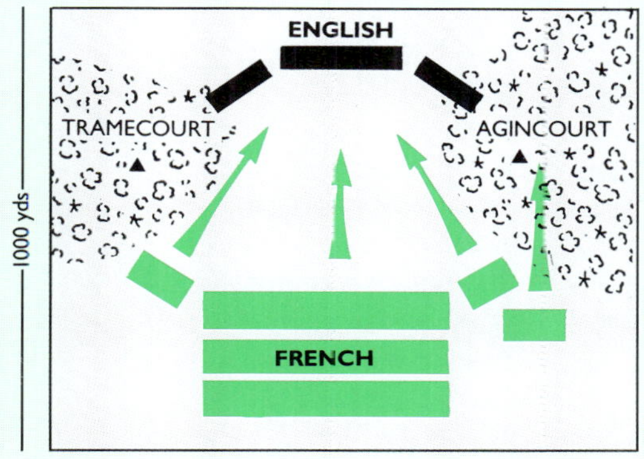

THE MEDIEVAL CASTLE: ITS CONSTRUCTION AND USE

(Above) The motte-and-bailey consisted of a mound (motte) furnished with a wooden tower and an attached defended enclosure (bailey) wherein lay the chapel, storehouses and living quarters for its inhabitants. Such a castle could be built in a week. (The Bayeux Tapestry shows the Normans achieving this at Hastings, in 1066.)

THE CASTLE WAS the fortified residence of a lord, someone who exercised political and judicial authority over territory. It used to be supposed that the timber and earth "motte-and-bailey" was the earliest form, but stone towers were already being built in the Loire region of France in the tenth century: Doué-la-Fontaine (*c.* 950) and Langeais (*c.* 994). Timber castles were much favoured by the Normans in the early stages of their conquest of England, because they were quick to construct, but they obviously relied upon plentiful supplies of wood. This is why they were not an option in the Holy Land away from the coast.

In the 12th century, wherever they were sited, there was a tendency to rebuild in stone. Castle Rising, in Norfolk, is a fine example of such a tower keep, with each floor reserved for a different function. Fortifications began to become more complex as well. Curtain walls surrounded the tower, and barbicans (outworks) protected the main gate. The castles of the Crusader states and Edward I's Welsh fortifications represent the highest form of the art. Of course, they became enormously expensive, taxing the revenues of kingdoms. In Outremer it was only the wealthy military monks – Templar, Teutonic and Hospitaller – who could afford their upkeep.

Even the largest castles usually had very small garrisons. They were intended as residences, storehouses of food and supplies, places of refuge for their dependent peasantry and bases for attacks into enemy territory. This is what made them such a good investment for their owners. A handful of men, often commanded by their lord's lady, could hold large forces at bay until relief arrived. Until the development of gunpowder artillery able to breach walls quickly, investing a castle meant a great commitment of men, material and time for an attacker.

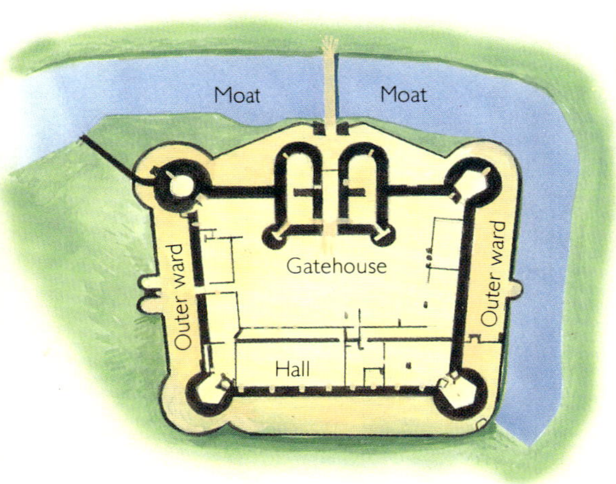

(Left) A plan of Harlech castle in Wales. Set on a huge crag above the estuary of the River Dwyryd, and further secured by a rock-cut ditch from the landward side, it is a model of the concentric castle. Four great drum towers at each corner supplement a powerful keep-gatehouse. Built between 1283 and 1290, Harlech is one of Edward I's finest achievements.

(Below) This cutaway drawing shows something of the layout and internal arrangements of a 12th-century castle where stone has replaced timber. The defended gateways were vital to its security. Invulnerable to fire, unlike its timber predecessor, the stone keep could only be defeated by undermining. Even then, at Rochester in 1215, the defenders fought on after a corner tower had fallen, secure behind an internal dividing wall.

(Right) Dover Castle: the keep. The heart of the defence, and also lavish living quarters equipped with lavatories (garderobes) and running water!

(Below) Krak of the Knights (Hospitaller) stands on a spur protected by a rock-cut ditch, its tall walls surrounding a massive citadel. The covered entrance to the castle makes two U-turns, leaving an attacker vulnerable to assault through hidden arrow-loops and from above. Krak defied all attacks until 1271, when there were too few knights to defend it.

SULTAN BAIBARS

Baibars, Sultan from 1260–83, was a product of the Mameluke system, a slave-soldier in the Bari regiment. He first achieved prominence for his role in the battle of Ayn Jalut (see page 78). Afterwards, he had Sultan Qutuz murdered and seized power himself. As a soldier-statesman he did much to extend Mameluke power. His campaign of conquest in Frankish Syria began in 1264 and within a year he took Caesarea, Haifa and Arsuf. In 1266 he took the strong castle of Safad, and Jaffa, an important port, in 1267. In 1268 Antioch and territories fell to him. In the face of the Crusade of 1270 Baibars chose negotiation with Prince Edward of England, but resumed his conquests the following year, taking Krak des Chevaliers and Safitha castles. Pressing on into Anatolia in 1275 he came up against the Mongols and defeated them in battle, and again in 1277. Baibars was renowned for the excellence of his military intelligence system and the secrecy with which he conducted his own affairs.

caliphate relied on Berber and Bedouin cavalry and Nubian foot-soldiers.

The Turkish nomads were such good warriors that they were soon recruited for their skills with bow and horse. Their traditional style of fighting was that of a cloud of skirmishers, but there was another tradition of fighting in the Middle East, that of the "cataphract" – man and horse both heavily armoured. This cavalry fought in regular ranks and preferred the bow to the lance. Furthermore, rulers had bodyguards of this type bound to them as slaves. Slavery did not have the same stigma as in the Christian West. It was a way of reaching the highest position in a state. Such soldiers had been known for a long time in the east as *ghulams* and in the 13th century under an alternative name of *Mamelukes*, a group seized power in Egypt, ousting Saladin's dynasty. This happened at a time of political crisis, the invasion of Egypt by King Louis of France and his Crusaders (1250). The results were enduring. The regime lasted until the Ottoman conquest in the early 16th century, and Mameluke cavalry even fought Napoleon's army at the battle of the Pyramids in 1798!

As a military dynasty the Mamelukes trained carefully for warfare. Their *furusiyas*, or training manuals, still exist showing how a Mameluke had to be a complete warrior with bow, sword and lance, both on horseback and on foot. They proved to be the only force in the Muslim East which could defeat the ferocious Mongols. This they did in 1260 after the destruction of Baghdad and the murder of the caliph there. The Mamelukes were also expert in siege warfare. Their second and greatest sultan, Baibars, travelled on campaign with an artillery train of siege engines. The last castles of the Crusader states could not hold out against them and by the early 14th century the Christians were driven back to Cyprus and Rhodes. The Mamelukes pressed on into Asia Minor, extinguishing the Christian Kingdom of Armenia in 1375. Here they faced their eventual conquerors – the Ottomans.

THE OTTOMANS

The Osmanli dynasty grew from one of the small confederations of nomadic Turkish tribes in north-east Asia Minor around 1300. It was a "ghazi", or frontier state of Islam, pledged to conquer lands for the Faith. In 1326 the Ottomans captured the important Byzantine city of Bursa, and then crossed over into Europe. In 1361 they took Edirne and began to conquer Greece and the Balkans. Their victory over the Serbs at Kosovo in 1389 reduced the Serbs to vassal status, and the noose began to close around their main goal – Constantinople. Defeat at the hands of Tamerlane, the Mongol conqueror in 1402, at Ankara, set back Ottoman expansion for half a century; but once recovered, the city's conquest was inevitable.

The reason for Ottoman success lay in their ability to combine all types of forces in their armies. Many of these were made up of Christian subjects fighting under their

1415

army then charged and routed the French. Late in the day, fears of French recovery persuaded Henry to massacre some of his prisoners.

CASUALTIES On the English side a few hundred men, including notables like the Duke of York; the French lost 5,000–6,000 killed and many thousands of captives, including their greatest nobles.

RESULT A huge blow to French military prestige which meant that they were unwilling to offer battle for many years.

SIEGE OF ROUEN

DATE 31 July 1418–19 January 1419

CAMPAIGN Conquest of Normandy by Henry V of England

OBJECT Henry needed to capture Rouen to complete his conquest of Normandy.

NUMBERS English – around 30,000; one-third fighting men, the rest siege experts and manpower; French – 5,000 men-at-arms, 15,000 militia, 70,000 populace.

DESCRIPTION Despite Henry's formidable

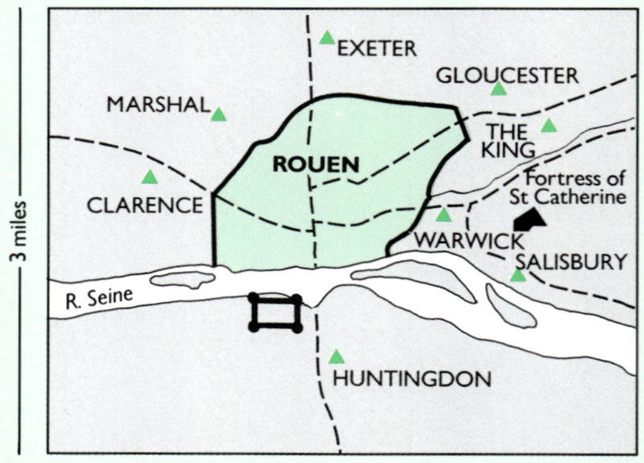

voynik lords. They also relied upon traditional nomadic Turkish cavalry for raiding and ravaging an enemy's territories and forcing him behind the walls of his towns and fortresses which could then be stormed or starved into submission. There was a strong element of religious fervour in Ottoman forces, spearheaded by the Dervish religious groups they sponsored and including *delis* (madmen), extravagantly costumed and fanatical warriors. The army was largely a cavalry force based on the nomadic horse-archer, but included more heavily armoured *spahi* (soldier) cataphract types, raised along feudal lines. Infantry also played an important role, both the ordinary Azab bow or spearmen and the elite Janissaries. Originally formed from prisoners of war, in 1438, the *devshirme* or round-up of young Christian boys was instituted. Brought up as Muslims they became fanatically loyal to their masters. They were better equipped than most infantry, specialists in the bow, crossbow and later arquebus, and wore distinctive tall white caps.

The Ottoman army included skilled technicians in siege warfare and artillery. The successful sieges of Constantinople (1453) (see page 84) and Rhodes (1480) bear witness to this. Artillery was also used in the field. Guns and wagons defeated the Mamelukes at Chaldiran in 1515, while chained guns and a solid Janissary line gave victory over the Hungarians at Mohacs in 1526. The Ottomans spelled the end of the crusading movement. Impetuous Western cavalry were defeated by Bayezit at Nicopolis (1396) and by Murat II at Varna (1440) and Kossovo (1448). This combiation of tactical and technical superiority made the Ottomans the greatest military force in the Mediterranean and Middle East until the end of the 16th century.

The art of fortification was not neglected in the East either. The Arab citadels of Cairo and Aleppo and the Rumeli Hisar, built by the Ottomans north of Constantinople on the Bosphorus, bear witness to this.

BOWS AND PIKES

Although infantry had always been important in medieval armies there is no doubt that their significance grew in relation to the knights from c.1300 onwards. The battle of Courtrai in 1302 is often taken as a decisive moment in the contest between cavalry and infantry. Flemish townsmen wielding long spears and *goedendags* ("good days", an ironically named ironbound club with a sharp spike) and crossbows saw off the flower of French chivalry, inflicting great loss. It should not be forgotten, though, that the Flemings were positioned behind dykes and ditches, and it was the tactical incompetence of the French, whose commander, Robert, Count of Artois, delivered frontal charges against this strong position, which led to the disaster. In the following year, faced with a hedgehog formation of spears the French attempted nothing more than piecemeal assaults by small groups. Scottish *schiltrons* of spearmen similarly

MEHMET II "THE CONQUEROR"

The conquest of Constantinople set the tone for Mehmet's reign, which lasted from 1452–80. He had a concept of world empire which he spent 30 years putting into effect. The Ottoman Empire had recovered from the humiliation of Ankara in 1402 when Bayezit was captured. Mehmet's personal slave troops numbered 7,000 and these were just the elite of vast armies. Between 1458–60 the conquest of Greece was completed. In 1459 Serbia and in 1463 Bosnia submitted, although Hungary held out under the leadership of John Hunyadi. War against Venice steadily reduced the Republic's territories and forced her to sue for peace in 1478. Mehmet won control of all the Black Sea, the Adriatic and the eastern Mediterranean. In Anatolia an army of 100,000 men was mobilized to defeat his Karaman enemies by 1474. Mehmet was a fanatic, pursuing religious, *ghazi* warfare to its logical conclusion; and this earned him the title "Conqueror".

1419

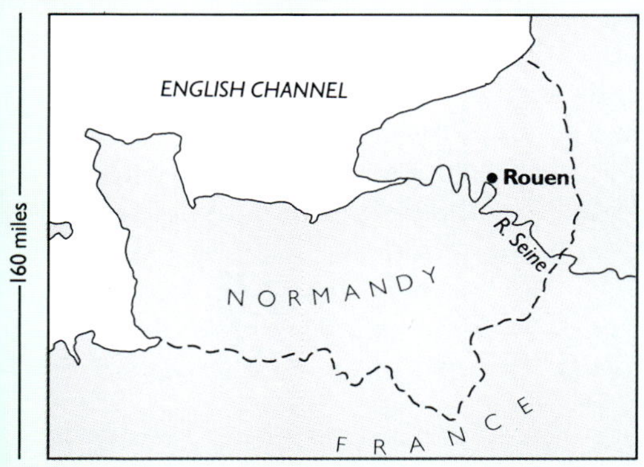

array of siege artillery, the size and fortifications of Rouen forced him to rely upon starvation tactics. First, he isolated the city by building a bridge upstream, a great engineering achievement, taking the fortress of St Catherine on 2 September, and the town of Caudebec a week later. Rouen was running short of food by late summer – only relief could help. The nearest a French force got was 20 miles away. The garrison expelled 12,000 useless mouths – women and children – who starved before the siege lines until surrender became inevitable.

CASUALTIES Unknown, but heavy amongst the civilians who continued to die even after Henry brought food into the city.

RESULT The capture of Rouen gave Henry a springboard for the conquest of the kingdom of France.

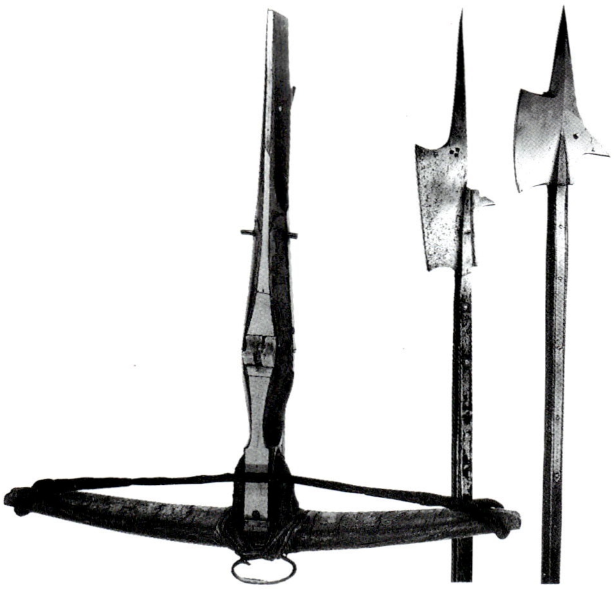

withstood English cavalry at Bannockburn in 1314. In a defensive position good foot soldiers were as impregnable as the British squares at Waterloo to the French cuirassiers, but they had the same weakness, they could not advance in the face of well-handled cavalry.

There was nothing new in the use of bodies of spear-or pikemen, but the English contribution to warfare was to be the exploitation of mass archery fire. Already the armies of Edward I had employed large numbers of Welsh bowmen. They carried a weapon usually called a longbow, a simple stave five to six feet long with an effective range of over 200 yards. Unlike the slow-firing crossbow, an expert archer could loose off six to 12 shafts a minute, depending on his needs. This put down a concentrated barrage of missiles which few could penetrate. Edward II's defeat at Bannockburn was largely due to his inability to bring his battle-winning force into action; something Robert the Bruce manoeuvred to prevent. At Halidon Hill in 1333 the Scots met defeat at the hands of well-deployed archers. This was the first of many victories to be won by English archers in the 14th and 15th centuries. They became the most sought-after troops in Europe.

They were put to good use in the long-running series of wars between England

(Above) A crossbow and two halberds, popular infantry weapons. Used in combination by the Swiss they were battle-winners. Unlike the longbow, the crossbow did not need years of training to acquire expertise, nor great strength to use, as the cranequin, a ratchet device, drew the string back in order to reload.

(Right) The king of France takes counsel at Sluys. This Flemish port was of great strategic importance in the naval war between England and France. It was also the site of Edward III's great victory which destroyed the French fleet in 1340.

1453

SIEGE OF CONSTANTINOPLE

DATE 5 April–29 May 1453
OBJECT Conquest of Constantinople by Turks
NUMBERS Turks – 100,000 including 12,000 elite Janissaries and many cannon; Byzantines – 7,000 men of which only *condottiere* Giustiniani's 500 Genoese were of good quality.
DESCRIPTION After establishing a blockade, the Turks made a naval attack, which was repulsed, on 12 April. Superior Venetian vessels also defeated the Turks on 20 April. But by the brilliant scheme of transporting ships overland into the Golden Horn, Mehmet outmanoeuvred the defenders. Meanwhile Ottoman cannon blasted holes in the 1000-year-old walls. Assaults on 7 and 18 May were repulsed, but eventually the Janissaries stormed the city.
RESULT Fall of Constantinople; death of Constantine amid the ruins.

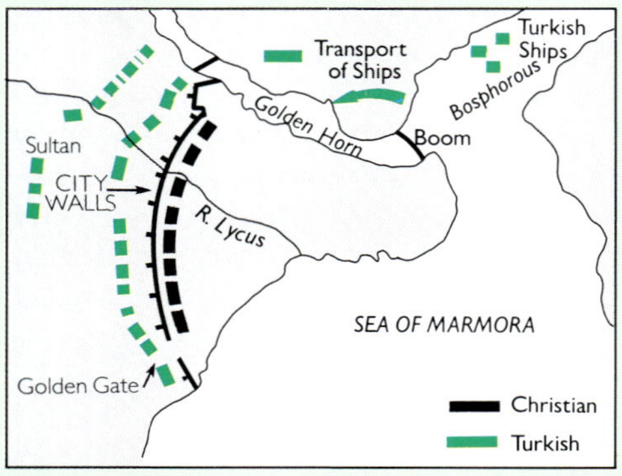

The impact of the longbow. A sallying English force, headed by archers, drives away a Scottish army. Although of lower social standing than the men-at-arms, trained archers were recognized as the best all-round soldiers of their age. In the foreground footmen engage in their favourite activity: pillaging.

and France known as the Hundred Years War (1338–1453). What started as a legal dispute between Edward III of England and Philip VI of France over Edward's possessions in Gascony became a struggle for the throne of France itself. The war began with French aggression; raids and the burning of towns on the southern English coast. This ended with the destruction of the French fleet at Sluys in 1340. Here too the archers had a part to play, as Sluys was fought very much like a land battle, with ships packed together, allowing the withering storm of arrows to sweep enemy decks. The English fought the war on land by the method known as *chevauchée*, which meant a ride through enemy territories, often sacking and burning town and countryside alike. This had the dual purpose of undermining the political allegiance of an area to the French crown, and, when it suited the English, of challenging the French to do battle.

This is probably what Edward III intended in the campaign of 1346. He marched his army of 11,000 men, three-quarters of whom were archers, towards Paris and then withdrew north. The French pursued and nearly trapped the English at the Somme, but Edward slipped across the fords of Blanchetacque near the river's mouth and took up position at Crécy. He dismounted all his men-at-arms, supported them with the archers and had pits dug to protect the battle-line. When the French arrived they hurled themselves into battle piecemeal, in a series of cavalry charges, and suffered a humiliating defeat. Ten years later, his son Edward the Black Prince, who

The Black Prince defeats and captures the French king at Poitiers in 1356. A rich manuscript, designed for an aristocratic audience, omits the base-born archers – the real architects of the English victory!

1461

TOWTON

DATE 29 March 1461

CAMPAIGN The Yorkist, newly crowned Edward IV challenged by Lancastrian forces under Henry VI's queen, Margaret

OBJECT Edward needed a decisive victory to secure his position.

NUMBERS c. 25,000 on each side.

DESCRIPTION Advancing in bitterly cold weather, the Yorkists forced a passage of the River Aire on the 28th. The Yorkists got the better of the archery duel, as snow was driving into their opponents' faces, but then Somerset's cavalry charge seemed to have won the day. Bloody fighting around King Edward lasted until Norfolk came up with reinforcements to decide the issue in favour of the Yorkists.

CASUALTIES Edward himself reckoned 28,000 in the combined armies, a chronicler, 9,000.

RESULT Edward secured his throne for a decade.

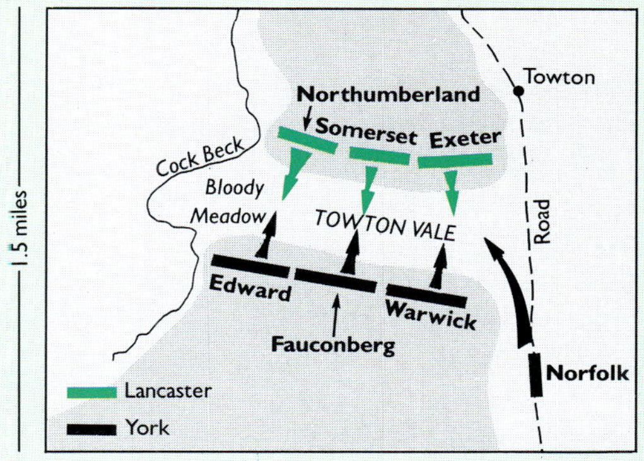

had won his spurs at Crécy, scored another great success. Following a very lucrative *chevauchée* south from Bordeaux to the Mediterranean in 1355, Edward decided to march north the following year. He was supposed to have met up with another English force on the Loire, but this did not transpire and the Black Prince led his army and its wagon-loads of booty back to just south of Poitiers. Here King John of France caught up with him. The French had 13,000 men, about double Edward's small force. Dismounting, the French came on towards the English position behind a small hedge and the hand-to-hand fighting was long and hard. An English mounted counter-attack won the day, and John and most of his nobility were captured.

Such victories as this won for the English the reputation as the foremost military nation in Europe and made their archers the most desirable as mercenaries. John Hawkwood's White Company won great renown in Italy, where city-states employed large numbers of such troops. Companies of mercenaries serving no one except themselves terrorized much of France at the time. They won the name of *Ecorcheurs*, or "flayers", for the devastation they wrought. The peasantry, already suffering from the ravages of the Black Death, had to band themselves together and attack such bandits. Mercenaries were an integral part of warfare now. Rulers who wished to raise troops for a campaign recruited paid soldiers rather than calling upon feudal obligation. In England this system was known as indenture. Men of all stations from prominent lords to local squires contracted with the government to bring along their retinues. Some men, like Sir John Fastolf, made a fortune from such contracts, receiving both money and grants of land in payment. Troops were divided between "lances" (that is to say men-at-arms and their bodyservants) and archers. An increasingly large proportion of archers were mounted. This gave the force great mobility, suitable for *chevauchée*. Indeed such bowmen were very like the later dragoons who took their firepower to where it could be used to best effect. The effectiveness of archery is shown by the increasing proportion of archers in English armies from 2:1 to men-at-arms in the mid-14th century to 10:1 in Edward IV's planned expedition of 1475.

The increasing importance of missile weapons had another result: the development of more sophisticated armour. Pieces of plate armour had been added to mail from the mid-13th century onwards, first at the knee, elbow and shoulder and then as a coat-of-plates not unlike a modern flak-jacket. In the mid-14th century developments in metalworking produced articulated coverings for the limbs and a heavy, visored helmet. By the early 15th century a complete suit was achieved, known as a "white armour" because the entire body was covered in polished steel. It was still possible for arrows to penetrate plate but only because arrows had developed as well, with bodkin heads which bored their way through the metal like modern

BERTRAND DU GUESCLIN

Du Guesclin rose from a family of Breton minor nobility to be Constable of France, the highest military position in the kingdom, from 1369 to 1380. With Charles V, he reversed the trend of the war with England. He had cause to know and rue English skill in war, being captured and ransomed several times, once at the battle of Auray in 1364. He led another army to defeat at the hands of English bowmen at Nájera in 1367, during the Black Prince's Spanish expedition. But he then replaced the battle-seeking strategy of the 1340s and '50s with "scorched earth" and the harrying of English *chevauchées*. In 1370, Sir John Knollys, and in 1373 John of Gaunt, both struggled home with their armies in tatters and no booty to show for it. Du Guesclin died, fighting English mercenaries in Languedoc.

The death of Du Guesclin.

1471

TEWKESBURY

DATE 4 May 1471

OBJECT The final showdown between Edward IV and the Lancastrians led by Queen Margaret and Somerset.

NUMBERS About 6,000 on each side.

DESCRIPTION After a cat-and-mouse game of marching through south-western England, Edward finally pinned the Lancastrians before they could escape across the River Severn. Somerset attacked in the centre and also pressurized the Yorkist left wing, under Richard of Gloucester. Then, by a clever manoeurvre, he drew off his right wing and brought it around to attack Edward in the flank. It almost worked; but Edward had left a mobile reserve of 200 men-at-arms who then attacked Somerset's flank. The Lancastrians were routed.

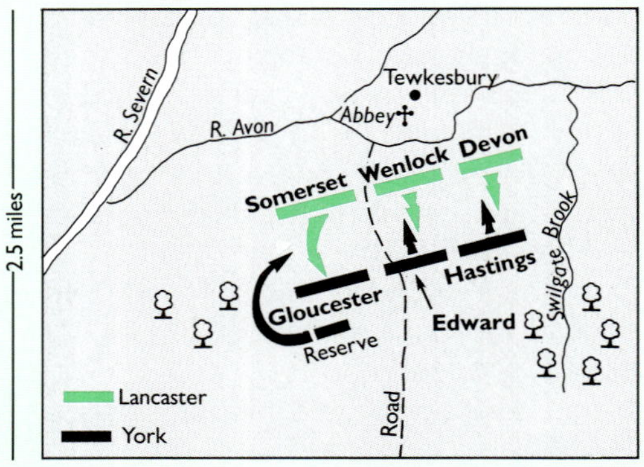

CASUALTIES Unknown, but quite heavy amongst the Lancastrians.

RESULT Edward was undisputed ruler until his death in 1483.

armour-piercing shells. At Agincourt (see page 79) the English archers were able to shoot into even the heavy French helmets at short range. But already there was appearing on the battlefields of Europe a weapon which was to supplant even the deadly longbow – the gunpowder handgun.

GUNS AND FOOT SOLDIERS

While the longbow dominated tactics in the Anglo-French wars, there were developments in central and southern Europe which pointed in another direction. Both were as a result of wars of independence from feudal overlords in Switzerland and Bohemia.

In 1315, at Mortgarten a small force of Swiss infantry had attacked and routed superior numbers of well-equipped Austrians. Admittedly this was an ambush, the Swiss attacked a marching column in a narrow defile, and broke the Austrian ranks by rolling down rocks and logs, but their ferocious follow-up attack with halberds tore the knightly opposition apart. In 1339, at Laupen the Swiss faced Burgundian cavalry and infantry, but the combination of pikemen and archers was more than enough to beat this force. The problem which many armies faced was the co-ordination of infantry and cavalry on the battlefield. One solution, as we have seen, was to dismount the knights and attack on foot. This is what the Austrians attempted at Sempach in 1386. The heavily armoured knights did force the Swiss phalanx back, but had no response to a Swiss counter-attack. Contemporaries commented on the Swiss bravery and discipline which gave them victory.

That infantry should possess these virtues came as something of a surprise to these writers, conditioned as they were to associate military values with the knightly classes. The events in Bohemia following the death of Jan Hus, condemned as a heretic at the Council of Constance in 1415, were to shake these assumptions still further. Bohemia rose in revolt against the Holy Roman Emperor and under the leadership of Jan Ziska a new method of fighting was developed. He took the ancient idea of the wagon fort and equipped it with artillery, handguns, crossbows and infantry carrying various vicious polearms. The most primitive of these was the flail, which symbolized the peasant nature of the revolt against authority. Now this was a good defensive formation, as his victory at Prague in 1419 proved, but Ziska developed mobile wagons which allowed him to attack at Kutna Hora in 1422. The Hussites defeated the Emperor's crusaders many times, even after Ziska's death in 1424. They were inspired by reformist religious fervour and even the sound of their hymns was enough to persuade the enemy to flee. They were irresistible in the field for two decades, but, like many revolutionaries, they were destroyed by internal dissension when the Moderates defeated the Taborites at Lipani in 1334. The artillery

Continued on page 90

HENRY V

Henry V, King of England from 1415 to 1422, was the foremost commander of his age. He had a long career in arms before his invasion of France in 1415. From the age of fifteen he fought Owain Glendwr for the control of Wales (1402–5). In 1403 he commanded the left wing at the battle of Shrewsbury against the Percy rebels. Having learnt the hard lessons of warfare he prepared meticulously for the siege of Harfleur in 1415 and took the town in five weeks. His *chevauchée* to Calais was nearly disastrous, but tactical cunning saw him through. The mature general emerged in the conquest of Normandy from 1417–20 where by determined sieges he subdued the duchy and forced Charles VI into the Treaty of Troyes, recognizing Henry as his heir. He died at the siege of Meaux in 1422.

Henry V of England.

1474

SIEGE OF NEUSS

DATE 30 July 1474 – 13 June 1475

CAMPAIGN Charles the Bold of Burgundy against a rebel city of the Archbishop of Cologne

NUMBERS Burgundians – 30,000 men and the best artillery train in Europe; Neuss – 3,000 "stout defenders with good artillery".

DESCRIPTION Neuss was swiftly encircled by well-organized and well-equipped ▸

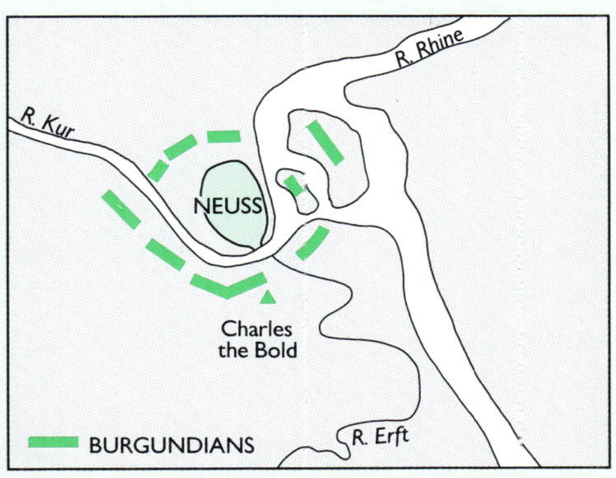

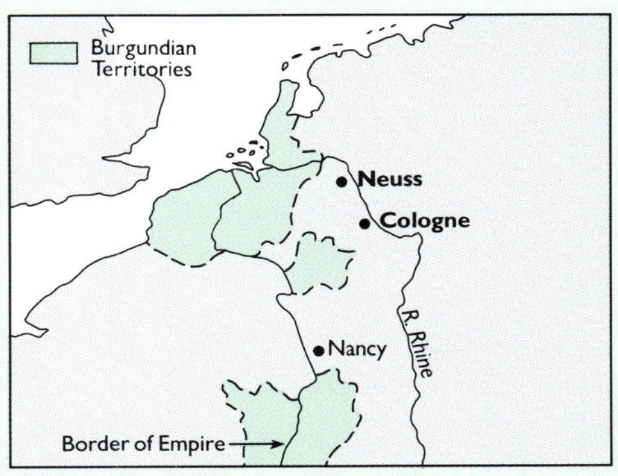

THE CONDUCT OF SIEGES: TECHNIQUES AND ARTILLERY

THE IMPORTANCE OF fortifications in medieval warfare ensured that careful attention was paid to the art of taking them. It was an area where techniques and technology made great advances throughout the period. In the 11th century the advantage lay with the defenders. It took William, as the young duke of Normandy, two years to reduce the castle of Brionne, secure in the middle of a river. He had to employ the most ancient, though eventually successful, approach of blockade. William was not so patient later in his career, overwhelming Exeter in 1067 in short order.

In this case, the choice was to go over or under the defenders' walls – or to combine the two. Mining was used throughout the Middle Ages but it was dependent on suitable conditions (a water barrier was the most difficult to overcome) and also the presence of the necessary specialists. Miners had to be brought from all over England for King John's siege of Rochester castle in 1215. In order to go over the walls, attackers built huge wooden siege towers moved up on wheels or rollers, which had bridges suspended from their upper stories to carry storming parties. This is how Jerusalem was captured in 1099.

Usually, any attack was preceded by a battering from artillery. Known as *mangonels* or *petraries* (stonethrowers) these were torsion-powered wooden engines. By the mid-12th century, as a result of contact with the Arabs, the Crusaders had developed the *trebuchet.* This was a counter-weighted machine which could hurl huge stones 200-400 yards. Such artillery was in use at the siege of Acre by the Crusaders in 1190. In the 13th century trebuchets were the foremost siege weapon.

By 1330 the weapon which was eventually going to transform warfare – the gun fired by exploding powder – made its appearance in the West. The Mongols had been using rockets and other incendiary weapons a century earlier, but it was the development of the technology, based upon bell-founding, of cast metal pots and tubes which produced a powerful artillery. These had the advantage of containing the force of the explosion and so increasing its propulsive force. Edward III used artillery at his siege of Calais after his great victory at Crécy in 1346, but the town was eventually taken by starving out its defenders.

Really heavy siege artillery took time to develop. Henry V terrorized France with it from 1415-22. Charles VII of France recovered his kingdom with an irresistible train in the 1440s. The possession of heavy guns like "Mons Meg" (shown opposite) by an attacker was enough to make most defenders surrender without a fight before their walls were shattered. In the East only the Ottomans paid attention to developing gunpowder artillery at this time. Employing Western experts, they used it successfully in the sieges of Constantinople in 1453 and Rhodes in 1480.

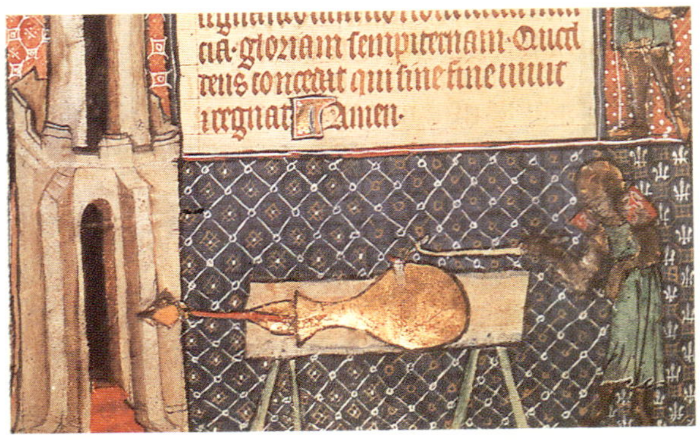

(Above) The earliest picture of a "fire-pot", a crude form of cannon, from the Millemete manuscript c.1326–27.

(Below) The siege of Calais by the English 1346–47. The ships in the background blockading the town are more important than the brawling soldiers!

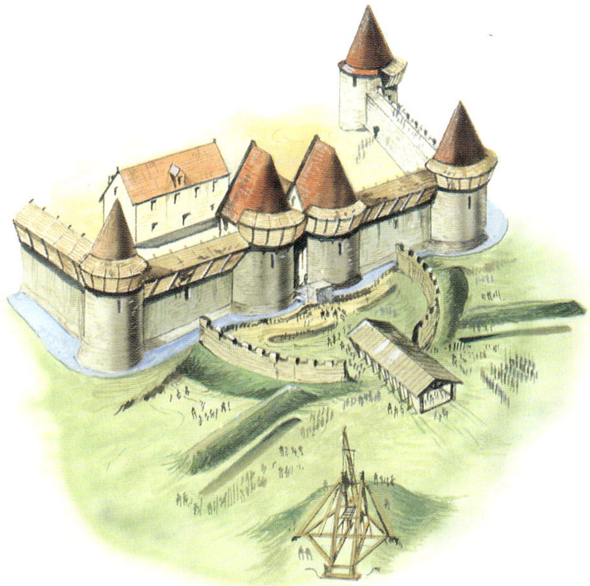

(Above) A siege. The attackers are assaulting the main gate using a combination of battering and mining in order to make a breach for storming. Trenches and wooden fences protect the attackers.

(Right) A huge trebuchet, its heavy counter-weight suspended between the massive uprights, the missile slung from the firing arm.

(Below) "Mons Meg" a massive bombard cast c.1450 in Flanders, now stands on the walls of Edinburgh castle. A gun like this could batter down castle walls with its huge iron or stone balls.

Henry VIII's foot armour. By 1400, plate armour had developed to such a degree that it covered the entire body in a flexible shell. It was not as heavy as is popularly supposed. A full field armour weighed between 45 and 55lbs, less than a modern infantry pack and better distributed over the body.

equipped wagon fort had made a permanent contribution to warfare though. John Hunyadi (1437–56) and his son Matthias Corvinus (1456–90) were able to defend Hungary from the Turks by its use.

Meanwhile in Western Europe a development was taking place which was to set the scene for the standing armies of the modern world. In France and Burgundy permanently maintained forces called Ordinance Companies were established. Initially this may have been an expedient by Charles VII, to try and exercise some form of control over the excessive numbers of professional soldiers in his kingdom in 1445 as a result of the war with England. He declared that there should be 1,800 men-at-arms, 3,600 archers and 1,800 lightly-armed horsemen. As well as providing a standing army this was an attempt to create a balanced force combining the strike power and mobility of knightly cavalry and the missile impact of the archers. His successor, Louis XI, recruited 8,000 Swiss foot to provide a solid infantry. In Burgundy, Charles the Bold created Ordinance Companies also. In 1472 they comprised 1,200 men-at-arms, 600 mounted crossbowmen, 3,000 mounted archers, 2,000 pikemen and 1,000 foot archers. This was a balanced all-arms force and Charles also experimented with light field artillery drawn on wheeled carriages.

English forces continued to contain large numbers of archers until the mid-16th century. Nor were they obsolete. During the latter stages of the Hundred Years War they provided victory as long as they were properly employed. The rashness of Thomas, Duke of Clarence pointed the moral at Baugé in 1421. Rushing on ahead of his archers he met defeat and death at the hands of the Armagnacs. The English had their revenge at Cravant in 1423 and at Verneuil in the following year. This battle was, to contemporaries, more important than Agincourt. It was also interesting from a tactical point of view because the French employed archers too – Scotsmen – who conducted a bloody shooting match with the English. The battle was eventually won by the English reserve, also bow-armed. The French revival began with Joan of Arc, whose inspiration led them to relieve the siege of Orléans and defeat the English at Patay in 1429. Even then English archery defeated the French at Beauvais in the following year. Recognizing the importance of archery the French king, Charles VII, instituted a native force of "free archers" as part of his army reforms.

The defeat of England in the Hundred Years War is often related to the development of gunpowder weapons. This is true insofar as the heavy siege artillery with which the Bureau brothers provided Charles VII assured the capture of English-held towns and fortresses, but not at a tactical level. At Formigny in 1450, when Sir Thomas Kyriell's *chevauchée* was trapped and annihilated by the French, artillery was present, but it was the arrival of a flanking force which decided the issue against the English. At Castillon in 1453, it was Sir John Talbot's hot-headed charge against an

1475

forces. But the defenders had strengthened their already good walls and moats and stripped all the lead off the roofs to make into cannon-balls. Dividing their forces into three they slept, ate and fought in turn, and awaited relief from the Holy Roman Emperor, Frederick III. Imperial forces approached in May but feared to attack. Though the defenders' supplies were almost exhausted by New Year 1475, they held on by severe rationing and Charles was forced to abandon the siege.

CASUALTIES Numbers unknown but casualties probably not heavy as no bloody assaults were attempted.

RESULT Although the siege, like so many medieval sieges was unsuccessful, Charles nevertheless gained prestige through his demonstration of his military power and the facing down of the Emperor.

NANCY

DATE 5 January 1477

CAMPAIGN Charles the Bold of Burgundy against René, Duke of Lorraine, and Swiss volunteers

OBJECT Following his defeats at Grandson and Murten, Charles was determined to take Nancy, which he besieged on 22 October.

NUMBERS Burgundians – 1,136 mounted men-at-arms, 1,788 mounted archers, 2,463

entrenched artillery park equipped with both large pieces and 700 handgunners, which led to an English disaster, rather than any intrinsic superiority of gunpowder weapons. More important in the long term to France's eventual victory was the end of the Anglo-Burgundian alliance in 1435, and Charles VII's effective royal control in contrast to the pathetic Henry VI.

Henry's weakness and the resulting noble faction-fighting led to the series of wars fought in England, usually called the Wars of the Roses. There were sixteen major engagements between St Albans in 1455 and Stoke 1487, when the Tudor Henry VII finally consolidated his rule. Tactically, they were unexceptional, often decided by the defection of an important noble and his following in the course of the battle. This was the case at Northampton in 1460, which enabled the Yorkists to storm an entrenched position defended with artillery, in the second battle of St Albans in 1461, a Lancastrian victory, and famously at Bosworth in 1485, where Lord Stanley's late intervention led to King Richard's death and Tudor victory. Edward IV, Yorkist king 1461–70 and 1471–83, was a commander of real genius, though. Returning from France (after his temporary deposition) in 1471, he won a victory at Barnet on 14 April. Only three weeks later (4 May) he had force-marched his army west to Tewkesbury to win another decisive victory and secure his throne.

The wars which pointed the way to the armies of the 16th century were fought not in the British Isles but Central Europe. Charles the Bold, Duke of Burgundy, had created a military force with which to turn his collection of possessions into an empire. This brought him into conflict with the Swiss cantons and it was their victory over the Burgundians which assured the dominance of the pike for the next 200 years. In fact, the Swiss infantry was still largely composed of halberdiers, although the proportion of pikemen had increased throughout the 15th century. It seemed as if Charles's "modern" army of cavalry, archers and mobile fieldguns would be invincible. However, at Grandson on 2 March 1475 he was unable to co-ordinate these elements in the face of a determined Swiss attack. Their infantry blocks, supported by smaller units of crossbows and handguns, attacked rather rashly, but unnerved Charles's mercenaries, who fled. The blow was to Burgundian prestige rather than any great physical loss. The next clash came before the walls of Murten, which Charles was besieging, on 22 June. The Burgundians had established a defensive entrenchment designed to be manned by guns and archers. But the Swiss surprised Charles's army. Three great columns of infantry manoeuvred with discipline to overwhelm the piecemeal attacks of the enemy, who suffered heavy loss. The final act was played out at Nancy six months later (see below), when Charles lost his army, his empire and his life. The Swiss went on to become the most popular soldiers and mercenaries in Europe for another three centuries.

Gunpowder weapons ushered in a new age. On the battlefield, in the form of handguns and mobile artillery, they finally rendered the fully-armoured knight (although not all cavalry) obsolete. In sieges, no old-style fortification with tall but thin walls, as shown above, could stand against their battering. In response, low, thick bastions were developed.

1477

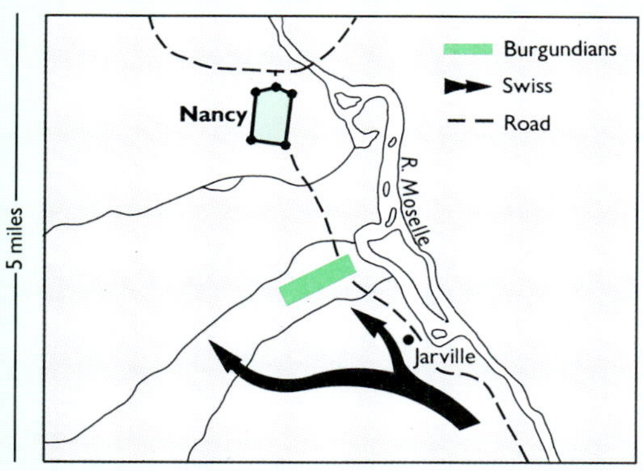

infantry plus a few other detachments making about 7,000 men; Allies – 20,000 men including 6,000 veteran Swiss.

DESCRIPTION Duke René had trouble winning support for a relief attempt from the Swiss cantons who did not wish to campaign in winter. Charles's determination bordered on madness; the Allies cut his supply lines in early December. He marched out to meet the relief force and barred the way with his artillery. Marching through terrible conditions of ice and snow the Swiss managed to outflank the Burgundian position. Then, co-ordinating their attack with the main body by horn blasts, they charged and routed the enemy.

CASUALTIES The Burgundian army was destroyed, Duke Charles being killed in the rout.

RESULT The end of independent Burgundy.

7

THE GUNPOWDER REVOLUTION

ALTHOUGH GUNPOWDER AND GUNS were to change the entire concept of warfare during the Renaissance, both had been in existence for a very long time. The first definite reference to gunpowder and its potential use in the West occurs as a cryptogram contained in a manuscript written in 1242 by the friar and alchemist Roger Bacon. From this it is clear that Bacon was aware of its explosive properties and that these could be controlled. His recourse to secrecy stems from the attitude of the Church which, the previous century, had laid an anathema upon any who made fiery substances for military purposes; this may refer to such products as Greek Fire, which had been known for many centuries, but equally its intention may have been to include black powder in the overall context of prohibited materials. Be that as it may, it is apparent from Bacon's text that some degree of development and experiment had taken place prior to 1242. It is thought gunpowder actually originated in China.

THE BLACK ART

The suggestion that the gun was invented accidentally by a German monk named Berthold Schwarz does not bear serious examination, for there is some doubt that he ever existed and the first documentary evidence of artillery in action appears in a manuscript of 1325 showing a primitive cannon firing at the walls of La Rochelle, pre-dating the period in which he is supposed to have worked. The first authenticated use of cannon in open warfare was at the Battle of Crécy in 1346, where Edward III employed three, and the first handgun had been developed by 1388.

Although presented with a *fait accompli*, the Church still did not like guns and warned those involved in their use that they were dabbling in the Black Arts. These early weapons were extremely expensive to produce and dangerous to friend and foe alike. Terrible accidents were frequent. During their training, gunners were told that it was "unseemly" to trample on powder which had been spilled around the gun, not

1485

BOSWORTH

DATE 22 August 1485
CAMPAIGN Wars of the Roses.
OBJECT The Yorkist king, Richard III, was attempting to intercept the Lancastrian claimant to the throne, Henry Tudor, who was marching on London.
NUMBERS Yorkists – 12,000, plus a small number of guns; Lancastrians – 10,000.
DESCRIPTION Richard's army was drawn up with its pikemen and billmen in the centre, flanked by cavalry, with an extended "forward" of archers and billmen in front; the position of his guns is unknown, but it is almost certain that they were aligned with the "forward". The majority of Henry's troops were cavalry, formed behind a "forward" of archers. On Ambion Hill, to the north of both armies, was a third and as yet uncommitted body of troops under Sir William Stanley. Henry had been promised the support of this, but Richard was fully aware of the Stanley

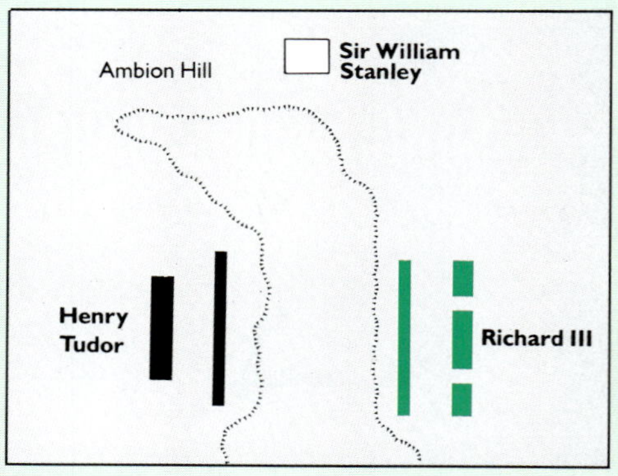

because this was considered unmannerly, but because the unstable compound could ignite and cause a major explosion. Rather than become involved in the heavy cost of establishing their own artillery park, kings setting out on campaign would hire their guns and gunners from contractors, much as a present day construction company hires in its plant.

Nevertheless, the quality of guns and the skill of artillerymen improved with the passing of time. At the battles of Formigny (1450) and Castillon (1453) the formidable English archers were defeated by artillery which outranged them. Moreover, as the 15th century drew to its close the feudal system was replaced by strong central administrations across Europe. Thus, for the first time national rather than private funds were available for the development and comparatively large-scale manufacture of artillery and other firearms, and it was this impetus which produced the revolution in the methods by which land and sea warfare were conducted. By modern standards the revolutionary process was slow, taking almost two centuries to complete, and its application was uneven, changes occurring at different times and in

COMPARATIVE RANGES

Longbow – accurate to 200 yards
Pistol – accurate to 10 yards
Matchlock arquebus – accurate to 50 yards
Flintlock musket – accurate to 75 yards
Light cannon (Saker) firing 5-lb shot – accurate to 350 yards, maximum range 1,700 yards
Medium cannon (Culverin) firing 17-lb shot – accurate to 400 yards, maximum range 2,500 yards
Heavy cannon (Cannon) firing 60-lb shot – maximum range 2,000 yards

A panoramic view of the Battle of Pavia, 1525. The Imperial army is shown breaking into the walled park on the French flank, with the French mounting their counter-attack. In the background are the defences of Pavia and the French siege lines, and the field works erected to block the original advance of the Imperialists.

1485

An imaginative view of the Battle of Bosworth Field, 1485.

family's sympathy for the Lancastrian cause and was holding Lord Stanley's son as hostage. For the moment, therefore, Sir William Stanley preserved a neutral stance.

The battle began with an exchange of arrow flights, and Richard's guns fired a few rounds. The two armies then closed in a general mêlée. Richard led a personal attack on Henry, but was killed in the process. At this point Sir William Stanley launched an attack on the Yorkist flank and ▸

A German gun of the mid-16th century with cast ornamentation. The lifting handles on top of the barrel were known as dolphins, for obvious reasons. The graduated marks on the barrel correspond with those on the rammer and powder ladle, indicating the position of the latter during loading. Unfortunately, the artist has shown the trunnions in a position which would destroy the balance of the weapon, and his wheels are much too small and flimsy for practical use.

different places. Taken as a whole, however, the period is extremely important in the history of warfare, covering as it does the difficult transition from medieval to modern methods. At Bosworth Field (1485 – see page 92) men thought and fought in the medieval manner; at Blenheim (1704 – see page 111), their thinking and actions were recognizably modern.

ARTILLERY AND LAND WARFARE

As the use of guns became commonplace, and exchequers were able to support the cost of their purchase, the possession of artillery began to reflect the status of monarchs and the old practice of hiring guns and gunners for campaigns and sieges was abandoned. For the moment, gun manufacture, some details of which are given elsewhere, remained in private hands, although the business was international in its scope. Many of the guns purchased in this way were given individual names; Henry VIII, for example, bought a great deal of ordnance from the Low Countries during the early years of his reign, including a dozen matched guns each of which was named after one of the Apostles. Normally, gunmakers also provided powder, ammunition and draught animals as part of the transaction. Once royal armies had been expanded by the addition of a permanent artillery park, it was entirely logical that the responsibility for this should rest with a corps of regular artillerymen, administered by master gunners and their assistants.

The roles performed by artillery in land campaigns were siege warfare, which employed the heaviest weapons, and field operations, in which lighter guns were used. The one problem which was never satisfactorily resolved during the period was the relative immobility of the arm. This was caused partly by the great weight of the weapons themselves, which in turn demanded heavy, cumbrous carriages from which they could be fired, and partly by the contemporary state of the roads, the best of which were little better than miry lanes. An additional complication was the fact that, while the professional status of the artilleryman had been recognized, the transport of the guns was still the responsibility of civilian contractors, who supplied oxen or horse teams and drivers. Needless to say, if a situation developed which was not to the contractors' liking, they were quite likely to make off with their animals and leave the guns stranded. Thus, the best speed at which artillery could be moved was walking pace, with the gunners trudging alongside, or even slower if oxen were employed. The munitions were carried separately, though as part of the artillery train, and everything depended on the powder and ammunition wagons reaching the right place at the right time. It has been calculated that a siege train of 100 guns and 60 mortars required the support of 3,000 wagons, the whole pulled by 15,000 horses, occupying 15 miles of road and travelling at about two miles per hour.

1485

the remainder of Richard's army fled.

While small in scale, the battle was extremely important as the new king, Henry VII, restored stability to England and established a strong central administration.

CASUALTIES Yorkists – 900; Lancastrians – 100.

RESULT A decisive victory for the Lancastrians which established the Tudor dynasty and ended the Wars of the Roses.

PAVIA

DATE 25 February 1525

CAMPAIGN War between Francis I of France and Hapsburg Emperor Charles V

OBJECT The Imperialists were attempting to break the French siege of the city.

NUMBERS Imperialists – total of 23,000 men under the Marquis of Pescara, including 12,000 German pikemen, 6,500 Spanish-Italian infantry and arquebusiers, 800 men-at-arms, 1,500 light cavalry and 17 guns, plus the 6,000-strong besieged garrison of Pavia; French – total of 22,000 men under Francis I, including 4,000 Swiss and 5,000 French pikemen, 6,000 French and 3,000 Italian infantry and arquebusiers, 1,200 men-at-arms, 2,000 light cavalry and 53 guns.

DESCRIPTION The Imperialist army approached Pavia at the end of January but found its path barred by entrenchments. It then entrenched itself and both sides engaged in an inconclusive bombardment

A 16th-century artillery train of the Imperial army on the march, including a field forge and other equipment. Horses could haul their loads quicker than oxen, but were not as strong and therefore larger numbers of them were required.

Artillery on the march in the 16th century. Oxen possessed the strength to haul the heavy weapons over the poor roads of the period, but were so slow that artillery trains often lagged far behind their armies. The ammunition is carried in panniers by pack animals.

This immobility was less of a disadvantage in siege warfare, unless the siege was broken, as at Pavia in 1525 (see below), when the guns could not be got away. On the battlefield, however, once the guns were emplaced they remained in position, the tide of battle ebbing and flowing past them, and because of this their capture came to be regarded as the tangible proof of victory.

Contemporary commanders were, of course, aware of the problem. Several attempts were made in the 16th century to standardize guns and, in the process of evolutionary development, somewhat lighter weapons and carriages were produced. The Swedish King Gustavus Adolphus introduced small battalion guns which could be manhandled by infantrymen and, towards the end of the period, light galloper guns, drawn by a single horse, made their appearance. During the 17th century trail wheels were also fitted to the carriages of some guns and by 1680 these had evolved into the limber, which was simply a pair of wheels on to which the trail could be hooked, thereby spreading the load between four wheels instead of two; the concept of the limber as an ammunition carrier lay 100 years in the future.

Field-artillery tactics for much of the period were very simple. The guns were

Continued on page 98

1525

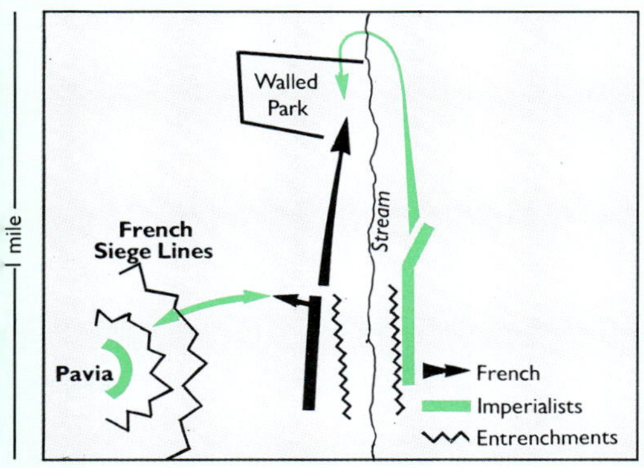

of each other across an unfordable stream. Under cover of a storm and artillery fire, Pescara broke the deadlock during the night of 24–25 February by marching north to cross the stream and penetrate a walled park lying on the French left, leaving a few men in his trenches to create the illusion that they were still occupied. Francis, taken completely by surprise, nevertheless led a determined cavalry charge against the Imperial left-centre while the rest of his army slowly changed front. His attack was at first successful, but the French horsemen were routed when a force of Spanish arquebusiers and pikemen fell on their rear while the Imperial cavalry counter-attacked from the front. As the French infantry entered the battle piecemeal it was destroyed in detail by superior numbers of halberdiers and arquebusiers. The French artillery played little part in the fighting as the unexpected redeployment masked the fire of the few guns that could be brought up in time. Observing the destruction of ▸

GUNS AND GUNPOWDER

THE FIRST PICTURE of what is indisputably a gun appears in a manuscript of 1325 (illustrated on page 88) and shows a soldier applying a red-hot iron to the vent of a bulbous container from which a large arrow is being propelled by an explosion of the contents. It was soon apparent that a tube shape would be more effective and at first this was made by arranging red-hot iron bars around a mandrel and hammering to weld them together; white-hot iron hoops were then shrunk onto the tube to give it strength. Another method was to make short iron tubes shaped like bobbins, then join them together to form a barrel and reinforce the joints.

Bar and bobbin guns were difficult to seal at the breech end of the barrel, so most early guns were breech-loaders, the breech consisting of a removable powder chamber closed at one end, secured by hammering a wedge between it and the rear of the gun cradle. Unfortunately, the major disadvantage of breech-loaders was a back-blast of gas and flame which progressively reduced the weapon's efficiency the longer it was in action. For this reason, large calibre siege guns were muzzle-loaders, the chamber being fitted into the rear of the barrel by means of a screw mechanism or lugs.

By the second quarter of the 15th century muzzle-loaders were being cast in one piece, using bronze. Shortly after, trunnions began to be cast with the barrels. This permitted the latter to be secured to wheeled carriages by cap-squares, and thus increased the mobility of artillery, enabling it to accompany armies in the field. Trunnions also permitted gunners to elevate or depress barrels and so obtain variation in range.

By 1600 the number of guns in service was rising dramatically. They began to be classified by size and given names such as cannon and culverin. The short-barrelled mortar, capable of high-angle fire, was also introduced during this period, being joined in the 17th century by another high-angle weapon, the howitzer. The difference between the two was that while the mortar's elevation was fixed and variations in range were obtained by adjusting the charge, the howitzer's charge was fixed and its elevation could be altered. Once the blast furnace had been brought into use, it became possible to cast sound iron guns, which were cheaper to produce and more robust. Breech-loading was eventually abandoned and the gun assumed the form it was to retain for 400 years.

Equally important to the new science of gunnery was the quality of the gunpowder. This varied widely and travelled badly until, early in the 15th century, someone hit on the idea of mixing the components in a wet state, allowing the result to dry and then passing it through a fine sieve to achieve a standard size of grain. The result, known as corned powder, was more powerful, travelled well and was resistant to damp. Despite this, it was only brought into common usage over a very long period, partly because it was extremely expensive, and partly because the older guns could not withstand the increased pressure.

(Above) A primitive bar gun (c. 1400) being fired using a red-hot iron applied to the vent. The recoil is absorbed by a wooden extension dug into the ground. (Right) A late 16th-century gun in a siege emplacement. The woven matting gave a firm footing for the gun and its crew, and the wicker gabions provided protection from the enemy's fire. (Below) A mortar of the same period engaging a fortress with high-angle fire. The shell has been fuzed to burst above the defences.

(Left) An unusual late 16th-century galloper gun on a four-wheeled carriage. The gun, though of small calibre, has a swivel mounting and can be trained in any direction. Galloper guns, used in support of cavalry, came into favour somewhat later than this early example.

(Below) Cannon and a mortar of the early 16th century. In the background is an Orgelshutz (organ gun), a primitive attempt to produce rapid fire by attaching several small-calibre weapons to the same mounting. In action, the barrels could either be fired together or in sequence – a remote ancestor of the machine gun.

ARTILLERY WEAPONS OF THE 16TH AND 17TH CENTURIES

	Weight lb	Calibre in	Shot lb
Falconet	400	2.25	1.125
Falcon	750	2.75	2.5
Minion	1.100	3.25	4.75
Saker	1.900	3.75	6
Demi-Culverin	3.000	4.5	11.75
Culverin	4.300	5.25	16.25
Demi-Cannon	5.600	6.5	32
Cannon	8.000	8	64

A number of intermediate classifications also existed. By the end of the 17th century, guns began to be classified by their weight of shot.

(Right) An artist's sketch of Swiss pikemen and halberdiers in action, almost certainly a preliminary for a larger painting, as little or no armour is shown.

(Below) A superb suit of English pikeman's armour, including helmet, breast- and backplates, and tassets to protect the thighs. Note how the tassets are hinged at the level of the hips.

drawn up in front of the army's battle line and their first task was to silence their opposite numbers; once this had been done, they could set about firing into the packed ranks of the enemy army. By the end of the 17th century, however, a more scientific approach had begun to prevail, with guns being grouped to support other arms during specific phases of the engagement.

INFANTRY

At the end of the 15th century the infantry element of most armies consisted of pikemen, halberdiers and archers. The pikemen and halberdiers, the latter armed with a spear incorporating an axe-blade just below its head, and sometimes a hook for dragging an opponent out of his ranks, wore helmet, breast-and-back plates and flexible thigh-pieces for protection during hand-to-hand fighting, although the archers were more lightly equipped. This medieval array, rooted in centuries of feudal warfare and as yet not seriously compromised by cannon, was forced to adapt to changing conditions very quickly by the development of the arquebus, evolved from a light anti-personnel gun normally mounted on the walls of fortifications.

1525

the French army, the garrison of Pavia made a sally and destroyed those units which Francis had left in the siege lines. The battle, in which the use of small-arms firepower had played a major part, lasted a mere two hours.
CASUALTIES Imperialists – approximately 500 killed and wounded; French – approximately 13,000 killed and wounded, 5,000 captured and all artillery lost.
RESULT The French army was destroyed, Pavia relieved and Francis I captured.

SPANISH ARMADA

DATE 19–30 July 1588
CAMPAIGN Naval war between Elizabeth I of England and Philip II of Spain
OBJECT The Armada, commanded by the Duke of Medina Sidonia, was to transport the Duke of Parma's invasion army from the Netherlands to England.
NUMBERS The Armada – 20 galleons, 44 armed merchant vessels, 23 transports, 35 smaller vessels, and four galleasses, manned by 8,500 seamen and galley slaves and 19,000 soldiers; 2,431 guns, of which 1,100 were in the heavy category, including 600 culverins, the remainder being light anti-personnel weapons. The English fleet – about 50 warships in all, including five of over 600 tons and 11 of 400–600 tons, manned by 6,000 men, of whom approximately three-quarters were seamen; over 1,500 heavy cannon, the majority being long-range culverins. A number of auxiliary vessels and supply ships, some

An arquebusier. His powder charges, measured and ready for use, were slung in a bandolier across his back and one can be seen just below his left forearm; a small horn of priming powder is suspended from his neck. He carries a sword and pistol for his own defence during close-quarter fighting.

Early versions of this weapon were tucked under the right arm and fired from an inclined rest spiked into the ground, later and somewhat smaller models being held against the chest and gripped with both hands. Both had very limited range and accuracy, but as early as 1503 Spanish arquebusiers under Gonzalo de Cordoba inflicted a convincing defeat on a conventional Franco/Swiss army at the battle of Cerignola. Cordoba preferred to position his arquebusiers in trenches or behind barricades which not only provided a degree of protection but also increased accuracy, with units of pikemen and halberdiers nearby to repel enemy attacks. In open country, however, the arquebusiers were clearly vulnerable and were forced to rely on pikemen for their defence. The system adopted by the Spanish, and copied by the majority of European powers, was to form integrated units knows as *tercios* in which the arquebusiers were stationed in front of or on either flank of the pikemen, supporting the advance of the latter with their fire or retiring under the long pikes if they were attacked.

Two types of soldier, the halberdier and the archer, had no place in the new scheme of things. The halberd was too short to be of use in the changed conditions and although halberdiers were present in considerable strength during the early battles of the period, their numbers declined steadily until, by the end of the 16th century, the use of the weapon was confined, largely but not exclusively, to the ceremonial role. The demise of the archer is more difficult to explain, since the protagonists of the longbow could claim, correctly, that the weapon had a much higher rate of fire, greater accuracy and longer range than infantry firearms, all of which remained true as late as the middle of the 19th century. The arrow, however, was less effective against plate armour than it had been against the older chain mail, whereas the kinetic energy stored in an arquebus or musket ball, which was far larger and heavier than a modern small-arms round, enabled the missile to penetrate plate with ease and knock man or horse flat with its impact. In consequence, while archers continued to be employed both on land and at sea, their numbers also declined and in 1595 a Royal Ordinance decreed that henceforth the English trained bands would arm themselves with firearms rather than the traditional longbow. Ironically, it was the introduction of firearms which led to the reduction of infantry armour to helmet and breastplate, worn only by pikemen for protection during close-quarter combat.

From the arquebus the musket was evolved, a more convenient weapon which could be fired from the shoulder, although at first a rest was still needed to support its 11 kg (25 lb) weight. Normally, arquebusiers and musketeers fought in ranks 10 deep, the front rank discharging its weapons and then filing to the rear, where they re-loaded as they made their way forward again by rotation, a system which enabled a continuous if proportionately narrow front of fire to be maintained. The earliest

1588

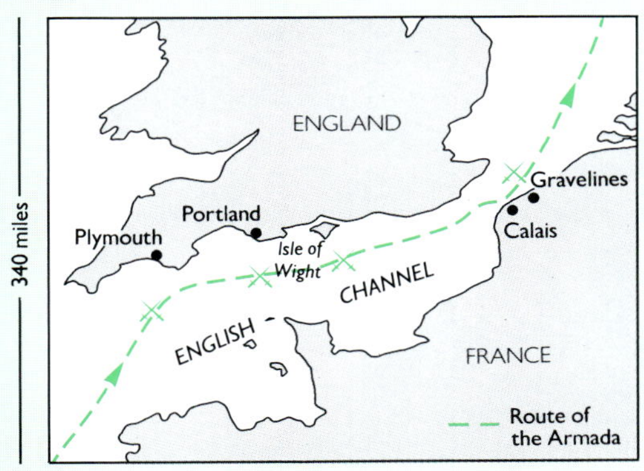

of them privately fitted out, sailed in support.

DESCRIPTION The Armada left Corunna on 12 July and was sighted by English scout vessels off the Lizard a week later. The English fleet, commanded by Lord Howard of Effingham with Sir Francis Drake as his vice-admiral, sailed from Plymouth on 20 July. The following day the Spanish formed a defensive crescent, the rear of which was harried by the English, setting the pattern of the battle as the fleets moved up-Channel. The gunnery of the English ships, coupled with their better sailing qualities and knowledge of local tides and currents, enabled them to inflict the greater damage. With the exception of their culverins, the heavy guns aboard the Spanish ships were more suited to siege warfare than to a naval engagement and the English fought beyond the range of the lighter anti-personnel weapons. ▶

This series of engravings shows five of the 36 positions to load and fire a 17th-century matchlock musket. Slung across the musketeer's bandolier are his powder charges. (Above left) Musketeer on the march, with musket over his left shoulder and match burning at both ends in his left hand. (Above middle) Ramming home the ball and wadding on top of the charge. (Above) Priming the flash pan. (Far left) Musketeer "blowing upon his coals" to improve the burn of the slow match. (Left) Aiming and firing from rest.

1588

Further heavy engagements took place off the Dorset coast and the Isle of Wight. Medina Sidonia abandoned his plan to effect a landing on the latter and proceeded to Calais, where he hoped to replenish his dangerously reduced stock of ammunition, but Parma, blockaded in Bruges by the Dutch fleet, was unable to assist him. Reinforced and replenished with ammunition, Howard followed the Armada to Calais and, during the night of 27–8 July, sent fireships among the anchored Spanish vessels, many of which cut their cables in panic.

Another major engagement took place off the Flanders coast on 28 July, strong winds pushing the fleets steadily north-eastwards. These same winds prevented the Spanish entering Dunkirk or Bruges, where a junction with Parma might have been effected. On 29 July the Armada was almost driven on to the lee shore of Zeeland and Medina Sidonia, his ammunition exhausted, decided to return to Spain by

The Spanish Armada engaged by the English fleet.

Sketches showing combat between cuirassiers, taken from a contemporary treatise on warfare. It is significant that in three of the four cases the lance or pistol is being used against the opponent's unprotected mount. The lance began to fall into disuse early in the Gunpowder Revolution.

firing mechanism was the matchlock, requiring the insertion of a burning slow match into the priming pan. The later wheel-lock incorporated a toothed wheel which, when activated by a trigger, struck sparks from a flint within the enclosed priming pan, thereby reducing the chances of an accidental discharge. The flintlock, in which a spring-loaded hammer containing a flint, again activated by a trigger, struck sparks into the pan, was less complex in its construction and cheaper to make. All three types of mechanism were used during the period, although by the end of the 17th century the matchlock had all but disappeared and the flintlock, because of its simplicity, had been generally adopted for military use, witness the Brown Bess musket, the basic design of which was to serve the British soldier well for over 150 years.

The first major changes in infantry tactics were introduced by Gustavus Adolphus. The weight of the musket was reduced to 5 kg (11 lb), so that it could be fired from the shoulder without a rest, and the fixed cartridge, incorporating charge and ball, was introduced. These measures increased the musketeer's efficiency to the point that his dependence on the pikeman was reduced and the proportion of musketeers to pikemen was therefore increased. Simultaneously, it was possible to reduce the musketeers' ranks from 10 to a maximum of six, so that units held a wider area of front than hitherto. The overall effect was to give the Swedish infantry a flexibility and firepower which the *tercios* lacked, amply demonstrated during the decisive Battle of Breitenfeld in 1631 (see page 102).

It was the introduction of the bayonet which spelled the end of the pikeman. Legend has it that sometime around 1640, possibly at Bayonne, a body of musketeers

sailing round Scotland and Ireland. Howard followed him northwards until lack of provisions forced him to return to port on 2 August.

The Armada had already lost 11 ships in action, from various causes. On entering the Atlantic it ran into severe gales which wrecked another 19 vessels on the Scottish and Irish coasts; the fate of a further 33 remains unknown. The survivors, their crews dying from hunger and thirst, straggled into Spanish ports in September.

The defeat of the Spanish Armada involved the most protracted sea battle ever fought and established the gun as the principal weapon of naval warfare for the next 350 years.

CASUALTIES 63 Spanish vessels lost from various causes during the engagement and its sequel, with personnel casualties in proportion; no English vessel of importance was lost and personnel casualties were light, given the protracted nature of the fighting.

RESULT The Armada failed in its purpose and Spanish naval prestige sustained a blow from which it never fully recovered; the prestige of the English Royal Navy, on the other hand, was now firmly in the ascendant. In overall terms, the battle vindicated those who favoured the fighting ship as gun platform rather than as a floating fortress, and had an immediate effect on warship design throughout the western world.

(Top right) Matchlock musket on firing rest. The weapon was fired with the musketeer's left foot forward, his left hand steadying the rest, and his right hand encircling the small of the butt, pulling it in towards his shoulder to absorb as much of the recoil as possible. When the trigger was activated the serpentine lowered the burning match into the priming pan.

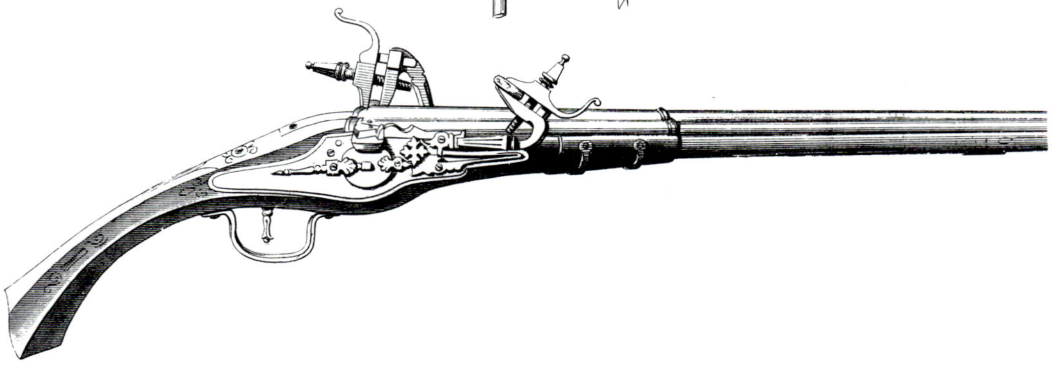

(Bottom right) Wheel-lock arquebus. Being smaller and lighter than the matchlock, the arquebus could be fired with both hands on the weapon; some were fired from the chest, some from the shoulder and others held under the right arm. This example is somewhat advanced in that it is fitted with a second dog containing a flint (iron pyrites) which can be brought into use if the first fails.

lacking pikemen for their defence solved the problem by plugging long knives into the muzzles of their weapons. The plug bayonet was in widespread use by the 1660s, but its obvious disadvantage was that the musket could not be fired while it was fixed. The answer to this was to fit the bayonet with a ring which could be slipped over the muzzle and then held in place by studs, leaving the musket free for firing and reloading. Ring bayonets first appeared in 1678 and their use quickly became general, eliminating the need for pikemen. With the pikemen went the last vestige of infantry armour, which would not reappear until the 20th century, and then for very different reasons from hand-to-hand combat. Instead, the infantryman wore a uniform coat of national colour, ornamented with distinctive facings and buttons intended to give his unit an *esprit de corps*.

As one type of infantryman began leaving the battlefield another, the grenadier, had already entered it. The function of the grenadier, as his name suggests, was to hurl grenades, which were then small spheres packed with gunpowder and fuzed by a length of burning slow-match. Because wide-brimmed or tricorn hats interfered with the swing of the arm, grenadiers wore a cap with trailing bag similar to a nightcap, but by 1700 several armies had begun to stiffen these to the shape of a bishop's mitre, ornamented with the regimental insignia or royal cypher. This work was performed best by the tallest and strongest men and grenadiers therefore came to

1631

BREITENFELD

DATE 17 September 1631
CAMPAIGN Thirty Years War
OBJECT Gustavus Adolphus and the Elector of Saxony sought to recover Leipzig from the Imperialist-Catholic faction.
NUMBERS Protestants – total of 40,000 Swedes and Saxons under Gustavus Adolphus and the Elector of Saxony, including 248 infantry companies, 170 cavalry squadrons and 60–70 guns; Imperialists – total of 32,000 men under Tilly, including 21,000 infantry, 11,000 cavalry and 30 guns.
DESCRIPTION Tilly chose to give battle in an area of treeless, undulating country which allowed easy deployment of his heavy *tercios* of pikemen and also permitted his cavalry to perform the *caracole*. His army was formed with 14 *tercio* blocks in the centre and cavalry on either flank. The Swedish army was also drawn up with its infantry in the centre and the cavalry on the flanks, but its smaller units were deployed in two lines with detachments of musketeers supporting the cavalry, and the infantry had the immediate support of 42 two-man battalion guns. The smaller and less flexible Saxon contingent was drawn up on the Swedish left.

The battle began with an artillery exchange, commencing at noon. From the outset, Tilly's intention was a double envelopment of the Protestant army. After about two hours the cavalry, on the left of

be regarded as an élite. Each battalion possessed a grenadier company, although in the field the practice was to brigade grenadiers together and employ them as assault infantry.

CAVALRY

The demise of the knight, already apparent during the previous 150 years in his encounters with English archers and Swiss pikemen, became a reality with the introduction of gunpowder, the great leveller; in fact, for much of the gunpower revolution, the mounted arm in general was in decline, despite the emergence of the professional cavalryman.

The essence of the problem was that cavalry was unable to perform its traditional role of shock action against infantry, being simultaneously vulnerable to the fire of arquebusiers and musketeers and kept beyond striking distance by massed pikes. In such circumstances the lance merely became an encumbrance and, save in Eastern Europe, had been discarded by the end of the 16th century, although the Scottish cavalry was still employing lancers some 50 years later.

An apparent answer was presented by the pistol, the type adopted at first being the wheel-lock, the matchlock mechanism being clearly unsuited to mounted action. Each trooper was equipped with two or three pistols and attacks were delivered at walking pace or, at best, the trot, in 10-deep formations. At point-blank range the front rank would discharge its pistols and then wheel to the rear to re-load and move forward by rotation, in the manner of contemporary musketeers, this type of cavalry manoeuvre being known as the *caracole*. Only when gaps began to appear in the enemy ranks did the troopers attempt to close with the sword. Once the pistol had been accepted as the principal cavalry weapon, the *caracole* was also employed against hostile cavalry, with the result that for many years the entire concept of shock action disappeared altogether, the only manoeuvre performed at the gallop being the pursuit of a broken enemy. Thus, the contribution made by cavalry during the 16th and the early years of the 17th centuries was only rarely decisive.

Once again, it was Gustavus Adolphus who rationalized the situation. Forbidden to perform the *caracole*, his cavalry attacked at a fast trot in four ranks, later reduced to three. Having fired their pistols, the two leading ranks closed immediately with the sword, followed by the remainder, who reserved their fire for the subsequent *mêlée*. Naturally, the effect of such a radical departure from the accepted drill was devastating. Furthermore, each Swedish cavalry regiment had the direct support of a 200-strong company of musketeers and light artillery, the fire of which created further gaps in the enemy ranks which could be exploited by the horsemen. During the English Civil War the achievements of Cromwell's Ironsides confirmed the

Continued on page 106

Cavalry trooper's armour, English Civil War. The helmet, known as a pot, was unlike the cuirassier's in that it relied on bars to protect the face and was fitted with a peak and a lobstertail neckguard. The cumbrous tassets were often discarded.

1631

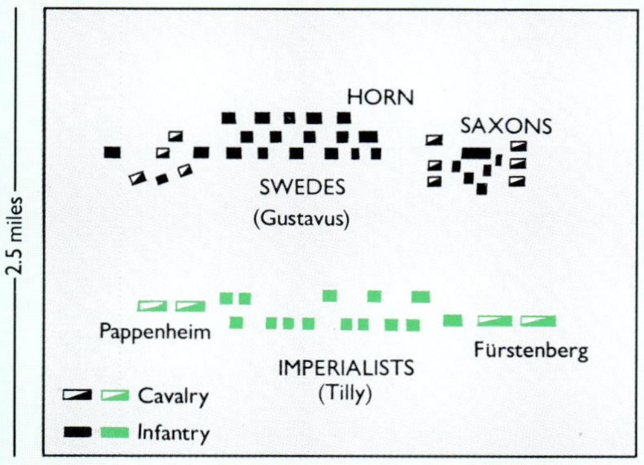

the Imperial army, commanded by Pappenheim, attempted to turn the Swedish right, but was balked when the Swedes simply extended their line by taking units from elsewhere; nor could Pappenheim make headway against the Swedish tactics of alternating musketry volleys with counter-charges by their own cavalry, athough fierce fighting raged for three hours. Meanwhile, the *tercios* had also advanced, covered on both flanks by the right wing of the Imperial cavalry under Furstenberg, swinging right to attack the Saxons, who were routed and driven from the field by 4pm.

With the Swedish left thus exposed, Tilly's victory seemed assured. However, its commander, Gustav Horn, immediately mounted a counter-attack which drove some of the Imperial cavalry back into the cumbrous *tercios*, which were attempting to reorganize. The time gained enabled the Swedes to extend their flank, their combination of firepower and shock action ▸

GREAT CAPTAINS: GUSTAVUS AND MARLBOROUGH

(Above) Gustavus Adolphus, King of Sweden 1611-32.

(Below) The Duke of Marlborough (right) gives orders during the Battle of Malplaquet. Marlborough maintained close tactical control in all his battles. In the foreground, a grenadier examines captured French colours.

(Right) A camp scene during the Thirty Years War. Much of central Germany was ravaged by troops such as these in their constant search for forage and plunder.

(Below right) Marlborough dictating to his secretary. Thorough administration and imaginative forward planning were the hallmarks of Marlborough's style of command.

GUSTAVUS ADOLPHUS came to the throne of Sweden in 1611, at the age of 17, and was almost immediately involved in a protracted series of local wars that established Sweden as the major military power in the Baltic. Sweden was poor and had limited manpower resources. Therefore, while the standing army which Gustavus formed was national in character, it needed to make up for small numbers with efficiency. It was raised by selective conscription, given uniforms for *esprit de corps*, humanely disciplined, paid regularly and, above all, trained. The key to improved tactics lay in weapons. Gustavus reduced the weight of the musket so that it could be fired from the shoulder, and introduced a fixed cartridge. This increased the rate of fire and the musketeers' ranks could be reduced from ten to six.

The flexibility of the Swedish infantry was provided by the internal organization of its units. A company had 72 musketeers and 54 pikemen; four companies formed a battalion; eight battalions formed a regiment; and two to four regiments formed a brigade. Gustavus trained his cavalry to charge home knee-to-knee and engage with the sword, so restoring shock action to the battlefield. Each cavalry regiment had the support of a musketeer company and light artillery which would be employed prior to and between charges.

The Swedish artillery assumed an importance equal to that of the infantry or cavalry. The most important development was in the field of regimental guns. Those in use were replaced by conventional 4-pounder guns firing fixed grape or canister ammunition a third as fast again as a musketeer. Each infantry and cavalry regiment was equipped with one or two such guns.

By 1630, Gustavus had spent about half his revenue on his armed services and it was the financial inducement offered by Cardinal Richelieu of France which prompted his direct involvement in the Thirty Years War. The superiority of the Swedish system was clearly demonstrated at Breitenfeld in 1631, but at Lützen in 1632, while the Swedes were again victorious, Gustavus was killed. His contribution to military science had been immense and his methods were quickly copied by every army in Europe.

THE DUKE OF MARLBOROUGH was born as John Churchill in 1650. As a junior officer he served in Tangier, at sea against the Dutch and for a while with the French Army. He was responsible for defeating the Duke of Monmouth's rebellion in 1685. On the outbreak of the War of the Spanish Succession William III appointed him Commander-in-Chief of the Allied armies and Ambassador to the Dutch United Provinces, concluding the treaty which established the Grand Alliance of the United Kingdom, Holland and the Austrian Empire. When Anne succeeded to the crown the following year she added the appointment of Captain-General to that of Master-General of the Ordnance, which he already held, and made him a duke.

Marlborough was both an excellent strategist and a master of

tactics. He increased the pace of the cavalry charge to a canter. This proved most effective against French cavalry, who were still performing a version of the *caracole*, and was followed by deep penetration and prompt rallying. He also personally ordered the deployment of artillery, massing his guns on a critical sector or sending them forward to provide close-quarter support during a general advance.

Above all, Marlborough was an inspiring leader. He recognized that most men were soldiers because they had no alternative and made officers responsible for the welfare of their men. The men responded. Marlborough was always quick to detect any flaw in his opponents' dispositions and concentrate overwhelmingly against their weaknesses. It was thus that he won his spectacular victories at the battles of Blenheim (1704), Ramillies (1706) and Oudenarde (1708), and was able to force his way through the formidable Ne Plus Ultra lines in 1711.

The War of the Spanish Succession ended in 1713. Marlborough had been recalled in 1712, but as a result of the alarm generated by the Jacobite Rising of 1715 he was again appointed Master-General of the Ordnance and, prior to his death in 1716, was able to place the artillery on a permanent footing. He was one of history's outstanding captains. Under Marlborough the prestige of the British Army reached a level unequalled since the longbow dominated the battlefield.

A cuirassier performing the caracole. Apart from the boots, his appearance is very similar to that of the medieval knight. Such expensive equipment could not be justified once the efficiency of firearms increased and by the middle of the 17th century the cuirassier's armour had been reduced to an open helmet, breast and backplate.

return of decisive shock action to the battlefield and also demonstrated the critical importance of rallying after a successful charge.

The heavy cavalry of the period were *cuirassiers*. At first their armour differed little from that of the medieval knight, although they wore long boots in place of lower leg armour. With the passing of time the thigh and arm pieces were discarded so that by the middle of the 17th century armour had been reduced to helmet, breast- and backplate. The dragoon, armed with a short musket known as a *dragon*, bayonet and sword also appeared about this time. His only armour was a helmet, generally discarded by 1700, and his role was that of a mounted infantryman who rode to the battlefield but could fight mounted or dismounted. Properly employed, he provided a valuable asset in conditions which witnessed the return of tactical flexibility. His contemporary the carabineer was a cavalryman armed with a lighter musket known as a carbine, pistols and sword. There was also a brief fashion for horse grenadiers. The backbone of the line cavalry, however, consisted of regiments of horse, armed with sword and pistols. In continental Europe the light cavalry roles, including scouting and "screening" (covering the army's movements), were at first performed by mounted irregulars recruited in the Balkans and Eastern Europe, but towards the end of the 17th century the first regular hussar regiments were formed for this purpose.

The last 50 years of the period, therefore, witnessed a restoration of the cavalry's ability to perform shock action. The French cavalry, in particular, acquired a reputation for dash, although during the War of Spanish Succession this was often eclipsed by Marlborough's ability to handle cavalry *en masse* at the higher level of command. Nevertheless, while cavalry had recovered its purpose on the battlefield, it had lost its former dominance and was now simply one of several arms which of necessity were forced to co-operate to achieve success. Indeed, the ratio of cavalry to other troops, already falling, continued to fall throughout the next century.

FORTIFICATION AND SIEGECRAFT

Unless it was situated on an inaccessible crag or surrounded by a wide body of water, no medieval fortress could hope to survive a siege conducted with artillery support, although as late as the English Civil War some castles were able to offer remarkably tough resistance. Equally, medieval siege methods were useless against a fortress armed with guns, which could destroy siege towers and other impedimenta at long range. Thus, gunpowder induced a major revolution in the opposed skills of fortification and siegecraft, just as it did in other forms of warfare.

For the fortress-builder, it was necessary to sink most of his defences into the earth, with only fighting parapets and gun embrasures visible above ground, sited to

1631

serving to compress the pikemen until they could no longer use their weapons. Advancing steadily, the Swedes recaptured the Saxon artillery, then took Tilly's own guns, which were turned upon the struggling *tercios*. At about the same time, 6pm, Gustavus Adolphus went over to the offensive on the right flank and, with the exception of some units which made a gallant stand until they were overwhelmed, the wreckage of the Imperial army was swept from the field. Tilly, wounded, had already been led away.

CASUALTIES Protestants – 4,000 killed and wounded; Imperialists – 7,000 killed and wounded, 6,000 captured and 8,000 surrendered subsequently in Leipzig.

RESULT Leipzig was taken, Tilly's army destroyed, the future of German Protestantism was assured and Sweden emerged as a major military power.

In addition to its important political consequences, Breitenfeld demonstrated that the older cavalry and infantry tactics could not prevail against an enemy who combined flexibility, mobility, firepower and shock action.

Of these elements, the most important were undoubtedly the flexibilty of the Swedish command system and the speed with which the smaller units of Gustavus' army could be re-deployed, which, together, prevented potentially dangerous situations developing on either flank.

sweep the approaches with their fire. Henry VIII constructed a series of defence works along the southern coast of England, designed specifically for all-round defence by artillery, the basic format of these being a circular central keep surrounded by interconnected semi-circular bastions mounting tiers of guns, the whole complex being encircled by a wide ditch.

The problem with circular bastions was that, though less vulnerable to cannon fire and able to provide a degree of support for each other with their crossfire, this still left areas of dead ground which could be exploited by the enemy. This same was not true of wedge-shaped bastions, which could be sited to provide mutual support covering every angle of approach. From this discovery the star system of fortification was evolved, so called because the overall design of a fortress consisting of bastions linked by curtain walls resembled a star. From their outer edge the permanent defences consisted of a sloped glacis, counterscarp, ditch, scarp and ramparts. To protect gateways and vulnerable sections of the curtain, ravelins and other outworks could be added, each with its own counterscarp, ditch and scarp, so producing an extremely complex ground plan. Very little detail of the defences was visible to an attacker as even the parapets were covered with a deep layer of earth which cushioned the impact of cannon balls and so reduced the danger from flying stone splinters.

To launch an assault on such a fortress without adequate preparation was to invite crippling casualties. Mining offered an alternative if the ditch was dry, but this involved tunnelling through the foundations of the counterscarp, then under the ditch and finally through the thickness of the scarp; even if the attempt was successful and a charge was laid and fired, the stone-fronted earth ramparts could absorb the effects of the explosion far better than could the walls of a medieval castle. The only method likely to guarantee success was to concentrate artillery fire against what was considered to be a weak sector of the defences, and then dig a sap towards it. The batteries would be emplaced 600 yards from the walls and then connected by a trench which became known as the First Parallel. From this zig-zag saps would be pushed out and guns brought forward to establish a Second Parallel 300 yards from the defences. This would be repeated until a Third Parallel existed within musket shot of the ramparts. Once the defences had been battered into silence and a breach in the walls effected, the garrison might surrender, or an assault might be launched if it rejected terms.

The master of this type of warfare was Sebastien le Prestre de Vauban, who received his commission as an engineer in 1653 and in 1687 became the French Army's Director of Engineering. Vauban consolidated the experience of the previous 100 years' fortification and siegecraft, applying mathematics to the former and logical

Marshal Sebastien le Prestre de Vauban, appointed Louis XIV's Director of Military Engineering in 1687. Vauban was a master of fortification and siegecraft, applying scientific principles to both.

1643

ROCROI

DATE 18–19 May 1643
CAMPAIGN Thirty Years War, campaign of 1643 in France and Belgium
OBJECT The French army under the Duc d'Enghien was attempting to relieve Rocroi, which was besieged by a Spanish army under Don Francisco de Melo.
NUMBERS French – 18 infantry battalions, 32 cavalry squadrons and 12 guns, total 23,000; Spaniards – 20 infantry *tercios*, 7,000 cavalry and 28 guns, total 27,000.

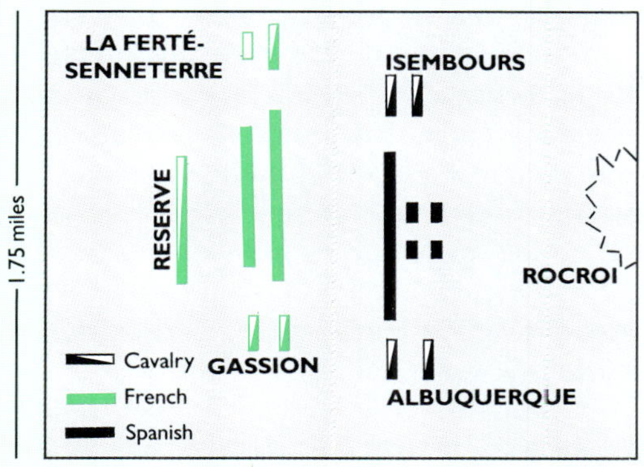

DESCRIPTION On 18 May both armies were drawn up in accordance with the conventions of the day, with the infantry in the centre and the cavalry on the flanks. The Spanish army, while larger than the French, occupied a shorter front as its infantry was massed in depth. The French had the worst of an artillery duel, sustaining 300 casualties, and the cavalry on their left wing, under La Ferté-Senneterre, attempted to ride round the Spanish right ▸

TERMS USED IN FORTIFICATION

Banquette – fire step behind a protecting parapet
Bastion – work consisting of two faces and two flanks, forming part of the main defences
Casemate – vaulted chamber within a rampart, containing an artillery port
Counterscarp – the exterior wall of a defensive ditch
Curtain – section of rampart connecting bastions
Ditch – excavation in front of ramparts; can be wet or dry
Embrasure – opening in parapet to permit artillery fire
Glacis – a clear slope on the enemy side of the ditch, covered by fire from the parapets
Parados – embankment behind a defensive position, protecting it against fire from the rear
Rampart – thick wall of earth and/or masonry forming the main defences
Ravelin – a work beyond the curtain consisting of two faces meeting in a salient, closed at the rear by the counterscarp; used to protect gates and the flanks of bastions. Sometimes called a demi-lune
Scarp – the inner wall of the ditch, leading upwards to the rampart

progression to the latter. He built over 100 fortresses and conducted some 40 sieges, some of them against fortifications of his own design. His systems of attack and defence were so precise that, given the number and type of guns employed, and the construction of the fortress, it was possible to predict with reasonable accuracy how long the latter might be capable of offering resistance. In such circumstances there was no disgrace in a garrison agreeing to march out with honour, provided it had done its utmost.

The complexities of fortification and siegecraft led to the establishment of permanent bodies of military engineers whose duties, in addition to the construction of defence works, also involved bridge- and road-building. Military engineering had barely existed in 1485, yet as a result of the gunpowder revolution it had attained the status of a science within 200 years.

CONDUCT OF OPERATIONS

Applying the new technology to the battlefield presented contemporary commanders with the sort of difficulties posed by mechanization in the inter-war years, 1919–39, in that no precedents existed and there was no experience on which to draw.

At first, even forming the battle-line was a slow and complicated process, since it required deploying pikemen and arquebusiers or musketeers to the mutual advantage of both, emplacing the artillery in the most favourable position and deciding how best the cavalry was to be employed.

The battles themselves tended to be fought with slow-motion, ritual formality, generally beginning with an artillery duel which might last an hour or two before the armies came to grips. The musketeers would fire in ranks by rotation, the pikemen would perform their cumbrous drill, culminating in the deadly "push of pike" with their opponents, and the cavalry would perform the *caracole* until one side or the other broke.

Armies were small, not simply because national populations were small, but also because they depended on agricultural economies which were labour-intensive. Living off the land was never a viable proposition, save in the very short term. Before planning a campaign, a commander therefore had to ensure that his troops could be properly fed and supplied, and for this he usually relied on civilian contractors. During the winter months, when the roads degenerated into mud wallows, armies tended to retire into billets to await better weather.

Another factor which concerned commanders during the 16th century was the composition of their armies. Although armies might be nominally French, Spanish, Dutch or Imperialist, the purely national element was comparatively small, the ranks being filled with contingents from other countries and bands of professional

1643

to relieve Rocroi, but were driven off.

Next morning d'Enghien feinted with some of his cavalry to the right and when the Spanish cavalry under the Duke of Albuquerque changed front to meet the anticipated attack he charged into its flank with the remainder of his right wing and dispersed it after an hour's hard fighting. On the French left, however, La Ferté-Senneterre was again defeated by Isembourg's Spanish cavalry which, joined by the leading *tercios*, then attacked the French infantry. The French artillery changed hands several times and was finally turned on its owners. The French began to give way but were rallied and counter-attacked with their reserve. At this point d'Enghien, having chased Albuquerque off the field, fell on the uncommitted *tercios* and routed them. The remainder of the Spaniards' army broke off their assault and began retiring slowly.

Reorganized, the French followed, led by their musketeers. Each side suffered severely from the other's fire, but d'Enghien massed his cannon against an angle of the enemy square and a final assault swept the Spanish army away.

The battle marked the replacement of Spain by France as the Continent's leading military power.

CASUALTIES French – 2,000 killed and 2,000 wounded; Spaniards – 7,500 killed, 7,000 prisoners and 6,500 missing.

RESULT Rocroi was relieved and the Spanish army was destroyed.

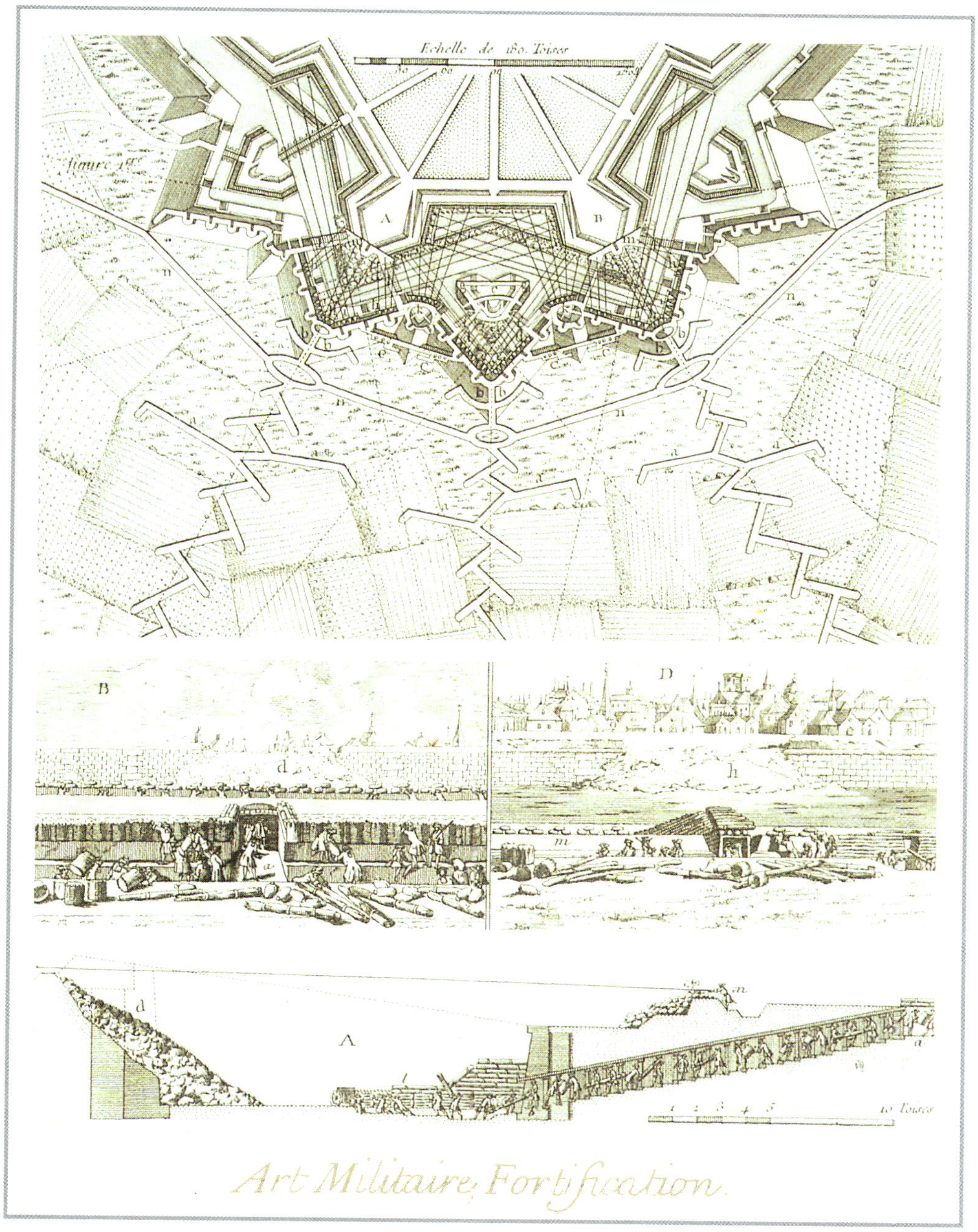

A contemporary print shows the complexities of fortification in the Vauban era. The "star system" and zig-zag "sap-and-parallel" trenches are illustrated in plan and elevation. Every approach to the defences is covered by fire from two or more sources.

1645

NASEBY

DATE 14 June 1645
CAMPAIGN First English Civil War
OBJECT The Royalist and Parliamentarian armies both sought a decisive action.
NUMBERS Royalists under King Charles I – 4,000 infantry, 5,000 cavalry and 12 guns, total 9,000; Parliamentarian New Model Army under Sir Thomas Fairfax and Oliver Cromwell – 7,000 infantry, 6,000 cavalry and 13 guns, total 13,000.

Sir Thomas Fairfax with Parliamentarian officers.

DESCRIPTION The two armies were drawn up with their infantry in the centre and their cavalry on the flanks, plus a reserve behind. The Parliamentarians also deployed a regiment of dragoons under Colonel Okey along the hedges leading to their left. The battle began with a simultaneous attack by the right-wing cavalry of both armies. Both attacks were successful, but while Prince Rupert's troopers pursued their enemy as far as the Parliamentarian wagon lines, where they were ▸

The growth of military engineering during the 17th century fostered more sophisticated surveying techniques as shown on the right. This in turn resulted in more accurate maps.

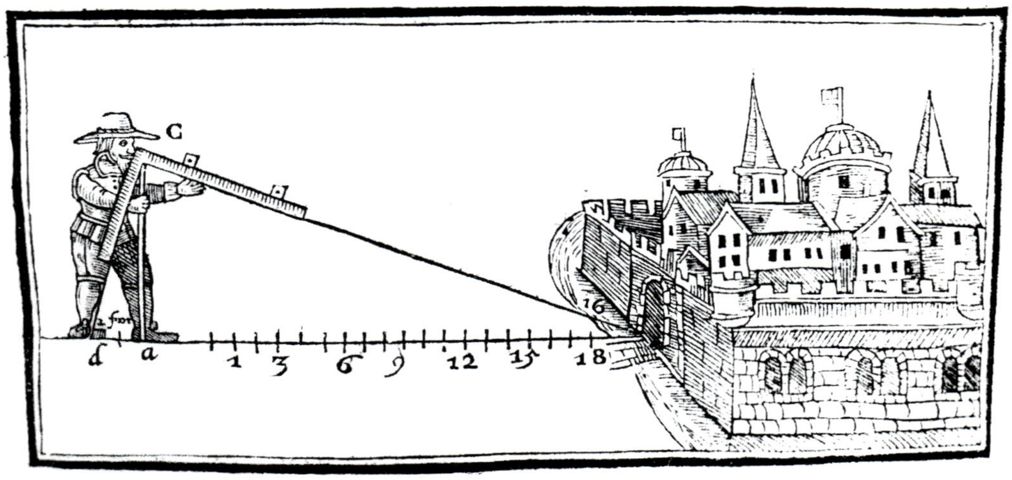

mercenaries. Some mercenaries, notably the Swiss, gave value for money, but the loyalty of others belonged to whoever paid best. The German *Landsknecht* and *Reiter* (mounted pistoleer) bands accorded a rough loyalty to their own captains, provided they could deliver pay and plunder, but acquired a reputation for brutality. Even worse were the *Condottiere*, employed by the Italian city states to fight their wars; they had no intention of becoming involved in anything as dangerous as a battle and, offered suitable incentives, would change sides at the drop of a hat.

Prominent among the military theorists of the day was Niccolò Machiavelli (1469–1527), author of *The Prince* and *The Art of War.* In many respects Machiavelli drew erroneous conclusions, notably in underestimating the effectiveness of firearms, but he condemned the mercenary system and advocated the Roman legion as a model for the infantry formations of the day, a direction in which the Spanish were already moving with their *tercios*. His intellectual heir was François de la Noue (1531–91), a Huguenot commander during the French Wars of Religion, who examined the strategic as well as the tactical aspects of warfare in his writings, the best known of which were his *Political and Military Discourses.*.

The reforms instituted by Gustavus Adolphus changed the face of the battlefield. Infantry were still deployed in the centre with cavalry on the flanks, but linear rather than columnar formations were adopted by both, a support line being formed behind the battle line. Individual units were smaller and more flexible, enabling them to be moved quickly where they were needed. This, in turn, placed greater emphasis on the role of the junior officer. Overall, the result was to accelerate the tempo at which operations were conducted.

1645

repulsed by musketeers, Cromwell exercised tighter control and after he had driven off Sir Marmeduke Langdale's Northern Horse he led his second line in an attack on the Royalist infantry which, under Lord Astley, was pushing back the Parliamentarian centre, despite its superior numbers. The chance now existed for the King to launch a decisive counter-attack into Cromwell's flank with his reserve and Langdale's rallied cavalry, but one of his supporters, believing the battle lost,

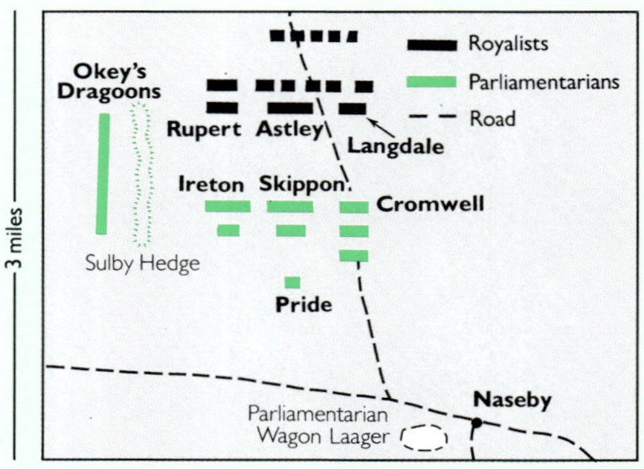

attempted to lead him away, and the reserve, subjected to misleading orders, was not committed. The critical moment passed and Okey's dragoons, which had fired a dismounted volley into the flank of Rupert's charge, now mounted their horses and joined in the attack on Astley. Most of the Royalist infantry, outnumbered and beset from three directions, surrendered, although one regiment at least fought to the bitter end. After this disaster, the remnant of the Royalist army fled, abandoning

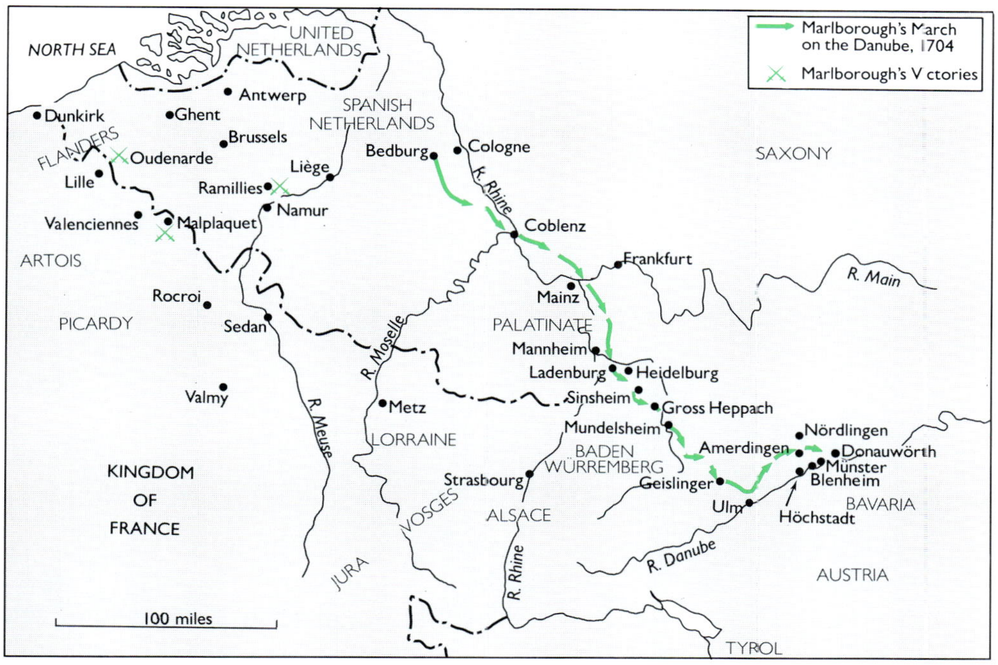

Map showing the area of Marlborough's campaigns. His great strategic march of 1704 was a masterpiece of planning and deception. The French were at first convinced that he intended advancing up the Moselle, then that he planned an invasion of Alsace, whereas his real intention was to effect a junction with Eugène's Imperial army and break the deadlock on the Danube front. This he succeeded in doing at Blenheim.

War had now become a matter for professionals, at every level, with officers and men alike needing to be trained in tactics and the most efficient use of weapons. By the latter half of the 17th century the concept of the nation state was firmly established and national standing armies were formed, providing regular pay, arms, uniforms and rations under the proprietary system, in which colonels were paid a sum of money by the central government to raise and equip their regiments and maintain them year by year. Officers purchased their commissions, which could be sold again, as could the proprietary interest itself. By and large, the system worked well enough in its time, although it was open to abuse. The need for foreign mercenaries was thus largely removed although, for internal security reasons, the reliable Swiss were still recruited by several monarchs for their personal guards, including the Papal Swiss Guard, which still exists. The internal efficiency of armies was improved by such matters as ordnance, engineering and procurement being administered centrally, and the establishment of permanent supply depots enabled greater numbers of troops to be maintained in the field.

It was under Marlborough (see feature pages 104-5) that the two centuries of painful transition from medieval to unmechanized modern warfare were consoli-

1704

its guns and baggage train.

CASUALTIES Royalists – about 6,000 including numerous prisoners; Parliamentarians – estimated at less than 1,000.

RESULT The battle effectively destroyed the Royalist cause in the Midlands. The north had been lost to the Crown the previous year at Marston Moor and after Naseby the few troops remaining to the King in the south and west were unable to halt the advance of the Parliamentary army.

BLENHEIM

DATE 13 August 1704

CAMPAIGN War of the Spanish Succession, Danube campaign of 1704

OBJECT The Duke of Marlborough and Prince Eugène of Savoy, commanding the Allied army, forced the battle on the Franco-Bavarian army under Marshal Tallard in order to break the strategic impasse on the Danube front.

NUMBERS Allies – 65 infantry battalions, 160 cavalry squadrons, 60 guns, total strength 52,000; Franco-Bavarians – 79 infantry battalions, 140 cavalry squadrons, 90 guns, total strength 56,000.

DESCRIPTION The early morning approach of the Allied army achieved complete tactical surprise, although this could not be fully exploited because Eugène's Imperial troops had a longer and more difficult route than Marlborough's British contingent. Tallard's flanks were protected by the Danube on the right and wooded hills on ▶

The British 16th Regiment of Foot advancing against the heavily fortified village of Blenheim. The French were forced to commit their reserves to contain the British assault, at the expense of their vulnerable centre. Heavy fighting continued around the village throughout the day and, whe the rest of the Franco-Bavarian army was defeated, the garrison surrendered that night.

dated. For infantry and artillery, the emphasis was on firepower, and for cavalry it was on shock action. The brigade, consisting of two or more regiments, became the tactical unit. Gone was the old formal array, replaced by a more flexible system of battle in which infantry, artillery and cavalry were deployed according to the terrain and the commander's intentions. The pattern was set for the next 150 years, and it is probably fair to say that an infantryman who fought at Blenheim, suddenly transported to a Crimean War battlefield, might well have regarded the artillery's mobility with wonder, but in other respects would have understood everything that was going on around him; indeed, he would have been able to take his place in the firing line, armed with a musket which differed little from his own.

NAVAL WARFARE

At the end of the 15th century the most important class of naval vessel in the Mediterranean was the galley, the basic design of which had not altered since classical times. Fitted with lateen sails for normal cruising, in action the vessel was propelled by banks of oars manned by criminals or prisoners of war who were chained to their benches. Galleys might attempt to sink or disable their opponents by ramming, but they also carried a large number of soldiers and their normal tactics were to board

1704

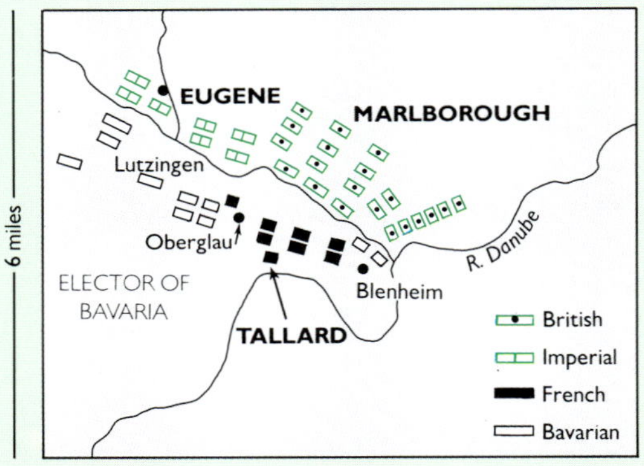

the left, and most of his infantry was positioned in three villages along his front – Blenheim (Blindheim) on the right, Oberglau in the left-centre and Lutzingen on the left. Marlborough noticed that the Franco-Bavarian centre, between Blenheim and Oberglau, was held by lightly supported cavalry and that between the French lines and the Nebel stream was a large area of undefended watermeadows. He therefore decided to mask the villages while his principal attack tore open the enemy centre, cutting the Franco-Bavarian army in two.

Marlborough and Eugène advanced simultaneously at 12.30pm. At Blenheim the attack by Lord Cutts' British battalions failed to break through the defences, but caused such concern that Tallard sent his reserve there, so that 21 battalions were penned uselessly in the village by a much smaller force. At Oberglau the spirited resistance of the garrison almost defeated the Allied attack force but Marlborough

after an exchange of missiles, which often included incendiary devices. In rougher Atlantic and northern waters, to which such narrow-hulled vessels were unsuited, the principal warship was the square-rigged carrack, with a beam approximately half its overall length, fitted with high fighting platforms known as castles fore and aft. These were manned by archers and men-at-arms whose task was to capture the enemy vessel by boarding. Engagements at sea, which rarely took place beyond the sight of land, were therefore simply land battles afloat in which the most important participants were the soldiers rather than the seamen.

This changed very rapidly with the advent of cannon and the growth of national exchequers which permitted a revolution in warship design. The galley, its narrow beam occupied by oarsmen, could only mount a few light guns forward, and was unable to adapt further. The carrack, on the other hand, was very suitable for employment as a gun platform, particularly after the hinged port was invented about the beginning of the 16th century, as this enabled cannon to be mounted broadside in tiers within the hull. Thereafter, warship design followed two schools of thought. The first envisaged the vessel as a floating fortress which employed her guns as a

The Battle of Lepanto was the last major decisive action fought between fleets of galleys. Although cannon were used extensively by both sides, the issue was decided by ramming and hand-to-hand fighting on the enemy's decks.

pushed reinforcements into the fight and by 3pm the village was contained. On the Allied right Eugène pinned down the Elector of Bavaria's troops in Lutzingen.

Meanwhile, in the centre, British troops were fording the Nebel and forming up on the meadows beyond. Suddenly aware of the danger, Tallard ordered his cavalry to charge them and for a while the issue was in doubt. It was resolved when Marlborough personally brought up a brigade of cuirassiers which Eugène had made available, defeating the counter-attack. The British infantry and cavalry then advanced and by 5.30pm had smashed through the weak French centre. Tallard was captured and the Elector of Bavaria withdrew, pursued by Eugène. At 11pm the French garrison in Blenheim surrendered.

CASUALTIES Allies – 12,000 killed and wounded; Franco-Bavarians – 20,000 killed and wounded, 14,000 captured, 6,000 desertions and 60 guns lost.

RESULT Two-thirds of the Franco-Bavarian army were destroyed, the French threat to Vienna was removed and the Allies over-ran Bavaria. The battle raised the reputation of British infantry to a level which had not been attained since the days of the longbow.

preparation for boarding and was adopted mainly but not exclusively by the Spanish. The result was the galleon, distinguished by its towering aftercastle, and such Great Ships as Henry VIII's *Henry Grâce à Dieu* of 1514, displacing over 1,000 tons and armed with 151 light and heavy guns. The second, supported by such great Elizabethan seamen as Sir John Hawkins, Sir Francis Drake and Sir Walter Raleigh, saw the warship as a weapon system complete in itself, capable of disabling and sinking its opponents with its own gunfire. To this end, slimmer vessels with trim lines and a more scientific sail plan were produced, their better sailing qualities enabling them to fight at ranges of their own choosing. When, during the defeat of the Spanish Armada (see page 98), the two concepts clashed, the latter emerged the undisputed victor and evolved into the ship-of-the-line, the design of which remained essentially unchanged until the advent of steam propulsion, armour plate and turret guns in the 19th century.

The technical problems facing the designers of the new warships were formidable. Because of the great weight of the guns carried, coupled with soaring top hamper, the need to preserve a low centre of gravity was essential, particularly in heavy weather or strong beam winds. Failure to recognize this led to the sinking of the *Mary Rose* (1545) and the loss of the Swedish *Vasa* in Stockholm harbour in 1629. Gunpowder itself posed a terrible hazard to wooden ships; in 1512, off Brest, the English *Regent*, close-grappled with the French *Marie la Cordelière*, was burnt out when the latter's magazine exploded.

At first gun mountings were fixed, the weapon's recoil being contained by a stout timber baulk or heavy ropes. This system produced difficulties in handling sponge and rammer staves and for this reason more primitive breech-loaders were to be found at sea than in land warfare; unfortunately, the back-blast of gases made them inefficient and dangerous and this area of development was abandoned for 300 years. By the middle of the 16th century it had been decided to let the recoil forces work for the gun crew. Guns were mounted on small four-wheeled trucks which rolled inboard on recoil, producing sufficient room in which to sponge, re-load and ram, and were then run out by means of tackles.

Meanwhile, the galley continued to soldier on. On 7 October 1571 a fleet of Christian galleys commanded by Don John of Austria inflicted a crushing defeat on a similar Turkish fleet off Lepanto. During this, the most decisive galley action since Salamis, ships were sunk by gunfire for the first time. It was, however, generally realized that flimsy galleys were no match for the new warships, save in the rare circumstances where the latter were completely becalmed, enabling the galleys to stand off their vulnerable quarters and pound them at will. Despite this, enthusiasts produced a larger intermediate design known as the galleass, combining oars with

1709

PULTAVA

DATE 28 June 1709
CAMPAIGN Great Northern War
OBJECT The Swedes, under Charles XII, were besieging Pultava; this battle was an attempt to defeat a Russian army under Peter the Great which was marching to Pultava's relief.
NUMBERS Swedes – 18 infantry battalions, 12 cavalry squadrons and a few guns, total 17,000; Russians – 30 infantry battalions, 30 cavalry squadrons and 40 guns, total 80,000.
DESCRIPTION As Peter approached Pultava, he established himself in an entrenched camp covered by a series of advanced redoubts. Charles, short of supplies and ammunition, wished to secure a quick victory and launched a night attack which was intended to pass between the redoubts and then assault the Russian camp. Unfortunately, he had been wounded in the foot some days earlier and was unable to exer-

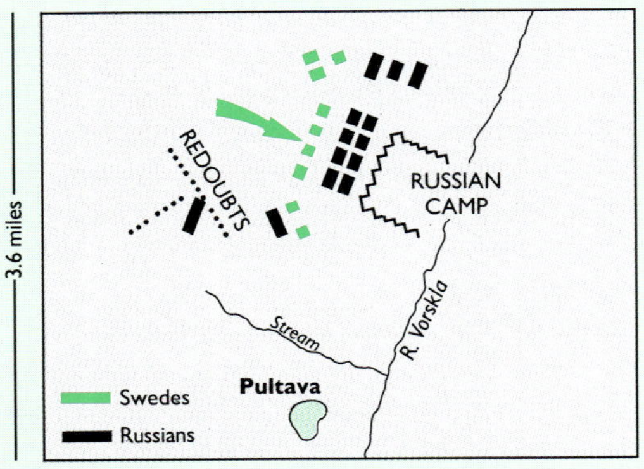

sail and mounting broadside guns. Most navies showed some interest in the idea, but by 1600 it was clear that the galleass could not be regarded as a first-line warship since the concept was inherently flawed. On the one hand, heavy guns could only be mounted deep in the hull, so that the oars had to be shipped when they opened fire, thereby reducing the vessel's speed and manoeuvrability; on the other, lighter guns could be mounted above the oars, but this reduced the weight of metal that could be thrown. The galley itself continued to serve in the Mediterranean and, later, in the Baltic, until the 19th century.

By 1600 the nature of sea power had become clearly apparent. It could be used to prey on an enemy's mercantile interests, as England regularly did against Spain's, using warships or privateers, which were privately fitted out vessels given official status by letters of marque, or it could be used to blockade the enemy's home ports, or to mount heavy and destructive raids. The naval aspects of the English Civil War introduced a new element, namely the often-disputed right of maritime powers to intercept neutral vessels trading with the enemy.

The three Anglo-Dutch wars fought between 1652 and 1673 stemmed from trade rivalry and were fought entirely at sea, producing the first major fleet actions since the Armada. They set the pattern of naval warfare for the next 150 years, for whereas fleets had formerly approached each other in line abreast, they now did so in line ahead, a formation which enabled their commanders to exercise the maximum possible control. To increase efficiency, the English produced a system of pre-arranged tactical manoeuvres which could be signalled by fleet commanders. Known as the *Fighting Instructions*, they first appeared in 1653 and, with appropriate modifications, remained in use in Britain for two centuries; although intended as a guide, some commanders chose to interpret them as strict rules, with the result that individual captains were often unable to exercise their own initiative when favourable opportunities presented themselves. Before an engagement commenced, both sides sought to put themselves up-wind of the enemy, which gave them freedom to manoeuvre as they wished. Whenever possible, the English sought to break the enemy's battle line, separating his ships into small groups which could be overwhelmed in turn.

The period which had begun with seamen possessing little or no status in warfare therefore witnessed such radical change that by its end standing navies and their supporting services were firmly established as instruments of national policy. From 1688 onwards the United Kingdom and France were to be at war, more or less continuously, for the next 128 years, during which the Royal Navy achieved an ascendancy at sea that was seldom lost and was not seriously challenged until the 20th century.

Another view of the British assault on the village of Blenheim, seen from the right flank. The troops in the left foreground are grenadiers, identified by their mitre caps. It was customary for the grenadier companies of individual regiments to be brigaded together as assault troops during this kind of operation.

1709

cise effective control of the battle from his litter. Thus, while his centre and left columns succeeded in passing through the redoubts at dawn and repulsing a covering force of cavalry beyond, that on the right fell behind when, contrary to his intentions, it became embroiled in a fight for the redoubts themselves. Spotting its isolation, Peter despatched a force of 10,000 men which quickly surrounded and eliminated it. The rest of the Swedish army reformed after a period of time-consuming wrangling among its commanders, and its infantry launched a series of attacks on the entrenchments. Despite the gallantry with which these were pressed, they were shot to pieces by superior Russian firepower. By the end of the day the Swedish infantry had virtually ceased to exist. The Swedish cavalry managed to leave the field but was overtaken and surrendered two days after the battle. Charles escaped into Turkish territory.

CASUALTIES Swedes – 7,000 killed and 2,600 captured; Russians – 1,300 killed and wounded.

RESULT A decisive victory for Peter which destroyed Swedish domination and established Russia as a European power. Although the war continued until 1721, Sweden was simultaneously beset by Russia and her Baltic allies and forced onto the strategic defensive. Peter himself commented that the foundation stone of St Petersburg was laid at Pultava.

FROM FLOATING FORTRESS TO SHIP-OF-THE-LINE

(Above) Henry VIII as a young man. Henry was keenly interested in military developments, and he placed the Navy on a sound footing which his daughter, Elizabeth I, used to good effect in establishing English sea-power.

THE RECOVERY OF the *Mary Rose* off the coast of southern England in 1982 was one of the most important marine archaeological operations ever: it led to the preservation of a ship which is a vital link between the converted merchantmen of the medieval era and the ships-of-the-line of the ensuing three centuries.

Built under Henry VIII in 1509–10, she was designed as a floating fortress that would first batter her enemies and then send over soldiers to board. A four-masted carrack with orlop, main and upper decks, she had fore- and sterncastles and fighting tops on each mast. She was square-rigged on the fore and main masts with lateens on the mizzen and bonaventure. Her displacement (700 tons) was given in "tuns burthen", a contemporary measure of cubic capacity. Her armament when launched consisted of 43 guns and 37 anti-personnel weapons.

In 1536 *Mary Rose* was extensively refitted. Compromises had to be made between the ship designers' ideas and those of her users – soldiers. Her fore- and sterncastles may have been raised and the armament was increased, leading to a larger ship's crew of 415.

Her trim was dangerously affected by these alterations. Shortly before she sailed to do battle with the French off the Isle of Wight on 19 July 1545, her crew was swelled by a further 300 soldiers, most of whom were placed on the upper decks, above her centre of gravity. The fleet left harbour in a light breeze but this freshened as the *Mary Rose* entered the Solent: she heeled over to starboard, water poured in through the open lower gunports, and she sank like a stone.

Sovereign of the Seas was the pride of Charles I's navy. She was launched in 1637 and cost £66,000, raised through the hated Ship Money tax. Characteristic of a ship-of-the-line (a warship designed to fight in the line of battle) her primary weapons were her guns, boarding being seen as secondary. *Sovereign of the Seas* was then the largest ship in the world, displacing 1,700 tons and the first to carry 100 guns. She served as the prototype for every British ship-of-the-line till 1860.

She had three gun decks flush throughout the hull, with extra guns on the beak, forecastle, half- and quarter-deck; gun crews on the upper decks were protected from falling debris by stout gratings. The upperworks of the hull were ornamented with gilded decoration known as gingerbread-work. Her sail plan was unique, including royal sails above the fore and main topgallants and a topgallant on the mizzen. In 1651 she was refitted by Peter Pett, the son of Phineas, her designer. Her forecastle and after superstructure were lowered to improve her weatherliness. In 1660 she was renamed *Royal Sovereign* in honour of the Restoration.

The *Victory* best embodies the concept first expressed by naval designers in the *Sovereign*. Appropriately, she is preserved within a short distance of the *Mary Rose* at Portsmouth.

(Left) The Sovereign of the Seas *was the largest ship in the world when she was launched in 1637, and possessed a sail plan a century ahead of her time. In 1660, following the restoration of the monarchy, she was renamed* Royal Sovereign.

(Above) The Mary Rose *as she might have appeared after she had been refitted. Her centre of gravity was dangerously high: note the contrast between the great bulk of the hull and superstructure above the water line and the small proportion of the hull below it.*

(Below) This manuscript illustration shows the Mary Rose *in full sail, after the refit. The principal flags flown are the Royal Standard, the St George's Cross of England, and pennants in the Tudor colours of green and white.*

8

THE BIRTH OF MODERN WAR

THE CENTURY which followed the end of the War of the Spanish Succession witnessed many important developments in military science, saw the emergence of a number of characteristics which might be ascribed to modern warfare and produced several of the greatest military commanders in history.

Certain factors remained constant for the first three quarters of this century. Until the beginning of the Industrial Revolution in the later part of the 18th century, economies were based largely upon agriculture, which was so labour-intensive that it was impossible to divert large numbers of workers into military pursuits without affecting radically the capability of a state to feed itself; thus armies remained small, and were drawn from the least productive members of society. This necessitated the imposition of the strictest discipline to control what the British Secretary at War in 1795 termed "men of a very low description", and led to the employment of mercenaries. These reinforced the fact that as wars were fought for the dynastic or personal motives of the monarchs who controlled the states, there was little overt "nationalism" beyond a personal loyalty to the monarch.

The conduct of wars was determined both by practicality and by ethical considerations. It is easy to overstate the latter, but the concept of limited war arising from the philosophy of enlightenment had an effect. (However, it is interesting to note that the most intellectually minded of the great captains, Frederick II of Prussia, whilst probably considering himself the model of the philosopher-king, was capable of a degree of ruthlessness which hardly accorded with his love of music, literature and philosophy.) Some elements of 18th-century warfare which corresponded to the theories of enlightenment were adopted for reasons of practicality. For example, in general armies were not allowed to subsist by foraging off the countryside but were dependent upon the provisions held by supply depots and magazines; not intentionally to protect the civilian population, but because the agricultural economies could not support such ravaging, and armies not support the indiscipline

1757

PLASSEY

DATE 23 June 1757
CAMPAIGN Anglo-French War in India
OBJECT The battle of Plassey arose out of Anglo-French rivalry in India, both nations endeavouring to exploit the riches of the subcontinent. The Nawab (prince) of Bengal, Siraj-ud-dowlah, with French assistance, opposed the operations of the British East India Company. In response to his temporary capture of the British base of Calcutta, the young British general Robert Clive (1725–74) marched against the Nawab who was encamped by a bend in the Bhagrathi river, at Plassey.
NUMBERS Clive's force comprised 10 small guns and 3,000 men, including only about 700 Europeans. Siraj-ud-dowlah had about 50,000 men and 53 heavy guns; but one of his generals, Mir Jafar, had been intriguing with Clive against the Nawab.
DESCRIPTION On 23 June Clive assembled his little army before the Nawab's camp,

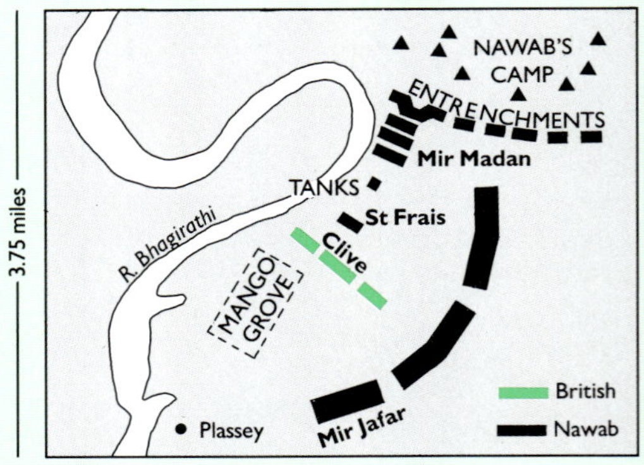

which would have resulted. (This is not to imply that civilians did not suffer: the passage of an army frequently brought with it violence and desolation.) Whilst enlightenment might suggest that the expending of human life was unjustified unless a specific goal was in view, it also made financial sense, in that trained soldiers were so valuable that they should not be hazarded unless an action had a reasonable chance of success. Such quasi-ethical considerations extended throughout the period; as late as the Napoleonic Wars a considerable body of opinion held that killing the enemy was unjustified unless a specific object could be attained by it.

In the first half of the 18th century there were few technological innovations in military weaponry; the musket remained basically unchanged to the end of the Napoleonic Wars, once the more substantial iron ramrod and socket-bayonet had been introduced at the beginning of the century, the latter allowing the musket to fire whilst the bayonet was fixed and thus finally dispensing with the pike as a means of defence. Armies remained small, professional and drilled to fight in rigid lines, with manoeuvre in action generally slow and limited. Few organizational developments were made, though the French Marshal Maurice de Saxe (1696–1750) experimented with legions composed of all arms (infantry, cavalry and artillery), which adumbrated the later concept of *corps d'armée* in producing autonomous formations capable of acting without support. Although Saxe was the finest general since Marlborough and Eugène of Savoy, his greatest influence was only felt after his death with the publication of his book *Mes Rêveries*, which was still being quoted as a manual even after the Napoleonic Wars.

THE AGE OF FREDERICK THE GREAT

The dominant character of the middle of the 18th century was Frederick II of Prussia (1713–86), "the Great". An immense influence upon military theory and one of the greatest generals of all time, he enjoyed two distinct advantages over many of his rivals: as a sovereign prince he was free of any strictures imposed by a superintending monarch or government; and he inherited from his father an extremely professional army and a state which was both prosperous and totally subservient, with a proficient internal organization which allowed his wishes to be enacted with a minimum of difficulty.

Prussia first became an influential state in northern Europe under Frederick William of Brandenburg (1620–88), "the Great Elector", whose financial reforms and creation of a professional army laid the foundations for the reforms of his grandson Frederick William I who moulded a state which was ultimately both prosperous and strong, and possessed of the finest army in Europe. He did not, however, commit this army to war; it was left to his son, Frederick II, who succeeded

1757

but retired to the cover of mango groves when the Nawab's artillery opened fire, Clive's light guns being unable to reply effectually, except to mortally wound Mir Madan, a general loyal to the Nawab. When a rainstorm soaked their gunpowder, the Nawab's forces began to retire; Clive advanced, driving back the Nawab's small French contingent under St Frais. Mir Jafar remained uncommitted, allowing Clive to storm the camp. Siraj-ud-dowlah fled and was murdered shortly after, to be replaced as ruler by Mir Jafar.

CASUALTIES The Nawab lost some 500 men, Clive lost 65.

RESULT The action was small but its effect was immense, opening India to Britain, and demonstrating that small bands of disciplined Europeans, resolutely commanded, could defeat huge native forces.

ROSSBACH

DATE 5 November 1757

CAMPAIGN Seven Years War

OBJECT Frederick the Great of Prussia was attempting to counter the advance through Prussian Saxony of the combined Franco–Austrian army of Prince Joseph of Saxe-Hildburghausen (Austrian) and Charles, Duke of Soubise (French).

NUMBERS Prussian – 21,000; Allies – 41,000. ▸

The Battle of Fontenoy (10 May 1745), shown in this painting by Pierre Lenfant, was a major combat during the Second Silesian War. Advancing into Flanders, the French army of Marshal Maurice de Saxe was opposed by an Allied army of British, Austrian, Dutch and Hanoverian contingents commanded by William Augustus, Duke of Cumberland. Despite heroic efforts by the British and Hanoverian troops, Cumberland was defeated, but withdrew in good order.

to the throne in 1740, to prove that the Prussian army was capable not only of automaton-like drill on the parade-ground but equally of stoic performance on the battlefield. Frederick's first campaign arose out of the conflict over the rights of succession to the Holy Roman Empire following the death of the Emperor Charles VI. Having no male heir, Charles decreed that his successor should be his daughter, Maria Theresa; this was disputed by other claimants, the Elector of Bavaria, Philip V of Spain and Augustus III of Saxony. In November 1740, six months after succeeding to the throne of Prussia, Frederick declared that he would support Maria Theresa's claim, but that in return for this unrequested aid he would occupy Silesia, pending the settlement of an old Brandenburg claim to this province of the Empire. On 16 December 1740 he invaded, precipitating the First Silesian War, which in turn led to the War of the Austrian Succession.

In the early part of 1741 Frederick consolidated his grip on Silesia, but in the spring an Austrian army moved to reoccupy the province and engaged Frederick on 10 April at Mollwitz. Early Prussian reverses caused Frederick to quit the field, only to return upon receiving news that the magnificent Prussian infantry had held firm and driven the Austrians from the field. In the aftermath of this, Frederick's first victory, the war expanded with Bavaria, France, Saxony and Savoy opposing Austria, whilst Britain and Holland supported Maria Theresa. Following another Prussian victory at Chotusitz (17 May 1742) Austria ceded Silesia to Prussia, which caused Frederick temporarily to leave the conflict.

Austrian fortunes improved in the following year, with George II of Britain winning a considerable victory with his Anglo-Allied-Hanoverian army against a French force at Dettingen (27 June 1743), thanks largely to the discipline and spirit of the British and Hanoverian infantry. Similar successes for the Austrian camp led Frederick to re-enter the war in August 1744, initiating the Second Silesian War. This finally turned the balance against Austria. Following Saxe's victory over an Anglo-Allied army at Fontenoy (10 May 1745), which resulted in the French conquest of Austrian Flanders, Frederick shattered an Austrian army at Hohenfriedberg (4 June 1745), and further Prussian victories (notably at Sohr, 30 September 1745) led Maria Theresa to confirm Frederick's possession of Silesia by the Treaty of Dresden (25 December 1745). Although campaigning continued in the Netherlands until 1747, to all intents the War of the Austrian Succession was ended, and hostilities were closed officially by the Treaty of Aix-la-Chapelle in October 1748.

THE ART OF WAR IN MID-CENTURY

Frederick's creative urge produced not only an outpouring of musical and literary work, but also two military treatises of immense significance, his *Military Instructions*

1757

DESCRIPTION The Allied army formed a column of march, preceded by a strong advance guard, to execute a wide turning movement against Frederick's left flank. They intended to defeat Frederick by using his own tactics against him, by massing against one of his flanks; but they neglected reconnaissance, and so laid themselves open to a counter-attack. Observing this, Frederick hastily broke camp, convincing the Allies that he was in retreat and causing them to press on more

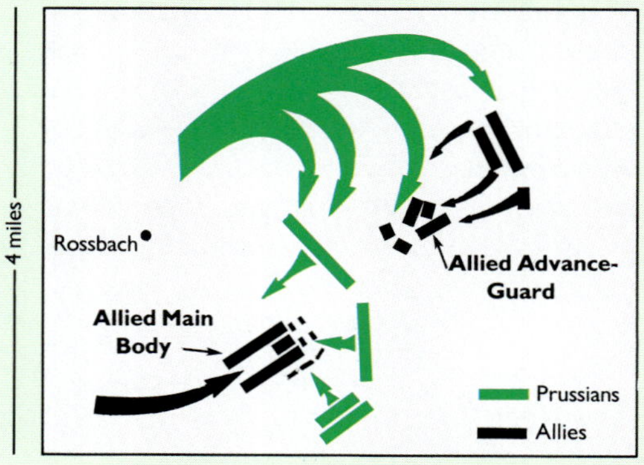

hurriedly. In fact, he was about to outflank the Franco-Austrians. His cavalry (commanded by his young general Friedrich Wilhelm von Seydlitz) advanced unseen and destroyed the Allied advance guard, while the Prussian infantry advanced in echelon to engage the head of the main body. Rallying his troopers, Seydlitz swung around to the right flank of the Allied column; as Frederick's artillery (a battery of 18 guns) devastated the head of the column, seven Prussian infantry

to generals of infantry and cavalry (1748). Initially secret documents, they were soon published and translated, and were of such great importance that even after the supersession of "Frederickian" methods by those of the Napoleonic era, they remained important references; a new edition was published in Britain as late as 1818. The *Instructions* contain much (though not all) of Frederick's military thought and, as befitted an enlightened monarch, emphasized the merits of limited war: "terminate every business prudently and quickly ... it is better one man perish than a whole people"; "To shed the blood of soldiers when there is no occasion for it, is to lead them inhumanly to the slaughter." The cornerstone of Frederick's military system was the rigid discipline and precise drill which became synonymous with his army, which was necessary to hold its members in the ranks and discourage desertion.

Contrasting with the somewhat sterile characteristics of conventional tactics, where linear formations dominated and which relied upon slow-moving advances and measured volley-fire, Frederick practised offensive actions of manoeuvre. By emphasizing that wars were decided by success in battle, he made a conscious effort to defeat his enemies in the open field, thus hastening the demise of fortress warfare which had enjoyed prominence in the preceding era. Frederick's most important development was the so-called "oblique order", adopted to counteract the disadvantage of the disparity in numbers under which the Prussian army often fought, and to utilize the discipline and ability to manoeuvre of the superb Prussian infantry. Instead of engaging an enemy along the entire length of his line as in conventional tactics, the oblique order involved Prussian units advancing in echelon against one of the enemy's flanks, so that a portion of the enemy force would be outnumbered and defeated before the remainder could assist. Frederick reasserted the importance of the shock effect in cavalry tactics, and although the earlier practice of intermingling infantry and cavalry was still employed by the French as late as Minden (1759), in general Frederick's lead was followed, and cavalry employed in concentration, their principal tactic being the charge with the sword. There was also a development in the classification of cavalry into heavy regiments used primarily for such shock action, and light regiments, epitomized by Frederick's hussars, with the additional skills of skirmishing, reconnaissance and raiding. Frederick devised the first truly mobile horse artillery, able to keep pace with and provide fire-support for cavalry. Most significant was Frederick's recognition of the importance of supplies. As a consequence, he paid great attention to the provision of supplies for his own troops and to the disruption of his enemies' lines of communication.

A development of this period not influenced by Frederick was the increase of light infantry, troops skilled in skirmishing, scouting and operating in "open order", i.e.

Frederick the Great's infantry was the mainstay of his army, and became the model for the armies of Europe. The regiment of Prussian infantry numbered as the 6th (shown here, c. 1759) was Frederick's Guard regiment, and composed entirely of grenadiers. All Prussian infantry wore blue uniforms, but the metal-fronted mitre cap was a unique distinction of the élite status of grenadiers.

1757

battalions poured in a most destructive fire, and the rout was completed in a few moments when Seydlitz charged them in the flank.

CASUALTIES Allied – approximately 8,000–10,000, casualties and prisoners; Prussians – 165 killed and 376 wounded.

RESULT Rossbach was a victory which established the reputation of Frederick the Great and his Prussian army, which had comprehensively defeated an enemy army twice its size.

LEUTHEN

DATE 6 December 1757

CAMPAIGN Seven Years War

OBJECT Frederick the Great of Prussia was advancing in Silesia to repel an Austrian force commanded by Prince Charles of Lorraine.

NUMBERS Austrians – approximately 65,000; Frederick – 35,000 of his magnificently-disciplined Prussian troops.

DESCRIPTION The Austrian army occupied a position about four miles long near the town of Leuthen, with their reserves strengthening their left wing in anticipation of a Prussian flanking movement. Largely concealed by low hills, Frederick formed his main body into four columns, advancing towards the Austrian line and inclining to his right, while his advance guard continued to move forward in a diversionary movement against the Austrian right. Imagining that this presaged the main attack, the Austrian ▸

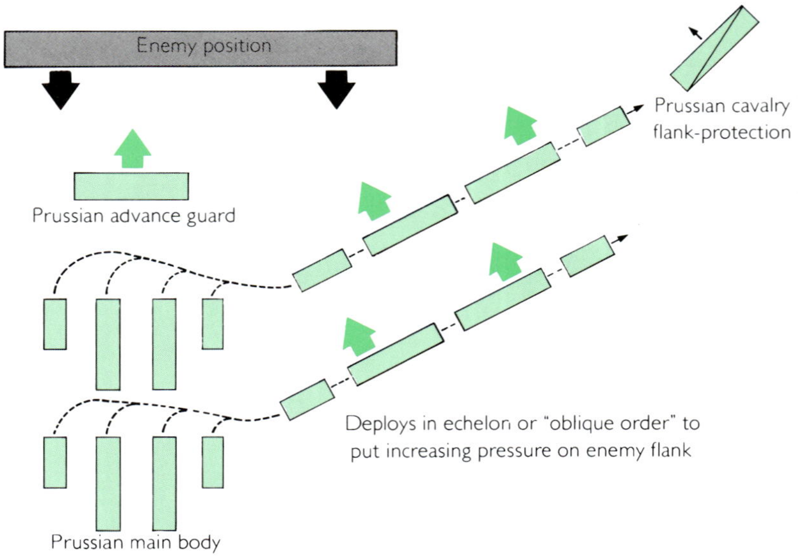

FREDERICK THE GREAT'S "OBLIQUE ORDER"

The "oblique order" of attack was one of the most important of Frederick the Great's developments. It required an army which was well disciplined and capable of executing manoeuvres under the most difficult of conditions. Initially, the army advanced towards the enemy line behind a strong advance-guard, which engaged or occupied the attention of the enemy army; ideally, the manoeuvres of the Prussians would also be screened from view by features of the terrain. The Prussian main body then deployed in echelon or "oblique order", to engage the enemy flank, upon which increasing pressure was put as each successive unit came into action. The enemy's flank would buckle; the Prussian cavalry stationed to protect the oblique attack could then exploit any collapse of the enemy's position.

not in the rigid line-of-battle; the most effective light infantry at this period were those maintained by Austria, mostly "irregulars" recruited from the Hungarian borders and using their indigenous skills of scouting and woodcraft. Although the Prussian army maintained some such units, Frederick never liked them, maintaining the belief that there was something faintly dishonourable about the tactics of such troops.

THE SEVEN YEARS WAR

The war which began in 1756 utlimately raised Frederick to a position of pre-eminence, but in the course of making his military reputation unassailable he almost destroyed his kingdom. Such were the demands made upon the Prussian state in repelling the coalition against Frederick that not even his genius could have saved the day had it not been for the superb quality of the troops he led: the campaigns proved the validity of what he had written in his *Instructions*, that "with troops like these the world itself might be subdued ..."

The Seven Years War arose principally from the perceived threat of a militant Prussia, to which end Austria allied with France, Russia and others; Frederick's only

1757

reserves were switched to that flank. As the marching Prussian columns (concealed by low hills) overlapped the Austrian left, Frederick switched them into two lines and attacked the Austrian flank, the pressure growing as successive battalions came into action. Seconded by artillery and the Prussian right-wing cavalry, the "oblique order" forced back the Austrian flank, and despite an effort to form a new defensive position the Austrian line was rolled up, their attempt to threaten Frederick's left

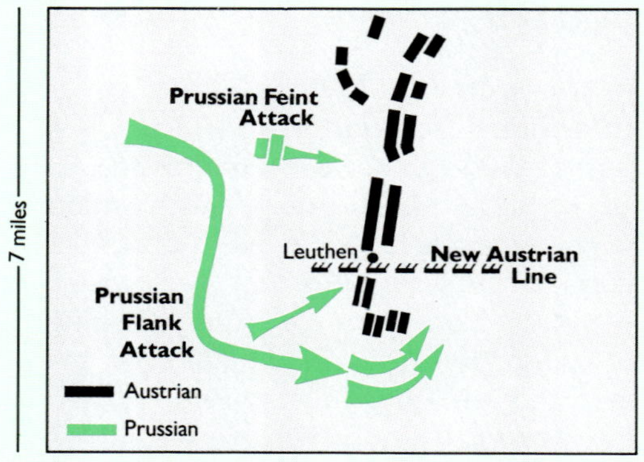

meeting with defeat. The Austrians were routed. Napoloen regarded Leuthen as a masterpiece of manoeuvre.

CASUALTIES Austrians – about 22,000; Prussians – about 6,000.

RESULT It was the greatest victory of the era and one which alone would have established Frederick as among the greatest generals in history.

ally was Britain, whose financial aid was essential. Seeing the threat of a coalition against him, Frederick invaded Saxony in late August 1756, that state falling into his possession after his defeat of an Austrian army at Lobositz (1 October 1756). Frederick temporarily occupied part of Bohemia, defeating the Austrians at Prague (6 May 1757) before having to evacuate Bohemia after a repulse at Kolin (18 June 1757). In the second half of 1757 Frederick was forced on to the defensive in the face of invasions by Austrian, French and Russian armies; from necessity, he was forced to revert to a reliance upon fortifications instead of the pure offence of his earlier career, perhaps demonstrating that, despite his tactical innovations, he was more a perfecter of accepted methods of war. He was aided greatly by his ability to use interior lines of defence (i.e. by operating in a more restricted area than the opponents who surrounded him, his lines of communication were shorter and he was able to concentrate at different points more quickly than his enemies). Although the Prussian army had increased from 80,000 in 1740 to almost double that number by the early 1760s, the multiplicity of threats against Frederick meant that his resources had to be divided widely, and thus his field army was generally greatly inferior to that of his opponents: 21,000 against 64,000 at Rossbach, 35,000 against 65,000 at Leuthen, for example. Such disparity makes his eventual success the more amazing, and confirms that he was a military genius.

As the Allies converged on Berlin, Frederick won two victories of immense significance: Rossbach (5 November 1757, against a combined Franco-Austrian army – see page 119) and Leuthen (6 December – see page 121). Having repelled this threat, Frederick had a brief respite until the middle of the following year, when he was again assailed, by Austrian and Russian armies. The two main actions of 1758 (Zorndorf, 25 August, against the Russians) and Hochkirch (14 October, against the Austrians) were inconclusive slaughters, but served to secure Frederick's position for a further year. 1759 saw one major success for Frederick's camp when Prince Ferdinand of Brunswick with an Anglo-Prussian army defeated a French army of twice their strength at Minden (1 August), another triumph for the resolute British infantry; but in other respects it was a bad year for Frederick, when his offensive against an Austro-Russian army broke down at Kunersdorf (12 August), a defeat which cost him over a third of his army.

In 1760 Frederick continued his desperate attempts to defend himself against overwhelming odds, outmanoeuvring his opponents and defeating an Austrian army at Liegnitz (15 August) and just winning a desperate action at Torgau (3 November) when his original offensive miscarried. By the end of 1761 Frederick was on the verge of defeat, able to assemble only about 60,000 troops in the face of overwhelming odds. His sustained resistance was almost in vain, until the death of

Continued on page 126

LIGHT INFANTRY

Originating in the middle of the 18th century, most notably in Austrian service and in the campaigns in North America, light-infantry tactics were the period's nearest equivalent to, and precursor of, modern tactics. Light-infantry service demanded a level of initiative greater than that of the automaton-like drill of the line, skill to take advantage of natural cover and a higher level of marksmanship. As stated by the British *Volunteer Manual* of 1803: "Vigilance, activity, and intelligence, are particularly requisite...a light infantry man...should know how to take advantage of every circumstance of ground which can enable him to harass and annoy an enemy, without exposing himself...To fire seldom and always with effect should be their chief study...Noise and smoke is not sufficient to stop the advance of soldiers accustomed to war; they are to be checked only be seeing their comrades fall..."

1759

QUEBEC

DATE 13 September 1759
CAMPAIGN Seven Years War
OBJECT British Prime Minister William Pitt the Elder wanted to expel the French from Canada; British attempts to capture Quebec, a principal French stronghold, were frustrated by the near impregnable position of that fortress.
NUMBERS British – 4,800; French – 4,500.
DESCRIPTION Quebec, "the battle which won Canada", was one of the most audacious operations of the period of the Seven Years War. The British army commander of the expedition to Quebec was the young and dynamic General James Wolfe, one of the most outstanding British soldiers of the period. Transported by a British fleet, Wolfe landed below Quebec in late June 1759 but was unable to establish an effective foothold near the city to engage the French defenders, until a precarious path was discovered up the cliffs just north of ▸

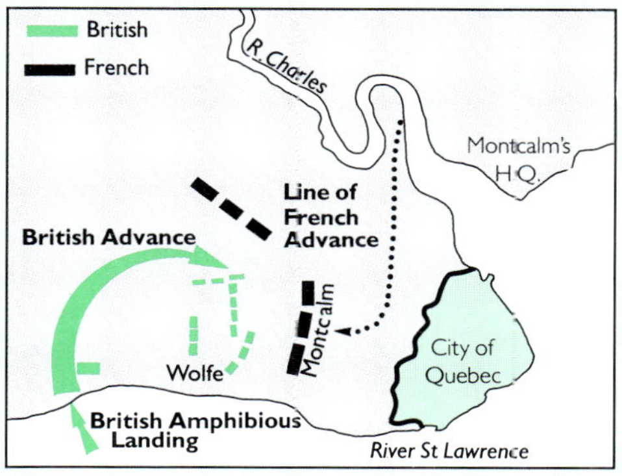

MUSKETS AND ARTILLERY

ALTHOUGH CERTAIN IMPROVEMENTS were introduced into the weaponry of the 1714–1815 period, with few exceptions the capabilities of armaments remained to a large extent unchanged. The principal weapon remained the smooth-bored musket or "firelock". Its accuracy was generally poor, so that although a maximum range of 700 yards might be attainable, at anything over 100 yards the chance of hitting a specific target was very small; as George Hanger, a noted British marksman, wrote in 1814: "as to firing at a man at 200 yards with a common musket, you may as well fire at the moon and have the same hope of hitting your object". Under the conditions of the warfare of the era, however, it was not necessary to hit a single man at this distance; as troops manoeuvred in packed formations, all that was needed was to register a hit at any point on a block of troops many yards long.

Infantry continued to manoeuvre in lines and columns; against cavalry, the universal defence was to form a square, all sides facing out, presenting an impenetrable hedge of bayonets on each side. The bayonet was carried by all troops armed with muskets, but was very rarely used except in the storming of fortified places or in isolated skirmishes. In battle, its merit was almost entirely psychological, bayonet-charges normally only being made when the enemy was already wavering as a result of artillery-fire or musketry.

Cavalry utilized the impetus of the charge, the sabres of the heavy regiments usually being straight but those of the light regiments often imitating Hungarian or central-European design by having curved blades. From the later 18th century the lance was reintroduced in a number of armies; generally a disadvantage in a cavalry mêlée against an enemy armed with sabres, against infantry the lance was a lethal weapon of execution.

Artillery remained smooth-bored and muzzle-loading. The principal ammunition remained the solid iron cannonball or "roundshot", with explosive "common shells" generally being restricted to howitzers, short-barrelled guns designed for high-angle fire. These were the only weapons capable of "indirect" fire; ordinary cannon had so low a trajectory that they could not fire over the heads of friendly troops, and thus had to be positioned among or in advance of the army's front line. Other projectiles included "canister" or "case-shot", musket balls packed into tin canisters which ruptured upon leaving the muzzle, turning the cannon into a giant shotgun; and grapeshot, of similar construction but using iron balls larger than musket shot.

The mechanics of targeting were improved greatly by the end of the 18th century with the invention of the "tangent sight" and the screw-elevator, but a practicable rate of fire remained at between two and three shots per minute. Projectiles could carry over a mile, but gunners generally reserved their fire until the target was within about half that distance, with canister being restricted to short range, rarely beyond about 500 yards.

(Above) Musket-drill: present arms, first motion (top); "present fire" (middle); "prime" (bottom), when the ignition-powder was poured into the pan. Prints from Thomas Rowlandson's Loyal Volunteers of London & Environs, *1798.*

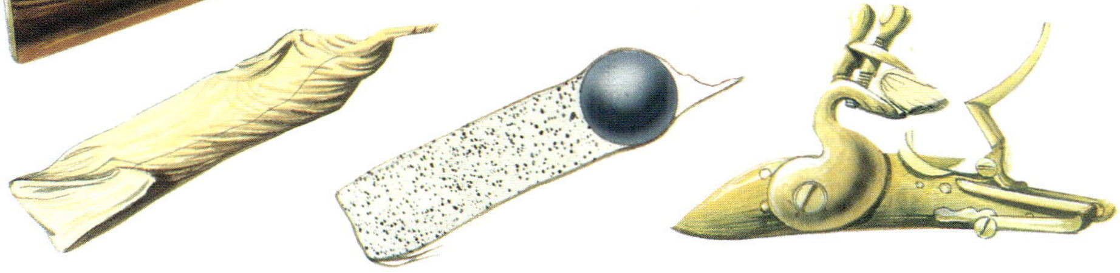

Most famous of the flintlock muskets were the British "Brown Bess" and the French "Charleville" (above). The musket was loaded via the muzzle with a lead ball and gunpowder in a cartridge (far left), and ignited by the flintlock mechanism (left) which, when the trigger was depressed, struck a spark, sent to the propellant charge via the touch-hole in the barrel.

(Above) Rifled muskets were used most effectively in British, Prussian and Austrian service. These men of the British 60th and 95th Rifles were armed with Ezekiel Baker's rifle, the most famous of the era.

(Above) British infantry at Fontenoy. Volley-fire was the almost universal use of the smooth-bored musket. Bayonets were seldom used: it was their threat which was most significant.

(Above) Grenadiers of the 1st, 2nd and 3rd regiments of British Foot Guards, depicted by David Morier (1751). The mitre cap indicated grenadier status; the tube on the belt originally contained match for igniting grenades.

(Below) French fieldpiece of the Gribeauval system, and coffret (ammunition chest). The construction of ordnance was improved with a lessening of weight but not of hitting power. Most effective was the French artillery designed by Jean-Baptiste de Gribeauval (1715–89). Artillery became more mobile: the light "battalion guns" of infantry units went out of use by about 1800, guns being employed in larger concentrations.

Frederick the Great and officers of his army. (Left to right) Dragoon officer in the light blue uniform adopted in 1745; general of cuirassiers, with the light blue facings of the 5th and 11th regiments; Frederick, in the uniform of his Guard Grenadiers; General Hans Joachim von Zieten in the dress uniform of his 2nd Hussars, including eagle-wing plume; officer, Guard Grenadiers. Frederick himself was careless of his appearance and dressed very plainly.

the Empress Elizabeth of Russia in January 1762 removed that state from the alliance against him. With Ferdinand of Brunswick continuing to hold off the French threat, Frederick was at last able to concentrate upon only one enemy, Austria, and after a further victory at Burkersdorf (21 July 1762) all participants were too exhausted to continue. The Seven Years War ended with an armistice in November 1762 and a treaty in February 1763; the result of so great an effusion of blood was that little had been achieved beyond the survival of the Prussian state, Frederick retaining Silesia. It did, however, guarantee Frederick's place in the pantheon of military geniuses, his survival against overwhelming odds and assaults on all fronts being little short of astounding. It is hardly surprising that in the following years his army was imitated by almost every European state, save France.

CONFLICT IN THE COLONIES

The Seven Years War spilled over into the existing confrontation between Britain and France as colonizing powers in North America and India. These campaigns confirmed the increasing importance of seapower, no longer simply a matter of the protection of trading routes but now the defence of a line of communication in support of the increasing military operations in distant colonies.

In India, Anglo-French rivalry was played out against a background of tribal and factional warfare within the subcontinent, with much of the French effort being maintained by allied Indian rulers. The interests of both major European powers were channelled through trading-agencies, the most powerful of which was the British East India Company, which had many of the powers of a sovereign state, including the right to declare war and to maintain its own army; thus the British war effort was run almost by proxy and at less expense to the treasury than if the entire venture had been run by the government. The most decisive action of the period was the victory of the young Robert Clive, originally an East India Company clerk, over the immense army of the Nawab of Bengal at Plassey (23 June 1757 – see page 118). The extinction of French interests in India was assured by the British victory of Wandewash (22 January 1760) and by the surrender of the main French base at Pondicherry (15 January 1761), the fall of which was inevitable after the French navy was unable to overcome the squadrons supporting the British presence in India, confirming the importance of maritime supremacy. Although Pondicherry was restored to the French by the Treaty of Paris (10 February 1763), the French trading organization, the *Compagnie des Indes*, was dissolved in 1769, leaving Britain with no serious European rival for the colonization and exploitation of the resources of India.

Anglo-French rivalry in North America had involved some considerable operations in King George's War (1740–48, contiguous with the War of the Austrian

1759

the city. On the night of 12–13 September Wolfe led an amphibious landing along the river St Lawrence and up a steep cliff, until by first light his men were drawn up before the city, on the Plains of Abraham. The French commander, Louis Joseph, Marquis de Montcalm, immediately marched his men from his camping-ground to oppose Wolfe. The armies being arrayed in opposing lines, the excellence of the British musketry drove the French away in moments; both commanders were wounded mortally, Wolfe dying on the battlefield and Montcalm that night.

CASUALTIES 58 British killed, 572 wounded; about 1,400 French killed or wounded.

RESULT Five days later Quebec capitulated, and although almost a year passed before the French rule of Canada was ended, the battle on the Plains of Abraham was the decisive action which ensured British possession of Canada.

YORKTOWN

DATE September – October 1781

CAMPAIGN American War of Independence

OBJECT The war between Britain and her rebellious American colonies had been in progress over six years when in August 1781 Charles, Earl Cornwallis, commander of the British forces in Virginia, retired to fortified positions on both sides of the York river, in the towns of Yorktown and Gloucester, to await reinforcement.

Succession), including the British-American capture of the French fortress of Louisbourg (1745), which was restored to France upon the conclusion of peace. The conflict was renewed before the outbreak of the Seven Years War, and is styled the "French and Indian War". Campaigning in North America involved very different skills from those required in Europe, the terrain being most suited to what were described as "irregular" operations, i.e. those involving the skills of scouting, skirmishing and woodcraft associated with light infantry, rather than line and volley-fire. The two methods came into contact at the battle of the Monongahela (9 July 1755), when General Edward Braddock's British army was ambushed and more than half killed by a numerically inferior force of French and Indians.

With the beginning of the Seven Years War, the British ministry determined to drive the French from Canada and extend British rule throughout the whole of colonized North America. In July 1758 a third British expedition re-captured Louisbourg (the second expedition had failed in 1757), but a British attack upon the French defenders of Fort Ticonderoga (held by the French commander in Canada, the Marquis de Montcalm) was a costly failure. Ticonderoga eventually fell in July 1759, but attempts to capture the French stronghold of Quebec, a position of immense strength, were frustrated until the young general, James Wolfe, led an amphibious British landing which surreptitiously established itself upon the Plains of Abraham, before Quebec (see page 123), on the night of 12–13 September 1759. In the battle which followed both Wolfe and Montcalm were mortally wounded, but the total defeat of the French led to the surrender of Quebec (see page 126), and in September 1760 to the complete capitulation of the French in Canada. British domination of North America was confirmed by the Treaty of Paris, and the merits of light infantry tactics were henceforth unchallenged by most forward-thinking military experts.

Cornet Thomas Boothby Parkyns in the uniform of the British King's Light Dragoons, 1776–81, painted by John Boultbee. The uniform of light troops exhibited similar features in many armies, often including short coat-tails and helmets. Featuring the traditional red coat of the British army, uniforms similar to this were worn by the British light dragoons which served in the American War of Independence.

THE AMERICAN WAR OF INDEPENDENCE

Barely a decade after the victory in Canada, Britain faced a new challenge to the domination of North America, in the rebellion of the 13 American colonies, the culmination of years of political dissent between the colonists and the home administration. The war which began on 19 April 1775 with skirmishes at Lexington and Concord was to have important implications for military developments in Europe, not least in the renewed confirmation of the value of proficient light infantry and the use of skirmish tactics in terrain which rendered European-style manoeuvre difficult; but it is not correct to view the War of Independence as exclusively a conflict between backwoodsmen armed with rifled muskets against the less enterprising, solid formations of redcoats.

1781

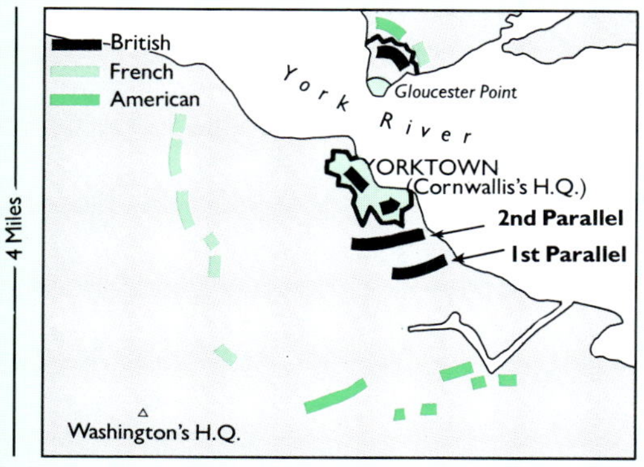

NUMBERS Cornwallis commanded some 7,500 men and 65 mostly light guns, but his provisions were not abundant and his army was sickly. Opposing the British were the American commander-in-chief, General George Washington (1732–99), with about 9,000 men, and about 7,000 French under Jean Baptiste, Comte de Rochambeau, together having 92 guns.

DESCRIPTION On 28 September 1781 the Allied forces began the investment of Yorktown, Cornwallis abandoning his untenable outer defences on 30 September, allowing the Allied artillery to bombard the whole of the Yorktown position. With his communications severed by the French fleet, Cornwallis was unable to receive help or evacuate his forces. The Allied siege-lines pushed closer, two British redoubts being stormed on 14 October; a spirited counter-attack by the British was repelled two days later. Almost out of ammunition and supplies, with almost 2,000 sick, Cornwallis was compelled to ▸

The emergence of the rifled musket was not a new development, for the greatly enhanced accuracy attained by a rifled (internally grooved) barrel which imparted a spin to the bullet had been known at least from the early 16th century, but had been neglected in most armies. With the light infantry tactics used in North America, the rifle was an ideal weapon and in the hands of trained marksmen most effective. The colonists' military forces, however, based on the existing militia organization and the so-called "minute-men" (capable of assembling at a moment's notice), while making limited use of rifled firearms, evolved into an army organized, equipped and trained upon European lines, with the predominant weapon being the smooth-bored musket as carried by the vast majority of their British opponents.

A further factor which emerged in the War of Independence was the growth of what might be termed a "national army", whose members (even if enrolled under a degree of compulsion) felt an enhanced degree of attachment to their cause, greater than if they had been simply professional soldiers who had enlisted for a livelihood.

Finally, the War of Independence differed from European conflicts in the lack of cavalry used by both sides, conditions and resources not being favourable for the employment of large mounted formations; and it demonstrated the difficulties of attempting to direct and supply an army from the opposite side of the Atlantic.

From the unpromising material of haphazardly organized and poorly equipped militia, the Continental Congress at Philadelphia announced the establishment of a "Continental Army" (i.e. one comprised of units not controlled primarily by their own states), to which George Washington was appointed as commander. Washington, a Virginian landowner who had previously served the British (he had escaped from Braddock's disaster), was the chief creator of the army which emerged from the original rabble, and was certainly the most able general who served in the war. Washington's organizational skills were considerable, as was his ability to recognize the salient features of the strategic situation. Loath to fight unless his chances of success were good, his introduction of foreign professional soldiers to provide an experienced cadre was instrumental in perfecting the American army. The most significant of the foreign recruits was the Prussian Baron von Steuben, trained in the school of Frederick, who produced the first American drill manual.

The first major engagement of the war was fought on 17 June 1775, at Bunker Hill overlooking Boston harbour, when an entrenched American position was carried by the British at the third attempt, confirming yet again the steadiness of the British infantry under intense fire, and demonstrating the great determination of the American colonists. The value to the Americans of Washington's presence in command became obvious in 1776, when his small army escaped entrapment and inflicted two sharp reverses upon the British at Trenton (26 December 1776) and

1781

surrender (19 October), the British marching out to lay down their arms to the appropriate tune of "The World Turned Upside Down".

CASUALTIES American-French about 400; British 600, with the rest captured.

RESULT Although the war continued for more than a year, to all intents Yorktown secured the independence of the American colonies, and demonstrated the crucial importance of the control of the sea.

FLEURUS

DATE 26 June 1794

CAMPAIGN French Revolutionary Wars

OBJECT Relief of Charleroi (captured previous day by French army under Jourdan) by Austro-German army (under Saxe-Coburg).

NUMBERS Jourdan commanded some 75,000 men; Saxe-Coburg about 52,000.

DESCRIPTION Jourdan believed his army to be greatly inferior to that of Saxe-Coburg,

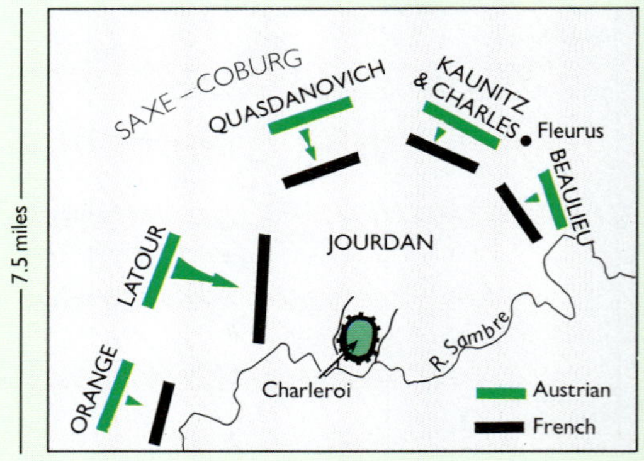

The surrender of Lord Cornwallis's British army to the US and French forces of George Washington at Yorktown, 19 October 1781; Washington's bodyguard (on foot) and his staff are arrayed under the Stars and Stripes, facing the French contingent. It was said that when the British chief minister Lord North learned of this surrender he exclaimed, "Oh God, it is all over!" It was: the defeat at Yorktown effectively secured the independence of the United States.

Princeton (3 January 1777), which probably saved the revolution from extinction.

Most actions in the American War were of small scale, but the results could be profound, such as the surrender of Sir John Burgoyne's outnumbered British army at Saratoga (17 October 1777). This not only put new heart into the American camp, but was followed by French recognition of American independence, leading to a French declaration of war on Britain (17 June 1778). This effectively turned the tide of the war. American fortunes were depressed in 1780, with serious reverses and unrest within the army; but Washington's appreciation of the strategic realities saved the day, and with the help of the French fleet and the Comte de Rochambeau, commander of the French army, he outmanoeuvred the British and by isolating them from support compelled the surrender of the army of Earl Cornwallis at Yorktown (19 October 1781 – see page 126). Although this was not the end of hostilities, it was the final major action of the war. The Treaty of Paris (30 November 1782) ended the American War, with the independence of the United States guaranteed and all British holdings evacuated.

THE ERA OF THE FRENCH REVOLUTION

The two decades and more of conflict which followed the French Revolution of 1789 resulted in radically new methods in the conduct of war. Some of these were developments of what had occurred earlier; some were deliberately innovative, and some arose from necessity.

The deposition of the French monarchy by the French revolutionary movement,

1798

so decided to hold a partly-entrenched and widely-spread position to the north and west of Charleroi. Saxe-Coburg made an error in his tactical deployment by attempting to attack all along the French line, instead of concentrating upon a single sector; consequently, five main columns attacked the French simultaneously. Jourdan was able to combat all the Austrian attacks (he was aided by the use of an observation balloon, the earliest example of aerial reconnaissance), so that an Austrian breakthrough was prevented. Saxe-Coburg made a number of territorial gains, but French counter-attacks drove him back, and after six hours' fighting the Austrians retired.

CASUALTIES The Austrians lost about 2,300 killed and wounded; Jourdan about 4,000.

RESULT Saxe-Coburg did not renew his attack; the French continued to advance and expelled the Austrians forever from the southern Netherlands, securing the northern frontier of France.

ABOUKIR BAY

DATE 1 August 1798 ("Battle of the Nile")

CAMPAIGN Napoleon's Egyptian expedition.

OBJECT The decisive action of Napoleon's expedition to Egypt was fought at sea. Transported in a French fleet, Napoleon's army evaded the British squadron of Admiral Horatio Nelson and disembarked in Egypt on 1 July 1798. Nelson wanted to destroy Napoleon's lifeline to France. Exactly a month later he found the French ▶

LINE VERSUS COLUMN

The diagram below, although a considerable simplification, illustrates the relative merits of the two principal battle-formations of this period, line and column. Infantry in line (1), usually two or three ranks deep, was able to bring every musket to bear simultaneously. An attack in column (2) was capable of much more rapid movement, but unless it was deployed into line before battle was joined it was at an immense disadvantage over the line since only the first two or three of its ranks were able to fire. (This weakness could be offset by preceding the attack with hordes of skirmishers, but this did not always occur.) The line might protect itself by stationing cavalry on its flanks or "refusing" (throwing back at an angle) the flank (3); and when the column had been engaged, part of the line could swing forward to enfilade the unprotected flank of the enemy column (4).

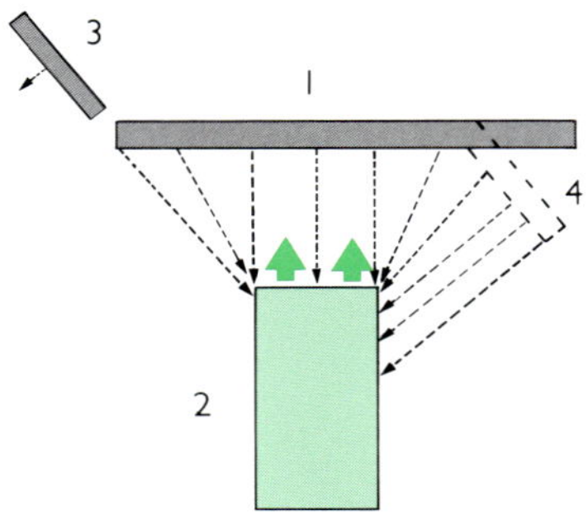

and its declared intention to export revolution to other states, caused the formation of a coalition, led initially by Austria and Prussia, determined to restore the *status quo ante* in France. The Revolution had left the French army in a parlous state; as its officer corps had been almost exclusively aristocratic, it was decimated by the emigration of fugitive nobility, so that only the experienced cadre of the ex-Royal army was left as a nucleus for the formation of the large army which was required to repel the coalition gathering to invade France. Although this core of disciplined troops were of great value, the mass of volunteers and conscripts swept into the army in the early years of the Revolutionary Wars could not be trained in conventional methods, mainly because of a lack of time but also because some political radicals equated established practice with subservience and inequality. The early French revolutionary armies, however, had one great advantage over their opponents, in their nationalistic and patriotic fervour which extended even to those conscripted compulsorily by the *Levée en Masse* of August 1793. This, enacted at a time when the French state was on the point of collapse, provided for the conscription of the entire male population, and thus produced the first truly "citizen army" of modern times. Although the first assault on France was repelled by the remnants of the old army, by the middle of the following year France was in chaos, riven by "the Terror", stricken by Royalist risings within as well as assailed from without, and controlled by the Committee of Public Safety whose political commissars frustrated the plans of even those generals who escaped execution.

The reorganization which followed not only saved France but set the style of tactics for the following 20 years. Lazare Carnot (1753–1823), war minister for the Committee of Public Safety presided over the enactment of the *Amalgame*, decreed in February 1793 and enacted in January 1794, by which each regular battalion of ex-royal infantry was allied to two volunteer or conscript battalions. The scheme was calculated to utilize the disciplined firepower of the regulars and the nationalistic fervour of the new battalions. By arraying the new battalions on either flank of the regular battalion in line, both qualities could be utilized simultaneously.

Two other tactical principles characterized the French revolutionary armies. The first was attack in column. Columnar formation (actually a succession of lines), could manoeuvre much more quickly than line, and although only the muskets of the first two or three ranks could be brought into play, the impetus of a charging column could burst through opposing lines of infantry. The second principle was associated with the column, and was the ultimate development of light infantry tactics. To protect the column from the enemy's view and to gall the enemy line, it was usual for vast hordes of sharpshooters or skirmishers *(tirailleurs)* to be deployed. Although the French army included units designated as light infantry, their difference from the

1798

warships anchored in Aboukir Bay, near the Rosetta mouth of the Nile delta.

NUMBERS The French fleet, commanded by Admiral François Paul Brueys d'Aigalliers, was anchored in line, protected by shoals and overlooked by a French battery; it comprised 13 ships-of-the-line, including the 120-gun flagship *L'Orient*, and four frigates. Nelson commanded 14 ships-of-the-line from his flagship HMS *Vanguard* (74 guns).

DESCRIPTION Instead of attacking by sail-

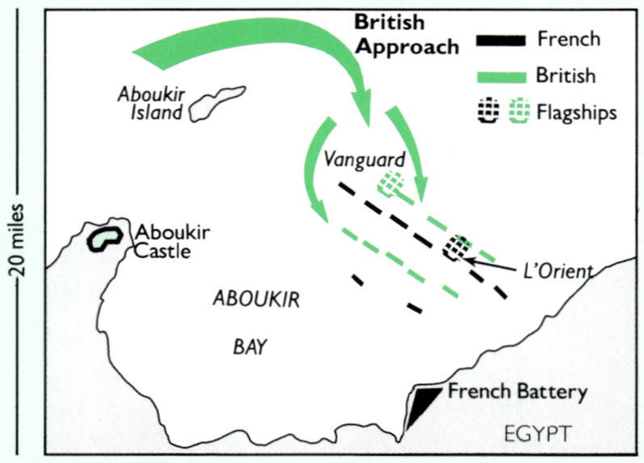

ing down the French line, a number of the 13 British ships (one, HMS *Culloden*, had gone aground on the approach) were able to pass between the anchored French ships and thus were able to subject them to a bombardment from both sides. The superior British gunnery and these audacious tactics destroyed the French fleet almost completely; two ships-of-the-line and two frigates escaped, nine were captured, one was grounded and burnt and *L'Orient* blew up at the close of the action.

ordinary line regiments was minimal, as all French troops were capable of fighting in "open order", and whilst some had enhanced skirmishing skills, it was possible for entire brigades to be deployed as skirmishers. In this, the French possessed a great superiority: the Austrian army's light troops declined in effectiveness, and the British army which had been so proficient in skirmish tactics in North America ignored these troops in favour of a Frederickian-style drill to such an extent that mercenaries had to be employed as light troops in the early campaigns of the French Revolutionary War, and not until the early 19th century did Britain possess a small light-infantry arm which was superior even to that of France. The other main Napoleonic combatants, Prussia and Russia, were never as proficient in skirmish tactics despite the tradition of rifle-shooting prevalent in Germany.

Another critical factor which emerged from the revolutionary period was the French method of supply. At first, the French republic was simply unable to provide enough food for its rapidly enlarged armies, so that troops had to resort to "living off the land" or foraging, and although they frequently went hungry, almost by chance it provided a great strategic advantage: by not being tied to supply depots, and not needing to guard lines of communication at all costs, French armies attained a freedom of movement totally surpassing that of their opponents, whose retention of the old system of supply lines and whose frequent halts to bake bread put them at an immense disadvantage. Such was the effect of this rapidity of movement that even when conventional methods of supply were possible, the French army retained the system of foraging, and only its total breakdown and literal starvation in the winter of 1806–7 led Napoleon to reintroduce a more effective means of supply.

The Battle of Fleurus, 26 June 1794, an illustration painted on to the lid of an ivory snuff-box. Many illustrations of Fleurus include the appearance of the French observation-balloon Entreprenant, *which had been used in the siege of Charleroi. At Fleurus Jean-Marie-Joseph Coutelle, commander of the French* Aërostier *(Aviation Company), took up General Morlot as an observer during the battle, the first use of aerial reconnaissance in warfare.*

THE RISE OF NAPOLEON

Having repelled the initial attacks, the French made such progress that a number of their enemies (including Prussia) were forced to make peace in mid-1795. France occupied the Netherlands and directed her operations against Austria, which together with Britain (which had entered the coalition against France in 1793) was to remain the most persistent opponent of the French throughout the period. (Only Britain remained at war continually, save for the brief Peace of Amiens, 1802–3.) From 1796 the war was waged on two principal fronts, in Germany and northern Italy, the campaigning in the latter giving rise to the dominant military personality of his generation, Napoleon Bonaparte. He first came to prominence in 1793 when as an obscure officer of artillery he was instrumental in ejecting an enemy expedition which had occupied Toulon, and his connections with the Directory (the new French government established in August 1795) led to his appointment to command the ragged and ill-disciplined French armies opposing the Austrians in Italy. Operations

1800

CASUALTIES The British lost no ships and a total of only 895 casualties. The French lost 11 ships-of-the-line and about 5,200 casualties.
RESULT The destruction of the French fleet isolated Napoleon's army in Egypt, and effectively decided the campaign, demonstrating the crucial influence of seapower and enhancing the reputation of Britain's greatest admiral.

MARENGO

DATE 14 June 1800
CAMPAIGN War of the Second Coalition
OBJECT One of Napoleon's most celebrated victories, Marengo was a battle which he should have lost. He was operating against the Austrian forces in northern Italy, in an endeavour to establish French dominance over northern Italy.
NUMBERS Napoleon had divided his forces and was encamped with only 24,000 men and 23 guns around Marengo, near Alessandria; the Austrians had 31,000 men.
DESCRIPTION The Austrian General Michael Melas succeeded in surprising the French in the early hours of 14 June 1800. Napoleon sent a frantic request for help to his scattered divisions, but by mid-afternoon the French had been driven back by three Austrian columns, and so confident of victory was Melas that he handed over the pursuit to his deputy, General Zach. Napoleon's ▸

The French passage from Switzerland to Italy via the Great St Bernard Pass occurred before the battle of Marengo (14 June 1800). Italy was the scene of Napoleon's early triumphs.

hinged around Austrian attempts to relieve their beleaguered garrison at Mantua, and by a combination of his military skill and the way in which he was able to galvanize his troops by the force of his personality, Bonaparte was able to defeat greatly superior Austrian armies with regularity, most notably at Lodi (10 May 1796), Castiglione (5 August 1796), Arcola (15–17 November 1796) and Rivoli (14 January 1797). Having compelled Austria to make peace and having established French satellite republics in northern Italy, Bonaparte attempted to create the foundation of a French oriental empire by his expedition to Egypt.

Although he defeated the Mameluke and Ottoman armies sent against him, the crucial nature of the command of the sea was demonstrated again when the French fleet was annihilated by the British admiral Horatio Nelson at Aboukir Bay (1 August 1798), isolating the French from resupply (see page 129). Their army was eventually defeated by a British expedition (1801), but Bonaparte had returned to France in late 1799 to establish himself as the country's leader with the title of "First Consul", the three-man Consulate having replaced the corrupt and ineffective Directory by a *coup d'état*. During Bonaparte's absence in Egypt, a Second Coalition had been formed against France, and Austro-Russian forces had driven the French from Italy. Assembling a new army, Bonaparte made an audacious advance through the Alpine passes into northern Italy, and defeated the Austrians convincingly at Marengo (14 June 1800 – see below), further defeats on the German front compelled Austria once again to make peace, and for a brief period even France's most intractable enemy, Britain, agreed to a cessation of hostilities, ending the French Revolutionary War. With his star now fully in the ascendant, Bonaparte was proclaimed as "Consul for Life" (2 August 1802), only a short step from his coronation as Emperor of the French (2 December 1804); he styled himself Napoleon I, from which the era takes its title. It was a meteoric rise and was proof of the validity of Napoleon's remark that, under the social conditions which arose from the French Revolution, if the talent were present then every soldier carried a marshal's baton in his knapsack.

NAPOLEON'S ART OF WAR

In assessing the reasons for Napoleon's successes, his own abilities are of paramount importance. His military capabilities are beyond question, to which were joined a capacity for unceasing hard work, ruthlessness, a grasp of political realities and an ability to engender not only respect and admiration among his followers but adoration verging upon idolatry. He also had the great advantage of "unity of command": he had no political masters to obey, both foreign and military policy being entirely in his hands. Although he inspired and led the army which achieved his great victories, he was not a great innovator, but rather refined the elements

1800

luck changed however with the arrival of his subordinate General Louis Charles Desaix, who without waiting for orders had begun to march his division towards Napoleon as soon as the cannonade was heard. Arriving after a forced march at about 5pm, Desaix declared that although one battle was lost, there was still time to win another, and attacked. He was seconded by a crucial cavalry charge led by General François Etienne Kellermann. Despite

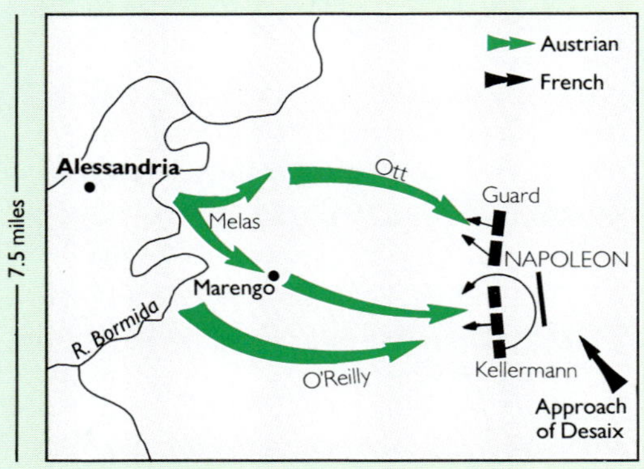

Desaix's death at the head of his troops, the weary French mounted a counterattack which turned the expected Austrian victory into a complete rout.

CASUALTIES French about 7,000; Austrians about 7,000 casualties and 7,000 prisoners.

RESULT Next evening Melas signed an armistice, and although the war lasted until February 1801, Marengo was the decisive blow. Napoleon made much of his victory; but in fact credit should have been accorded to Desaix and Kellermann.

The Battle of Austerlitz, 2 December 1805, was Napoleon's masterpiece. François Gérard's painting shows General Jean Rapp, left, presenting his prisoners to Napoleon, right, with his aides: chief-of-staff Marshal Louis Alexandre Berthier to the left of Napoleon; General Jean Andoche Junot, in the plumed shako, and, in oriental dress, Napoleon's Mameluke servant Roustam.

which were already in existence, including the reforms and reorganizations of Carnot as well as earlier ones. The artillery, for example, one of Napoleon's most effective arms, had been modernized radically from 1765 by Jean Baptiste de Gribeauval, whose artillery system remained the finest in Europe until well into the 19th century. Artillery employment changed during the period in a manner common to several armies, with the realization that, where sufficient guns were available, a concentration of artillery fire was more than the sum of its parts. This led to the general discarding of so-called "battalion guns" (lighter field-pieces which accompanied individual battalions to provide immediate fire-support) and the assembly instead of larger formations, "massed batteries" which became an offensive arm, blasting a hole in the enemy line which infantry or cavalry could exploit, rather than, as previously, acting basically as a support for the other arms.

Napoleon's cavalry attained great significance, but although the French cavalry at the outset of the Revolutionary Wars was wretched, the basic tactics and classifications were established before Napoleon.

1805

TRAFALGAR

DATE 21 October 1805
CAMPAIGN Napoleonic Wars
OBJECT To execute his intended invasion of England, Napoleon planned to decoy away as many British warships as possible by sending his own fleet to the West Indies, and then return in time to support an invasion before the British could catch up. The plan miscarried and the invasion scheme was abandoned, but Napoleon compelled his admiral Pierre de Villeneuve to leave the safety of Cadiz to raid the Mediterranean.

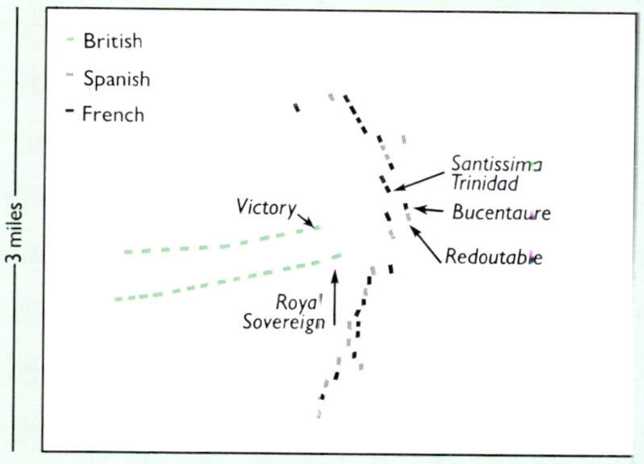

NUMBERS The combined Franco-Spanish fleet had 33 ships-of-the-line, while Horatio Nelson's fleet comprised 27 ships-of-the-line.
DESCRIPTION Nelson intercepted Villeneuve as the latter attempted to regain the safety of Cadiz; the fleets met off Cape Trafalgar. Nelson adopted a refinement of the tactic of "breaking the line" by attack- ▶

A grenadier of Napoleon's Imperial Guard, shown in a contemporary print by Pierre Martinet. The Imperial Guard was perhaps the most famous military formation of the Napoleonic era, originating as a bodyguard and increasing in size until it became the army's most valuable reserve in the later campaigns. The Grenadiers of the Guard – mostly part of the "Old Guard" of the most stalwart veterans – were known by the nickname grognards *(grumblers).*

The beginning of the 19th century witnessed another development of crucial significance in the creation of semi-permanent higher formations. Previously, the largest tactical unit had usually been the regiment, or sometimes a temporary association of two or more in a brigade. Although some nations were remarkably slow in introducing even permanently organized brigades, they were soon followed by the organization of two or more brigades into divisions, which usually included their own cavalry detachment (for reconnaissance), artillery and supporting services. The existence of such formations greatly facilitated the transmission of orders, so that with the establishment of a "general staff" of trained administrative and command officers, the general's orders could be enacted very much more rapidly than orders transmitted to each regiment from one central source. Equally, the organization of supply was facilitated, a factor vital to the management of armies of ever-increasing size. Napoleon took this one stage further with the creation of autonomous *corps d'armées* of two or more divisions, each complete with all its supporting services and each capable of fighting a battle unaided. Allied with the capacity for rapid marches made possible by the practice of "living off the land", this was perhaps the most important feature of Napoleon's system of war. Its efficacy was demonstrated by his advances upon Austria in 1805, which completely outmanoeuvred the Austrians and led to the surrender of a large part of their army, and upon Prussia in 1806.

Aspects of the French system were copied by many of Napoleon's enemies, but rarely with equal success (Austrian attempts to institute a system of partial foraging were disastrous, for example). Austria, Prussia and Russia all adopted a system of *corps d'armée*, but only Britain devised an effective counter to the French method of attack, in Wellington's use of the "reverse slope" tactic. By concealing his troops on the reverse slope of a low ridge and behind proficient light infantry, they were shielded both from the fire and from the view of the attacking French; thus when the British advanced in line to the crest just as the French attack approached, their appearance was a surprise, the French were unable to deploy and their columns were defeated by a brief burst of British musketry followed by a controlled bayonet-charge upon the wavering French ranks. Despite the success of the tactic, it was not adopted by other nations opposed to Napoleon.

As a strategist, Napoleon was the nonpareil of the age. His aim was always to destroy the enemy's field army rather than embark upon protracted campaigns based upon the occupation of territory; the French capacity for rapid movement and the comparative freedom resulting from their system of supply permitted the most audacious manoeuvres and resulted in a number of speedily decided campaigns. Against numerically superior enemies he manoeuvred his opponents into two bodies, concentrating first against one and then against the other, each time

1805

ing the Franco-Spanish line-of-battle almost at right-angles with two columns of British ships, led respectively by his own flagship HMS *Victory* and his deputy Admiral Sir Cuthbert Collingwood's *Royal Sovereign*. This audacious plan overwhelmed Villeneuve's centre and rear before his van could return to aid the remainder, and in forcing the "pell-mell battle" Nelson desired it allowed the greatly superior British ship-handling and gunnery to destroy over half the enemy fleet (17 captured, including Villeneuve's flagship *Bucentaure* and the gigantic Spanish *Santissima Trinidad*, plus one burnt) for the loss of no British ships. Nelson was mortally wounded by a marksman aboard the French *Redoutable*.

CASUALTIES Villeneuve – 18 ships and 14,000 men, half of whom were prisoners of war; British – no ships, 452 killed, 1,141 wounded.

RESULT Henceforth, a French invasion of Britain could never again be contemplated.

AUSTERLITZ

DATE 2 December 1805

CAMPAIGN War of the Third Coalition

OBJECT To break up the coalition of major powers resisting Napoleon's ambitions.

NUMBERS Napoleon had 73,200 men and 139 guns, with his army at the peak of efficiency; he was opposed by Czar Alexander I of Russia and the Emperor Francis I of Austria with 85,400 men and 278 guns, the army actually commanded by the Rus-

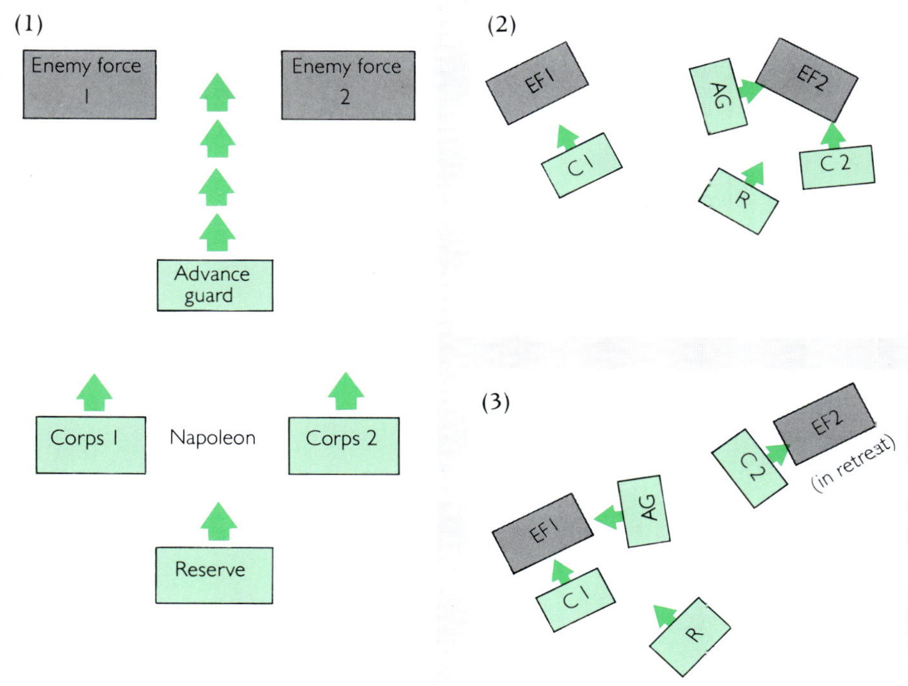

NAPOLEON'S TACTICS

Napoleon's method for defeating one or more enemy forces of greatly superior strength consisted of the seizing of the so-called "central ground", and depended upon the ability of each of Napoleon's *corps d'armée* to be able to operate without support for a considerable time. Initially (1), a rapid march would establish Napoleon's force between the two enemy bodies, hence the "central ground". One autonomous corps would then fight a holding action against one enemy force (2) whilst Napoleon concentrated the rest against the second enemy, enabling him to defeat it by achieving local superiority of numbers. When this enemy force was in retreat, one French corps would be assigned to pursue (3), whilst Napoleon force-marched the remainder to the assistance of the corps fighting the holding action, and then defeat the second enemy by again achieving local superiority of numbers.

achieving "local superiority" of numbers and defeating them in turn. Alternatively he would engage the enemy with a minority of his army and swing around their flank with the bulk of his force, the so-called "strategy of envelopment", cutting the enemy's communications and forcing them to fight upon his, Napoleon's, terms. As a strategist, Napoleon's only real failing was his inability to grasp the essentials and significance of sea power.

THE NAPOLEONIC WARS

The war between France and Britain resumed in 1803. Napoleon's initial aim was an invasion of England, to which end he had to divert as much of the British navy as possible to allow him temporary domination of the English Channel. His plan to decoy the British fleet to the West Indies failed, and a considerable proportion of his

Continued on page 138

1805

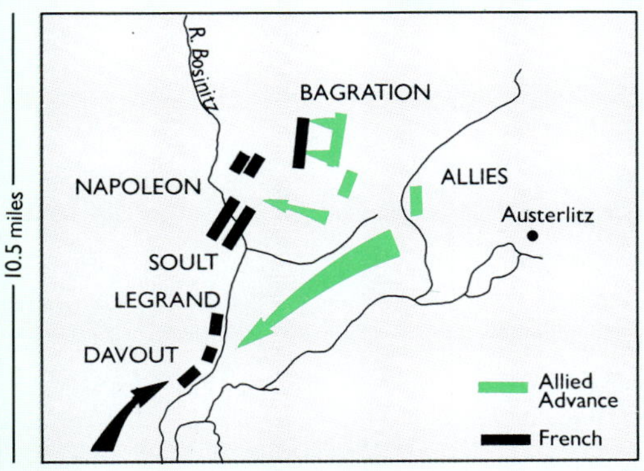

sian General Mikhail Kutuzov, who was unable fully to exercise his considerable skill due to the overbearing presence of the two emperors.

DESCRIPTION Austerlitz was Napoleon's masterpiece, following a brilliant advance against his Austro–Russian enemies that had moved at so rapid a pace that he had isolated and compelled the surrender of much of the Austrian army at Ulm (20 October). Then, by feigning weakness, Napoleon persuaded the Allied commanders to advance against him before they had been reinforced. The armies met at Austerlitz, near Brunn in Moldavia. The Allied army manoeuvered exactly as Napoleon had hoped: General Peter Bagration's secondary attack to the north was contained by the French Marshal Lannes, and as the main Allied force advanced Napoleon counter-attacked with Marshal Soult's corps. The Allied army was split in two, and as Napoleon reinforced Soult and drove back an attempted counter-attack by ▶

NAVAL WARFARE

(Right) A sailor of the British Royal Navy. Most sailors wore the costume of ordinary mariners, including short jackets and loose trousers which could be rolled up.

WARSHIPS IN THE 18th century were divided into two basic categories. The larger vessels, "ships-of-the-line" (originally "of-the-line-of-battle") were two- or three-decked craft, essentially floating gun-platforms designed to batter the enemy with their heavy armament. They were classified according to the number of guns they carried, which varied according to nationality and period; but typically "first-raters" would have 110 guns or more, "second-raters" 98, "third-raters" 64 to 80 and "fourth-raters" from 50 to 64. Naval artillery was generally heavier than that used on land; cannon firing a 32-lb shot were the standard arm. The carronade was introduced in the later 18th century (named from the place of its original manufacture, Carron ironworks at Falkirk, Scotland), a short-barrelled gun used for close-quarters action, so terribly efficient that it gained the nickname "the smasher".

The smaller warships were the frigates of 32 to 44 guns ("fifth-raters"), "sixth-raters" of up to 28 guns and smaller sloops, brigs and gunboats.

Naval tactics were determined by the fact that a ship could only discharge its guns from the sides (producing "broadsides"), and thus originated the "line-of-battle" in which opposing fleets would assemble in line astern and batter each other with broadsides. Fights would often be conducted at extremely close range, and when locked together a boarding-party might be sent on to the enemy ship, the crews fighting hand-to-hand. In general, the "line-of-battle" was a sterile formation which precluded decisive victory.

For a decisive action, a revised tactic was necessary, which took advantage of the comparative helplessness of a ship attacked from bow or stern, where its gunnery could not respond. The application of this tactic in a major action was postulated by a British writer, John Clerk, who printed privately a treatise on naval tactics, which advised that the fleet should deliberately break the enemy's line, overwhelming that part astern of the break before the remainder could change their course and return to help. The theory was perfected by Horatio Nelson, who at Trafalgar broke the enemy line in two places, by attacking in two columns. Once the line-of-battle had devolved into a number of close-quarter, ship-to-ship actions, superior discipline, ship-handling and gunnery were the deciding factors, in which the British navy at this period surpassed all others. A further factor was the conflicting theory of targeting. The French aimed to destroy the enemy's rigging and masts, to render them incapable of pursuit, in accordance with the French policy of seeking combat only when a definite objective was in view. For the British, the destruction of enemy ships was sufficient in itself to justify combat, and their gunnery was thus targeted on the enemy's hull, to destroy guns and kill the crew, and render the ship incapable of further operation.

(Below) A naval gun, mounted on a wooden "sea service" carriage. Recoil was absorbed by a system of ropes and pulleys, which kept it in position and allowed it to be run out of the gun port.

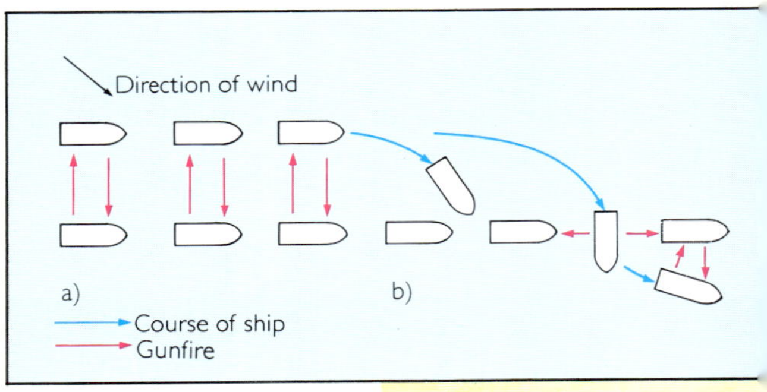

(Above) In the "line-of-battle" broadsides were exchanged (a). "Breaking the line" (b) permitted closer combat.

(Right) Rodney used this tactic at the Battle of the Saints, 12 April 1782. T. Whitcomb's painting shows the surrender of the Ville de Paris.

(Above) A typical "ship-of-the-line". These were the most effective naval vessels, with between 50 and 110 guns; the larger ships with three gun decks. The smaller ships, especially frigates, were equally useful in duties such as reconnaissance and raiding. Probably the most famous ship-of-the-line of the era is HMS Victory, *built at Chatham in 1765; a 100-gun "first-rater", which served as Lord Nelson's flagship at Trafalgar.*

Napoleon's Europe exhibited the results of successful French campaigns from the mid-1790s. Military conquest expanded the borders of the French Empire into the Netherlands and northern Italy, with client states between France and his enemies. Most significant of these was the Rheinbund *or "Confederation of the Rhine". Ultimately, the attempt to impose his brother Joseph as king of Spain and the continued conflict with Britain, undid him. This map, showing Napoleon's Empire, demonstrates his strategic problems. Napoleon was unable to supervise more than one campaign in person, and the conflict in the Iberian peninsula was a constant drain on his resources.*

fleet and that of his ally, Spain, was destroyed at Trafalgar (21 October 1805 – see page 133), which ensured that the scheme of invasion could never be resurrected. Even before Trafalgar, however, Napoleon had postponed the invasion and turned instead upon Austria, which with Russia had joined Britain in the Third Coalition against France. In one of the most brilliant operations of his career, Napoleon made a lightning march to the Danube, enveloping a large part of the Austrian army which was forced to capitulate at Ulm (20 October 1805 – see page 135), a strategic victory

1805

the Russian Guard, the Allied army disintegrated.

CASUALTIES French losses were almost 9,000, those of the Allies 26,000.

RESULT The battle's consequences were immense: Austria capitulated two days later and the Russians retired to their own territory. Austerlitz was a tactical masterpiece ranking with the greatest victories in history, a product of Napoleon's own genius and the magnificent quality of his army.

BORODINO

DATE 7 September 1812

CAMPAIGN Napoleonic Wars, invasion of Russia

OBJECT Part of Napoleon's campaign to eliminate Russia conclusively as a threat to a French Europe.

NUMBERS The Russian commander, Mikhail Kutuzov, had some 120,000 men and 640 guns; Napoleon 133,000 and 587 guns.

DESCRIPTION One of the largest and most sanguinary battles of the era occurred during Napoleon's advance on Moscow in his Russian campaign of 1812. The Russian forces retired before the advancing *Grande Armée* but made a stand some 70 miles from Moscow, at Borodino. Kutuzov's First and Second West Armies (commanded by generals Barclay de Tolly and Bagration) were drawn up in a strong position behind earthworks, the Shevardino redoubt (captured by Napoleon on 5 September), the

without parallel. He completed his most successful year by smashing the main Russo-Austrian field army at Austerlitz (2 December 1805 – see page 135), which led almost immediately to Austria's exit from the war.

In 1806 Napoleon turned upon Prussia, which had finally decided to join the opposition to France, partly from disquiet over Napoleon's establishment of an organization of French satellite states in Germany, the *Rheinbuna* or Confederation of the Rhine. With another advance of amazing swiftness, Napoleon destroyed the main Prussian army at Jena and Auerstädt (14 October 1806), removing Prussia from the war in little over a week. He followed this by engaging the Russians at Eylau (8 February 1807) and, much more decisively, at Friedland (14 June 1807). The peace terms which Napoleon dictated to the Czar at Tilsit in the following month made him master of almost all of western and central Europe.

This left Britain alone in opposition to France, and in an attempt to strangle British trade Napoleon devised his "Continental System" by which British goods were prohibited from all the states over which Napoleon exerted influence. Due to the British domination of the sea, however, this had hardly any economic effect on Britain, whereas the British naval blockade and actions against French trade wrecked the French maritime economy. In an attempt to impose the Continental System throughout Europe, Napoleon invaded Portugal (Britain's last supporter) via his ally, Spain, following which he decided to depose the ineffectual Spanish monarchy and replace it with a Bonapartist regime under his brother Joseph, who became king. This had two important consequences: first, it inflamed the Spanish population in a widespread revolt, a further example of the new concept of "patriotic war", for though the calibre of the Spanish army was low, the popular risings which resulted in a most brutal guerilla war occupied vast numbers of French troops. Second, it led to British intervention in the Iberian Peninsula, turning the war into a "Spanish ulcer" which ultimately bled Napoleon's empire to an insupportable degree. Napoleon intervened in the Peninsular War only briefly in person, being otherwise occupied in eastern Europe; although he had many capable subordinates, command in Spain was never unified under a general approaching Napoleon's stature, and the French defeat proved that Napoleon's possessions were too widespread for a war to be waged successfully on more than one front simultaneously.

The Peninsular War also produced the other dominant general of the age, Arthur Wellesley, Duke of Wellington. Wellesley came to prominence in India in a number of successful campaigns which had taught him the basics of his art, his most important victory being Assaye (23 September 1803, against the Marathas). Although Wellesley learned his trade in a continent where the most successful tactic was a rapid attack by a small European force against immensely more numerous but

Two members of Wellington's infantry wearing the British army's traditional red coat. Left, a private of the 23rd (Royal Welsh) Fusiliers and right, a private of the 6th (1st Warwickshire) Regiment, in their campaign uniform of 1812, as depicted by Charles Hamilton Smith in his Costume of the Army of the British Empire *(1812–14).*

1812

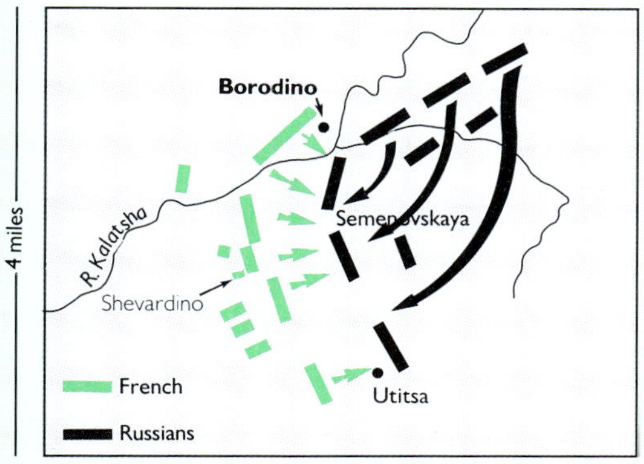

Raevsky redoubt and the *flèches* (arrow-shaped fortifications). Napoleon adopted a most unenterprising plan, little more than a frontal assault against the dour Russian defenders, with only token attempts to outmanoeuvre Kutuzov. The battle began in the early morning and continued until late afternoon, an action of appalling butchery. Napoleon made some progress after the Russians were driven from the Raevsky redoubt, the *flèches* and the village of Semenovskaya, but although the Russian centre was thus pierced they hung on grimly until both sides were exhausted.

CASUALTIES Russian losses were about 44,000 men and Napoleon's about 33,000.

RESULT Kutuzov withdrew during the night and a week later Napoleon was in Moscow, an untenable position which he abandoned and lost his army totally in the disastrous retreat from Moscow. By failing to destroy the Russian field army at Borodino, the campaign was effectively lost and Napoleon's downfall became inevitable.

ill-disciplined Indian armies, the limited nature of his resources in the peninsula resulted in his adoption of a defensive mode of warfare until he was strong enough to take the offensive, from 1812. It also demonstrated his mastery of tactics, which (although his strategical skill was probably not as great as that of Napoleon) firmly established him as one of the greatest commanders of his or any age. The British army's pre-eminent reputation was confirmed by these campaigns: as Wellington observed, the force which he moulded and commanded with such genius was for its size probably the most complete military machine then existing.

Despite the evacuation of one British army (that of Sir John Moore, killed in the battle of Corunna on 16 January 1809) from the peninsula in the face of enormous odds, Britain retained a foothold at Lisbon, through which port her army was supplied, further confirmation of the enormous advantage accorded by British command of the sea. Wellesley attempted an offensive into Spain, winning a hard battle at Talavera (28 July 1809), but the impossibility of co-operation with the ineffectual Spanish forced him on to the defensive. He retired behind the Lines of

(Above) Lieutenant-General Sir John Moore (1761–1809), commander of the British expedition to the Iberian peninsula which was evacuated after the retreat to Corunna (1808–09).

(Right) Marshal William Beresford (1768–1854), the British officer who reformed and commanded the Portuguese army. At the Battle of Albuera (16 May 1811), where Beresford commanded the Anglo-Portuguese, he unhorsed a French lancer who attacked him, as shown in this print after William Heath.

1813

LEIPZIG

DATE 16–19 October 1813
CAMPAIGN Napoleonic Wars
OBJECT After Napoleon's defeat in Russia in 1812, he was assailed by a coalition of Russia, Austria, Prussia and Sweden, intent on driving the French from their client-states in Germany. Having failed to defeat the Allied forces in detail, Napoleon concentrated around Leipzig, upon which the four Allied armies advanced.

NUMBERS Napoleon's army, numbering about 120,000 on the day before the battle, was reinforced to about 195,000 with 700 guns; the Allies' original force of 250,000 increased to 365,000 men and 1,500 guns.
DESCRIPTION Napoleon intended to hold a defensive perimeter around the city of Leipzig, while the Allies attacked in four main columns. Their first attack was made on 16 October, but the key action took place on the 18th, when a massive Allied attack was mounted upon all parts of

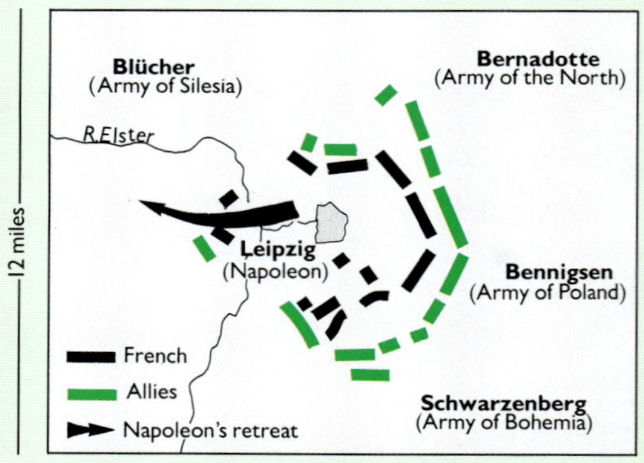

The battle of Polotsk, 17–18 August 1812, during Napoleon's disastrous Russian campaign, painted by Wilhelm von Kobell. The French Marshal Oudinot and General St Cyr with their French and Bavarian corps drove back General Wittgenstein's Russian army. Taking command after Oudinot was wounded, St Cyr was rewarded with a marshal's bâton. Wittgenstein was defeated again in another battle near the same location on 14 November 1812.

Torres Vedras, a fortification he devised to secure the Lisbon peninsula. By the British operation of a scorched-earth policy in front of the Lines, the French were starved into retreat, a major triumph for the most effective fortification of the period. By 1812 Wellesley (now Lord Wellington) was sufficiently powerful to mount an offensive against the French forces weakened by the diversion of resources to the east and by continual harassment by Spanish guerrillas. Wellington won a major victory at Salamanca (22 July 1812), advanced again in the following year, destroyed King Joseph's army at Vittoria (21 June 1813), crossed the Pyrenees and invaded southern France before the war ended. British financial aid to others of Napoleon's opponents was crucial, but the Peninsular War was of major significance in Britain's contribution to Napoleon's downfall.

Napoleon's personal efforts in Spain ended in early 1809 when he had to return to Germany to face a renewal of the war by Austria. He was not immediately successful, for although he captured Vienna the main Austrian army eluded him, and in an attempt to engage them by bridging the Danube Napoleon suffered his first serious reverse at Aspern-Essling (21–2 May 1809). A renewed and better-organized

1815

Napoleon's line. Hopelessly outnumbered, Napoleon had no option but to order a retreat westwards. Though he managed to extricate much of his army, the defeat he had suffered was of major proportions.

CASUALTIES Napoleon sustained about 73,000 casualties (killed and wounded) and the Allies about 54,000.

RESULT The defeat at Leipzig cost Napoleon control of Germany – his Saxon allies actually deserted him during the battle – and laid France open to invasion in 1814.

WATERLOO

DATE June 1815

CAMPAIGN The Hundred Days of Napoleon's restoration

OBJECT Napoleon escaped from his exile on Elba on 26 February 1815 and very quickly re-established his rule in France. It was imperative for him to score an early victory to improve his bargaining position.

NUMBERS Napoleon – 105,000 men; Wellington – 68,000 Anglo-Allied troops; Blücher – 89,000 Prussians.

DESCRIPTION Napoleon advanced rapidly, sending a minority of his force under Marshal Michel Ney towards the Anglo-Allied outposts at Quatre Bras, while he led 80,000 men against Blücher's Prussians. Stubborn British defence and an uninspired performance by Ney left the Anglo–Allies at Quatre Bras undefeated, but Blücher was severely mauled at Ligny and the Prussians withdrew. Napoleon ▸

attempt successfully crossed the Danube and inflicted a comprehensive defeat upon the Austrians at Wagram (5–6 July 1809), ending the war.

In 1812, in the face of renewed Russian hostility, Napoleon assembled an immense *grande armée* drawn from all the states under his influence, a multi-national force of quite exceptional size, with which he invaded Russia in June (over 450,000 men were used in the invasion, not including supporting formations). Unable to win a decisive victory over the Russian army despite an action of rarely parallelled butchery at Borodino (7 September 1812 – see page 138), Napoleon advanced to capture Moscow but, with much of the city burned by Russian incendiaries, he had to retreat in the late autumn and winter. A combination of severe weather and Russian harassment destroyed his army almost completely. From this point Napoleon's fall was inevitable. As he gathered a new army in 1813, the Russian success led to the revolt of Prussia, encouraged by a vociferous German nationalist movement, and in 1813 the "war of liberation" began which ejected the French from Germany, the Allied forces against Napoleon being joined by Austria and Sweden. The Allies closed in around Napoleon and in the "Battle of the Nations" at Leipzig (16–19 October 1813) Napoleon was fortunate to escape with part of his army. With Germany lost and his erstwhile satellites turned against him, Napoleon prepared to defend France in the following year. He had been suffering from worsening ill-health from at least 1812, but for a time in 1814 his old skill and vigour returned; yet his skilful manoeuvres against the converging Allied forces served only to postpone the inevitable. Assailed on all fronts and with his resources collapsing, Napoleon abdicated on 11 April 1814.

At the same time as the later Napoleonic campaigns were being waged, another conflict occurred in North America between the United States and Britain, the "War of 1812". Although its actions were small in comparison with the huge actions fought in Europe, it was significant in diverting considerable British resources from the war against Napoleon, and for the series of remarkable "frigate actions" in which the Americans were successful, denting the prestige of the British navy for the first time in the period. American attempts to invade Canada were repelled, as were British landings in the United States, though a considerable success was the burning of Washington's public buildings (including the White House) by a British expedition. The last and most famous action of the war, the repulse of a British force at New Orleans (8 January 1815), was fought before news of the signing of peace was received by the opposing armies.

Peace in Europe was short-lived; exiled by his enemies to the Mediterranean island of Elba, Napoleon brooded for some months before returning to France. He re-established control quickly and determined to take the offensive immediately, to

1815

detached a portion of his army under Marshal Emmanuel Grouchy to pursue the Prussians, whilst he joined Ney and moved upon Wellington, who retired from Quatre Bras to a position at Mont St Jean, near to the village of Waterloo on 17 June. Despite his defeat, Blücher determined to support his ally and retired on Wavre.

By the evening of 17 June Wellington's 68,000 Anglo-Allied troops and 156 guns awaited Napoleon's attack at the head of 72,000 men and 246 guns. Blücher left

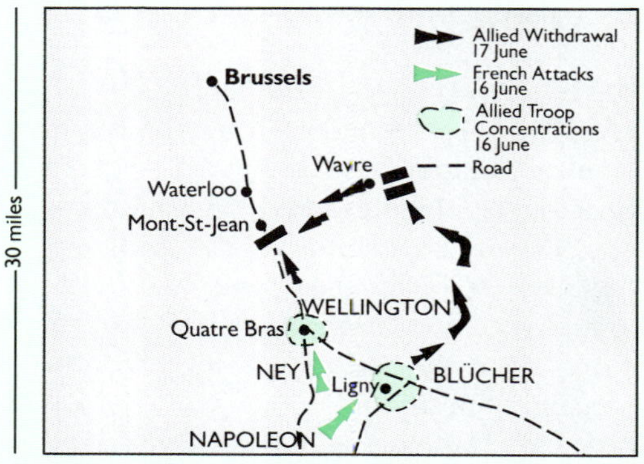

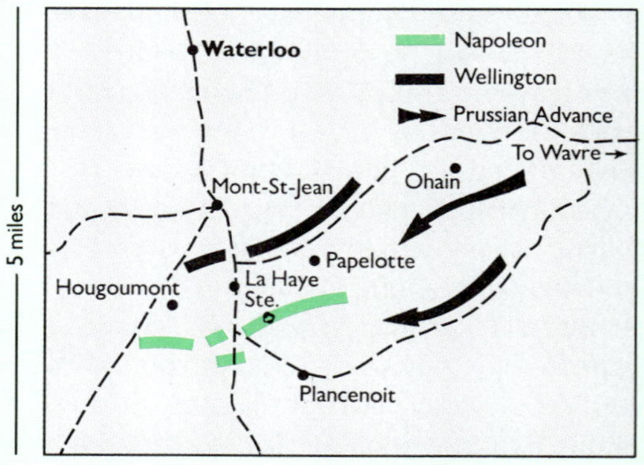

endeavour to achieve one major victory to strengthen his bargaining position before he was overwhelmed by the coalition again formed against him. He invaded the Netherlands, intending to defeat in detail the Anglo–Netherlands and Prussian armies under Wellington and Blücher respectively; but though he defeated the latter at Ligny (16 June 1815), Blücher extricated his army and, determined to support his ally at all costs, marched to support Wellington's position at Waterloo. The battle fought there on 18 June (see page 141), which destroyed the French army and ended Napoleon's career, is probably the most famous of modern times, and was a climactic end to an era in which the nature of warfare changed radically and in which many aspects of modern warfare can be recognized.

The Battle of Queenston (13 October 1812) was one of the first actions in the Anglo-American War of 1812, in which the American General Stephen Van Rensselaer attempted to invade Canada; the assault was repelled by the British commander, Sir Isaac Brock (1769–1812), who was killed in the battle.

1815

17,000 men and 48 guns to engage Grouchy's 33,000 and 80 guns, and marched with 72,000 and 44 guns to Wellington's relief. Wellington's position was upon a low ridge, anchored by the fortified château of Hougoumont and the farm of La Haye Sainte. About 11.30am Napoleon launched a furious assault against Hougoumont, hoping to compel Wellington to commit his reserves and weaken his centre for a breakthrough; but Hougoumont held throughout the day, and successive French attacks were beaten off by Wellington's beleaguered army. Not even a concentrated bombardment by the French artillery and repeated massed cavalry charges could break through, despite the loss of La Haye Sainte; and by about 4pm Blücher's leading elements were in action on Napoleon's right wing, diverting an increasing amount of his strength. The crisis came when Napoleon launched his reserve, part of the fabled Imperial Guard, at Wellington's centre; its repulse was the signal for the complete disintegration of the French army.

RESULT Blücher's Prussians pressed on with the pursuit of the routed French; Wellington's army was in no state to move, having suffered so severely for so long. The most famous battle of modern history ended Napoleon's long career; and, though a result of Allied co-operation, the chief reasons for its outcome were the skill of Wellington and the dour determination of his British contingent.

GREAT COMMANDERS

FREDERICK II OF PRUSSIA (Frederick the Great) was undisputedly the greatest commander of his generation, yet was an unlikely subject for a great soldier: slight of build, he suffered a most wretched youth at the hands of his boorish father, Frederick William I, who attempted to beat out of Frederick the artistic and intellectual qualities which were his natural characteristics. Frederick remained absorbed with music, literature and philosophy (which included a long and ultimately acrimonious association with Voltaire), but despite these ideals he was openly aggressive as a politician and a commander. His early campaigns in particular relied heavily upon offence, and only in later years did circumstances force him to operate in a more defensive mode. Frederick had exceptional qualities as a commander, though his inventiveness declined as years of attritional warfare reduced the abilities of his troops. Both king and army became the models for much of the remainder of Europe as a result of his outstanding victories.

NAPOLEON BONAPARTE, who was born in Ajaccio, Corsica, of minor and impoverished aristocracy, was an obscure officer of artillery in the French army until his plan for evicting the Anglo-Spanish-French expedition to Toulon brought him to public notice. His rise was amazingly rapid: after his "whiff of grapeshot" saved the National Convention from a royalist mob, his connections with influential personalities and his own immense talent made his future secure. In his early years he made an exhaustive study of his profession which, together with an appetite for relentless labour and a belief that he was destined for greatness led to his astonishing successes in Italy, followed by a *coup d'état* which established him as dictator of France and ultimately Emperor. He was a strategist of the highest order, formulating a method of warfare against which his opponents initially had no answer. Among his greatest talents was his ability to motivate his followers and to instil in them a feeling nothing short of adoration; though much of his apparent concern for them was artifice which concealed his ruthless nature. Later in his career his powers began to wane, and he over-reached himself with the invasion of Russia in 1812. Despite a return to his old vigour in 1814, his end was inevitable: he was marooned by his enemies on the Atlantic island of St Helena, an embittered and lonely fate for a man who had been master of half Europe.

ARTHUR WELLESLEY, the first Duke of Wellington, was the greatest British soldier since Marlborough, and arguably the greatest of all time. The offspring of Irish nobility whose family connections only eased the early stages of his career, his progress was due to his own immense talent and a selfless attitude to public service. Winning his early reputation in India, he led the most successful British army for a century when given command in the Iberian peninsula. Beset with immense difficulties and unreliable allies, and sometimes hindered by political considerations at home, the successful conclusion to the

(1)

(2)

(3)

(4)

Four of the most outstanding commanders in history, shown in contemporary portraits. (1) Napoleon Bonaparte (1769-1821) was not only a general of immense skill but an astute politician, the effects of whose civil reforms are still evident in France today. (2) Frederick the Great of Prussia (1713-86), known as "Old Fritz", one of the most influential figures in the development of tactics, raised Prussia and its army to a position of prominence. (3) Arthur Wellesley, 1st Duke of Wellington (1769-1852) was a highly talented general who succeeded despite unfavourable conditions in all his campaigns, and crowned his military career with the defeat of Napoleon. (4) Horatio, 1st Viscount Nelson (1758–1805), probably the greatest of all naval commanders, refined naval tactics and met an heroic death.

(Right) Napoleon surveys the battlefield of Wagram, in this painting by Horace Vernet. Wagram (5–6 July 1809), in which Napoleon defeated the Austrian Archduke Charles (1771–1847), concluded the last campaign in which Napoleon was victorious.

(Below) Horatio Nelson wounded at Tenerife, 24 July 1797; a painting by R. Westall. This injury resulted in the loss of Nelson's right arm; he had previously lost the sight of his right eye at Calvi in Corsica (1794), and was also wounded in the head during his victory at Aboukir Bay (the battle of the Nile) on 1 August 1798.

Peninsular War, and the final defeat of Napoleon at Waterloo, were due entirely to his genius and the solid, reliable character of the British troops he led. Sometimes criticized as being a defensive commander, when circumstances allowed he showed his talent for offence, and his organizational skills were no less extensive than his tactical ability. Giving the appearance of a cold and austere personality, he engendered no real affection among his army but instead their total trust and loyalty to "Our Arthur". His later career encompassed every office of state, including Prime Minister, which duties he discharged with the same selfless concern for the public good that had marked his military career, so that upon his death he was mourned as the nation's greatest servant, "the Iron Duke".

HORATIO, 1ST VISCOUNT NELSON was the greatest British sailor of the age, and probably the most innovative naval commander in British history. Born into minor Norfolk gentry, he entered the Royal Navy as a boy and rose to command a ship-of-the-line at the outbreak of the French Revolutionary Wars. In 1794 he lost the sight of an eye in Corsica; in 1797 he was largely responsible for the victory of St Vincent by his audacious manoeuvres, and later in the year lost an arm at Tenerife. He wrecked Napoleon's attempt to create an oriental empire by annihilating the French fleet at Aboukir Bay, and in 1801 destroyed the Danish fleet at Copenhagen. In 1805 he commanded the fleet which ended the prospect of a French invasion of Britain at the Battle of Trafalgar, tragically dying at the moment of his victory. His influence was not simply as a tactical innovator (refining the theory of "breaking the line" to its ultimate) and a strategist of the first rank, but as a quite exceptional character who imbued a reverence among his followers matched only by that of Napoleon, though without Napoleon's dissembling or lack of sincerity. The mutual affection between Nelson and his subordinates (whom he styled his "band of brothers") was an important factor in the successful execution of his plans.

9

INDUSTRY AND WAR

AS THE GLARE of Napoleon's comet sunk over the horizon towards St Helena, Europe sought to come to terms with the events of the past quarter century. The peace settlement which followed the Napoleonic Wars, largely the work of the Congress of Vienna, was essentially conservative, setting much store by the principle of legitimacy. The Quadruple Alliance (Britain, Austria, Russia and Prussia) underwrote the peace, agreeing to future joint action should it be needed to preserve "the Concert of Europe".

THE LEGACY OF NAPOLEON

But there were good reasons for the peace to prove fragile. The French Revolution had unleashed, across the whole of Europe, enthusiasms which could never again be quelled. The new French constitution declared that: "Frenchmen are equal before the law, whatever their titles or ranks." However, the unequal distribution of political and economic power, in France as elsewhere, helped inspire revolutionary upheavals. The conservative powers intervened to suppress revolutions which threatened to disturb the peace of Europe in the 1820s, although in 1830 the restored Bourbons were ousted by the "July Monarchy" of Louis-Philippe.

In 1848, which became known as the "Year of Revolutions" because of the general upsurge of rebellion, there were serious outbreaks in Paris, Berlin, Vienna and elsewhere. The Prussian and Austrian dynasties survived, but Loius-Philippe was removed, to be replaced first by a republic, and then by the Second Empire of Napoleon III. Even Russia, that most conservative of states, witnessed a failed revolt in the winter of 1825, although this was an attempted coup by upper-class army officers, the Decembrists, rather than a genuinely popular outburst.

The disturbances of 1815–48 reflected more than resentment at economic exploitation or political inequality; they also bore testimony to the growing strength of nationalism. Two areas were especially vulnerable to the joint pressures of

1854

INKERMAN

DATE 5 November 1854
CAMPAIGN Crimean War
OBJECT A Russian relieving force was to collaborate with a large-scale sortie from Sebastopol and launch a surprise attack on the British and French besiegers.
NUMBERS Russians – 19,000 men from the Sebastopol garrison, under General Soimonov, 16,000 men from the field army, under General Paulov. Another 22,000 soldiers from the garrison feinted at the Allied siege-line to prevent the sector under attack from being reinforced. Allies – about 8,000 in the threatened sector.
DESCRIPTION Both Russian forces were under the command of General Dannenbeg when united. The Allied armies were under the overall command of Lord Raglan and General Canrobert, and Major General Pennefather, commanding the British 2nd Division, played a leading role in meeting the attack. The Russian attackers were

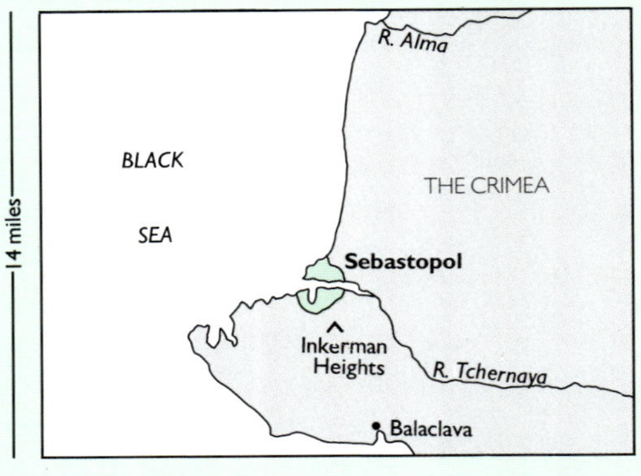

liberalism and nationalism. The Austrian Empire, huge and unwieldy, stretched from the Carparthians to the Mediterranean and from the Balkans to the Alps: the centrifugal tendencies of its national minorities threatened to pull it apart in 1848, and for the remainder of the century its instability was to have far-reaching consequences. Germany, in contrast, enjoyed greater national identity, but little in the way of political unity: Prussia was the most important of its numerous states, but in 1848–50 she failed to assert her dominance of the German-speaking world.

Thus, despite the conservative settlement of 1814–5, European stability was to be threatened by the combined effects of liberalism and nationalism. By mid-century these forces had already brought about marked political change in France; they had rocked the Austrian Empire, and had fuelled demands for German unity, creating pressures which, as the century wore on, were to pit the rising power of Germany against the waning strength of France. In short, the Vienna settlement was to prove less durable than its authors had expected. As has so often been the case, the world arising from the ashes of one war was all too soon to be scorched by other conflicts.

Conscription was one of the most potent legacies of the Napoleonic period. The French *levée en masse* of 1793 established a principle of universal military service which was to make possible the mass armies of the 19th and 20th centuries. True, its application was by no means universal. It was often politically convenient to stress the theory of universal obligation and the practice of generous exemptions, and it was only Prussian victory in the Franco-Prussian war of 1870–1 that proved, beyond dispute, that the effective mobilization of a nation's manpower played a leading role in the quest for victory.

JOMINI AND CLAUSEWITZ

Some military theorists, too, harked back to the Napoleonic age. General Antoine Henri Jomini, although Swiss by birth, had served in the French and Russian armies, and in the *Précis de l'art de la guerre* (1836) he analysed Napoleon's conduct of operations. Jomini was heavily influenced by 18th-century theorists like Lloyd and Bülow and looked back with affection to an era of small armies and controllable wars. He identified the importance of applying mass to the proper point at the decisive moment – the quintessence of Napoleon's style – and in his concern for the geometry of operations he deduced the importance of "interior lines", which enabled a centrally placed army to deal with external threats in turn. Although he recognized the value of genius amongst leaders and robust morale amongst the led, Jomini's great strength was his ability to make war seem dependent on principles which could be distilled and taught. He was enormously influential, not only in Europe but also in North America, and as late as 1914 the commander-in-chief of the British

1859

badly co-ordinated and lost their way in the fog and broken ground. Despite the patchy visibility, artillery played an important part in the battle. The British brought up two long 18-pounder siege guns, and their range and accuracy enabled them to silence the artillery supporting the attack.
CASUALTIES Russians – about 12,000; French 1,726, British 2,505.
RESULT The Allies fought a classic "soldiers' battle" and repulsed the Russians with disproportionately heavy loss.

SOLFERINO

DATE 24 June 1859
CAMPAIGN French campaign in northern Italy, 1859
OBJECT The French and their Piedmontese allies were advancing into Lombardy with the expectation of meeting the Austrians east of the River Mincio. The Austrians, for their part, hoped to secure the ground east of the River Chiese to block the French advance. An encounter battle took place on the hilly ground between the two rivers.
NUMBERS Austrians – 150,000, under the Emperor Franz Josef I; French and Piedmontese – approximately 120,000 under the Emperor Napoleon III.
DESCRIPTION After a hard-fought battle the French took Solferino and Cavriana in the Austrian centre. The Austrians fell back, their retreat covered by a sudden storm. They soon established themselves in "the quadrilateral" – the fortresses of Verona, Mantua, Legnano and Peschiera. The ▸

A contemporary print shows Union infantry of the 63rd Ohio Volunteers at the battle of Corinth, Mississippi, in October 1862. Well-entrenched Union troops were driven back by a Confederate assault, but rallied to mount a victorious counter-attack. The firepower of muzzle-loading rifles, the chief infantry weapon of the war, gave a marked advantage to the determined defender.

Expeditionary Force was dissuaded from embarking on a potentially suicidal course of action by remembering a line from a book written by a disciple of Jomini.

General Karl Maria von Clausewitz, on the other hand, enjoyed fewer plaudits in his lifetime. He had served in the Prussian and Russian armies in the Napoleonic wars, and been chief-of-staff of a Prussian corps at Waterloo. Although he became director of the Prussian *Kriegsakademie* after the war, he had little impact on the school's syllabus or teaching, and died of cholera in 1831 while serving as chief-of-staff of a force sent to put down the Polish insurgents. His great work *Vom Kriege (On War)* was published after his death, and many of its defects stemmed from the fact that its author never had the opportunity to revise it properly. Clausewitz saw war in quite different terms from the structured, measured conflict described by Jomini. It was the realm of physical exertion, chance and danger, characterized by constant friction, which made even the simplest things difficult. Clausewitz placed war firmly in its political context, emphasizing that it was the continuation of state policy by other means. It was the business of three distinct elements: the people, the army and the government. The people injected violence and passion. Armies had to cope with the uncertainty which overshadowed war, and politics was the business of the government. He saw the defensive as the stronger form of war and described a vigorous defence – "a shield of blows" – as the defender fell back until his opponent had outrun himself, when the culminating point of victory was reached and the counter-attack – "the flashing sword of vengeance" was unleashed.

There can be no doubt that Jomini enjoyed far more influence than Clausewitz for most of the 19th century, and it was not until after the Franco-Prussian War that Clausewitz was discovered by a Europe eager to find the touchstone of Prussian success. Yet Jomini and Clausewitz, in their very different ways, link the Napoleonic era with the First World War. Jomini codified the experience of the past, while Clausewitz looked forward to the age of total war. His writings were all the more relevant because, alongside the heady passions of liberalism and nationalism, which were to provide the emotional mainsprings of conflict, the onrush of industrialization was to fill the arsenals of Europe and North America with weaponry whose quantity and effectiveness was, quite literally, to change the face of war.

THE IMPACT OF TECHNOLOGY

Industrialization was the essence of 19th century war. Up to that time the pace of military change had been slow. The "Brown Bess" musket carried by Wellington's infantrymen at Waterloo was not markedly different from that used by their grandfathers under Marlborough, and the Swedish king, Gustavus Adolphus, killed at Lützen in 1632, would not have found the armies of 1832 totally strange. Infantry,

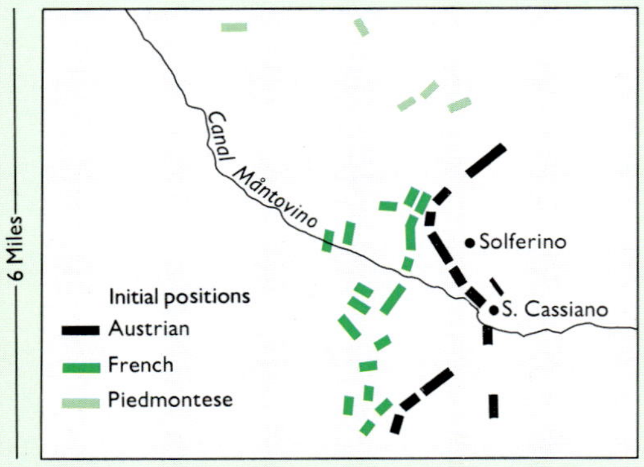

Allies were preparing for siege operations when an armistice was concluded, in part because Napoleon was sickened by the carnage of Solferino.

CASUALTIES French – 11,000, Piedmontese – 5,400; Austrian – 22,000.

RESULT The dreadful plight of the wounded and the inadequate provision made for them inspired the Swiss Henri Dunant to found the Red Cross, and to bring about the conference which resulted in the Geneva Convention (1864).

CHANCELLORSVILLE

DATE 2–4 May 1863

CAMPAIGN American Civil War

NUMBERS Hooker's Army of the Potomac – 150,000 men, including some 40,000 under Major-General John Sedgwick at Fredericksburg; Robert E. Lee's Army of Northern Virginia – 60,000, with only 10,000 at Fredericksburg.

DESCRIPTION Major-General "Fighting Joe" Hooker, who had recently taken com-

A French infantryman on the eve of the Franco-Prussian War aims his "Chassepot" rifle. The experience of campaigning in Algeria, where natural resources were scarce, had led to French soldiers carrying heavy packs with cooking and camping equipment. These were usually dumped before troops went into action. In 1870–71 a low képi *replaced the taller shako for field service, and a long blue overcoat was often worn instead of the tunic. The red trousers remained the hallmark of French infantry until the replacement of colourful uniforms by "horizon blue" in 1915.*

1863

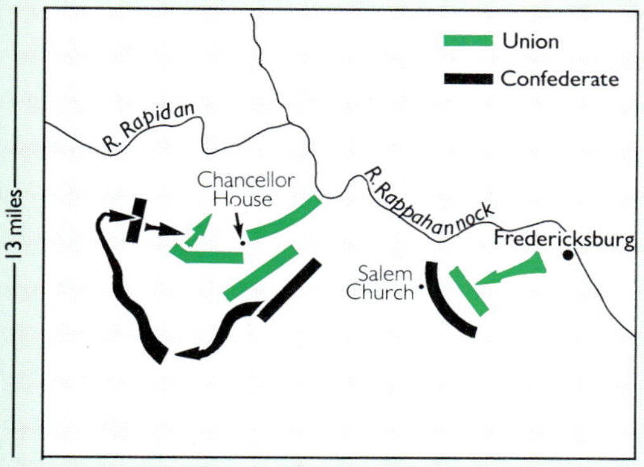

mand of the Army of the Potomac, left a strong force facing his opponents on the Potomac at Fredericksburg, scene of an earlier unsuccessful Union offensive. He then took the remainder of his army upstream to cross near Chancellorsville, turning the Confederate flank. Hooker crossed the river successfully but paused, and was vigorously counter-attacked by Lee, who unleashed Jackson against Hooker's right. The resultant flank attack mauled the Union XI Corps: Hooker's nerve broke and he fell back across the river. He was replaced in command of the Army of the Potomac by Major-General George G. Meade the following month.

CASUALTIES Confederate – 13,000, including the mortally wounded Thomas J. "Stonewall" Jackson. Union – 17,000.

RESULT Hooker had failed to encircle and destroy the Confederate Army of North Virginia. The battle is a good illustration of the importance of moral forces in war. Even after the success of Jackon's flank attack, ▸

(Above) Niklaus von Dreyse's Needle Gun, adopted by the Prussian Army in 1840, finally showed that breech-loading was a viable system. Its success pioneered the way for all subsequent bolt-action rifles. The gun's name came from the long, spring-propelled firing needle with which it was fitted.

(Top) The French equivalent was the Fusil Mle, which became the standard French infantry weapon in 1866. Designed by Antoine Chassepot, this was a distinct improvement on the Dreyse design. The whole firing mechanism was considerably simplified, with the needle becoming a fixture inside the bolt, being automatically cocked as the latter was closed.

the most numerous arm, delivered massive short-range firepower from dense formations. Under ideal circumstances a soldier might hit a man-sized target at 80 yards, but the conditions were rarely ideal. The dense and stinking smoke that shrouded the battlefield reduced visibility, the fouling of burnt powder clogged musket barrels and locks, and the unreliability of the flintlock mechanism meant that perhaps a quarter of all shots were misfires.

Artillery had remained a direct fire weapon, which did most of its killing at well below 1,000 yards. Gustavus might have been impressed by the fact that some field guns now fired bursting shells, but he would have observed that these were very much in the minority and that roundshot, or multiple rounds like grape or canister, still enjoyed pride of place. The cavalry, an arm Gustavus understood so well, had retained its two old roles. Light horsemen carried out scouting and reconnaissance, and joined in the pursuit of a beaten enemy, while heavy cavalry, often part armoured in cuirass and helmet, strove to break their opponents by shock action on the battlefield.

Between Waterloo in 1815 and Mons 99 years later technology intervened to transform this time-honoured picture – and much else besides. The process had, in fact, started in the 18th century, when numerous innovations – most notably James Watt's development of the first commercially viable steam engine in 1776 – had improved coal-mining and iron-founding alike. Iron production increased enormously over the period: in Germany alone it rose from 85,000 tons in 1823 to more than 1,000,000 tons in 1867 and a staggering 15,000,000 tons on the eve of the First World War. The Bessemer Converter made possible a fourfold increase in steel output in Britain and Germany between 1865 and 1879.

New production methods marched alongside this burgeoning output. In the 18th century small arms were produced by techniques which had changed little since the Middle Ages. Individual craftsmen in small workshops or larger factories assembled weapons, filing a lock here, straightening a barrel there. Despite the existence of official specifications, no two weapons were exactly alike, and the system's dependence on skilled labour made rapid increases in production difficult to achieve.

ARRIVAL OF THE MASS-PRODUCED RIFLE

During the 19th century this process was transformed. First, government arsenals, like Enfield in England, Harper's Ferry in the USA, Chatellerault in France and Tula in Russia, devoted themselves to arms production, and at the same time a number of commercial companies, with Krupp and Vickers prominent amongst them, applied the full entrepreneurial zeal of the age to the manufacture and marketing of weaponry. Secondly, the techniques used by government arsenals and private

1863

Hooker's position was far from hopeless, and a more dogged general might have fought it out. But as the Union commander himself admitted: "I just lost confidence in Joe Hooker."

GETTYSBURG

DATE 1–3 July 1863
CAMPAIGN American Civil War, Lee's invasion of the North, June–July 1863
OBJECT After defeating Federal forces at Chancellorsville, Virginia, in May, General Robert E. Lee decided to invade the North in hopes of further discouraging the enemy and possibly inducing European countries to recognize the Confederacy.
NUMBERS Union – Major-General George

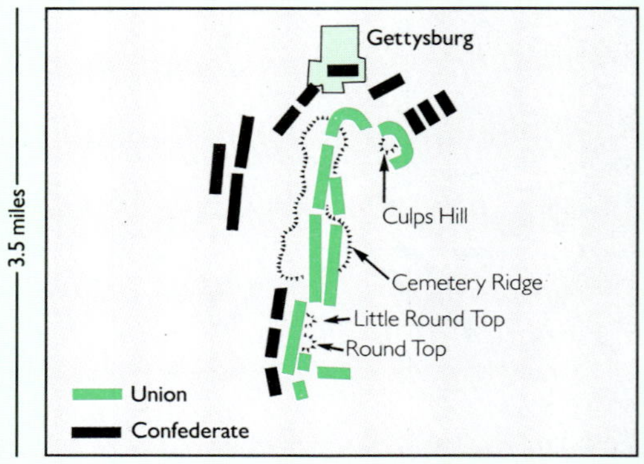

manufacturers alike made possible the swift production of standardized weapons with interchangeable parts. Precision machine-tools made for finer manufacturing tolerances, and the beginnings of industrial automation saw weapons and spares clatter off the new production-lines. One case points up the general trend. In 1866 France decided to equip her army with the "Chassepot" infantry rifle. By the time the Franco-Prussian War broke out four years later, over a million of these rifles, hundreds of millions of rounds of ammunition, not to speak of bayonets, cleaning-kits and cartridge-boxes, were ready for use.

And there were more young men to use them. Improvements in medical science, with Lister's work on antiseptics, Pasteur's on bacteriology and vaccination, and Jenner's experiments with smallpox vaccine, all helped improve life expectancy. The population of Europe grew rapidly, from 187 million in 1800 to 266 million in 1850, 401 million in 1900 and 468 million in 1913. The picture was not altogether rosy, however, for despite advances in medicine, disease remained more deadly than the bullet. It was not until the 20th century that the soldier was more likely to die from enemy action than from illness. In the American Civil War the Union army lost 96,000 men in battle, while 183,000 died of disease, and for the 4,285 British soldiers who were killed or died of wounds in the Crimea, another 16,422 died of disease or exposure.

Technology affected war in three main areas. It increased the range and lethality of weapons; improved transport and communications – from railway, through steamship to electric telegraph; and, finally, it strengthened defences, from the armoured turret to the concrete fortress carapace.

Improvements to weapons in the first half of the century showed the way ahead. In 1805 Alexander Forsyth, a clergyman with an interest in wildfowling and chemistry, had developed a lock which used fulminate of mercury, rather than a flint, to ignite a weapon's main charge. The percussion lock was improved over the next 30 years and by 1840 all major armies were replacing their flintlock muskets with the more reliable percussion weapon. If the percussion lock enhanced the reliability and simplicity of infantry weapons it did nothing for their accuracy. That depended on the adoption of rifling. It had long been understood that cutting spiral grooves in a weapon's barrel imparted a spin to the bullet and greatly increased accuracy; riflemen had performed creditably in North America during the American War of Independence and in Spain during the Peninsular War. But there were problems with early rifles which prevented their widespread introduction. It was important to have a tight fit between bullet and rifling, but what was comfortably tight with a clean weapon became difficult or impossible as fouling clogged the rifling.

The problem of having a bullet which was tight-fitting on firing but could be

Continued on page 154

WAR ON RAILS

Armies were quick to recognize the military potential of the railway. In 1840 the British took a battalion from Manchester to Liverpool by train, and six years later the Russians moved a corps of 14,500 men 200 miles by rail. The French made great use of the railway in the 1859 campaign, moving a total of 604,381 men and 129,227 horses.

The railways were particularly useful to Prussia. In 1866 nearly 200,000 men were sent to the frontiers by railway, and the numerous lessons learnt stood Prussia in good stead in 1870.

The evidence of the American Civil War allied to that of 1870–1 to emphasize the railway's vital role. By 1914 railways, and the specialist troops who maintained and managed them, were an indispensable part of national mobilization plans.

Military railroad construction in 1864.

1863

G. Meade's Army of the Potomac, 88,000 men. Confederate – General Robert E. Lee's Army of Northern Virginia, with J.E.B. Stuart's cavalry detached, 70,000 men.

DESCRIPTION Lee opened the campaign by taking the war out of Virginia, into Union territory. Stuart's cavalry, the eyes of the army, were out of contact with Lee's main body, and Lee thus encountered Meade's army by accident. A leading Confederate divisional commander had heard that there were large quantities of shoes in Gettysburg, and asked permission to obtain them. This brought him into contact with Union cavalry and provoked a general engagement. Once battle was joined, Lee sought first to outflank the Union army from his right, and, when this failed in fierce fighting around Little Round Top (2 July), he launched a frontal assault – known as Pickett's Charge – against the Union centre on 3 July. After coming very close to success in the Round Top fighting on 2 July, the Confederates were bloodily repulsed from the Union centre on the next day. The defeat did savage damage to the Army of Northern Virginia and Lee rapidly fell back to Virginia.

CASUALTIES Confederate – between 20,000 and 28,000 men; Union – 23,000.

RESULT In itself Gettysburg was inconclusive. But on 4 July, as Lee's beaten army recoiled, Ulysses S. Grant took the Confederate stronghold of Vicksburg on the Mississippi after a long siege. Between them, ▸

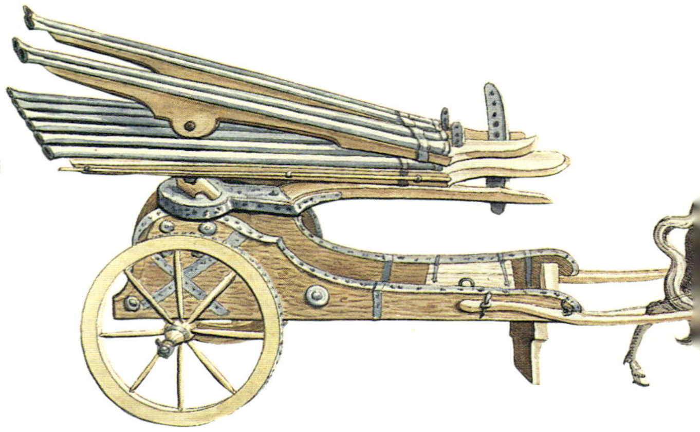

CONCENTRATED ESSENCE OF INFANTRY: THE MACHINE GUN

(Above) A 16th-century Portuguese illustration of the "Death's Organ Gun". This is typical of early attempts to produce multiple-fire weapons: the barrels, laid side by side like organ-pipes, had to be loaded individually and, while the gun might set off a useful salvo, reloading was a lengthy business.

THE IDEA OF PRODUCING multiple shots from a single weapon had existed almost as long as the firearm itself. The first mention of ribauldequins or "Organ Guns" occurs as early as 1339. These had a number of barrels laid side-by-side, and could be sited to command entrances or defiles or, if mounted on wheeled carriages, brought into an army's battle-line. Yet their real value was decidedly limited. They could only deliver a single volley, for it was usually impracticable to reload each barrel in turn in the heat of battle. James Puckle's machine gun, patented in 1718, worked on the revolver principle, with a single barrel fed from a revolving chamber. It was neither a technical nor a commercial success.

The first militarily useful machine guns appeared in America in the mid-19th century. In 1861 the American Union army bought a small number of Ager machine guns, but these were never fully tested in action. The Chicago dentist Richard Gatling developed his revolving machine gun in 1862, and in 1866 the US Army placed a large order. Britain followed suit the following year.

(Right) The Gatling, like many early machine guns, was multi-barrelled. As the barrels were rotated, each in succession came level with the magazine, where a cartridge dropped into its loading-tray. The cartridge was then forced into the chamber by a rammer, was fired and had its spent case extracted as the barrels turned (see inset).

The French adopted a machine gun of their own. The *Mitrailleuse* was developed in the artillery workshop at Meudon, and in 1865 it went into mass production: 215 guns were available by 1 January 1870. The weapon looked like a conventional field-piece, mounted on a wheeled carriage. Its bronze tube contained 25 13mm barrels, which were loaded simultaneously with a block containing 25 rounds, fired in a *rafale* or burst. The gun's performance in 1870 was disappointing. *Mitrailleuse* batteries were often mishandled, being held back with the artillery where superior Prussian guns could deal with them: this was in part because few *Mitrailleuse* battery commanders had received training on the weapon, which had been kept scarcely less secret from its friends than from its enemies.

As long as machine guns relied upon gravity feed and black-powder cartridges they remained unreliable. With the advent of the metallic cartridge and smokeless powder new developments were possible. The American Hiram Maxim hit upon the idea of using the recoil of one round to load and fire the next. Cartridges were contained in a fabric belt which was cranked automatically into the action: the Maxim was a genuine machine gun in that it did not depend on the firer operating its mechanism, merely in keeping the trigger pressed. Maxim demonstrated his gun in England in 1884, and went into partnership with Vickers the same year: the British army adopted the Maxim in 1891, and many others followed suit.

Maxim's design established the pattern of machine guns for the next 30 years. His fellow-countryman John M. Browning made his own contribution by using some of the gas which fired the bullet to assist the loading process, and the Vickers, adopted by the British army in 1912, incorporated this addition. The Vickers was water-cooled, with a water-filled jacket surrounding its barrel.

(Below) This late 19th-century photograph shows British Gatling guns on the North-West Frontier of India. The machine gun increased the advantage enjoyed by Western armies engaged against many of their tribal opponents. Each weapon is hitched to its limber, whose chest contains ammunition. The escalating consumption of ammunition was one consequence of the increase of firepower.

(Above) Men of the 3rd London Rifle Volunteers with a Gatling gun, 1893. This smartly-posed photograph shows the weapon's drum magazines, one mounted on the gun and another held by the third soldier from the right.

(Left) An early Maxim machine gun being test-fired. The fabric belt holding the ammunition can be seen clearly, as can the cocking handle on the firer's right, and the backsight, in its elevated position.

In 1914 a British battalion usually had two Vickers guns. In the German army, a three-battalion regiment had six guns, forming a machine-gun company which put strong centralized firepower at its commanding officer's disposal. The standard German weapon was the 1908 Spandau, a belt-fed, water-cooled 7.92mm gun. As the First World War went on, the number of machine guns grew rapidly, and there was a tendency to group medium machine guns in specialist units: the British Machine Gun Corps was founded in 1915. Secondly, light machine guns were developed. Some, like the Lewis, were purpose-built. Others were derived from existing weapons. In 1915 the Spandau was modified to become the 08/15 by the addition of a wooden stock and the replacement of the heavy mount by a small bipod. The machine gun made unsupported assault suicidal, and helped drive the infantryman into the troglodyte world of trench warfare. Well might the Machine Gun Corps' memorial at Hyde Park Corner proclaim:

> Saul has slain his thousands
> But David his tens of thousands.

Chassepot-armed French infantry defend a street during the Franco-Prussian war. The figure with the baggy red trousers is a zouave, from a unit raised among European settlers in the French colony of Algeria.

loaded easily was solved in France, where a series of experiments resulted in the projectile known, from the name of its inventor, as the Minié bullet. This was conical, with a hollow base (in early patterns containing an iron or wooden plug) and flanged rim. It slipped easily down even a heavily fouled barrel and, on firing, the gases of the explosion drove into the hollow base, forcing the flanges to bite into the rifling. In the 1850s the Minié became the first rifle issued to the infantry as a whole, and, corrupted as "minny", was the characteristic infantry weapon of the American Civil War.

Between 1830 and 1860 infantry weapons had at least doubled in reliability, and their effective fighting range had increased to between 300 and 400 yards. Over the next 30 years the pace of change was to be no less rapid. The disadvantages of loading a weapon from the muzzle had long been recognized: not least amongst them was the fact that it was extremely difficult to load a muzzle-loading weapon lying down. Some militarily useful breech-loaders had been produced before the 19th century, but it took that century's industrial developments to make the breech-loader feasible on a large scale.

Prussia led the way. In the 1840s she equipped her infantry with the Dreyse bolt-action needle gun, so called because of the needle-like firing pin which entered the base of the cartridge to strike the primer and fire the round. Although the Dreyse suffered from numerous defects, short range and a poor gas-tight seal at the breech amongst them, it gave a startling demonstration of its prowess in the Austro-Prussian War of 1866, when its sheer rapidity of fire cut swathes through the Austrian infantry. Thereafter all major armies sought to re-equip with breech-loaders. The French 1866 "Chassepot" was infinitely better than the needle gun. A rubber obturating ring diminished the problem of gas leakage at the breech, and the weapon's effective fighting range was some 600 yards. At St Privat on 18 August 1870 the Prussian Guard launched an ill-conceived frontal attack on the French 6th Corps, and lost some 8,000 men, mainly to "Chassepot" fire, in 20 minutes.

The enormous success of the "Chassepot" increased the speed of change. Several armies converted their muzzle-loaders to breech-loaders as a temporary expedient (the British Snider was a classic case in point) while the search for the most effective breech-loader went on. The hunt was no simple one, and led down a number of blind alleys. The single-shot breech-loader, with a falling breech-block like the Martini-Henry or a turning one like the Remington rolling-block, was able to cope with the radical reduction in calibre made possible by the development of the metallic cartridge and cupro-nickel bullet. But it could not be modified to permit rapid fire, and so it was the bolt-action rifle, with a box magazine at the breech or a tubular magazine below the barrel, that eventually became the standard infantry weapon across the world.

1863

Gettysburg and Vicksburg marked the climax of the Civil War. Though the North could still lose the war through incompetence or war-weariness, the South no longer had the power to force a decision in its own favour.

Pickett's Charge was a graphic illustration of the effects of defensive firepower: the remarkable fighting qualities of Confederate infantry were no answer to the fire that Union troops poured down the slopes of Cemetery Ridge.

THE MARCH TO THE SEA

DATE Winter 1864–5
CAMPAIGN American Civil War, Sherman's campaign in Georgia and the Carolinas
OBJECT Having taken Atlanta in September 1864, Sherman planned to march through the heartland of the Confederacy, crippling its resources and striking a powerful blow at southern resolve.
NUMBERS Sherman left Atlanta with 62,000 men. He was not opposed by

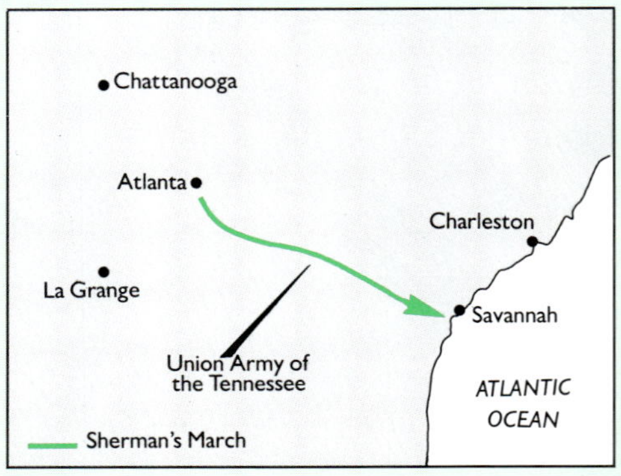

In the 1880s the bolt-action magazine rifle, with a calibre of around .303 inch or 7.92mm, was universally adopted. Most were known from the arsenal where they were developed or produced, like the US Springfield; from the name of their inventor, like the French Lebel, or from a combination of both, like the British Lee-Enfield. The introduction of smokeless powder – the way was led by France, with *Poudre B* in 1885 – set the seal on the process, and by the turn of the century the infantry rifle had attained the form it was to retain through one world war and well into a second. Mass-produced, accurate and reliable, it had an effective fighting range of up to 1,000 yards against a mass target. Its magazine held five to 10 rounds and permitted very rapid fire: the average British infantryman, a regular soldier with thorough training, could get off 15 rounds a minute, and some of his more experienced colleagues could do even better. Alongside this went the perfection of what Liddell Hart was to call "the concentrated essence of infantry" – the machine gun.

IMPROVEMENTS IN ARTILLERY

Artillery had developed along lines similar to small arms, with the introduction of breech-loading rifled weapons as the crucial line of departure. But the scale of the technical problems to be solved, the importance attached to the projectile as well as to the weapon itself, and the difficulty of absorbing recoil – so simply accomplished by the firer's shoulder in the case of the rifle – meant that the development of artillery often lagged behind that of infantry weapons.

Advances in metallurgy solved the first problem facing artillery manufacturers. Bronze was costly. Cast-iron gun barrels, a cheaper alternative, were unmanageably heavy if thick and dangerous if thin. Wrought iron, hammered into shape around a mandrel, and sometimes with strengthening bands shrunk on at points of maximum pressure, was an improvement. During the American Civil War the smooth-bore 12-pounder "Napoleon" was the mainstay of Union artillery, supported by a variety of rifled cannon, notably 10- and 20-lb "Parrots", their cast-iron barrels reinforced by wrought-iron bands. But the real answer had already been found. The German manufacturer Krupp exhibited steel cannon at the Great Exhibition of 1851: although their barrels were originally made up of several components, soon they were machined from solid steel.

The second difficulty, producing a gas-tight breech, was half-overcome once guns were made of steel and manufacturing tolerances could therefore be finer. Several workable solutions were produced, amongst them Krupp's sliding breech-block and the "interrupted thread" perfected by the French engineer de Bagne. The superiority of German artillery in the Franco-Prussian War encouraged swift imitation and, though the British army briefly switched back from breech-loaders to muzzle-

Union heavy guns in Fort Brady on the James River. The piece in the foreground, the reinforcing band on its cast-iron barrel clearly visible, is on a fortress mount: the two guns immediately behind it are on field carriages. Shells are stacked in the left foreground, and handspikes, to help the gun's detachment to traverse the weapon, stand ready.

1866

formed units of significant size.
DESCRIPTION Sherman wanted to "make Georgia howl" and he certainly succeeded in doing so, reaching the coast at Savannah on 21 December. In early February he set off again, leaving a trail of destruction through the Carolinas. This was a more difficult operation, for terrain and weather were worse, and resistance was stiffer. However, Sherman defeated J.E. Johnston, forcing him to surrender near Goldsboro.
CASUALTIES Relatively few casualties were suffered by either side. Much more important was the damage done to Confederate industry, agriculture and communications.
RESULT Sherman made an important contribution to Union victory, gnawing at the Confederacy's vitals while Grant beat its armies in northern Virginia. His achievements – burned mills and ravaged railroads – left bitter memories in the South.

KÖNIGGRÄTZ (SADOWA)

DATE 3 July 1866
CAMPAIGN Austro-Prussian War
OBJECT Prussia, under Otto von Bismarck, challenged Austria for the leadership of the German Confederation – a carefully planned stage in the unification of Germany under Prussia's Hohenzollern dynasty.
NUMBERS Prussians – approximately 200,000; Austrians and Saxons – approximately 200,000. ▸

The changing face of war. Canadian troops, dressed in utilitarian khaki uniforms and armed with long Lee-Enfield magazine rifles, climb a rock-strewn kopje during the Boer War of 1899–1902.

loaders, rifled breech-loaders were in general use by the 1880s. Producing a shell which would take the rifling without wearing out the barrel had caused problems similar to those experienced in small-arms design. The eventual solution was to add a copper driving band, flexible enough to mould to the rifling, ensuring a gas-tight seal without abrading the inside of the bore.

This left only the question of recoil unanswered. As long as the barrel was fixed directly to the carriage, the shock of firing was transmitted through the whole weapon, causing it to spring backwards: its detachment had to manhandle it back into position and re-lay it before firing again. The "recuperator" interposed a hydraulic buffer – with a plunger working inside an oil-filled chamber – between barrel and carriage. Although the barrel still leapt back sharply, the recoil was absorbed by the recuperator, and the carriage scarcely moved. The famous French 75mm, the *soixante-quinze* of 1897, used not only the recuperator but also "fixed" ammunition – projectile and cartridge joined in a brass case – and could hammer out an unprecedented 20 rounds a minute.

Advances in the gun were paralleled by improvements in the projectile. New propellants and burster charges gave better performance and less smoke. Shells could be fitted with percussion fuses to burst on the ground, or with time fuses to burst in the air. The shrapnel shell, named after its inventor, Lieutenant Henry Shrapnel of the Royal Artillery, was intended to explode above enemy infantry, showering them with small balls, while high explosive – HE in military shorthand – ripped holes in buildings or ground and turned woods to debris. Some HE shells were very large indeed and were intended for use against fortifications. The sloping glacis in front of a fortress and the armoured turrets that began to sprout from its top offered obdurate targets to guns that fired directly at them. They were more vulnerable to heavy howitzers, whose shells rose high on steep trajectories to drop with devastating force on top of the fortifications.

OTHER EFFECTS OF TECHNOLOGICAL ADVANCES

At the same time that it increased the range and lethality of weapons, technology also transformed communications. The development of the railway was of immense significance, for it speeded up strategic transport and enabled a country like Germany, with potentially hostile powers on both flanks, to use "interior lines" to her advantage. Steam was scarcely less crucial at sea. In 1807 Robert Fulton's steamboat made the 150-mile journey up the Hudson from New York to Albany in 32 hours. Steam was soon used by naval vessels, first to power the paddle-wheels and later to drive underwater propellers. The Battle of Navarino, when a British, French and Russian force destroyed a Turkish fleet in 1827, was the last general action fought

1866

DESCRIPTION Feldzugmeister Ludwig von Benedek's Austrians and their Saxon allies held a strong position along the line of the Bistritz north-west of the fortress of Königgrätz. The Prussian First and Elbe armies, under Prince Frederick Charles and General Herwath von Bittenfeld respectively, attacked from the west. Fierce fighting was already in progress when the Prussian Crown Prince's Second Army, which had pursued a quite separate line of advance, appeared on the Austrian right flank. This turning movement proved decisive and the Austrians were heavily defeated, though the courageous performance of Benedek's cavalry and gunners enabled him to extract his surviving troops.

CASUALTIES Casualties were utterly disproportionate, in great measure because of the effects of the needle gun used by the Prussians. Prussians – 9,000. Austrians and Saxons – 44,000, including 22,000 prisoners.

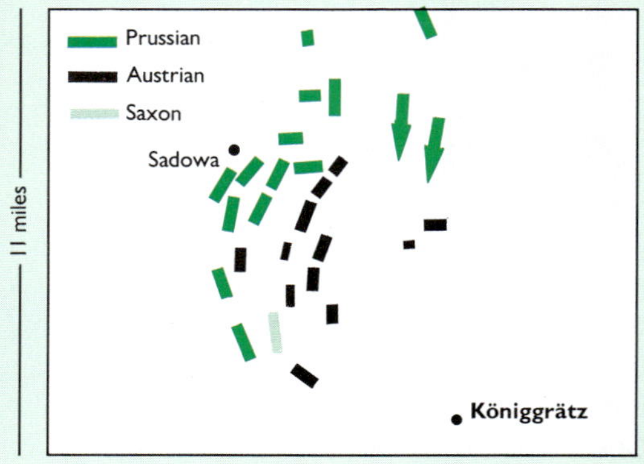

An idealized view of the British attack on Russian positions at the first battle of the Crimean War, the Alma, fought on 20 September 1854. Although outnumbered, the Allies carried the heights above the river, but failed to mount a quick attack on the Russian fortress of Sebastopol.

between wooden sailing ships. Natural conservatism, allied to a desire to save coal when the breeze would serve, meant that for much of the century warships remained full-rigged. Nevertheless, fleets were at last freed from the tyranny of the wind and were able to manoeuvre freely.

By the close of the century the internal combustion engine was beginning to make its presence felt. Between the Boer War of 1899–1902 and the outbreak of the First World War in 1914 armies made cautious experiments with automobiles and lorries, although the overwhelming majority of land transport continued to be horse-drawn. It was the application of the internal combustion engine to the aircraft that foreshadowed the most dramatic future developments. Armies had already put balloons to military use, but in 1911 the heavier-than-air machine came of age when the Italians flew reconnaissance and bombing missions against Turkish troops in Tripolitania.

Not only did technology enable troops and supplies to move faster and more efficiently: it also permitted commanders to communicate with growing ease. The semaphore telegraph had been widely used in the Napoleonic Wars, but its limitations were considerable. In 1829 the electric telegraph was perfected, and with the development of Samuel Morse's code in 1850 it became a valuable means of strategic communication. The telephone, patented by Alexander Graham Bell in

1870

RESULT Although the Prussians had failed to encircle the bulk of the Austrian army, largely because of Bittenfeld's failure to press his victory over the Austro-Saxon left wing, the battle was decisive. Benedek fell back rapidly on Vienna, where he met the Archduke Albrecht's Army of the South, which had moved up from Italy after defeating the Italians at Custozza. But it seemed clear that a continuation of hostilities could only result in another Austrian defeat and peace preliminaries were signed on 26 July. The battle was no less decisive in political terms. Prussia had asserted her right to the leadership of Germany, from which Austria was excluded. Königgrätz was the single most important step on the road to German unification, a path which was to lead directly to war with France in 1870 and thereafter to the First World War.

REZONVILLE–MARS-LA-TOUR

DATE 16 August 1870
CAMPAIGN Franco-Prussian War
OBJECT Marshal Bazaine's French Army of the Rhine, having been defeated at Spicheren on 6 August, sought to withdraw from Metz towards Verdun. The Germans wanted to impede that withdrawal.
NUMBERS French – 160,000 men, mostly within reach of the battlefield but not all ▸

Three hirsute veterans of the Crimean War. These Coldstream guardsmen are equipped with the .577-inch three-band Enfield rifled muzzle-loader, and wear the Crimea medal, each of its bars denoting their presence at a battle. The Coldstream played a distinguished part at the Alma and Inkerman.

1876, was better yet, and in 1885 the Germans experimented with linking artillery observers to their guns by field telephone, making indirect fire possible for the first time. Marconi's work on the wireless was to be of immense long-term importance, but during the period in consideration wireless was in its infancy, bulky, prone to jamming and insecure. Indeed, poor security over the wireless was to contribute to the great Russian defeat at Tannenberg in August 1914.

The third area of military affairs affected by the technology of the 19th century was fortification. The great engineers of the 18th century had established the importance of low, geometrical works, which offered poor targets to an attacker's artillery, and always presented assaulting infantry with ditches, steep walls and flanking fire. The principles of classical fortification evolved little in the 19th century, but technology came to the fortress-builder's aid. It enabled him to add concrete (often with a sand "burster layer") to the stonework of yesteryear and, finally, to put the fortress guns in armoured turrets. The offensive technology of siege artillery tended to change quicker than the defensive technology of the fortress, as the rapid fall of the Liège forts in 1914 was to demonstrate. Nevertheless, permanent fortifications were to be of considerable importance in the First World War. Nor should we forget that very simple piece of defensive technology, barbed wire, developed in the United States as a means of cattle control. Less dramatic than the steel turret or the concrete casemate, barbed wire was, in its way, to have more awesome military consequences than either.

It was at sea that defensive technology really came into its own. Adding armour plate to the hulls of wooden warships enabled them to sustain punishment which would have sunk a conventional vessel, and the clash between the USS *Monitor* and CSS *Merrimac* in Hampton Roads, Virginia, on 9 March 1862 was the first battle between steam-powered ironclads. Neither ship was really ocean-going, but this said more about the circumstances of the American Civil War than about marine engineering, for France had launched the seagoing ironclad *La Gloire* in 1858. Britain replied with HMS *Warrior*, her main guns, boilers and engine enclosed in an armoured box composed of wrought-iron plates 4½ in thick bolted to 18 in of solid teak. *Warrior* herself was soon outdated, and by the end of the century naval guns were, increasingly, mounted in revolving turrets rather than in an armoured hull.

THE ART OF WAR

The new military technology of the 19th century fitted into a world increasingly overshadowed by war. But apart from minor campaigns against insurgents, and the more widespread upheavals of 1848, it was not until 1854 that large-scale hostilities broke out. A dispute over the Holy Places in Jerusalem, and instability resulting from

1870

directly engaged. The Germans deployed 76,000 by nightfall.

DESCRIPTION The German Second Army (under Prince Frederick Charles) crossed the Moselle south of Metz, and two of its corps jabbed up against the French line of retreat. They realized that they had brought the main French army to battle and maintained their attacks in order to persuade Bazaine not to press his advantage and force his way towards Verdun. Bazaine, increasingly obsessed by the threat to his left rear, failed to push on and carry out his planned retreat on Verdun or, more enterprisingly, to defeat the German Second Army in detail.

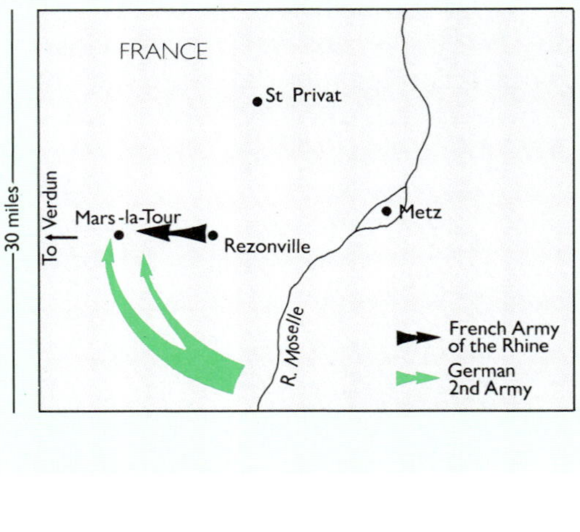

CASUALTIES Germans – 16,000, French – 14,000 (including about 5,000 missing and prisoners).

RESULT On the night of the battle Bazaine decided to fall back on a strong defensive position outside Metz and to restock with supplies and ammunition before making another attempt to leave the city.

shrinking Turkish power, produced war between Britain, France and Turkey on the the one hand and Russia on the other. The Allies sent an expeditionary force to the Black Sea, landed in the Crimea, beat the Russians on the River Alma and laid siege to the naval base of Sebastopol. Russian attempts to relieve the city led to the battles of Balaklava and Inkerman (see page 146), and after costly assaults on Sebastopol in the autumn of 1855, the Russians at last evacuated it.

The Crimean War was described by Philip Guedalla as "one of the bad jokes of history", and it did indeed have an air of black comedy. Yet its consequences were far-reaching. It convinced the new czar, Alexander II, of the need for internal reform, and the abolition of serfdom in 1861 freed some 40 million peasants. It established France, once again, as a first rank military power. French soldiers were no longer "the beaten men of Europe", and their achievements drew admiring comments from friend and foe alike. The toughness and resource displayed by French soldiers in the Crimea was largely a product of long experience of campaigning in Algeria and it stood out in stark contrast to the privations endured by the British as they wintered on the bare uplands outside Sebastopol. The lamentable performance of her administrative services lent fresh impetus to military reform in Britain. The campaign also drew attention to the shortcomings of military hospitals; and Florence Nightingale, who did so much to organize the hospital at Scutari, emerged as a popular heroine.

The French army was in action again only four years later. In 1858 Napoleon III had made a secret agreement with Count Cavour, prime minister of the north Italian state of Piedmont, to come to Piedmont's support if the Austrians, in possession of the neighbouring states of Lombardy and Venetia, could be provoked to attack. Napoleon hoped to gain prestige and the French-speaking Piedmontese territories of Nice and Savoy: Cavour, for his part, saw the ejection of the Austrians as a key step towards Italian unification. In 1859 the Austrians were duly duped into attacking and a French army moved into northern Italy, winning scrambling victories at Magenta and Solferino (see page 147). Then, much to Cavour's fury, Napoleon made peace without ensuring that Venetia was relinquished by Austria, but over the next two years all Italian states, with the exception of Rome and Venetia, came under the sway of Piedmont, which duly became the Kingdom of Italy in early 1861.

Victory in 1859 revealed numerous shortcomings in the French army. While it excelled at "the small change of war", mobilization had been inefficient and the higher conduct of operations clumsy. Magenta and Solferino had been won by the aggressive determination of the French infantry, whose charges swept away the Austrians before they were able to make best use of their excellent Lorenz rifles. Yet the experience did not deter Napoleon from further military adventure. In 1862 he sent an expeditionary force to Mexico, and two years later installed an Austrian

Continued on page 162

UNIFORM: FROM DRAMATIC TO DRAB

Uniform had long tended to be flamboyant but impractical, though wartime alterations often modified its more extreme aspects. During the 19th century there were demands for simpler uniform, in part as a response to the growing importance of concealment on the battlefield, and in part because of calls for utility and economy.

Armies bowed to the pressure. Some British units wore khaki (from the Urdu for dust-coloured), in the Indian Mutiny of 1857–8, and it replaced scarlet for field service after the First Boer War of 1880–1. The Russo-Japanese war persuaded its belligerents to adopt khaki too, and the US army took to olive drab in 1902. In 1909 the Austrian army wore "pike grey", while the Germans adopted "field grey" between 1907 and 1910. The French stood fast against the trend. On the eve of the First World War a minister proclaimed *"Le pantalon rouge, c'est la France"* (the red trouser is France), and French infantry took the field in 1914 in red trousers and long blue greatcoats. This finery did not survive the first clashes, and 1915 saw it replaced by "horizon blue".

1870

GRAVELOTTE–SAINT PRIVAT

DATE 18 August 1870
CAMPAIGN Franco-Prussian War
OBJECT Following the indecisive battle of Rezonville–Mars-la-Tour, Bazaine's Army of the Rhine had taken up a strong defensive position on the rolling uplands west of the Moselle, covering the fortress of Metz. He intended to refit his army before making another attempt to retreat on Verdun.

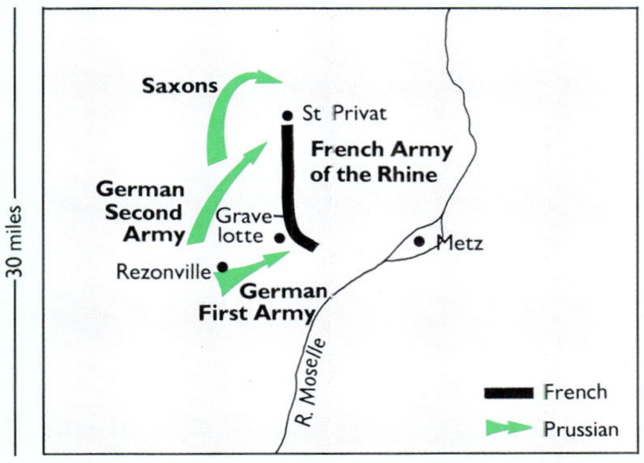

NUMBERS Germans – 188,500; French 113,000.
DESCRIPTION The German Second Army, under Prince Frederick Charles, marched across the front of Bazaine's position in an effort to find its right flank, and the German First Army, under General von Steinmentz, launched a series of frontal attacks against the French left. Towards nightfall the Saxon Corps turned the French right at Saint Privat. Although his left and centre had held their ground, the collapse of his right ▸

THE RISE OF THE DREADNOUGHT

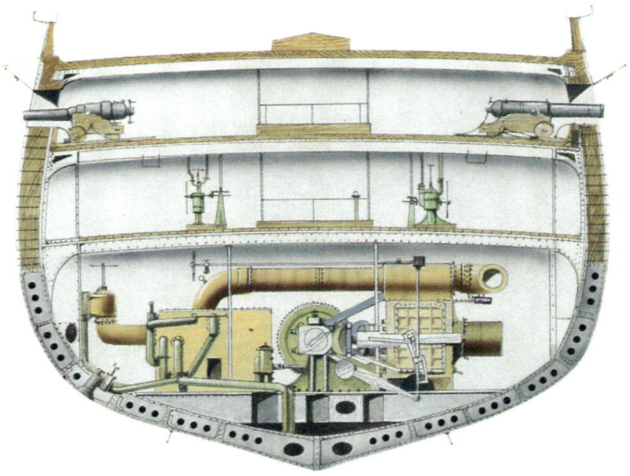

(Above) This cross-section through HMS Warrior shows two of her ten 110-pounders. Her main gundeck is protected by 4½-inch wrought iron plates, backed by 18 inches of teak. Warrior's engines could push her along at 14½ knots. (Right) The battle between the sail-powered Merrimac and ironclad Monitor, March 1862.

IN THE 1840s, ships-of-the-line differed little from those which had fought at Trafalgar. They were full-rigged wooden sailing vessels, their muzzle-loading cannon firing through ports in three gun-decks. Just as technology transformed land war, it also revolutionized warship design, and the ships of the 1840s were soon to be obsolete. Developments took place in three areas – propulsion, protection and firepower. In 1807 the American engineer Robert Fulton proved that steam-powered vessels were commercially viable, but the vulnerability of the paddle-wheel limited the application of the steam engine to the warship. In 1843 the first screw-driven warship, the USS *Princeton*, was launched.

Developments in France led to dramatic increases in firepower. Naval guns had traditionally fired solid shot at hostile ships, supplementing this with grape- or case-shot for close-range work against crew or rigging. In 1837, however, the French began to arm their warships with exploding shells. The French launched the ironclad battleship *La Gloire* in 1858. The British response, launched in 1861, was HMS *Warrior*, a massive ironclad which rendered all other warships obsolete. Although *La Gloire* and HMS *Warrior* enjoyed armoured protection, were powered by screws, and had mounted guns which fired exploding shells, in one important respect they remained backward-looking. Their guns fired broadside, just as Nelson's had. The battle between the USS *Monitor* and the Confederate *Merrimac* (renamed *Virginia*) in March 1862 showed just how helpless sail-powered wooden warships were against ironclads – *Merrimac* destroyed two the day before *Monitor* arrived. It also suggested that a revolving turret, like that housing *Monitor*'s guns, was a better way to mount main armament than the traditional broadside gun.

(Above) The French battleship Jauriquiberry. Along with her centre-line turrets, she carried some heavy guns in barbette turrets, one visible amidships.

The weight of early turrets meant that ships equipped with them tended to ride perilously low in the water, and were suitable only for inshore operations. Moreover, the Battle of Lissa (1866), in which a technologically inferior Austrian fleet defeated a superior Italian force, encouraged designers to equip warships with armoured rams. As the century drew to its close the pace of innovation increased, with successive warships gaining a decisive technological edge, only to be rendered obsolete.

Study of naval developments overseas encouraged Admiral Fisher, appointed Britain's First Sea Lord in 1904, to set up a committee to design the "all big gun battleship". The result was HMS *Dreadnought*. She was the model for the mighty battle-fleets that waited to contend for mastery of the seas during the First World War. But like the armoured knight at the very height of his power, they contained the seeds of their obsolescence. They were cripplingly expensive: and there were growing threats, beneath the sea, and in the air above it, against which they were increasingly vulnerable.

(Above) France's director of naval construction, Stanislas Dupuy de Lôme, built mostly wooden-hulled vessels with iron armour. This painting shows the first of these, La Gloire, *launched in 1858. Britain's HMS* Warrior *was built in response.*

(Below and right) Study of naval developments and the evidence of the Battle of Tsushima encouraged Admiral Fisher, appointed Britain's First Sea Lord in 1904, to set up a committee to design the "all big gun battleship". The result was the 17,900-ton Dreadnought, *launched in 1906. The fastest battleship in the Royal Navy, she was well protected against attack by torpedoes. Her five turrets housed ten 12-inch guns; smaller quick-firers were provided to deal with torpedo-boat attacks. With* Dreadnought's *appearance, all other battleships became obsolete, but she was overtaken by new developments and was scrapped in 1920.*

King William I of Prussia, right, and his staff at the battle of Königgrätz. Moltke is second from the right, and Bismarck third from the left, in the front row. Although Moltke had been Chief of the General Staff since 1857, his name was not a household word in the Prussian army. At Königgrätz one general commented that a written order seemed to be all right, "But who is this General von Moltke?" After the battle the question was not asked again.

Archduke, Maximilian, as emperor. But the Mexican escapade turned sour. Maximilian's new subjects were anything but loyal, and Union victory in the American Civil War was followed by vigorous protests about European intervention in the New World, which was seen as contrary to the principles of the Monroe Doctrine of 1823. Prussia's victory over Austria in 1866 was the last straw, and the French withdrew from Mexico to concentrate on the worsening situation in Europe. The unlucky Maximilian was captured and shot, and the episode did much to weaken the prestige of Napoleon's gaslight empire.

THE ASCENDANCY OF PRUSSIA

The waning of French power gave Otto von Bismarck, prime minister of Prussia, the opportunity to proceed towards his aim of German unification. He believed that this first required the defeat of Austria, so that Prussia could become the basis for a united state which would exclude the German-speaking elements of the Habsburg Empire. In 1864 he manoeuvred the Germanic Confederation into war with Denmark over the duties of Schleswig and Holstein. The Convention of Gastein (1865) left these under the Prusso-Austrian condominium, which resulted in friction between Prussia and Austria, exactly as Bismarck had expected. He bought off Napoleon, hinting that French neutrality would be rewarded by territorial gains along the Rhine and, with French help, concluded an agreement that would bring Italy into an Austro-Prussian war, forcing the Austrians to fight on two fronts.

The spectre of Prussian aggrandizement alarmed many German states, who sided

1870

persuaded Bazaine to withdraw into Metz.
CASUALTIES Germans – 20,000, including over 8,000 casualties suffered by the Prussian Guard in its premature attack on the French 6th Corps at Saint Privat. French – at least 12,500.
RESULT Moltke left a force to blockade Metz and to set off in pursuit of the Army of Châlons with the newly created Army of the Meuse and the Third Army. Bazaine remained in Metz until he surrendered in October.

SEDAN

DATE 1 September 1870
CAMPAIGN Franco-Prussian War
OBJECT Marshal MacMahon intended to relieve the French Army of the Rhine, trapped at Metz. Moltke wished to use the German forces to surround the French army.
NUMBERS Germans – Moltke commanded 150,000 men of the Third Army (under the Crown Prince of Prussia) and the Army of the Meuse (under Crown Prince Albert of Saxony). French – 120,000 men of the Army of Châlons, commanded by Marshal MacMahon and, after his wounding, by General de Wimpffen.
DESCRIPTION The fighting of 16–18 August had resulted in Bazaine's Army of the Rhine taking refuge in the fortress of Metz. Marshal MacMahon's Army of Châlons, consisting of troops defeated in Alsace in the opening battles of the war and fresh forces from elsewhere, left Châlons in an

with Austria when war broke out, after disputes over the federal structure of Germany and the administration of the duchies, in 1866. Conventional wisdom favoured the Austrians and their allies, but this reckoned neither with the needle gun nor with an even more decisive weapon – Helmuth von Moltke, chief of the Prussian general staff. Moltke and the war minister von Roon had carried out far-reaching reform of the Prussian army, whose arrangements for conscription and mobilization were later to become the models for other European armies.

Moltke's conduct of operations was bold but risky. An ambitious "forward concentration" by railway led to his armies crossing the frontier in widely separated columns, the Elbe Army swinging down through Austria's ally Saxony while the First and Second Armies pushed into Bohemia from the north. The Austrians had split their forces to face the Italian threat, and though they were victorious in Italy all the determination of their robust infantry, resolute gunners and flamboyant cavalry was to no avail against Moltke's huge concentric attack and the savage firepower of the needle gun. On 3 July the Austrians were defeated at Königgrätz (see page 155) in a single battle that decided the war. The peace excluded Austria from active participation in the new German world. The old Germanic Confederation was disbanded, and the states north of the River Main formed the North German Confederation under Prussian leadership. Although the treaty was generous to Austria, defeat in 1859 and 1866 left her weakened, and in 1867 the empire was reorganized to form the Dual Monarchy, with separate Austrian and Hungarian governments, united in the person of the reigning Habsburg who was both Emperor of Austria and King of Hungary.

France was defeated, indirectly, at Königgrätz. Napoleon failed to obtain any compensation for his neutrality, and found himself facing an increasingly nationalistic Germany whose army had given recent proof of its prowess. His own attempts at military reform were marred by his weakening grip on political power, for it was difficult to sustain both the new "Liberal Empire" and the thoroughgoing reform which the French army urgently demanded. The new military service law, the *Loi Niel* of 1868, went part of the way, and the introduction of the "Chassepot" and "Mitrailleuse" put powerful new weapons in the hands of French soldiers. But the underlying flaws remained. Mobilization arrangements were archaic and the command structure relied upon a single controlling will which Napoleon, already painfully ill, was never able to provide.

In the summer of 1870 France stumbled into a war which more astute diplomacy might have averted. A German prince was offered the throne of Spain. Although he eventually withdrew his candidacy, Bismarck phrased reports of the King of Prussia's refusal to guarantee that similar candidacy would not be repeated in such way that

POLITICAL GENERALS

Both American Civil War armies, faced with the task of raising troops in a nation with little military experience, granted commissions liberally. Men whose political connections would strengthen the government and aid recruitment were especially favoured.

Prominent Union political generals included Benjamin F. Butler, a Massachusetts state senator, and the New York Democratic politician Daniel E. Sickles, who lost a leg as a corps commander at Gettysburg. Franz Sigel, a former Baden artillery officer, enjoyed immense influence with the Germans of the North.

The Confederate political generals included some of real military ability. John C. Breckinridge, a Kentucky lawyer, rose to the rank of major-general before becoming Secretary of War. South Carolina planter Wade Hampton raised "Hampton's Legion" at his own expense, and ended the war as a lieutenant-general.

Not all politicians aspired to high rank. Colonel Frank Wolford of the 1st Kentucky Cavalry was a small-town lawyer and politician. Known as "Old Meat Axe" to his men, his phraseology owed little to the drill-book, but it was hard to mistake his cries of "huddle up", "scatter out" or "get up and git".

1870

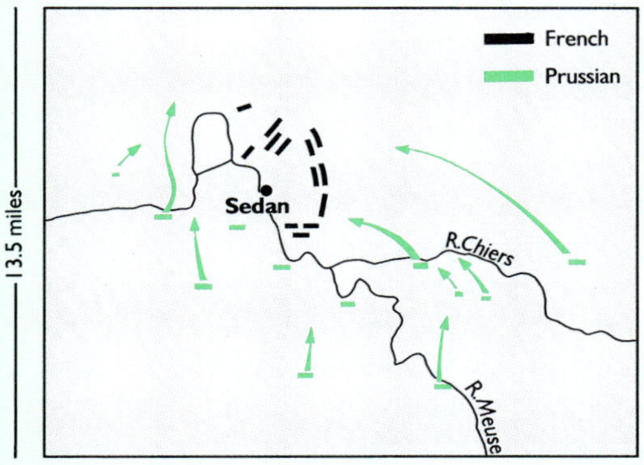

effort to join Bazaine, who was expected to break out of Metz. The French advance was beset by contrary orders and poor logistics, and on 31 August MacMahon took up a defensive position at Sedan, hoping to resume his march after a day's rest. Moltke had set off in search of MacMahon with the Third Army on his southern flank and the Army of the Meuse to its north. His cavalry did not find MacMahon till 26 August, and on 30 August an isolated French corps was beaten at Beaumont. Moltke then ordered his army commanders to pin the French against the Belgian frontier, the Army of the Meuse moving up from the east and the Third Army from the south: he aimed at a battle of encirclement, trapping the whole French army. The Germans succeeded in surrounding the French. Neither resolute defence of the eastern end of the position, nor heroic attempts by their cavalry to break out to the west, helped the French, who were forced to capitulate.

CASUALTIES German – 9,000. French – ▸

The world's first militarily successful submarine, the CSS Hunley, *at Charleston, South Carolina, 6 December 1863. The* Hunley *was armed with a contact mine at the end of a bow-mounted spar. On 17 February 1864 she sank the USS* Housatonic *off Charleston, but then went to the bottom too.*

the exasperated French declared war. The first phase of the war was reminiscent of 1866. The French, spread out along the frontier, were defeated on 6 August at Froeschwiller in Alsace and Spicheren in Lorraine. The forces in Alsace withdrew to Châlons under Marshal MacMahon, while those in Lorraine came under the command of Marshal Bazaine. Bazaine tried to withdraw form Metz to Verdun, was defeated at Rezonville on 16 August, and fell back into Metz after the inconclusive battle of Gravelotte-St Privat on the 18th. MacMahon, marching to relieve him, was trapped at Sedan on 1 September (see page 162) and compelled to capitulate: Bazaine surrendered Metz in late October.

The second phase of the war tried Moltke's talents more severely, as the government of National Defence, which replaced the fallen Second Empire, raised troops in the provinces and vigorously defended the besieged capital. The efforts of the Armies of National Defence prolonged the war but could not win it. An armistice was concluded on 28 February 1871, and France made peace on humiliating terms. These included the loss of Alsace and Lorraine, a painful blow which made for a high likelihood of another Franco-German conflict. The war not only confirmed German unity under Prussian leadership, but also helped accelerate the militarization of German society, another dangerous portent for the future.

THE AMERICAN CIVIL WAR

By the time that the Franco-Prussian War was fought in Europe, a conflict in North America had foreshadowed many of its developments. The American Civil War, which broke out in 1861, pitted the largely agricultural, agrarian South against the industrial North. The weight of resources was to tell heavily in the North's favour. In 1860 it had 110,274 industrial establishments to the South's 18,026, and had $949,335,000 of capital investment against the South's derisory $100,665,000.

It is easy to argue that the North's formidable industrial muscle must eventually

1870

13,000 killed and wounded and 21,000 prisoners. The surrender of the French army added another 83,000 prisoners to this total.

RESULT The Emperor Napoleon III, accompanying his last army, surrendered. Revolution in Paris replaced the Second Empire by the Government of National Defence. Although the war ground on until February 1871, Sedan was its decisive battle.

PAARDEBERG

DATE 17–27 February 1900

CAMPAIGN Boer War 1899–1902

OBJECT The British army wished to re-establish control over areas taken by Boer General Piet Cronje.

NUMBERS British – 40,000 in all, rather more than half engaged. Boers – 5,000.

DESCRIPTION Early February 1900 saw the British stuck fast on the Modder river south of the besieged town of Kimberley. Lord Roberts was commander-in-chief with Lord Kitchener as his chief-of-staff. Lieutenant-General French commanded the cavalry. Roberts left a division to pin Cronje's main Boer army to the river and hooked around Cronje's left flank in a wide turning movement led by French's cavalry. French crossed the Modder on 13 February and relieved Kimberley on the 15th. Cronje, meanwhile, set off eastwards along the Modder in an effort to escape encirclement. French cut his line of retreat

have proved decisive. However, it took time for the North to gear its strength to a single cohesive plan, and it was not until Ulysses S. Grant remorselessly applied the Union's bludgeon to the Confederacy's rapier that Union victory was assured. Moreover, if the South lacked human and industrial resources it possessed some commanders of outstanding ability, Robert E. Lee and Thomas "Stonewall" Jackson among them. Thus the early years of the war were marked by Union defeats, some of which seemed to leave the Confederacy on the very brink of victory. But all Lee's brilliance could not save the Confederacy from being ground down in a battle of resources. The North's blockade of southern harbours made it increasingly difficult for the South to import arms, and her own factories and battlefield captures were never sufficient to keep the Confederacy's armies fully equipped. In 1864–5 the combination of Grant's relentless pressure in Northern Virginia and William T. Sherman's destructive march from Atlanta, through the heart of the Confederacy, to the sea (see page 154), sounded the South's death-knell. The war showed that industrial and economic resources, if properly applied, were decisive.

THE RUSSO-JAPANESE WAR

The American Civil War, with its widespread use of railways and startling

A Japanese print shows infantry cutting the railway line at San-Tai-Tzu, north of the Manchurian city of Mukden, during the Russo-Japanese War of 1904–5. There was heavy fighting around Mukden, which was eventually taken by the Japanese. Defeat in Manchuria, loss of Port Arthur, and disaster in the naval battle of Tsushima compelled Russia to make peace, weakening the autocracy's hold at home and its prestige abroad.

1900

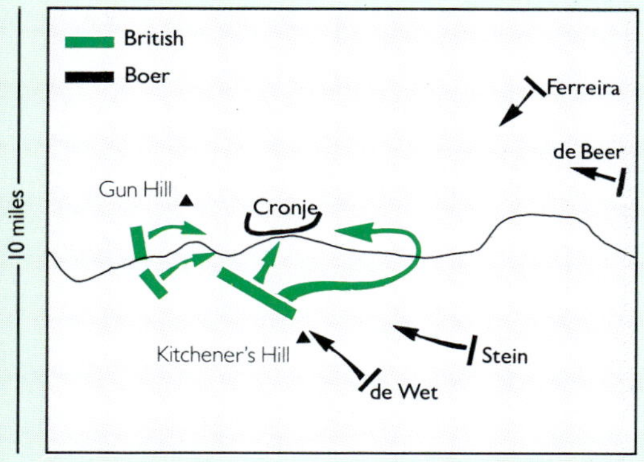

on the 17th, and kept him in check while the infantry divisions marched up. Thereafter Cronje remained in his laager on the river at Paardeberg, while the British first attempted a series of unwise attacks and then settled down to starve Cronje into submission. On 18 February the British suffered 1,200 casualties, the heaviest of any single day of the war; the Boers lost fewer killed and wounded, but Cronje surrendered with 4,000 men on 27 February.

CASUALTIES British – more than 1,200; Boers – up to 1,000.

RESULT Cronje's force was captured, removing about one-tenth of Boer fighting strength at a blow. However, the battle proved inconclusive, and it was to be Boer irregulars, rather than formed Boer armies, that caused the British their most serious problems.

The Japanese battleship Asashi, *part of Admiral Togo's fleet, opens fire on the Russians at Tsushima. Superior Japanese communications and gunnery played an important part in bringing about the almost complete destruction of the Russian squadron.*

demonstrations of the effectiveness of infantry firepower and field defences, pointed the way ahead to both 1866 and 1870–1. The Russo-Japanese War of 1904–5 did much the same for the First World War. The Japanese attacked the Russian fortress of Port Arthur without warning in February 1904, and for the next year they besieged Port Arthur and fought the Russian field army in Manchuria. Although the fighting in Manchuria was inconclusive, it gave graphic proof of the effectiveness of magazine rifles and machine guns. The siege of Port Arthur was every bit as significant. Determined Japanese infantry suffered frightful casualties in their attacks on Russian forts and field defences, but the plunging fire of Japanese heavy howitzers proved murderously destructive, not only to the forts themselves but also to Russian ships at anchor in the harbour.

An attempt by a Russian fleet sent from the Baltic to break the siege of Port Arthur failed miserably. On 27–8 May 1905, in the largest sea battle since Trafalgar and the first fought with steam-powered turreted warships, Admiral Togo utterly defeated Admiral Rozhdestvensnki in the straits of Tsushima (see below). Port Arthur had already fallen by the time Rozhdestvensnki appeared and the demolition of his fleet led the Russians to make peace. Russian defeat had profound consequences. It once more revealed the limitations of the autocracy, encouraging internal opposition and inspiring a cautious move towards parliamentary democracy. It also highlighted Russian military weakness, and at the same time picked out the rising power of Japan. The latter point was not missed by colonial populations, for whom the defeat of a Western power was especially portentous.

Colonial wars had been in almost constant progress throughout the 19th century. The picture was usually a consistent one. Western powers – the British in India and Southern Africa, the Russians in Central Asia, the French in North Africa and Indo-China – were usually able to defeat indigenous populations by the application of superior technology. There were times when technology was not enough and most colonial powers incurred at least one serious reverse: in 1879 the British suffered a bloody defeat at the hands of the Zulus at Isandalwana and in 1896 Baratieri's Italian army was routed by the Abyssinians at Adowa. Moreover, as Western technology spread into Africa and Asia, contests were less unequal. A small British force was defeated by the Afghans at Maiwand in 1880, in part because the Afghans' Krupp guns outperformed British artillery. The most serious colonial confrontation was the Anglo-Boer War in 1899–1902, when it required the sustained military might of the British Empire to defeat the largely irregular forces of the Boer republics and then to cope with a long and exhausting guerrilla war. From the British point of view, however, the war was not without its uses, for it inspired a serious reorganization of the army, which emerged much better prepared to face the challenge of 1914.

1905

TSUSHIMA

DATE 27–8 May 1905
CAMPAIGN Russo-Japanese War
OBJECT The Japanese, under Admiral Togo, wanted to disrupt Russia's hope of regaining mastery of the sea.
NUMBERS Russian – 4 modern and 4 obsolescent battleships, 9 cruisers, 9 destroyers, 8 auxiliaries; Japanese – 4 modern battleships, 8 cruisers and a strong torpedo-boat flotilla.

DESCRIPTION The Russian 2nd Pacific Ocean Squadron under Admiral Rozhdestvensnki was making for Vladivostock after a long voyage from the Baltic. The original intention had been for this Second Fleet to relieve Port Arthur, Russia's main naval base in the Far East and join up with the Far Eastern Fleet, which was bottled up in the port. However, the fall of Port Arthur on 2 January 1905 necessitated a change of plan.

On the morning of 27 May, the

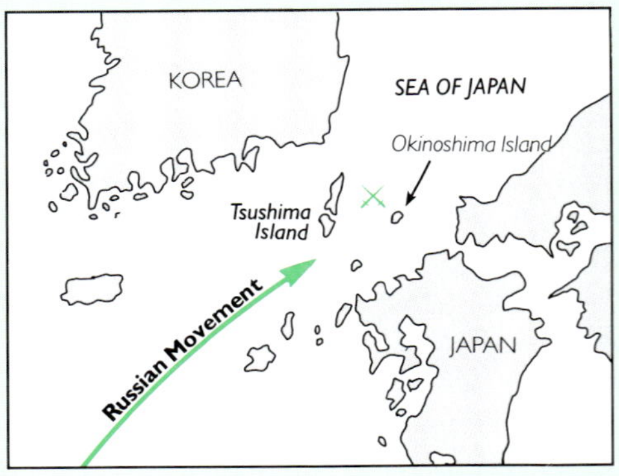

THE ROAD TO ARMAGEDDON

The seeds of disaster had begun to sprout while the new century was still in its infancy. An ominous confrontation between France and Germany was an enduring legacy of the Franco-Prussian War. Anglo-German naval and economic rivalry helped push Britain towards an unofficial understanding with France, and the need to counterbalance a powerful Germany encouraged France, for her part, to look towards Russia. Austria-Hungary, riven by the problem of nationalities, was wary of developments in the Balkans, where the decline of Turkish power and the Balkan wars of 1912–13 had aroused new and destabilizing national passions.

The military developments of the late 19th century ensured that these political concerns inspired fine-tuned preparations for war. All major European powers recognized the potentially decisive contribution to be made by conscription and mobilization plans, the railway and the general staff. The techniques of mass production enabled the huge armies swept together by conscription to be armed and fed. And the new armies had abundant firepower at their disposal. Their infantry and artillery looked so unlike the men who had fought at Waterloo as to be unrecognizable: only the cavalry, striving to confer mobility to a battlefield soon to be locked solid by firepower, still resembled the dashing horsemen of yesteryear. And, despite the beliefs of generals such as Britain's Douglas Haig, who stated that bullets "had no real stopping power against the horse", 1914 was to show that cavalry had lost its place on the modern battlefield.

A mixture of the intellectual currents of the 19th century, nationalism high amongst them, and the industrialization of war had made possible a new sort of conflict, fought between powers with prodigious human and industrial resources at their disposal. It is small wonder that men looked at the prospect of future war with utter disbelief, arguing that it would prove so destructive as to be impossible: others, like Britain's Lord Kitchener, prophesied that once the battle of the giants had been joined it could end only in the exhaustion of the weakest.

A late First World War German cavalryman still sits on his horse and carries the lance like his forefathers, but a plain steel helmet and field-grey uniform have replaced the elegance of only a few years before. The gas mask bears testimony to the threat posed by poison gas. The photograph underlines the involvement of the horse in war.

1905

Russians approached the Tsushima Strait, between Japan and the island of Tsushima, where it was intercepted by Admiral Togo's Japanese battle fleet. The Russians enjoyed an advantage in heavy guns, with 43 10–12in pieces to the Japanese's 16, but the Japanese were superior in 6–8in guns. The Japanese fleet was able to steam more quickly than the Russian, and Togo made the first use of wireless communications in battle. Togo first "crossed the T", steaming across the path of the Russians, and then used his fleet's superior flexibility to position it parallel to the Russians and slightly ahead, concentrating on their leading vessels. Rozhdestvensnki's flagship, the Suvorov, was badly damaged and the admiral himself seriously wounded. As the Russians grew increasingly confused, Togo "crossed the T" again, this time at close range. Though the battle lasted through the night, the Japanese mopping up the next day, there was no recovering from the rout. Only two Russian destroyers and a light cruiser managed to disengage and reach Vladivostock; the old battleship *Oslyaba* and the modern vessels *Alexander III*, *Borodino* and *Suvarov* were all sunk.

CASUALTIES The Japanese lost only three torpedo boats. Russians – 5,000 killed, 6,000 wounded or captured; Japanese – 700.

RESULT The total defeat of Rozhdestvensnki's force struck the final blow at Russian fortunes in the Russo-Japanese War and peace soon followed.

MEN OF STEAM AND STEEL

GENERAL ULYSSES S. GRANT (1822–85) passed out of West Point in the bottom half of his class. Although he served with distinction in the Mexican War, boredom with garrison duty led to hard drinking, and he resigned from the army in 1854 to avoid court-martial. He was working in his brothers' Illinois store when the Civil War broke out, and he obtained command of the 21st Illinois Volunteers.

Promoted to brigadier-general in command of a district based in Cairo, Illinois, Grant found himself playing a crucial role in Union strategy. General Winfield Scott's "Anaconda Plan" demanded seizure of the line of the Mississippi as part of a general attempt to throttle the Confederacy to death. Grant's first thrust down the river failed at Belmont in November 1861, but early the following year he took Forts Henry and Donelson. In April he was surprised at Shiloh on the Tennessee River, but recovered from a disastrous first day's fighting to win a costly victory. His initial attempt to take Vicksburg was thwarted in December 1862, but in a methodical amphibious operation he took the city in July 1863.

Grant's success at Vicksburg encouraged Lincoln to appoint him commander of all Union forces in the western theatre of operations, and he swiftly transformed the situation in Tennessee. In March 1864, Grant was promoted lieutenant-general and appointed general in chief. He accompanied the Army of the Potomac, and set about moving "all parts of the Army together and, somewhat towards a common center". This policy produced a costly slogging-match in the Wilderness fighting of May–June, followed by the long siege of Petersburg. Sherman, meanwhile, took Atlanta and marched to the sea to bisect the Confederacy. In early April 1865 Lee led his dwindling army out of Petersburg, but was cornered at Appomattox Court House, where he surrendered.

Victory brought Grant immense authority, first as commanding general of the army in the rank of full general, and then as Secretary of War in President Johnson's administration. He served two terms as a Republican president but the malpractices of his colleagues discredited him.

GENERAL ROBERT E. LEE (1807–70) passed out second of his class at West Point and was commissioned into the engineers. As chief engineer of the central column in the Mexican War he was severely wounded at the storming of Chapultepec. He was superintendent of West Point in 1852–5 and greatly improved the establishment's efficiency.

Colonel Lee was serving in Texas when the first Confederate states seceded from the Union in March 1861. He felt duty bound to "go with his state" when Virginia seceded, and accepted the command of the state's forces. He prepared the defences of Richmond, and then opposed Rosecrans in West Virginia, before being summoned back to the eastern theatre to take command in the Seven Days' Battles around Richmond in the spring of 1862. Thereafter, at the head of the Army of Northern Virginia, he

(Below) Robert E. Lee's style and bearing in this formal portrait are indicative of his origins in the Virginia aristocracy. His father, "Light-Horse Harry" Lee had commanded cavalry under Washington and served as state governor.

(Above) On campaign Ulysses S. Grant rarely looked as well-trimmed as in this portrait. But he had few rivals in his grasp of the essentials of war.
(Right) Grant rides amongst soldiers during the Wilderness battle, May 1864.

repeatedly thwarted the Army of the Potomac's advances on the Confederate capital, and twice took the war into the North. His defeat of Hooker at Chancellorsville in May 1863 was a stunning achievement, and though he narrowly failed at Gettysburg this was in part due to the slowness of his "Old War Horse", James Longstreet.

Indeed, reluctance to assert himself with reticent or headstrong subordinates is the only flaw in Lee's military character. He excelled at manoeuvre, but showed himself no less adept in contending with Grant's bludgeon-work in the Wilderness battles of 1863 and in protracting the siege of Petersburg. Appointed commander of all Confederate armies in February 1865, Lee eventually surrendered only when his own Army of Northern Virginia was worn to a thread by casualties and desertion, and its last line of supply was cut.

FIELD MARSHAL COUNT HELMUTH VON MOLTKE (1800–91) was commissioned into the Danish army, but transferred to the Prussian army in 1822 and almost immediately attended the elite *Kriegsakademie.* In 1835 he was given leave to travel to Turkey, and served with the Sultan's army at its disastrous defeat at Nisib. He published an account of his travels in 1839.

Foreign service and literary skill helped bring Moltke royal patronage, and in 1857 he was appointed Chief of the Great General Staff. He served as chief of staff to the Austro-Prussian force in the Schleswig-Holstein war of 1864, and in 1866 Prussian victory over Austria-Hungary at Königgrätz made him a figure of European importance. In 1870 his was the directing brain behind the German defeat of France, an achievement which brought him his field-marshal's baton and the title of count. He was retained in his post, against his wishes, until 1888.

An accomplished planner, von Moltke was especially swift to recognize the military potential of railways. His conduct of operations in 1870 marks him out as a great general.

(Above) Alphonse de Neuville's painting shows a battalion of Garde Mobile *retaking Chenebier during the Franco-Prussian war, 1871. Despite a few French successes, Von Moltke ensured German strategic victory. (Right) Von Moltke was proverbially stony-faced. It was said that he smiled only twice in his life: once on seeing some obsolete Swedish fortifications, and again when his mother-in-law died.*

10

THE FIRST WORLD WAR

IT IS IMPORTANT to emphasize that the First World War began in August 1914 much as soldiers had expected, with a fluid war of movement. In the west, the German strategic design for the rapid defeat of France prior to the transfer of German strength to the Eastern Front to confront Imperial Russia – the Schlieffen Plan – was highly old-fashioned in the way that it unfolded in August and September 1914. Indeed, the German chief-of-staff who had originally masterminded it, Alfred von Schlieffen, had been much taken by the classic encircling movement executed by Hannibal at the Battle of Cannae.

THE SCHLIEFFEN PLAN

Although modified by von Schlieffen's successor, the younger Helmuth von Moltke, the plan still resembled a great revolving door in which the arc of the German advance would sweep through Belgium and carry the German right wing around Paris and back towards the Rhine. Unfortunately, the Schlieffen Plan took little account of any military realities. The arc of advance would always be within reach of the French strategic rail network while Schlieffen had hardly considered possible enemy reaction at all in demanding a rigid adherence to a timetable that would commit the German First Army on the extreme right to a 300-mile march at a constant 15 miles a day for three weeks.

Schlieffen had assumed that use would be made of the Belgian and French railways but the former were extensively damaged during the German advance and the critical distance between the marching columns and the railheads stretched to an average of 70 to 80 miles in the case of von Kluck's First Army. Compared with the small British Expeditionary Force (BEF) of 75,000 men with the comparatively lavish total of 1,485 motor vehicles of all kinds, the five northern German armies operating between Luxemburg and Brussels had but 500 motor lorries between them. As they marched deeper into France the intense summer heat took its toll of the German

1914

MONS

DATE 23 August 1914
OBJECT British rearguard action in the face of the advancing German army.
NUMBERS British Expeditionary Force – 70,000, and 300 guns; German First Army – 160,000, and 600 guns.
DESCRIPTION Advancing from its concentration area at Mauberge in support of a limited French move towards the Sambre and Meuse rivers, the one cavalry and four infantry divisions of Field Marshal Sir John French's BEF unknowingly came into the path of General Alexander von Kluck's First Army on the extreme right of the German invasion of Belgium and France. After making contact with German patrols on 21 and 22 August, the BEF was dug in along the Mons–Conde canal where it was attacked on 23 August by von Kluck's army. In nine hours of fighting, the brunt of the German assault fell on the British II Corps which suffered most of the British casualties. Unable to advance in face of heavy British fire, the Germans lost heavily. However, with von Kluck having hardly committed his army and with news that the French were already retreating, the BEF also retired that evening.
CASUALTIES British – 1,638; German – heavy, though precise figure unknown.
RESULT While the retreat was to continue until 4 September, Mons and the BEF's subsequent delaying actions imposed crucial delays on the Schlieffen Plan.

infantry and the poor roads of their boots. German High Command (OHL) steadily lost contact with its forward elements. Initially located at Koblenz, OHL was 206 miles from von Kluck. Von Kluck had two wireless transmitters but OHL had only one receiving set. Codes were slow to decipher and, in any case, the French were using the Eiffel Tower transmitter to jam German transmissions. OHL was thus forced to communicate with army commanders by despatching staff officers in motor cars.

Poor communications and lack of co-ordination between the German First and Second Armies led von Kluck to abandon the original plan and to pass east rather than west of Paris. He exposed his right flank in doing so and enabled the Allies to counter-attack in what became known as the First Battle of the Marne. This coincided with German loss of confidence and, on 9 September 1914, the Germans began to retreat. Improvised field fortifications had appeared at an early stage with, for example, the BEF digging in along the Mons–Conde canal on 23 August in its first major engagement (see page 170). On 13 September, however, the French Fifth Army encountered something new in an organized trench system before Reims. In a matter of days the other Allied armies had similarly come up against a more systematic entrenchment on the part of the Germans. Von Moltke had not actually intended that these trenches should do more than gain a temporary respite for his armies. Therefore, in search of renewed mobility, each side began to attempt to outflank the other, leapfrogging to the north in turn. By mid-November this "race to the sea" had resulted in a continuous front from the Alps to the Channel.

New recruits in Britain being measured for their uniforms in the early days of the First World War. Such men would have been among those who volunteered in response to the appeal of the new Secretary of State for War, Earl Kitchener of Khartoum. At this stage, however, khaki was rarely available and, more often that not, men were clothed in so-called "Kitchener blue".

PEACE BY CHRISTMAS?

On the Eastern Front, where there had also been an initial search for a decisive envelopment, positions had similarly stabilized by the end of 1914 although the distances involved – it was over 600 miles from the Carpathians to the Baltic – ensured that the line was not continuous and the war always more fluid. In the Balkans, Serbia had thrown back three major Austro-Hungarian offensives. Clearly, the widespread assumption that the war would be over by Christmas was mistaken and, despite the essential familiarity of much of the early fighting, there were already indications of a new kind of warfare. Losses had greatly exceeded expectations, the Germans suffering 750,000 casualties in the first five months in the west and the French some 900,000. Moreover, the sheer expenditure of ammunition was so far above pre-war estimates that most belligerents were to suffer "shell shortages" in the course of 1915. The increased demands for artillery shells in particular also significantly changed pre-war logistic patterns. Most logistical systems were geared to carrying food and fodder and were still dependent upon horsed transport. Now more ammunition was required which, in turn, required more horses and more fodder.

1914

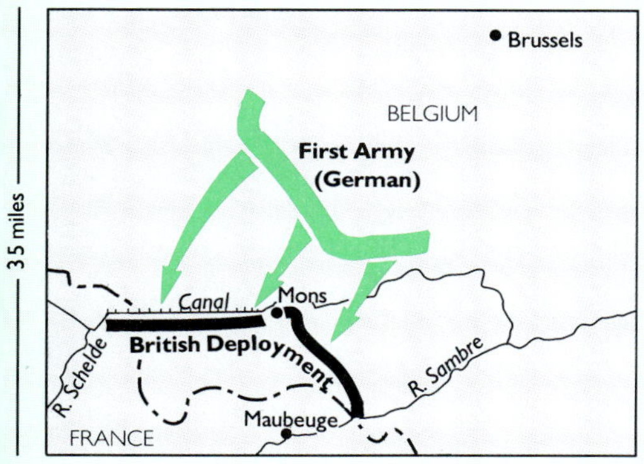

TANNENBERG

DATE 26–30 August 1914
OBJECT German counter-offensive to defend East Prussia against the Russians.
NUMBERS Roughly equal – approximately 150,000 men and 700 guns on each side.
DESCRIPTION Faced with the invasion of East Prussia by the Russian First Army commanded by General Paul Rennenkampf and the Second Army of General Alexander Samsonov on 17 August 1914, the commander of the German Eighth Army, Max von Prittwitz, ordered a retreat. Prittwitz was subsequently convinced by his staff that the Germans could exploit their superior communications to defeat Samsonov before Rennenkampf could come to his assistance but OHL was not made aware of the change of plan and dismissed Prittwitz. His successor, General Paul von Hindenburg, arrived on 23 August with Major-General Erich Ludendorff as chief of staff and approved the plan ►

Thus, between 1914 and 1918 the 5.9 million tons of fodder sent to France for the BEF's animal transport actually exceeded the 5.2 million tons of ammunition also despatched. Inevitably, the war saw an increase in the ratio of men required in support units to those actually deployed as combat personnel in the front line, a ratio that has continued to increase through the 20th century. At least the soldiers of the First World War did not yet require vast amounts of petroleum and petroleum-related products but the BEF was still supported by no less than 447,000 motor vehicles by 1918.

AIR POWER

Apart from the logistic revelations and the realization that firepower had now determined that the power of the defence would be greater than ever before, the first campaigns also witnessed a number of innovations, not least the rapid development of airpower. During the Allied retreat from the Belgian and French frontiers in August and September 1914, British and French aircraft provided a vital reconnaissance function and had detected the German turn east of Paris. In fulfilling the reconnaissance role, airmen had also begun experimenting with improvised

British soldiers of the 2nd Battalion, Royal Warwickshire Regiment being transported in requisitioned London Transport "Old Bill" buses from Dickebusche to Ypres during the First Battle of Ypres between 15 October and 22 November 1914. The battle marked the climax of the "Race to the Sea", the British Expeditionary Force having been withdrawn from the Aisne and brought back into the line in Flanders in order to be able to maintain better communications with its bases at Calais, Boulogne and Le Havre.

1914

already drawn up by Colonel Max Hoffmann to transfer the Eighth Army to the southern frontier of East Prussia, leaving only a cavalry division to cover Rennenkampf. Having concentrated approximately an equal number of men against Samsonov's forces, the Germans commenced a double envelopment of the Russian army on 26 August. This was completed in four days; Russian losses were high, including 300 guns, and Samsonov committed suicide.

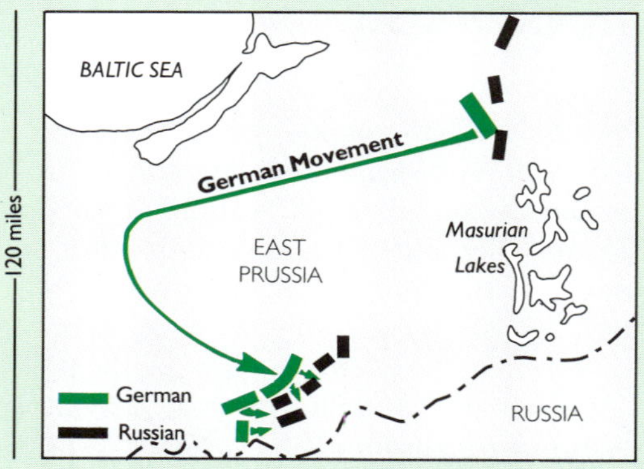

CASUALTIES Germans – 10,000–15,000; Russians – 70,000 and 55,000–75,000 captured.
RESULT A reinforced Eighth Army then turned north to defeat Rennenkampf around the Masurian lakes in September 1914, a double victory which thoroughly established the reputations of Hindenburg and Ludendorff.

Officers and men of the newly-formed Royal Air Force, in front of an equally new twin-engined Vickers Vimy heavy bomber at a French airfield at Cramaille on the Aisne, some time in 1918. The French commandant of the base stands fourth from right in the front row.

weapons to down their opponents. Three Royal Flying Corps (RFC) machines became the first to force down an opponent on 25 August 1914. Although no wireless was as yet available for aircraft, the RFC also undertook its first aerial spotting for artillery on 13 September above the Aisne battlefield.

Air power also made its debut at sea. The Royal Naval Air Service (RNAS) had been the first successfully to launch a torpedo from the air just prior to the outbreak of war but, on 25 December 1914, German Zeppelins undertook the first actual aerial attack on ships. Ironically, they engaged the British naval force that was itself launching the first seaborne air attack on the Zeppelin sheds at Cuxhaven. Earlier, on 8 October, RNAS aircraft had carried out the first genuine strategic bombing mission in attacking other Zeppelin sheds at Düsseldorf and Cologne. Submarines were making a similar impact, the German U-21 becoming the first submarine to sink a ship in action at sea when attacking HMS *Pathfinder* in the Firth of Forth on 3 September 1914. The first merchantman to fall victim was the *Glitra* to U-17 on 20 October, while HMS *Birmingham* became the first vessel to sink a submarine by ramming U-15 in the North Sea on 9 August 1914.

BREAKING THE IMPASSE

The air and sea conflict, however, would not yet make any decisive impact on the war as a whole and, as 1915 opened, the armies of Europe still faced the same problem as in 1914 – how to cross the zone of fire. It was a task made doubly difficult by the appearance of trenches. Primarily, the creation of static entrenchments robbed the attacker of the element of surprise since it required a lengthy build-up of supplies and

STRATEGIC BOMBING

The first air raid on a civilian target was mounted by German Zeppelins on Great Yarmouth on 19 January 1915, London being attacked first on 31 May. On 25 May 1917 came the first German air raid using conventional aircraft, when Gotha aircraft attacked Folkestone. A raid on London on 13 June 1917 by 14 Gothas caused 162 deaths and near panic in the capital's East End, foreshadowing the strategic bombing raids of World War II. The raid played a decisive role in creating Britain's Royal Air Force (RAF), one element of which, the Independent Force, was formed in June to undertake raids against Germany: 242 British raids were carried out by November. German raids on Britain left 1,413 civilian dead.

1915

ANZAC COVE

DATE 25 April 1915
CAMPAIGN Gallipoli Peninsula
OBJECT The Australian and New Zealand Army Corps (ANZAC) were to support the main landing at Cape Helles by coming ashore a mile north of Gaba Tepe and moving inland to seize the commanding Sari Bari heights.
NUMBERS British and ANZAC – 75,000; Turkish – 4,000.

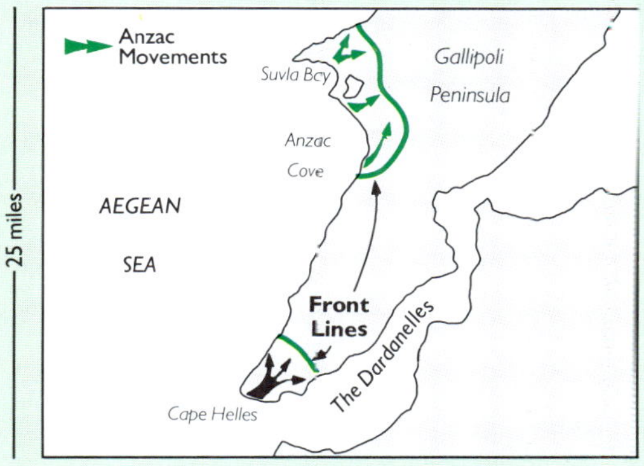

DESCRIPTION Following the failure of the British and French fleets to force the Dardanelles in March 1915, there was little alternative to attempting an amphibious landing on the Gallipoli peninsula although only 75,000 men of the British 29th and Royal Naval Divisions and the Anzacs were available to General Sir Ian Hamilton. The German general, Liman von Sanders, had some 84,000 troops in defence but only about 700 men from the Turkish 19th Division were in the area of ▸

THE SIDE SHOWS

The First World War was a global conflict. While the Central Powers eventually embraced Germany, Austria-Hungary, Turkey and Bulgaria, no less than 22 states eventually comprised the Allies including Japan and the United States. It was thus inevitable that the war would not be confined to the main Western and Eastern Fronts. Even within Europe, there was the war between Italy and Austria-Hungary after the former joined the Allies in May 1915, while the Allied landing at Salonika in October 1915 opened a separate Balkan front against Bulgaria. It could also be argued that the fall of Serbia and Romania to the Central Powers in December 1915 and December 1916 respectively were campaigns separate from the main German and Austro-Hungarian struggle against Russia. The Allied war against Turkey embraced the Dardanelles campaign in 1915, the Russian campaign in the Caucasus and the British campaigns in Egypt, Palestine and Mesopotamia. There were also the campaigns against German colonies such as the Cameroons, Togoland and German East and South-West Africa which extended to Japanese participation in the conquest of German possessions in China and the Pacific.

manpower in preparation for any attempt to break through an opposing trench line. The place of assault could frequently be determined by the intended victim and arrangements made accordingly. Moreover, the ability of the attacker to protect his infantry as it crossed what soon became known as "No Man's Land" was limited to the range of the artillery available. Artillery could not readily be brought forward from its fixed positions behind the lines in order to extend any breakthrough made by the infantry and the attacker generally lacked the mobility required to fully exploit any success. Of course, artillery could reach the opposing infantry in its trenches if they had no overhead cover such as bunkers or tunnels, but the artillery available was still not sufficiently powerful to totally destroy a defensive system. Indeed, even when heavier artillery was deployed, sufficient numbers of infantry usually survived to break up an infantry attack, particularly by the use of machine guns sweeping the oncoming ranks. Increasingly, the Germans were to protect their machine guns in bunkers or deep dug-outs with something of a race developing at the end of any Allied bombardment between the German machine gunners and the Allied infantry to determine who reached the German parapet first. Invariably, it was the German machine gunners, with results that are unmistakably associated with the image of the Western Front.

To a very large extent, the problem of overcoming the defence was that of the Allies and not the Central Powers. On the Western Front in particular, the Germans had successfully occupied much of Belgium in the opening campaign and a good deal of the most industrially productive regions of northern France. It was thus a strategic necessity for the Allies to win back such lost ground while the Germans could afford to stand on the defensive and indulge in positional attrition in the West while pursuing territorial ambitions in the East. The Allied difficulty was that the Germans had also occupied commanding geographical positions in 1914 which gave them both strategic and tactical control of the Western Front.

The first real British offensive aimed at breaking through the German front line was that at Neuve Chapelle on 10 March 1915. It was a highly innovative attack in terms of such techniques as aerial reconnaissance of German defences, the issue of objective maps to the infantry and the co-ordination of artillery fire by timetable to fit the projected lines of advance. A narrow front was selected where the German line formed a salient and where the German trenches lacked real depth or much barbed wire, itself becoming a major obstacle in such positional warfare. The British enjoyed a numerical superiority of something like 35:1 and had assembled the unprecedented number of 340 artillery pieces for a short preliminary bombardment. However, despite the laying of an experimental network of field telephones, communications broke down almost immediately the infantry had left the British trenches, mist also

1915

the proposed Anzac landing. The first Anzacs landed at 4.30 am on 25 April but 2 miles north of the intended destination in what became known as Anzac Cove, an inlet surrounded by steep cliffs. Despite administrative confusion, they had captured the immediate beachhead by 6 am and came within just 3½ miles of the Straits before being pushed back by counter-attacks organized by the future president of the Turkish republic, Mustapha Kemal.
CASUALTIES By nightfall the Australians had suffered 2,000 casualties and were fighting simply to retain a foothold on the beach.
RESULT The Australians were pinned down for almost a year, as were the British at Cape Helles. A further landing at Suvla Bay also failed. Both Anzac Cove and Suvla Bay were evacuated on 20 December; Allied troops left Cape Helles in January.

VERDUN

DATE February – December 1916
OBJECT At the beginning of 1916 the German Chief of Staff, von Falkenhayn, appears to have sought a battle of attrition in the Verdun salient. Whatever his precise aim, this was the result as the French were to defend it desperately as a key fortified frontier zone.
NUMBERS Not known precisely, but more than 500,000 in total.

conspiring to obscure much of what was happening beyond the British front line. A breakthrough was achieved and that in itself was not usual on the Western Front – other comparable breakthroughs by the British were confined to the first day of the battle of Loos on 24 September 1915, the first day at Vimy (by the Canadians) on 9 April 1917 and the first day at Cambrai on 20 November 1917 (see page 187). But the success could not be reinforced rapidly enough and the attack was broken off on 12 March, the cost being 12,000 casualties for the gain of just 4,000 square yards.

Unfortunately, the lesson drawn from Neuve Chapelle was not the psychological value of the brief preliminary bombardment but the need for an even longer bombardment both to cut the German wire and to neutralize the opposing defenders. Therefore, it was assumed that greater firepower would do a more comprehensive job while it was also believed that future attacks must be made on a far wider frontage. Thus, opening bombardments such as those fired by the British before the opening of the Somme battle on 1 July 1916 (see page 180) or the opening of the Passchendaele offensive on 31 July 1917 (see page 181) became heavier in the expectation that this would achieve the task. One refinement of artillery support introduced as a result of the initial experience on the Somme was the creeping barrage to take infantry right up to the opposing front line and beyond under a curtain of protecting fire. But, in turn, this presented difficulties since it only

Continued on page 178

THE ARTILLERY WAR

As early as the first campaign of the war, it was apparent that artillery was becoming the decisive weapon of land warfare. In the Russo-Japanese War only 10 per cent of the total casualties had been caused by artillery fire but, between 1914 and 1918, this would increase to an estimated 70 per cent of total casualties. Nevertheless, sufficient numbers of defenders still often survived a bombardment to break up an infantry attack. Thus, the British fired 1.7 million shells in eight days prior to the opening of the Somme offensive in July 1916 and 4.2 million shells in 14 days prior to the Passchendaele offensive a year later without suppressing the defence. Subsequently, advances in instrument location of enemy batteries rendered long bombardments unnecessary.

General Sir Henry Horne commanding the British First army inspecting the 24th Motor Machine Gun Battalion at Dieval on 12 June 1918. Formed in 1916, the Machine Gun Corps was a belated recognition of the weapon, but motorcyclists only became effective once trench deadlock was broken.

1916

DESCRIPTION After a nine-hour opening bombardment, the German Fifth Army attacked along an 8-mile front on 21 February. The lack of armament in the surrounding forts and the loss of the largest – Fort Douaumont – on 25 February almost proved fatal to the defence which was entrusted to General Pétain's Second Army on 26 February. Having reached their initial objectives on the east bank of the Meuse, the German advance came to a halt before being renewed on 29 February in an attempt to seize the west bank. Two German offensives towards the Mort Homme feature were halted on 6 March and 9 April but General Nivelle, who succeeded Pétain on 19 April, had to face repeated assaults during June. The fall of Fort Vaux on 7 June made the situation difficult once more but the Russian Brusilov offensive and the British Somme offensive both sucked away German reserves and the French recaptured Douaumont on 24 October and Vaux on 2 November.

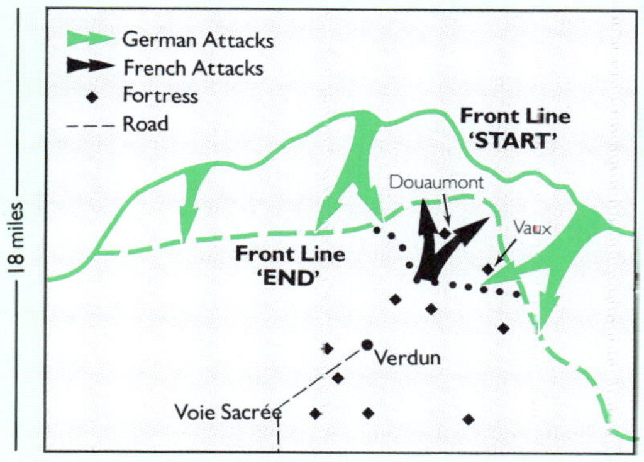

LIFE IN THE TRENCHES

EVEN AFTER THE ALLIES and the Germans settled into static winter positions after the conclusion of the "Race to the Sea" on the Western Front, it was some months before the trenches became continuous or systematically organized on all sectors over the 475-mile front from Switzerland to the sea. There were also perceptible differences between the armies.

Initially, for example, the Germans concentrated troops in their front line with little immediate support beyond some machine gun bunkers. By contrast, the British began almost at once to adopt a three-line system of front, support and reserve trenches linked by zig-zag communications trenches. The French constructed strong points enfilading less well-defended stretches of line, backed by a support line. Artillery tended to be placed as ranges dictated behind the front line, although the French had a tendency to site their guns farther forward than the British or Germans.

Nonetheless, the pattern of trench warfare became much the same for all the soldiers on the Western Front, despite the fact that the terrain varied greatly from the wooded heights of the Vosges and the flooded coastal plain of the Yser to the dry chalklands of the Somme and Champagne, which alone were suitable for large-scale operations. But, in fact, such operations were comparatively rare and there could often be tacit truces between the opposing front lines in some "quiet" sectors. There were dangers, of course, from artillery, snipers and mortars, which contributed to a constant dribble of casualties, and there was also the ever-present threat of disease resulting from cold, damp or vermin. However, there were regular rotations between front, support and reserve positions, ready access to letters or parcels from home and, in the British army at least, an extensive programme of recreational activities which substantially assisted the maintenance of morale and, to a degree, promoted a "community" of shared experience.

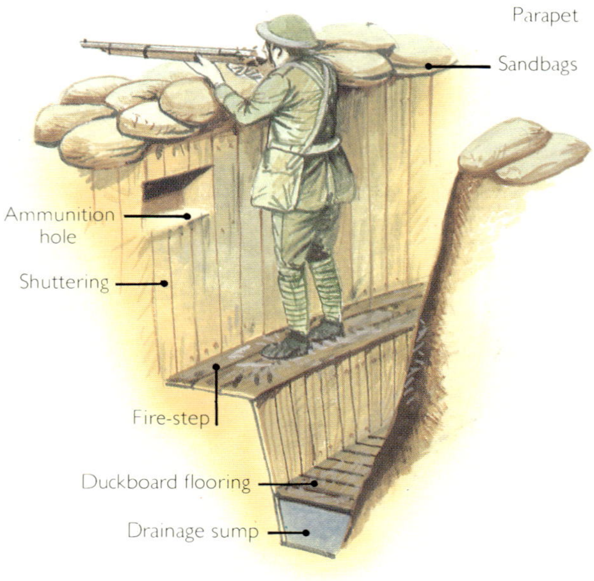

(Above) An idealised trench of some 10 to 12 feet in depth with sandbag protection and wooden firestep, shuttering and floor.

(Below) A man of the 1/7th Sherwood Foresters guards a barbed-wire gate in the front line at Cambrin, 16 September 1917.

(Left) Princess Patricia's Canadian Light Infantry defending a trench against a German attack during the Second Battle of Ypres, April 1915.

(Above) Wounded and dead from the American 53rd Battalion, hit while advancing through a gap in the wire near Anvil Wood on 2 September 1918.

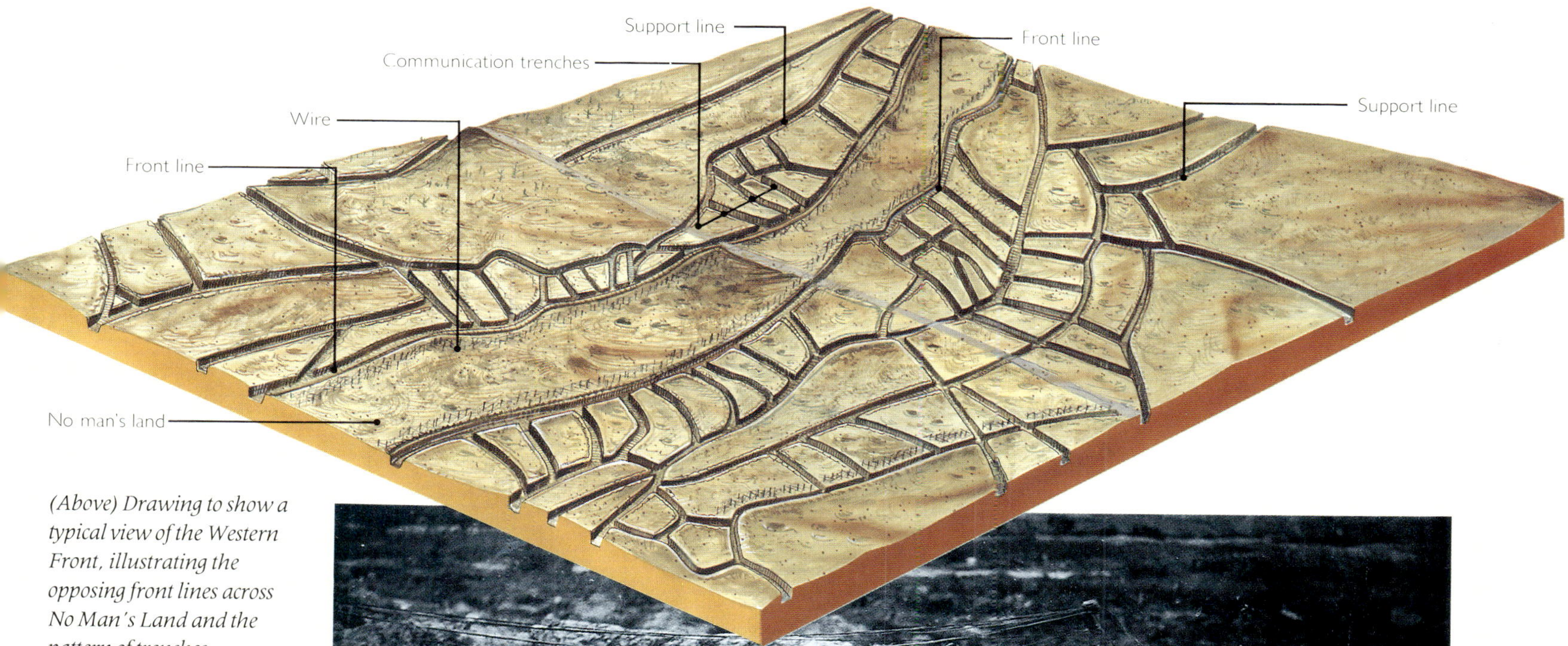

(Above) Drawing to show a typical view of the Western Front, illustrating the opposing front lines across No Man's Land and the pattern of trenches.

(Right) Men of the British 34th Division resting in a communication trench near Elverdinge, 19 August 1917.
(Below) British Cavalry crossing a bridge over a communication trench near Neuve Eglise on 7 May 1917, with Australian signallers moving up in the foreground.

(Left) A French soldier preparing to fire an old pattern Model 58 Mk 1 trench mortar some time during 1915.
(Right) Machine gunners of the 11th Leicesters in 6th Division, in a captured German second-line trench near Ribecourt during the first day of the Battle of Cambrai, November 1917.

A general view of the battlefield of Third Ypres below Passchendaele Ridge in October 1917, showing a British tank stranded in one of the many water-filled shell holes which resulted from artillery bombardment destroying the drainage system in an area with a high water table. For many in the inter-war years, this kind of image of a battle literally drowned in mud was instantly recalled by the very name of Passchendaele.

encouraged linear formations and the infantry failed to keep up with a moving barrage that could not be recalled due to the lack of communications. While telephone wires and cables were dug ever deeper they were still cut by artillery fire and, of course, they could only be extended forward of the front line into No Man's Land as the infantry advanced.

An even more unfortunate effect of heavier bombardments was that, in attempting to destroy the barrier of the wire, it merely created a new obstacle in breaking up the ground. In those areas most suited to offensive operations, such as the Flemish plain where the water table was high and the drainage systems were close to the surface, this had disastrous results. Indeed, the very name of Passchendaele invokes visions of a British army floundering in mud. In such conditions, even if a breakthrough occurred, it was all but impossible to move reinforcements forward sufficiently quickly to exploit it. The only arm of exploitation available was the cavalry, but on the Western Front horsemen were an anachronism. On 14 July 1916, for example, the 20th Deccan Horse and the 7th Dragoon Guards were brought into attack at High Wood on the Somme – machine guns destroyed them. Similarly, at Arras on 11 April 1917 British cavalry was swiftly halted before

1916

CASUALTIES French – 270,000; German – 240,000.

RESULT By December the French had regained almost all the positions lost in February. But the battle had cost both sides very heavy casualties in what has become a lasting symbol of an attritional battle taken to the extremities of suffering.

JUTLAND

DATE 31 May 1916

OBJECT Faced with the superiority of the Royal Navy, the German strategy was to isolate and destroy a portion of the British Grand Fleet. Thus, whereas Admiral Jellicoe intended to manoeuvre the Grand Fleet so as to allow its heavy guns to bear on the German High Seas Fleet in any naval engagement, his German opposite number, Vice-Admiral Scheer, had no intention of becoming involved in a gunnery duel. The conflicting intentions were to contribute to the inconclusive nature of the only great naval battle of the war.

NUMBERS Britain – 151 ships; Germany – 103 ships.

DESCRIPTION Rear-Admiral Hipper's battlecruisers were designated as bait to draw Vice-Admiral Beatty's battlecruisers on to the main High Seas Fleet before Jellicoe could come to Beatty's support. The first clash between the battlecruisers took place

A British cavalry trooper resting somewhere in Belgium on 13 October 1914 as the British Expeditionary Force advanced towards Ypres. It was almost the last occasion on the Western Front when horsed cavalry would be able to perform its traditional function of reconnaissance let alone that of shock action. Mounted divisions were maintained awaiting a breakthrough in the trench deadlock but, on those few occasions when it was brought up, cavalry had no answer to wire and machine guns.

Monchy. On the Eastern Front, however, there was still a role for cavalry, as well as in peripheral campaigns such as that in Palestine. Indeed, over 4,000 cavalry charges took place on the Eastern Front during the war including the shattering of the Austro-Hungarian Seventh Army by Russian cavalry at Gorodenko on 27–8 April 1915.

The maintenance of cavalry divisions in the British and other armies epitomized the transition through which the high commands were passing in a painfully gradual learning process. They were effectively isolated from the front line by the new managerial problems that had emerged with mass armies, yet contrived to live close to the front in the old style. Through the greater extent of the battlefield and the primitive means of communications available to cover its extent, the war was the first and last fought without voice control by the commander in the traditional manner. "Château generalship" by army commanders marked the real tensions that existed in the transition to a new professionalism.

It would be wrong to assume that all generals and all armies failed to appreciate what was happening on the Western Front. Small-units tactics – the attempt by infantry to advance in small groups using their own firepower – had suggested itself to some British officers during the Somme campaign as a means of avoiding the

1916

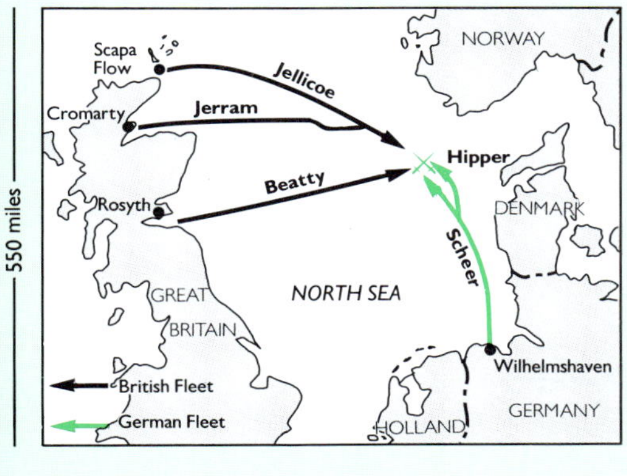

at 1548 hours on 31 May off Jutland, Beatty losing *Indefatigable* and *Queen Mary* and suffering damage to *Lion*. However, upon sighting the main High Seas Fleet, Beatty turned back towards Jellicoe at 1726 hours and almost succeeded in luring Scheer in turn. Scheer promptly executed a "battle turnaway", in the process of which another British battlecruiser, *Invincible*, was sunk. The two fleets again clashed in fading light at 1915 hours upon which Scheer covered his retirement by a massed torpedo attack which forced Jellicoe to turn away.

CASUALTIES Britain – 14 ships; Germany – 11 ships.

RESULT Having sunk 14 ships including the three battlecruisers for the loss of 11 of their own ships including the battlecruiser, *Lutzow*, the Germans could claim a tactical success; but the strategic advantage still lay with the Royal Navy.

A British officer and his soldiers await "zero hour" in a trench on the Somme during the summer of 1916. The first day of the offensive that began on 1 July was to cost over 57,000 casualties as men "went over the top" in the face of machine guns not knocked out by bombardment as anticipated.

carnage of the first day. However, these ideas were not to be fully implemented until late 1917 and Passchendaele was characterized by the same linear tactics as on the Somme but with longer intervals between lines and individuals. It was no easy task for any army totally to change its doctrine in the midst of a major war but one army did so – the Germans. Having suffered heavily from the opening British bombardment on the Somme, a new concept of "elastic defence in depth" partly based on captured French documents was implemented during the winter of 1916–17 by Colonel Fritz von Lossberg, Captain Hermann Geyer and others at OHL. The front line would now be thinned in terms of manpower but considerably deepened from

1916

THE SOMME

DATE July–November 1916
OBJECT A decisive breakthrough for the Allied forces.
NUMBERS Allies (initially) – 24 divisions; Germans (initially) – 11 divisions.
DESCRIPTION It was agreed in December 1915 that the Allies would mount a series of offensives in 1916. The main British effort was to take place along the line of the River Somme marking the junction of the British and French armies. In the event the opening of the German Verdun offensive in February forced the British to take pressure off the French, with the result that Lieutenant-General Sir Henry Rawlinson's Fourth Army lacked real strategic purpose in its attack opposite General Fritz von Below's German Second Army. The situation was not improved by disagreements over the objective of the offensive between Rawlinson and his commander-in-chief, Sir Douglas Haig. After an eight-

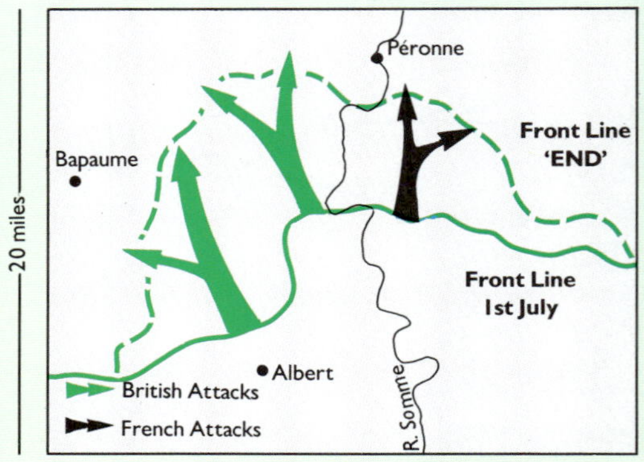

GAS

The Germans first attempted unsuccessfully to use irritants in shells in October 1914. Shells containing xylyl bromide gas were then used at Bolimov on the Eastern Front on 3 January 1915 only for the liquid to freeze in the sub-zero temperatures. However, on 22 April 1915 the Germans released chlorine gas in the area of Pilckem and Langemarck near Ypres, the gas cloud tearing an 8,000-yard gap in the line held by terrified French colonial troops. But gas was a fickle weapon when released from cylinders and, when used by the British at Loos in September 1915, little reached the German lines. Increasingly, therefore, gas was put into shells, some 63 different types being utilized by 1918. In July 1917 the Germans tried the first of the vesicant or blistering agents – mustard gas – which caused 20,000 British casualties in six weeks. In all, gas resulted in an estimated 1.2 million casualties during the war.

A line of British soldiers blinded by tear-gas during the German Spring Offensives (1918).

front to rear defensive positions. This enabled a more mobile defence and the possibility of surrendering ground tactically. The defence zone would now extend to between 6,000 and 8,000 yards in new *Stellung* (positions) constructed behind the existing front. The most formidable was the *Siegfriedstellung* between Cambrai and St Quentin but the whole system was collectively known to the BEF as the "Hindenburg Line" extending from Arras to Soissons. The new concept also saw special counter-attack divisions placed behind the lines, to which the Germans retired in February and March 1917. The main Hindenburg Line was not effectively broken until August and September 1918 although it was breached by the British at Cambrai in November 1917.

TECHNICAL INNOVATIONS

In many respects, the innovations which led to the initial success at Cambrai marked the culmination of the BEF's learning process on the Western Front; but it was not the first attempt to use new tactical methods of weapons in order to break the opposing trench lines. Some weapons were revolutionary in concept but still others, such as the flamethrower and chemicals, actually looked back to medieval siege

1917

day preliminary bombardment in which 1.7 million shells were hurled at the German positions, the British attacked on 1 July 1916, the battle being the first real blooding of the "New Armies" of volunteers who had responded to Kitchener's appeal in 1914.

CASUALTIES Almost 500,000 on each side.

RESULT On the first day alone the Allied Fourth Army suffered over 57,000 casualties, including over 19,000 dead, making it the bloodiest day in the history of the British Army. By the time the battle officially ended on 19 November, an area of approximately 25 miles long by 6 miles wide had been won. The Germans suffered as many losses as the Allies and what began, at least as far as Haig was concerned, as a battle for a decisive breakthrough, rapidly became transformed into a battle of sheer attrition.

PASSCHENDAELE

DATE July–November 1917

OBJECT The British commander-in-chief, Field Marshal Douglas Haig, wanted to reach the Belgian coast.

DESCRIPTION Officially known as the Third Battle of Ypres, the Passchendaele campaign took the form of eight separate efforts to push the British forward in the Ypres salient between 31 July and 10 November 1917. The offensive was partly justified by ▸

Two days after the dramatic breakthrough by the British Fourth Army at Amiens on 8 August 1918 – the so-called "Black Day of the German Army" – officers and men of the Tank Corps, which had spearheaded the assault, examine a captured German .5-inch anti-tank rifle. Tanks remained as vulnerable to anti-tank fire as they were prone to mechanical failure.

warfare. It is perhaps appropriate in any case to liken the war on the Western Front to a protracted siege operation. Developed by a Berlin engineer, Richard Fiedler, in 1900, the modern flamethrower used gas pressure to shoot out inflammable oil for a distance of some 65ft. Some attempt appears to have been made to use the weapon against the French in both October 1914 and February 1915 but its effective debut came at Hooge near Ypres on 29 July 1915 when six *Flammenwerferapparate* were used to dislodge men of the British 41st Infantry Brigade from Hooge crater as part of a wider attack. It was extremely successful but the proximity of the opposing lines – a mere 15 yards – was an important factor and it would not have such a decisive impact again. By contrast, the use of gas was to have much more lasting effect.

Yet older siege weapons re-appeared in a new form with the development of tunnelling as a means of breaking through the trench lines. Not all areas were suitable for mining but, where possible, tunnelling companies pursued their own specialized and terrifying conflict. The most spectacular success was undoubtedly the explosion of 19 British mines under German positions on the Messines ridge on 7 June 1917, which resulted in a swift advance and the capture of 7,000 stunned Germans. However, new weapons also emerged. At the level of personal weapons, the trench mortar was improvised with the British eventually deploying 11 different types. The Germans developed steel-cored bullets to pierce sandbags while the grenade and tin helmet equally became a feature of trench life. The new weapon with the greatest strategic and tactical potential was, of course, the tank.

The British commander-in-chief, Sir Douglas Haig, was keen to use tanks at once and 49 were used for a renewed attempt to break through on the Somme on 15 September 1916. Of the 32 machines that reached the start line, however, five had to be ditched, nine broke down and nine failed to keep up with the infantry. Thus, only nine spearheaded the actual advance on Flers-Courcelette. A breakthrough was partially achieved but it was an uncertain beginning and the tank was to continue to experience severe technical limitations. They were vulnerable to artillery and far too slow to exploit any breakthrough they might achieve: all their potential lay in the future. In fact, the Germans distrusted tanks and made no significant attempt to use them until the action at Villers Bretonneux on 24 April 1918 when they used 13 tanks. The action also saw the first duel between tanks when three British Mark IVs engaged three German A7Vs.

The tank was not the war-winning weapon sometimes supposed but Cambrai did show its potential when used in conjunction with small groups of infantry. Cambrai also heralded the future in other ways since the British had learned the virtue of reverting to a short preliminary bombardment. Steady advances in instrument

1917

the threat allegedly posed to Britain by German submarines operating out of the Flanders ports of Ostend and Zeebrugge, and partly by the fact that only the British remained capable of applying direct pressure on the Germans after the collapse of Russia and of French military morale in the spring of 1917. The offensive also appeared to the British commander-in-chief, Haig, to offer the opportunity of a real strategic objective in the ports for which the Germans would need to fight. A highly ambitious plan was advanced by which General Sir Hubert Gough's Fifth Army, supported by the Second Army, would be able to advance 15 miles in just eight days and on to the coast and the Dutch frontier although, subsequently, some confusion ensued as to the precise objective. After a 10-day preliminary bombardment, the offensive opened against the German Fourth and Sixth Armies on 31 July but broke down against the German defence in depth with 31,000 casualties. By the time

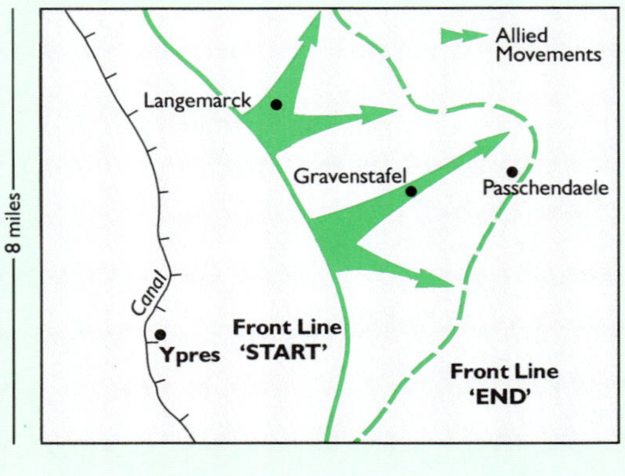

location of enemy batteries, including sound-ranging and aerial photography after the introduction of the Thornton-Pickard camera in 1915, immeasurably improved artillery accuracy. Aerial wireless had first been used by the RFC to assist the direction of artillery fire at the battle of Aubers ridge on 9 May 1915. By 1917 the Germans had come to fear British counter-battery fire, which was especially effective both at Arras in April and at Cambrai in November. Such accuracy now rendered long preliminary bombardment and pre-registration of batteries unnecessary.

Communications had also improved with a combination of telephones and spark wireless. Indeed, a wireless deception plan was used for the first time by the Canadians in August 1918. British infantry firepower had also improved through wider distribution of the Lewis light machine gun down to platoon level by 1917. The RFC had undertaken some training in ground attack and the co-ordination of artillery, infantry, aircraft and tanks in attack proved a potent combination at Cambrai even if the BEF essentially remained an infantry force supported by other arms. But the model was there and the techniques employed at Cambrai would bear fruit in 1918: in fact, British artillery techniques as refined during 1917 did not change again until 1942.

Cambrai also saw another attempted solution to the problem of ensuring breakthrough in the German method of counter-attack on 30 November 1917. It was the product of a second remarkable transformation in doctrine and, again, it was inspired by Lossberg and Geyer and based upon captured French manuals. On this occasion, the Germans had captured during 1916 a pamphlet by Captain André Laffargue dating from May 1915 which advocated a sudden attack by specially trained troops using automatic rifles or light machine guns. Other French experience also appeared relevant since the French had rediscovered the merit of short

Continued on page 186

(Above) British soldiers stand above one of the huge craters caused by gigantic mines detonated under the German lines on the Messines Ridge on 7 June 1917. The sound of the explosions could be clearly heard in London. (Below) Miners and sappers from the Royal Engineers digging one of the large shafts used in the attack, which proved to be one of the most spectacular successes of mine warfare on the Western Front, fought out deep under No Man's Land. General Plummer's troops advanced with minimal loss against the demoralized Germans.

1917

the battle ended on 10 November, it had become even more grisly than the Somme. Indeed, the "battle of the mud" would remain the very evocation of the seeming futility of the war on the Western Front.

CASUALTIES British – c.238,000; Germans – c.220,000.

RESULT Both sides were weakened by attrition but, in the long term, the Germans were less able to afford such losses.

CAPORETTO

DATE 24 October 1917

OBJECT German offensive to assist Austria-Hungary knock Italy out of the war.

NUMBERS Central powers – 35 divisions; Italy – 41 divisions.

DESCRIPTION With the Austro-Hungarian armies being forced back by an Italian offensive in August 1917, the German Fourteenth Army commanded by General von Below was despatched to the Italian ▸

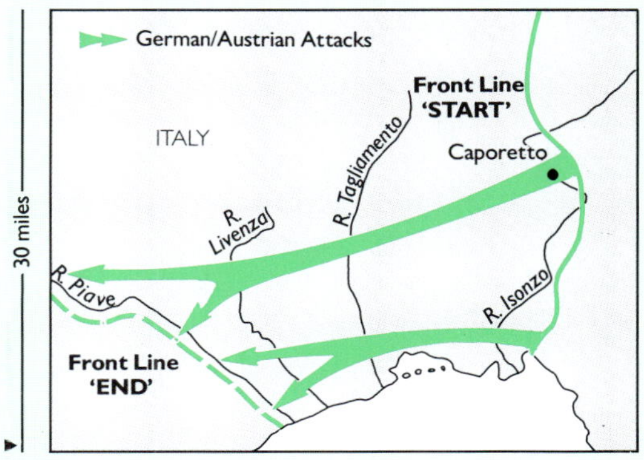

EASTERNERS, WESTERNERS

THROUGHOUT EUROPE in 1914, politicians of the belligerent countries either willingly surrendered responsibility for the strategic conduct of the war to the professional soldiers or found it effectively wrested from their grasp. The latter was true, for example, of Imperial Germany where the tradition of von Schlieffen inherited by the younger von Moltke assumed that politicians had no role once war had begun. In Britain, by contrast, the office of Secretary of State for War was given to Earl Kitchener of Khartoum who, having served most of his army career overseas, had virtually no knowledge of pre-war arrangements for expanding the home army and, on one occasion, memorably expressed his distaste for discussing strategic options with gentlemen with whom he was unacquainted, by which he meant the remainder of the Cabinet.

Inevitably, when the deadlock and sheer cost of war on the Western Front became apparent in the late autumn of 1914, politicians in Britain and France were motivated to seek not so much a new weapon to break the deadlock as an alternative strategy. At that point, however, they had cause to regret the easy transference of their control over strategy to the soldiers, for most professionals regarded any attempt to divert manpower from the Western Front to other theatres as "sideshows", irrelevant to the main effort to defeat Germany's strongest army in the west. Thus, in Britain and France leading soldiers such as Sir William Robertson, who became Chief of the Imperial General Staff in December 1915, and Sir Douglas Haig, who took command of the British Expeditionary Force (BEF) the same month, were "westerners" seeking a decisive victory in the west. Politicians such as Winston Churchill and David Lloyd George, who became prime minister in December 1916, were "easterners" who were convinced of the desirability of finding an "indirect approach".

In one sense the division was artificial since both "westerners" and "easterners" were committed to defeating Germany by raising and deploying a large British army whereas there were some British politicians, such as Reginald McKenna and Walter Runcimann, who believed only in a war of "limited liability". Nonetheless, if the aim was the same, the means to achieve it differed radically. Unfortunately for the "easterners", the indirect campaigns they managed to initiate such as the Dardanelles campaign against Turkey between February 1915 and January 1916 and the Salonika campaign against Bulgaria between October 1915 and September 1918 failed to undermine Germany through her allies. Failure enabled the "westerners" to prevail and, even as prime minister, Lloyd George was reduced to contriving to deny troops to Haig in France by attempting to divert manpower elsewhere.

The division in strategy was also paralleled in Germany, where von Moltke's successor as Chief of the General Staff, von Falkenhayn, was committed to a decision in the west while Hindenburg and Ludendorff sought it on the Eastern Front.

(Above) General Sir William Robertson, right, with the commander of the VI Corps in the British Army of Occupation at Cologne on 17 May, 1917.

(Below) Douglas Haig, commander of the BEF from December 1915 who, with Robertson, formed a formidable combination of British "westerners".

(Left) Haig and Joffre in conversation with Lloyd George at Meaulte on 12 September 1916 watched by Thomas, the French munitions minister.

(Below) Joffre and Sir John French depicted with Haig (left) and Smith-Dorrien (centre rear) and French generals, de Castelnau and Pau (right rear).

(Below) General Sir Hubert Gough, commander of the British Fifth Army, whose defeat in March 1918 was blamed by the "westerners" on Lloyd George's supposed denial of troops to Haig.

The strategic options considered by British "easterners" in the winter of 1914 included a descent on the island of Borkum as well as expeditions to the Dardanelles and Salonika. Borkum was rejected but the others were mounted in an attempt to undermine Germany by knocking out her allies and advancing through them. Later, when these expeditions failed, Italy became the favoured alternative front.

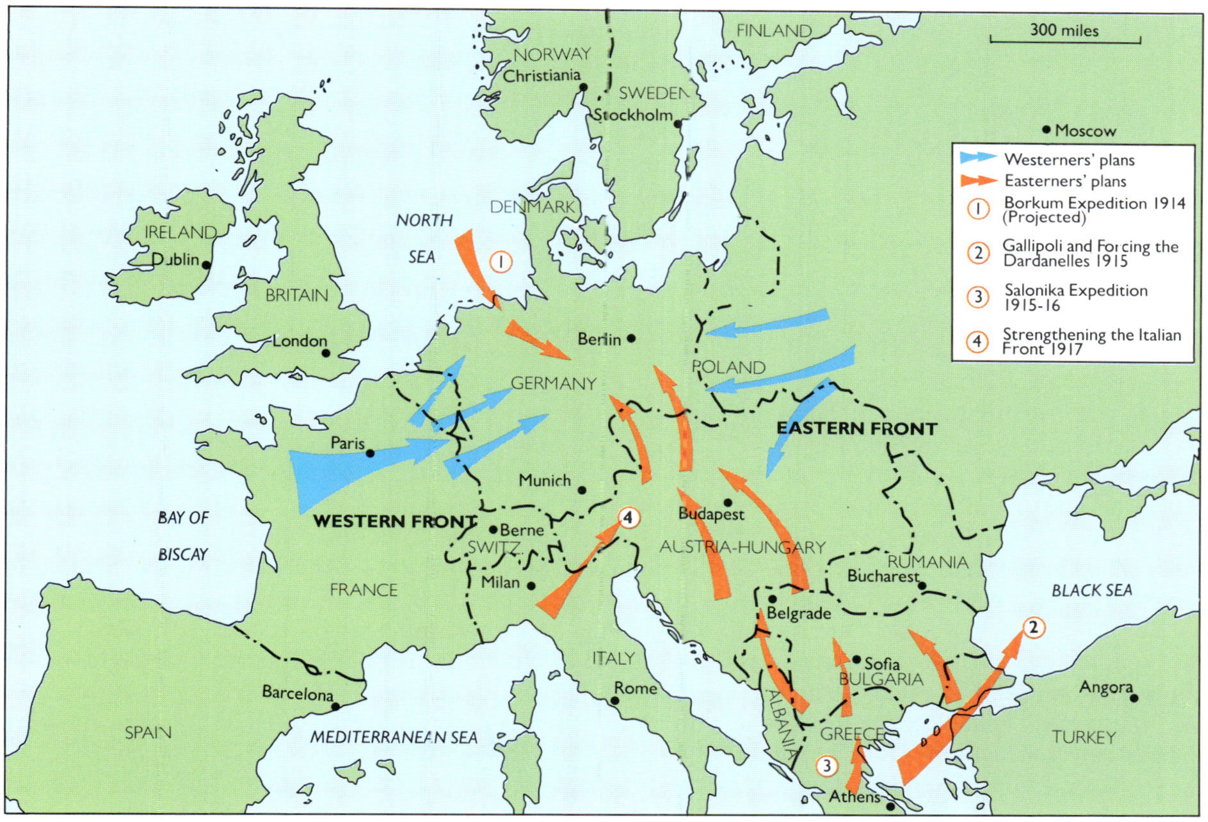

A German soldier accompanies captured Russian infantry with their machine guns, being marched to the rear in September 1915. As in the 1914 campaign, the Germans enjoyed some spectacular victories on the Eastern Front, bundling the Russians out of Poland and taking 750,000 prisoners in the process. However, the Russians still represented a danger.

bombardment in limited operations at the end of the Verdun battle in 1916 (see page 174). Similarly, there had been only limited artillery bombardment when General Alexei Brusilov had launched Russia's South Western Armies into an offensive on 4 June 1916. Lacking large reserves of ammunition, Brusilov had relied on surprise, little or no preliminary bombardment and a combination of separate attacks over a wide front to disguise his objective and disrupt enemy defensive plans. His four armies had attacked on a frontage of not more than 20 miles each between the Pripet marshes and the Dniestr river and had shattered two Austro-Hungarian armies. By 12 June some 192,000 Austro-Hungarian troops were prisoners but Brusilov had been forced to disperse his own reserves to disguise his plans and the breakthrough could not be sufficiently exploited.

TACTICAL DEVELOPMENTS

Drawing on such examples, the Germans struck back at Cambrai with great success. Specially trained *Sturmtruppen* (stormtroopers) led the attack supported by rapid and accurate artillery fire in a short hurricane bombardment. They bypassed strong points and left these for the ordinary infantry following. Thus, deep penetration was achieved by the tactics of infiltration, with the stormtroops maintaining mobility by means of machine guns drawn on sledges, horse-drawn light artillery and lorry-borne observation balloons to spot for the artillery as a whole and an elaborate series of light signals to mark the advance. They were also equipped with the new Bergmann light machine gun, which had been introduced in 1917.

Elements of these tactics had been introduced by the Germans before November 1917. Assault troops, for example, had been used as early as August 1914. Similarly, the short but heavy preliminary bombardment, intended not to destroy the enemy but to disrupt his command structure, had also been evolved prior to Cambrai. It owed much to Colonel Georg Bruchmüller, who had tried it first at Tarnopol on the Eastern Front on 19 July 1916 and at Riga on 1 September 1917. It was again used when the Germans broke the Italian army at Caporetto in October 1917 (see page 183) as well as at Cambrai. Thus, when the German spring offensive began on the Western Front in March 1918, some 6,473 guns were used in only a five-hour opening bombardment of enormous intensity. Ultimately, however, the Germans still faced problems in trying to exploit the initial breakthrough and their defeat then opened the way for more mobile warfare. At last, the Allies were content to attempt a progressive loosening of the front by a series of limited operations rather than pursuing the grand strategic breakthroughs of the past. The final Allied offensive broke the German army but at a cost, the British losing as many casualties between August and November 1918 as in the previous two years.

1917

front to stabilize the situation. In all, some 35 German and Austrian divisions were concentrated against 41 divisions of the Italian Second, Third and Fourth Armies on the Isonzo. The brunt of the Central Powers' counter-attack fell on General Capello's Second Army around Caporetto on 24 October 1917. Neither Capello nor his commander-in-chief, Cadorna, had anticipated the German offensive and the line was weakly held at this point despite information from deserters that an attack was likely. In addition, Capello himself was a sick man and had taken to his bed although he refused to relinquish his authority.

Using infiltration tactics, liberal amounts of gas and the kind of hurricane bombardment perfected on the Eastern Front, the Germans smashed the Italian front and advanced up to 12 miles on the first day. The Third and Fourth Armies fell back in better order towards the Piave but a measure of the overall Italian collapse was the fact that while they suffered only relatively light battle casualties, over 275,000 Italians surrendered.

CASUALTIES Italian – 30,000.

RESULT With the arrival of British and French reinforcements and the replacement of the Italian commander-in-chief, Cadorna, by General Diaz, the Central Powers broke off the general offensive on 25 November. They were soon to use the same infiltration tactics on the Western Front.

Symbol of a new era in warfare: the German Zeppelin L-12. Nonetheless, the size of the rigid airship made it a relatively easy target for anti-aircraft guns and prevented the Zeppelin from achieving the rapid manoeuvrability necessary to escape aircraft.

It was probably only on the Western Front that it was possible to impose a sufficiently comprehensive defeat on the Germans to force their surrender, given that Germany maintained her strongest army there. However, the sheer cost of warfare on the Western Front prompted some politicians and soldiers to seek alternative fronts. What were regarded by most Allied soldiers as "sideshows" did not produce the key to breaking deadlock on the Western Front but developments in the air and at sea did appear to offer a more viable alternative by allowing the belligerents to bypass an opponent's army and to strike at the heart of a state and its people. An early taste of what was to come was the brief German naval bombardment of Great Yarmouth on 3 November 1914 and the more sustained attacks on West Hartlepool, Scarborough and Whitby on 16 December 1914 which resulted in 133 civilian deaths. A similar attempt to break civilian morale was the German long-range artillery bombardment of Paris between March and August 1918, which compelled 500,000 people to flee.

An even greater opportunity to attack civilians was provided by air power, Great Yarmouth scoring another hapless first as the target of German Zeppelins in January 1915. The main lesson drawn from the bombing of England by dirigibles and, later, by heavy bombers was that most air battles would take place only by mutual consent and that aircraft could hide in the vast space of the skies. Indeed, it appeared exceptionally difficult to win command of the air without seeking constant battles that an opponent could choose to avoid. For much of the war, the RFC's policy was one of "strategic offensive", although this would now be regarded as a tactical use of airpower in which British aircraft sought to fight for and to win command of the air over the German lines. Inevitably, this resulted in casualties both from direct losses

AIR FIGHTING

Initially, aircraft were seen merely as reconnaissance machines and air fighting emerged as a means of protecting one's own machines. In February 1915, two Frenchmen experimented with firing a machine gun forward from the cockpit. Roland Garros and Raymond Saulnier fixed steel plates to the propeller in the hope that they would deflect the 7 per cent of bullets fired that they expected to hit it. In April 1915 the Dutch-born Anthony Fokker invented an interrupter gear based on pre-war Swiss designs and close inspection of Garros' machine. His resulting Fokker aircraft was the first true fighter and ushered in the era of the air-to-air duel. This was short-lived, as formation flying and large-scale air battles became the norm. By 1918 the RFC had also become adept at ground attack.

1917

CAMBRAI

DATE 20 November–7 December 1917
OBJECT Originally large-scale British tank raid, later transformed into an attempt to break through the German Hindenburg Line.
NUMBERS Allies – 24 divisions; Germans – 6 divisions.
DESCRIPTION At 6.20am on 20 November, ten days after the end of the Passchendaele offensive, General Byng's British

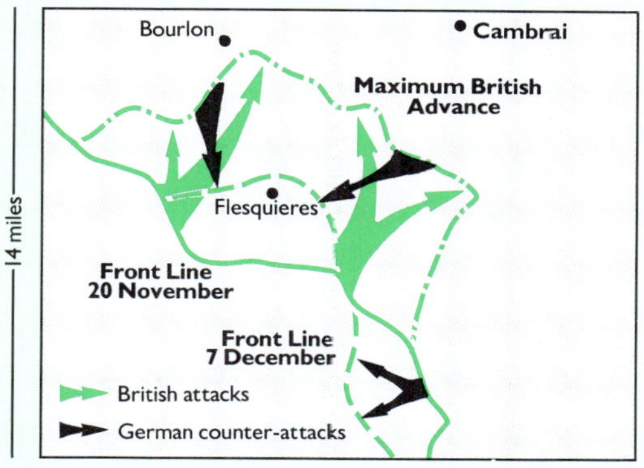

Third Army, spearheaded by the Tank Corps, attacked the German line at Cambrai. Launched without a preliminary bombardment and utilizing some 378 tanks closely supported by infantry, the attack achieved complete surprise. Unfortunately, however, the original concept of a large-scale tank raid had been transformed into another attempt at a decisive breakthrough, without sufficient reserves being available to exploit any breach in the formidable Hindenburg Line. Moreover, ▸

Commander Samson, holding a Webley Mk 1 automatic pistol, standing next to his Spad fighter prior to one of his missions over Turkish lines. The aircraft itself has a Vickers machine gun mounted on the upper wing centre-section. One of the most effective demonstrations of air power in the First World War was the destruction of a Turkish column on 21 September 1918.

and from the failure of machines to make their way back to Allied lines if in technical difficulties against the prevailing westerly winds. Continuous standing patrols were thus maintained regardless of the situation on the ground, while the Germans chose to concentrate their aircraft to gain local superiority as required. By 1917, therefore, British air losses were four times those of the German air force. The difficulties were compounded by an over-reliance on the products of the Royal Aircraft Factory, which trailed behind German production machines in efficiency, and by the refusal to consider parachutes on the grounds that they were unreliable, too bulky and might lead airmen to abandon their aircraft too readily.

Despite the poor quality of many British machines, new lighter aircraft with better speeds and higher rates of climb constantly evolved and presented new challenges to each side. In fact, the personalized air-to-air duel was relatively short-lived as formation flying became the norm in 1916 and 1917. Ground attack had also evolved by 1918, the potential of aircraft in this regard perhaps being best illustrated by the destruction of a Turkish column by seven British squadrons at Wadi el Far'a in Palestine on 21 September 1918. The actual casualties sustained by the Turks were surprisingly few but vehicles and guns were abandoned and morale shattered.

Morale was the prime target, of course, of the strategic use of airpower but another way to strike at the will of a society to continue the war was provided by the development of sea power. While the Allies blockaded Germany by means of patrols and mines, the Imperial German Navy increasingly retaliated with submarine warfare against merchant ships. But submarines also posed a challenge to naval vessels and, together with mines, ensured that the First World War was the last conflict in which the battleship would be regarded as the main instrument of sea-power. A single line of mines was sufficient to wreck the attempt by the Allies to force the Dardanelles on 18 March 1915, three capital ships being sunk and a fourth damaged by mines or shore-battery fire. Yet another challenge to the capital ship was the aircraft, a German guardship being the first vessel sunk from the air when attacked by Japanese aircraft at Tsingtau in October 1914. Mines were also laid by air in the Baltic during the war and an aerial torpedo attack was attempted at the Dardanelles in March 1915. During the same campaign, HMS *Triumph* became the first ship to fire at an opposing vessel it could not see when aircraft spotted for it over the Sea of Marmara on 25 April 1915. The first capital ship to be sunk by aircraft was an old Russian pre-*Dreadnought* in April 1916.

THE WAR AT SEA

Large-scale naval engagements were few and far between, that at Jutland in May 1916 (see page 178) seeing both the Royal Navy's Grand Fleet and the German High

1917

tanks were still thoroughly unreliable and only 92 remained serviceable by 23 November, the only effective arm of exploitation remaining cavalry. Thus, although the defence of General von der Marwitz's German Second Army was penetrated to a depth of 3 miles along a 6-mile front, little more could be achieved and a fierce struggle developed around the German positions in Bourlon Wood. On 30 November the Germans counter-attacked using the techniques that had brought such success at Caporetto, and by 7 December the net British gain on the first day had been all but wiped out.

CASUALTIES Some 45,000 casualties on both sides.

RESULT While a stalemate, the "first modern battle" had demonstrated the tactics that would finally end deadlock on the Western Front.

THE GERMAN SPRING OFFENSIVE

DATE 21 March–5 April 1918

OBJECT German victory in the west.

NUMBERS Germany – 65 divisions; Allies – 27 divisions.

DESCRIPTION Variously known as the Ludendorff Offensive or the Kaiserschlacht ("Emperor's Battle"), the German March offensive was a last gamble to achieve victory in the west. Of the five separate

THE AIR ACES

The emergence of fighter aircraft on the Western Front brought a relatively short period when air fighting became a romanticized contest between individuals. Removed as it was from the all-too-obvious carnage on the ground, such an aerial war caught the public imagination to such an extent that the often tragically short-lived pilots became overnight legends. For Germany, the earliest "ace" was Oswald Boelcke, who was killed in October 1916. But Boelcke's fame was surpassed both by his former pupil, Max Immelmann, who was killed even before Boelcke, and, of course, by the "Red Baron", Manfred von Richthofen. The latter had shot down a record 80 aircraft by the time of his death in April 1918. French "aces" included René Fonck, Georges Guynemer and Henri Navarre, who was actually the first to paint his aircraft a distinctive red. British airmen to achieve similar status – none were to survive – included Albert Ball VC, James McCudden and Edward "Mick" Mannock, whose 73 "kills" placed him second only to Richthofen.

Richthofen's Circus on an airfield.

René Fonck.

The Red Baron, von Richthofen (right).

The British ace, Albert Ball, VC.

The flamboyant Henri Navarre.

1918

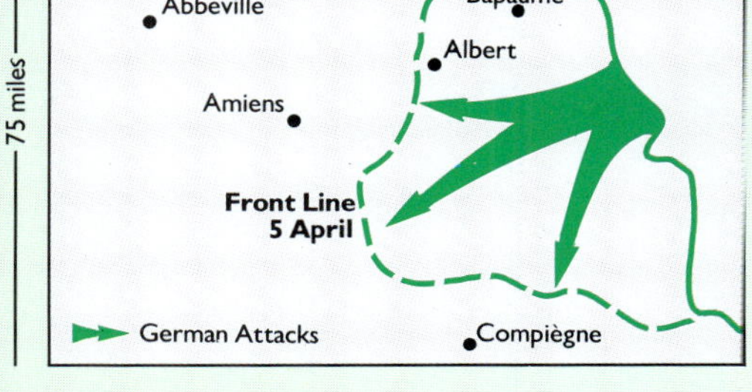

offensives mounted by the Germans over five months the first and largest was Operation Michael which in 16 continuous days of fighting finally broke the deadlock in France and Flanders. Planned by Ludendorff, Michael hurled 65 divisions from the German Second, Seventeenth and Eighteenth Armies against a maximum of 27 divisions of the British Third and Fifth armies, the latter commanded by General Sir Hubert Gough, at 4.40am on 21 March 1918. Under cover of mist and assisted by an unprecedented concentration of artillery along a 43-mile front, German stormtroopers took 98.5 square miles (and 21,000 prisoners) in a single day, or approximately the same amount of ground taken by the Allies over 140 days on the Somme in 1916. However, while the German losses were comparatively light at 39,000, they were still more than they could afford among élite troops. Moreover, they met increasingly dogged British resistance as the Allies finally created a ▸

SUBMARINE WARFARE

Unrestricted submarine warfare was introduced by the Germans in British waters on 18 February 1915 but, due to protests from neutral powers, it was suspended in September. However, full unrestricted submarine warfare was subsequently resumed by Germany on 1 February 1917 and resulted in a dramatic increase in Allied shipping losses. The solution was the re-emergence of the convoy. An experimental convoy was run from Gibraltar on 10 May 1917 and by November the convoy system had become fully operational, with U-boats forced to attack underwater and escorts able to locate them with the assistance of increasingly reliable hydrophones. By 1918 the Allied Submarine Detection Committee had also invented a new submarine-tracking sonar device named after it – ASDIC. The U-boats had been effectively beaten, the Germans losing 192 out of the 372 submarines they deployed during the war.

Seas Fleet sailing in line ahead, firing broadsides and seeking the weather gauge (to get the wind to clear the smoke of the guns) as if in the midst of a battle of the age of sail. The future lay with naval air power and the submarine. In terms of the former, a conventional aircraft was successfully flown off HMS *Vindex* in August 1916 while the first conventional aircraft successfully to land on a ship was flown on to HMS *Furious* by Flight Commander E.H. Dunning on 2 August 1917. However, Dunning was killed trying to repeat the feat and the number of obstacles on a ship's deck which could obstruct landing was not finally resolved until the commissioning of the first true aircraft carrier – HMS *Argus* – in October 1918, too late to get into the war.

The emergence of the *Argus* is an illustration of the nature of the First World War. In a very real sense, it was a new kind of conflict. Compared to the wars of the previous century, which had been localized and limited in many ways, the First World War was a total conflict fought on a global stage. In order to survive the challenge of war, states were required to transform their societies, economies and even their political structures. It required the total mobilization of a state's resources on an unprecedented scale with increased intervention in all aspects of its citizens'

The German battlecruiser, Seydlitz, *in dry dock at Wilhelmshaven on 14 June 1916 displaying the damage caused by two of the 15 hits it sustained during the battle of Jutland on 31 May. Generally, German shells and armour-plating appeared superior to those of the British, but it was the German High Seas Fleet that suffered a strategic defeat at Jutland.*

1918

supreme command to handle the crisis. Once Ludendorff switched objectives on 27 March, momentum was lost and Michael ground to a halt on 5 April 1918 without achieving a decisive breakthrough.

CASUALTIES German – 250,000; Allied – 254,000.

RESULT Whereas the Allies could afford their losses, Germany could not, and Michael's failure squandered her only strategic reserve.

MEGIDDO

DATE 19 September 1918

OBJECT To defeat the Turks, and so end Ottoman power.

NUMBERS British – 44,000; Turkish 8th Army – 8,000.

DESCRIPTION Although Jerusalem had fallen to General Allenby's forces in November 1917, the British campaign in Palestine did not end. Nevertheless the despatch of 60,000 veterans to the Western

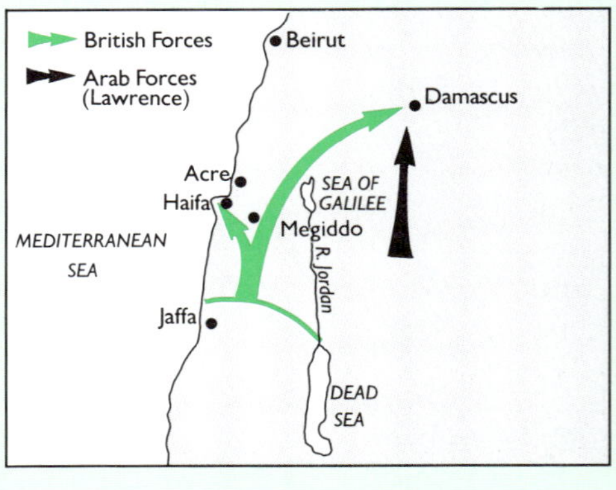

Commander E.H. Dunning's Sopwith Pup goes over the side of the carrier HMS Furious *on 4 August 1917, despite attempts by the deck party to save the aircraft. Dunning was drowned in the accident, two days after he had become the first man to land an aircraft successfully on a ship. The American, Eugene Ely, had been the first to take off from a ship successfully in November 1910, but the vessel had not been under power, and the first flight from a moving vessel had been off HMS* Vindex *in August 1916. Landing was rather more hazardous.*

lives, from relatively minor changes such as the introduction of licensing laws and summer time in Britain – both designed to increase war production – to direction of labour and conscription. The war provided new opportunities at a variety of levels and resulted in radical social changes, particularly for women.

The First World War also wrought global disruption and enormous loss of life and property, although it is worth noting that medical advances were such that it was the first war in which deaths from battle wounds exceeded those from disease. It is estimated that the war may have resulted in 10 million dead (excluding 1.5 million Armenian victims of Turkish genocide and a possible 27 million victims of the influenza pandemic of 1918), 20 million being maimed or seriously wounded, nine million children becoming orphans, five million women becoming widows and 10 million persons becoming homeless. Four empires – those of Imperial Germany, Austria-Hungary, Imperial Russia and Ottoman Turkey – were destroyed and a shattering blow dealt to European global dominance.

Yet, for all the ways in which science and technology had been harnessed to the war effort in the belligerent nations, there was much that was traditional in the way the war was fought from the line of battle at Jutland to the great cavalry battles on the Eastern Front. The tank, the manned aircraft and the aircraft carrier had all emerged on the military stage for the first time but their potential would only be realized in the future. In that sense, therefore, the First World War was essentially a transitional conflict at the dawn of a new age of warfare.

1918

Front and the assimilation of replacements drawn from the Indian Army necessitated a considerable lull in operations and it was only in September 1918 that Allenby felt ready to resume his offensive towards Damascus. Having effected a comprehensive plan of deception to persuade the Turkish commander, the German General Liman von Sanders, that he intended to attack inland, Allenby surprised the Turks by striking along the coast. Concentrating some 9,000 cavalry and 35,000 infantry on just a 15-mile front opposite some 8,000 men of the Turkish 8th Army, Allenby attacked on 19 September. With the infantry opening the way and supported by aircraft mercilessly strafing Turkish columns, Allenby's armoured cars and horsemen raced into the Turkish rear towards Megiddo, the site of the ancient battle of Armageddon.

RESULT The entire Turkish line collapsed and Allenby's forces swept on to Damascus by 1 October and to Aleppo on 25 October. In 38 days the Egyptian Expeditionary Force had advanced 350 miles.

CASUALTIES 75,000 Turkish prisoners were taken, the Desert Mounted Corps alone taking 47,000 prisoners for only 533 casualties of its own.

THE BIRTH OF THE TANK

MOST ELEMENTS OF the tank were developed prior to the First World War. Indeed, the concept of a caterpillar track originated as early as the late 18th century although, of course, the internal combustion engine was only invented in 1885. Steam tractors were common before the war and, in fact, the British army had utilized a number for transport purposes during the South African War. Armoured cars had also made their appearance in warfare during the Italo-Turkish conflict in Libya in 1911 and some civilians, including an Australian named de Mole in 1912, had actually suggested tracked armoured vehicles.

However, during the war itself the idea of utilizing the pre-war Holt agricultural steam tractor as a means of overcoming barbed wire and broken ground first occurred to the official British war correspondent, Colonel Ernest Swinton, who submitted his ideas both to General Headquarters (GHQ) and the Committee of Imperial Defence on 20 October 1914. GHQ rejected Swinton's proposals but the secretary to the CID, Colonel Maurice Hankey, submitted a paper of his own and the concept was taken up by the First Lord of the Admiralty, Winston Churchill. The Royal Naval Air Service (RNAS) had enjoyed some success with armoured cars operating out of Dunkirk in the opening months of the 1914 campaign. The Germans had attempted to obstruct the RNAS cars by digging trenches across the roads and Churchill had encouraged Admiral Bacon to find a solution to the problem. The work of Swinton and Hankey thus happily coincided with this initiative and an Admiralty Landships Committee was established in February 1915.

After some setbacks, a prototype known as "Little Willie" was built by the agricultural engineer William Tritton and Lieutenant W.G. Wilson at the Foster Works in Lincolnshire of which Tritton was managing director. The next prototype, "Big Willie", was then tested at Hatfield Park in January and February 1916 and, as a result of the trials, 40 and then 100 were ordered by GHQ. The first six reached France in August 1916.

(Above) A sketch of a British Mk IV tank. "Male" tanks, as shown here, had two six-pounder guns and four machine guns and "female" tanks six machine guns.

(Above) Tanks of the 2nd Brigade, Tank Corps on railway trucks at Fins, 6 December 1917, after their return from the Cambrai battle. Large numbers broke down before even reaching the start line.

(Right) The "Mother" or "Big Willie" (HM's Landship, Centipede) prototype which went through its trials at Hatfield Park in Hertfordshire in January and February 1916, becoming the forerunner of a series of tanks which ran to nine marks.

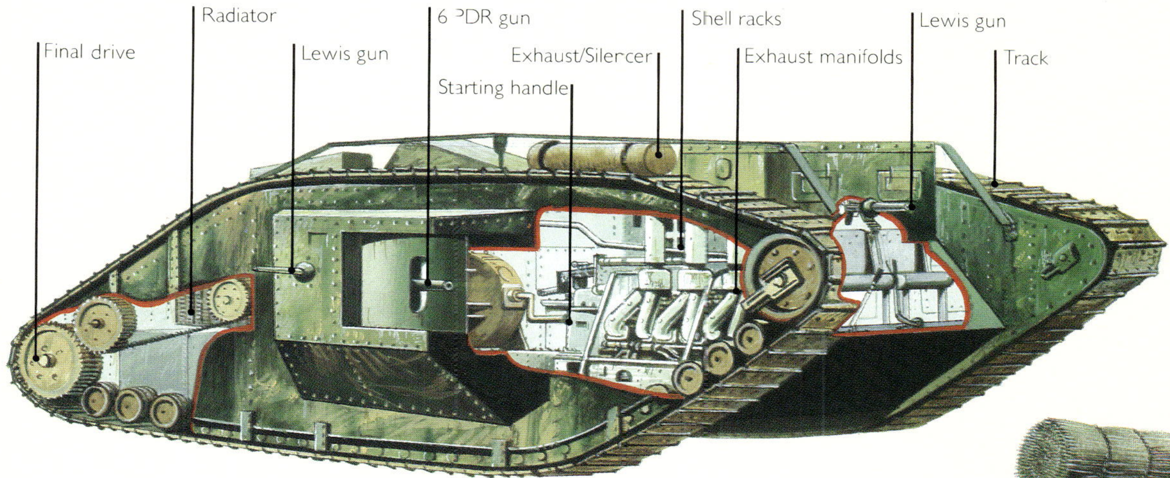

(Above) A section through a Mark IV tank. Prone to mechanical failure of engines, gears or rollers, it was a cramped, hot, noisy and fume-ridden environment for its eight-man crew.

(Right) A Mark IV adapted to lay fascines – large bundles of wood – over trenches, to enable tanks to cross.

(Right) A representation of the tactical plan for the use of tanks at Cambrai. The first wave crushes gaps in the wire and fans out to fire down the enemy trenches while the second wave drops fascines and advances towards the enemy support tanks then gathering to advance towards the rear, infantry grouped in platoons would follow in files to clear the trenches and prepare the way for a general advance.

(Right) An illustration of both a new weapon and a modern adaptation of an older idea: German infantry, probably storm-troopers, using a modern version of a medieval weapon – man-portable flamethrowers – against an entirely new weapon – a British tank – during the Spring Offensives of 1918.

11

THE SECOND WORLD WAR

THE LEGACY OF THE GREAT WAR in terms of strategy was an important one. The Western Front during 1914–18 had demonstrated the superiority of defence over attack. No one wanted to repeat the costly experience of trench warfare, but during the last part of the war the tank and the German stormtroops had pointed the way to an antidote. Two other weapons also displayed potential for winning wars more quickly in the future. At sea the U-boat had during 1917 almost throttled Britain's maritime lifeline, while in the air the German air attacks on London had had an effect on civilian morale out of all proportion to the size of the raids.

The significance of these weapons was recognized by the Allies when they drew up the Treaty of Versailles, which formally ended the war with Germany. Apart from reducing her navy to 15,000 men and her army to 100,000, she was forbidden an air force. Tanks, U-boats and capital ships were also proscribed. As for the Allies themselves, they speedily dismantled their vast wartime armed forces. The USA resumed her prewar isolationism, and France and Britain, especially the latter, turned their attention once more to the empires. The belief that the Great War was the "war to end all war" encouraged widespread pacificism and this was reflected in a desire for general disarmament. The first positive indication of this was the 1922 Washington Naval Treaties, by which the major naval powers agreed to suspend capital ship-building for 10 years, as well as agreeing to maintain their fleets in the existing strength proportions to one another. During 1927–33 there were further disarmament conferences at Geneva, but they achieved little apart from banning poison gas.

Undeterred by the disarmament environment, a number of theorists were considering the shape of war in the future, recognizing the revolutionary effect that the tank and the aircraft could have. In Britain General J.F.C. Fuller, who had been on the Tank Corps staff in France during the war, and Captain Basil Liddell Hart wrote copiously on how the petrol engine could revolutionize the battlefield, enabling the

1936

SPANISH CIVIL WAR

DATE 1936-39

This began in July 1936 when army garrisons in Spanish Morocco, led by General Franco, revolted against the left-wing government in Spain. Within a few months Germany and Italy had sent air and ground forces to help Franco, while the Russians did the same for the Republicans. This enabled all three countries to test their latest weapons in combat and the war became a technical laboratory. Amid the inevitable atrocities that civil war brings, the German bombing of the Basque town of Guernica on 25 April 1937 was the most prominent, and confirmed people's worst fears of what a major European war would be like. Though the Republicans, aided by foreign volunteers (the International Brigades) managed to hold Madrid throughout most of the war, Franco's Nationalists gradually brought the whole country under their control. Britain and France

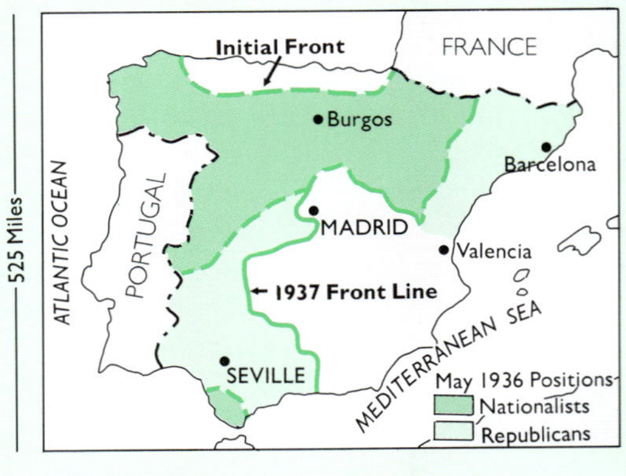

attacker to defeat the enemy through sheer pace. Although the British and US armies did experiment, on a small scale, with mechanized forces, lack of money and the international climate at the time inhibited the formation of these forces to any significant degree. More note was taken of their writings, especially those of Fuller, by the two outcasts of Europe, Germany and Russia. Through secret clauses in the 1922 Treaty of Rapallo the Russians allowed the Germans covert armoured and air-training facilities in Russia in return for technical guidance. By the early 1930s the Russians, largely under the guidance of chief-of-staff Mikhail Tuchachevsky, had developed large armoured forces. Once Hitler came to power, the Germans would do the same.

The air prophets took a more extreme stance. Led by the Italian General Giulio Douhet they argued that future wars could be won by airpower alone. Aircraft would be able to do what armies and navies could not, strike directly at seats of government, industry and the civil population. In the USA General Billy Mitchell declared that aircraft could destroy capital ships and hence make navies vulnerable to airpower, while in Britain, General Hugh Trenchard used the airpower argument to preserve the newly won independence from the other two services of the Royal Air Force. As for the general public, their view was summed up by Stanley Baldwin, soon to be British prime minister, in his often quoted comment of 1932: "The bomber will always get through."

Once Hitler came to power in Germany in 1933 he quickly threw off the remaining shackles of Versailles with a wide-ranging rearmament programme. The German navy was given legitimacy through the 1935 Anglo-German Naval Agreement. While this limited Germany's surface fleet to a third of that of the Royal Navy, she was significantly allowed parity in submarines on the basis that convoying, ASDIC (Sonar) and agreements on restricting submarine warfare (1936 London Protocol) had much reduced the threat of this weapon. The German army underwent a massive expansion, while the Luftwaffe grew from nothing to one of Europe's largest air forces in the space of just a few years.

By the mid-1930s growing tension in Europe, largely created by Hitler, forced Britain and France into a degree of rearmament. France pinned her faith on fixed defences on her border with Germany, the Maginot Line, believing that this would be sufficient to deter aggression. Britain, on the other hand, put priority on maintaining her naval supremacy and in strengthening the RAF in order to match Hitler's Luftwaffe. The Army was a poor third, with the main effort going into anti-aircraft guns, but much progress was made in replacing the horse by the petrol engine. Yet, while Germany mechanized from the front, Britain motorized from the rear. As for the Soviet Union, the impressive progress that the Red Army had made in developing

A Maginot Line casemate in winter 1939–40. Named after the French war minister of the time, work on the Line began in 1928. Much of it was underground and in many places all that could be seen from the east was a series of small steel cupolas. Its weakness was that it could be outflanked through neutral Belgium.

1940

adopted a non-interventionist policy and attempted to enlist German and Italian help in mounting a naval blockade to prevent arms and men being shipped to both sides. Hitler and Mussolini, however, ignored this and it was their ability to supply at a much greater rate than the Russians that became decisive.

FALL OF FRANCE

DATES 10 May–22 June 1940

While Army Group C masked the Maginot Line, Army Group B overran Belgium and Holland, forcing the Dutch to surrender on 15 May and the Belgians on 27 May. Army Group A, led by three Panzer Groups, passed through the Ardennes and secured crossings over the Meuse on 13 May. As the German armour exploited these the French tried to mount counterstrokes in their southern flank, but with little success. A British armour attack at Arras on 21 May did cause a momentary German panic, but on the 20th the first German tanks had reached the mouth of the Somme, cutting the Allies' armies into two. Meanwhile, the northern Allied armies, now aware of the threat to the rear, withdrew from Belgium, pressed closely by Army Group B. By 27 May the bulk had been trapped around Dunkirk and were being hastily evacuated back to England. ▶

Hitler reviewing the SA, his political shock troops, in 1933. Their power threatened the army, and even Hitler himself, and so he removed their leadership in the infamous Night of the Long Knives. This and its rigid observance of the traditional Prussian code of Honour, Duty, Loyalty bound the army high command to him.

concepts of armoured warfare came to naught. During the great purges of the late 1930s Stalin removed all the best brains in the armed forces and the tank formations were largely broken up.

The flower of the Polish army was its cavalry. Napoleon had had a high opinion of his Polish Lancers, and their successors had distinguished themselves against the Red Army cavalry during 1920–21, but they were no match for the German Panzer divisions.

THE *BLITZKRIEG* YEARS

The years 1939–41 were marked by a series of spectacular German victories. The secret of the German success lay in a new doctrine, *Blitzkrieg* or lightning war. The concept behind this lay in a move away from the 1914–18 philosophy of defeating the enemy by engaging his armies frontally and destroying them by weight of fire. Instead, the object was dislocation of the command and control system. This was achieved by fast-moving armoured formations slicing through the enemy's defences and penetrating deep into his rear. Having achieved this they would then trap the withdrawing enemy armies in pockets. These would then be reduced by the bulk of the German Army, the infantry, who still relied on their feet. In order to help the Panzer divisions get through the defences, techniques were evolved by which they could quickly call on Luftwaffe support, normally in the shape of the Junkers Ju87 Stuka dive bomber, which was used as aerial artillery. One other aspect was the

1940

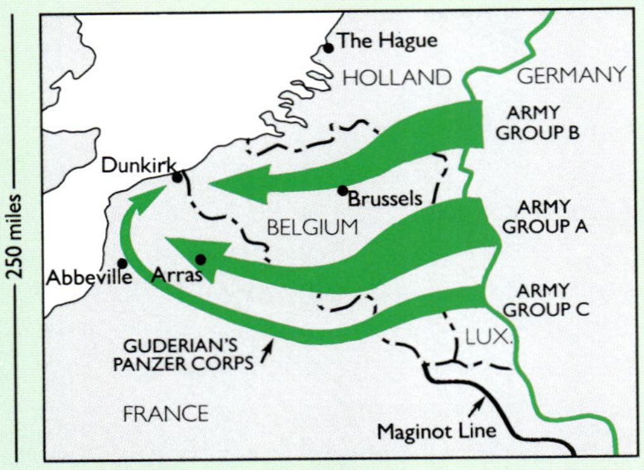

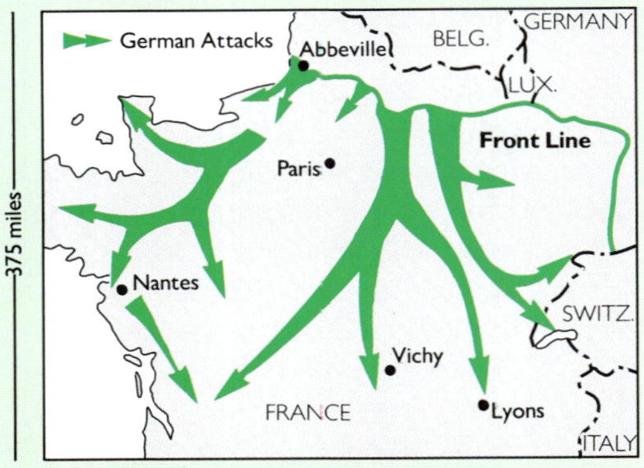

Most got away, partly because the German armour had been halted to enable the infantry divisions to catch up, and also because Goering foolishly declared that the Luftwaffe could finish the job. The Germans now turned south. Once they had got across the Somme and Aisne rivers progress was rapid and an armistice was signed on 22 June. German casualties were 45,000 killed and missing compared to 100,000 fatal Allied casualties.

German tanks in France, June 1940. The Allies had roughly the same number of tanks, but the Germans kept their armour concentrated, using it as a mailed fist. Good radio communications also helped it exploit Allied weaknesses.

THE STUKA

The *Blitzkrieg's* "aerial artillery" had its origins in the Curtiss Hawk, which had been developed as a dive bomber for the US Navy. This had been seen by Ernst Udet, Great War German fighter ace and soon to head the Luftwaffe's Technical Office. He persuaded Goering to back development of a dive bomber for use against pinpoint targets and the Junkers Ju87 Stuka, first blooded in Spain in 1937, was the result. Its top speed was only some 250 mph and, armed with 500 kg (1,100 lb) and 50 kg bombs, it attacked its target in a near-vertical dive, its siren wailing, pulling up at the very last moment. However, it was highly vulnerable to fighter attack. Later in the war it became a highly effective "tank buster" on the Eastern Front.

A Ju 87B Stuka during the Polish "blitzkrieg".

1940

BATTLE OF BRITAIN

DATE 10 July–31 October 1940
CAMPAIGN Western Europe
OBJECT To achieve air supremacy over southern England as a prerequisite to a cross-Channel invasion.
NUMBERS (at beginning of the battle) Germans – 2,600 aircraft of all types; RAF – 644 fighters.
DESCRIPTION The battle consisted of five distinct phases. The first, which lasted until 7 August, was known as the "contact" phase. The Luftwaffe, by attacks on Channel convoys, tried to tempt the RAF into battles close to the French shore. The RAF policy at this stage was conservation and they largely refused to be drawn. During the period 8-23 August the Germans switched their attention to fighter airfields and the RAF's vital early warning radar system, Chain Home. The Luftwaffe came close to seriously crippling RAF Fighter Command's infrastructure, but Goering, ▸

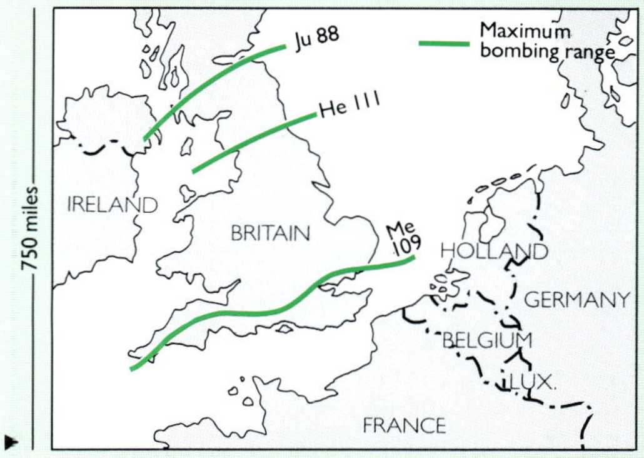

A major threat to Allied armour, especially in the close country of north-west Europe, during the last part of the war was the German Panzerfaust, *a hand-held weapon. It fired a hollow charge projectile and, although of very limited range, its penetrative capability was impressive. The British and US equivalents were the PIAT and Bazooka.*

importance of radio communications, much stressed by *Blitzkrieg*'s prime practitioner, General Heinz Guderian. These gave armoured commanders the ability to react quickly to any given situation.

The first victim of *Blitzkrieg* was Poland, which was overrun in a campaign lasting just five weeks. While the Poles fought with great bravery, they were under grave disadvantages from the outset. Poland's long frontiers with Germany, including those with the geographically isolated East Prussia, had been lengthened still further by Hitler's annexation of Czechoslovakia in March 1939, and she was forced to deploy the bulk of her armies on them. Another factor which compelled this was that the main industrial region was in Polish Silesia. This resulted in insufficient reserves being available to counter the German thrusts. The Polish army had few tanks and was short of artillery, while the air force was small and its aircraft obsolete. Given these factors, the result was inevitable and any hope that the Poles might have had of prolonging resistance and encouraging a positive response from her allies, Britain and France, was dashed when the Russians invaded eastern Poland on 17 September. As it was, apart fröm a very limited advance into the Saarland, the French refused to be drawn away from the Maginot defences.

The Western Allies were, on paper at least, a much more formidable opponent and Hitler's generals needed much more time to prepare than Hitler was initially prepared to give them. But the bad weather of winter 1939–40 came to their aid. While the Allies could match the Germans in tank strength, they did not concentrate their armour, but distributed it along the whole front. The long period of inactivity also did little for the morale of the French army, and the Allied plan for an advance into Belgium to meet and hold the Germans on the line of the River Dyle on the assumption that Hitler would repeat the 1914 Schlieffen Plan, played into the hands of the eventual German plan. This called for the main thrust to be made in the centre, creating operational surprise by passing the bulk of the tanks through the wooded and hilly Ardennes, believed by the Allies to be impenetrable by large quantities of armour. When the blow fell on 10 May 1940, the Allies were caught wrong-footed from the outset and never recovered from this. The sheer pace of the German operations was too much for the creaking Allied command structure to react to in time. This was especially true when it came to mounting counterstrokes into the ever-lengthening flanks of the German armoured rapier. The German high command itself constantly worried about flank vulnerability and the need for the follow-up infantry to catch up, and this resulted in a number of temporary halts, culminating in that before Dunkirk. Even so, it only took a week longer to overcome France and the Low Countries than to subjugate Poland.

The overrunning of Yugoslavia and Greece in April 1941, although spectacular,

not believing that his attacks against the radar stations were effective, began, from 24 August, to be drawn towards London, concentrating on airfields and aircraft factories. The more inland the target, however, the less able were the German fighters, because of their limited range, to protect the bombers. Then, from 7 September, came the offensive on London, primarily by day. Finally, during October the bombing effort switched to night as the Blitz got properly underway, with day nuisance raids, taking advantage of poorer weather, on airfields.

CASUALTIES 1,700 German and 600 British aircraft lost.

RESULT The failure to gain air superiority quickly made Hitler lose enthusiasm for invasion. Instead he tried to bomb Britain into submission, but his desire to invade Russia brought this to an end in May 1941.

CAPE MATAPAN

DATE 28 March 1941

CAMPAIGN Mediterranean

OBJECT To intercept British convoys to Greece.

NUMBERS Italian naval task force of one battleship, eight cruisers, nine destroyers. British Mediterranean Fleet, including three battleships and one carrier.

DESCRIPTION The Germans had been complaining of lack of Italian effort to prevent

were *Blitzkrieg* campaigns on a much smaller scale. What they did do, however, was to force a postponement of the attack on Russia. This was to be fatal, since the German plan relied on the ultimate objectives being gained before the onset of winter. Initially the Germans were helped by Stalin's refusal to take practical precautions against invasion for fear of provoking Hitler, and the major reorganization of the Red Army as a result of its poor showing against Finland during the winter of 1939–40. Consequently, during the first weeks of the invasion there were dazzling successes in the form of enormous pockets being created. This was helped by Stalin's refusal to accept large-scale withdrawals. Hitler, however, increasingly meddled in operations, changing his mind over where the ultimate priority lay, the flanks or the seizing of Moscow. This, the effect of poor road/rail communications and ever-lengthening supply-lines caused progress to fall behind schedule. The autumn rains and subsequent snows caused further aggravation. Consequently, the Germans, ill equipped for winter, were not only halted in front of Moscow, but thrown back in a series of counter-attacks. *Blitzkrieg* had met its match.

German anti-tank gun crew in the Libyan Desert. While on the surface this theatre was ideal for the tank, being very open and with few natural obstacles, cleverly deployed anti-tank guns could often neutralize their effect. Both sides mounted them on vehicles, "porteeing", as it was called by the British, to increase their flexibility.

NORTH AFRICAN SEE-SAW

For three years after the fall of France the only area in which Western Allied ground forces were actively engaged against the Axis was in North Africa. The fighting in the Egyptian-Libyan desert was characterized by each side making long rapid advances, only to be halted by overstretched supply-lines, and then, in turn, being driven back. The desert made the tank seemingly the dominant weapon, but the generally better success enjoyed by the Axis armour was not so much to do with technical superiority, but Rommel's better handling of it. Too often, British armoured commanders tended to emulate their horsed-cavalry forebears in unsubtle charges at the enemy or failed to take timely advantage of windows of opportunity. Rommel's sixth sense, something he shared with the other panzer commanders, for being at the critical point at the right time, and his tactic of drawing the British armour onto his formidable 88mm anti-tank guns time and again won the day for him. The German ability to quickly form ad hoc all-arms battle groups was also significant. In the end, it was the virtual throttling of the Axis supply-lines across the Mediterranean and quantitative superiority in material, aggravated by the fact that in German eyes North Africa was always a very minor campaign, that eventually brought Allied victory in May 1943.

THE RECONQUEST OF EUROPE

The lessons of *Blitzkrieg* initially caused the Western Allies drastically to increase their numbers of armoured divisions, although their programmes were later cut back with

1941

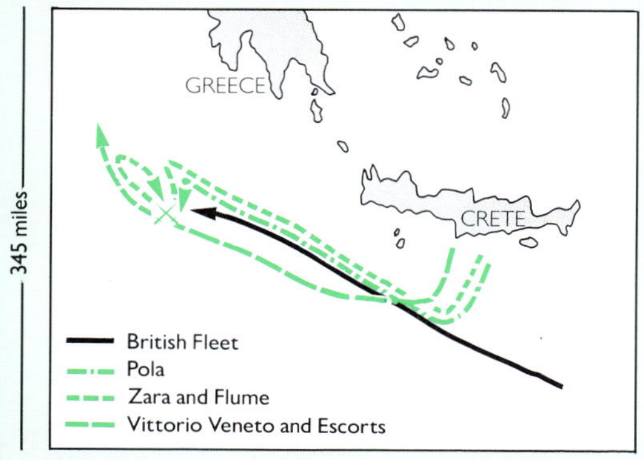

British troops and supplies being sent from Egypt to Greece to support her in her war against Italy, which had begun with an Italian attack from Albania the previous October. The Greeks had successfully driven the Italians back into Albania and Mussolini was forced to appeal to Hitler for help. The resulting blitzkrieg, launched in the spring, was the last unqualified success scored by the Nazi war machine.

In response to the German complaints, an Italian task force under Admiral Iachino began to sweep north and south of Crete in the hope of contacting convoys, but was spotted by an RAF flying boat. The Mediterranean Fleet under Admiral Cunningham therefore set sail from Alexandria to intercept Iachino. The Italians now contacted a British cruiser-destroyer task force covering the convoys. This drew them onto the main fleet. Aircraft from the carrier *Formidable* hit the battleship *Vittorio Veneto* with a torpedo, but she was able to limp back to port. Later they also struck a ▸

(Above) Deutsches Afrika Korps armoured car in North Africa. In mobile warfare these acted as the eyes of the armoured formations.

(Above right) Another important form of reconnaissance was the aircraft. Here, also in North Africa, a camera is loaded into a German Me-110.

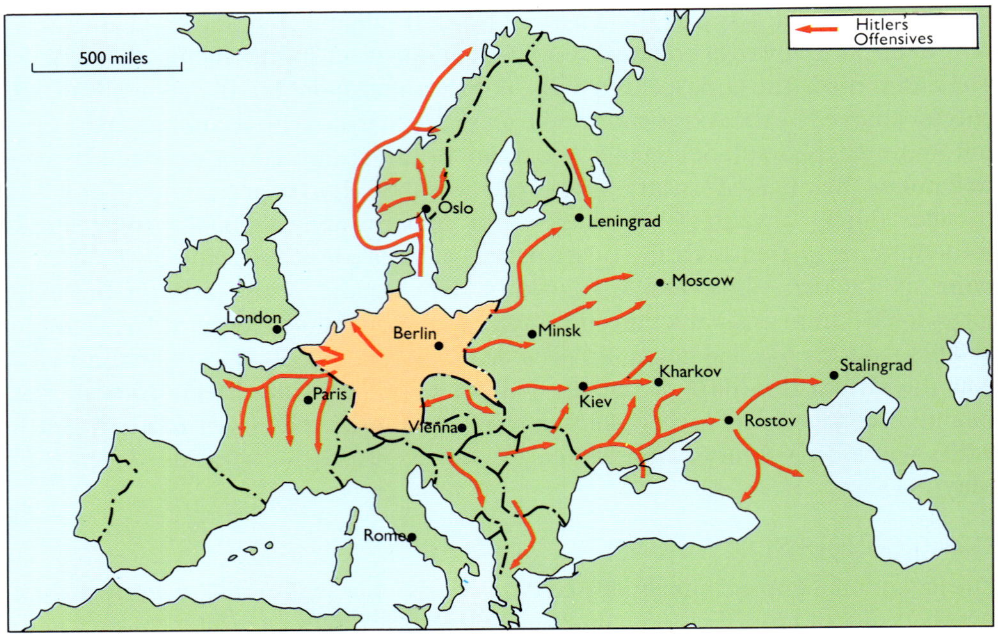

(Right) Map to show Hitler's offensive campaigns in Europe. Comparing Hitler's invasions of northern, western and south-eastern Europe to that of the Soviet Union makes clear the vastness of this undertaking. From June 1941 until the end of the war in Europe, never less than 70 per cent of the German army's combat power was committed to the Eastern Front. No wonder the Russians claim they bore the brunt.

cruiser and, in the course of trying to extricate her, the Italians lost further ships.
CASUALTIES Three Italian cruisers and two destroyers sunk. One Italian battleship damaged.
RESULT This kept the Italian fleet in harbour for some months, but the British success would only be temporary. The increasing Luftwaffe presence would make much of the eastern Mediterranean virtually an Axis "lake".

INVASION OF CRETE

DATE 20 May–1 June 1941
CAMPAIGN Mediterranean
OBJECT To capture the island
NUMBERS 40,000 Germans; 30,000 British and Dominion troops.
DESCRIPTION A significant proportion of the Allied troops on Crete had recently been evacuated from Greece and were still somewhat disorganized. The Germans began to bomb the island on 13 May and invaded it a week later. Their initial target was the airfields in the north-west of the island and paratroop forces were dropped to seize these. Ground resistance was initially bitter and the German paratroops suffered heavy casualties, with many aircraft also being shot down. The paratroops were followed by glider-borne elements. A further force was sent by sea, but was intercepted by the Royal Navy and much of it was lost. After two days, however, the vital airfield of Maleme was in German

(Left) Italy became very much a backwater, especially after the Allied landings in France. Nevertheless, apart from keeping German troops tied down, it witnessed some of the fiercest fighting of the war in Europe. This was especially so at Monte Cassino during the first part of 1944. Here a Polish Bren gunner fights in the monastery ruins.

the realization that the generally close terrain of north-west Europe needed a high proportion of infantry. Much effort was also made to perfect systems for employing close air support on the battlefield which came to fruition during 1944 campaigns, where, through the "cab rank", ground-attack aircraft circled overhead waiting to be called down to attack targets of opportunity. In spite of the increasing quantitive Allied superiority in all departments, the Germans showed themselves to be as tenacious in defence as they had been adventurous in attack, *vide* Cassino and Normandy in 1944 and the winter 1944–5 campaign in NW Europe. The tank, too, proved as effective in defence as in attack, especially the German Tiger, which outgunned all Allied tanks. The German principle of training all ranks to be able to assume the responsibilities of two levels higher was also a factor, especially since operational orders allowed subordinate commanders greater freedom of action within the constraints of a mission than on the Allied side. The Allies' greatest problem was, as was so often the case in warfare driven by the petrol engine, logistics. Hitler had decreed that all the English Channel and Atlantic ports were to be held to the last man. Consequently, when the Allies finally broke out of the Normandy beachhead in August (see page 224) they were still reliant on all supplies coming through here. Thus, their spectacular dash across France on the broad front on which Supreme Commander Dwight Eisenhower insisted, for political reasons as much as

A German Pz Kw-III in Russia. During 1941–2 the German Panzer arm enjoyed even more spectacular successes than in the West, but the problems of keeping them supplied with fuel and ammunition during their thrusts became ever more difficult. This was aggravated by the Russian "scorched earth" strategy and the partisans.

1941

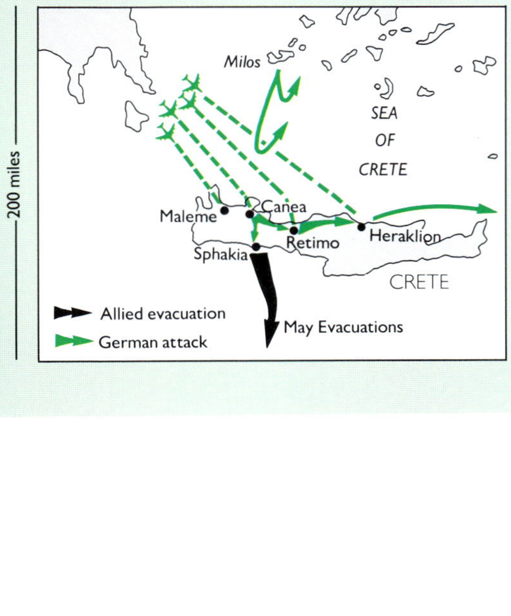

hands and reinforcements were brought in by aircraft. With the Germans enjoying air supremacy the defenders began to withdraw to the south of the island and the Royal Navy prepared for another evacuation. It began on the night 28-29 May, but ever-spiralling losses in British warships brought an end to it three nights later and some 12,000 men were forced to surrender. **CASUALTIES** German 6,200 men; British 16,500 men, including prisoners. The Germans also lost some 400 aircraft and the British three cruisers and six destroyers sunk, as well as three battleships, one carrier, six cruisers and seven destroyers damaged.

RESULT The capture of Crete strengthened the Axis hold on the east Mediterranean. The high loss in transport aircraft, however, deterred the Germans from mounting any more major operations. In contrast, the Allies began to use airborne forces as a major spearhead. As such they took part in the landings in French North Africa (Nov- ▸

More Russian prisoners are marched off to the rear. In June 1941 the Russian troops were caught unprepared by the German invasion. This was largely thanks to Stalin, who did not want to do anything that might antagonize Hitler, despite many warnings of what the Germans intended. Once the initial shock had passed, the Russian soldier proved to be an equal match for his German counterpart.

anything, could not be sustained. Only when the port of Antwerp was opened up at the end of November 1944 did the situation improve, but by then winter and a coagulating German defence put paid to final victory before the end of 1944.

On the Eastern Front, the German summer 1942 offensive in the south tried to complete what had been left unfinished in December 1941. It failed partly because the Russians, learning from their 1941 mistakes, traded space for time, and destruction of their forces in large pockets did not occur. Also Hitler, instead of concentrating on overrunning the Caucasus, became increasingly mesmerized by Stalingrad and his attacking forces found themselves thrusting in divergent directions. The Soviet counter-offensive in front of Stalingrad in November 1942, which cut off Paulus's German Army and brought about its eventual surrender three months later, marked the debut of the reborn Red Army. Re-equipped both through weapons sent by Britain and the USA ("lend lease") from the West and the Russian armaments industry safe behind the Urals, it relied on success by initially achieving overwhelming superiority, especially in artillery, at the point of attack. Once the door of the defences had been forced slightly ajar, mechanized formations, known as

1941

ember 1942), Sicily (July 1943) and Normandy (June 1944), by which time they had created a large airborne army. Their most spectacular operation was at Arnhem (September 1944), a failure largely because the ground forces took too long to link up with the paratroops.

CRUSADER

DATE November 1941
OBJECT Britain wanted to relieve Tobruk, besieged by Axis forces, and to drive Field Marshal Rommel out of north-east Libya.
NUMBERS British – 90,000 men, 760 tanks; Axis – 105,000 men, 320 tanks.
DESCRIPTION This battle is a prime example of the fluidity of desert warfare. Auchinleck's aim was to relieve Tobruk, which had been under siege since April,

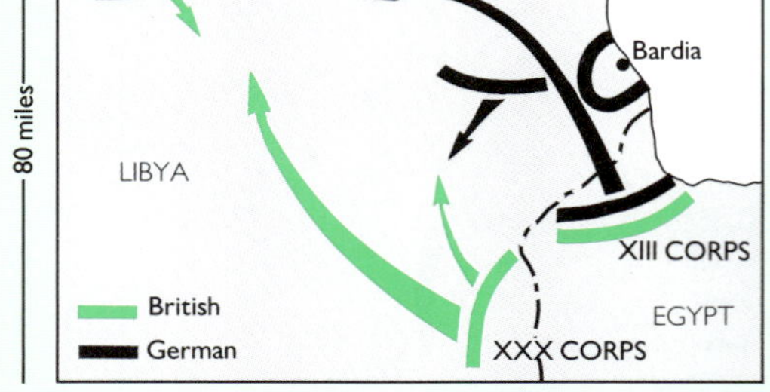

mobile groups, would be passed through to penetrate deep into the rear, seizing key terrain to aid the advance of the follow-up forces, disrupt command and control and encourage precipitate enemy withdrawals. Echelonment of forces helped sustain the exploitation of the breakthrough, but when one thrust began to lose momentum the Russians would launch a fresh offensive in another area, thus preventing the Germans from reinforcing a threatened sector from elsewhere along the front. The German counter was to increase the depth of their defences. Once the Russians did break through, the German forward forces were to accept being bypassed and cut off and to rely on relief by armoured forces striking the Russians in the flank. This worked to a degree, but growing Russian superiority in resources, especially manpower, proved too much (see Kursk, page 221).

THE JAPANESE WAY OF WAGING WAR

The successes enjoyed by the Japanese army in the months immediately following the strike at Pearl Harbor were equally dramatic as those of the German Army in

Continued on page 206

(Below) Pearl Harbor, 7 December 1941. The Japanese recognized that the greatest threat to their ambitions in the Far East and the Pacific was the US Pacific Fleet. If this could be destroyed, they could consolidate their gains. The attack caught the Americans by surprise, but missed the Pacific Fleet's two aircraft carriers, which were at sea – a fatal omission.

1941

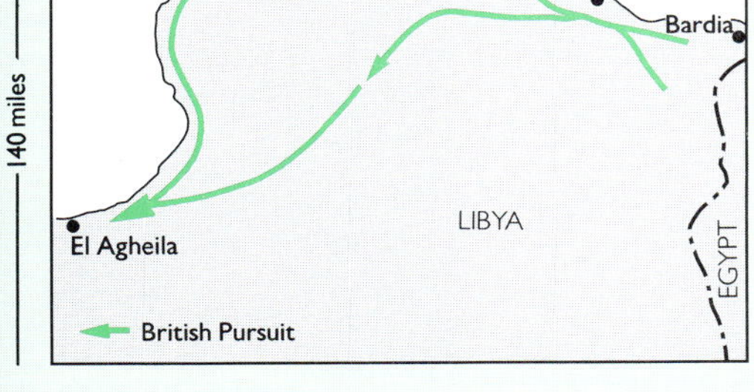

and to drive Rommel out of Cyrenaica. The British armour, concentrated in XXX Corps in the south, was to tie down and destroy the Axis armour while XIII Corps enveloped the Axis defences on the Egyptian frontier and then advanced on Tobruk. The attack opened on 18 November, initially taking Rommel by surprise, and on the 20th the Tobruk garrison was ordered to break out. Rommel concentrated his armour and in a two-day battle around Sidi Rizegh caused it heavy casualties. The Tobruk break-out was halted and Rommel then dashed for the frontier to cut the British Eighth Army's supply lines. Cunningham, its commander, wanted to halt the offensive, but Auchinleck overrode him, replacing him. Rommel, after causing some confusion, ran short of fuel and, heavily attacked from the air, began to withdraw, especially since a link-up had now been made with the Tobruk garrison. Rommel then withdrew his besieging forces and fell back on Gazala, but fear of ▸

KEY COMMANDERS

THOSE WHO LED the air, sea and land forces of each nation between 1939 and 1945 represented many different command styles.

At the very top were the supreme warlords, the national leaders. Of the dictators, Hitler and Stalin displayed many similarities. Both immersed themselves in the minutiae of operations and took personal control of them. Hitler relied on his commanders' observance of the traditional Prussian code of Duty, Honour, and Loyalty; Stalin controlled his generals, as he did the whole of the Soviet Union, through fear. Mussolini merely postured. In Japan the Emperor was treated as a god, but the power lay with the generals, especially war minister Hideki Tojo, nicknamed "The Razor".

Winston Churchill undoubtedly inspired not only the British but others as well with his famous speeches, but he, too, could not resist meddling at times in operational matters. The bond forged between Churchill and Franklin D. Roosevelt became crucial in coordinating Anglo-US strategy, but Roosevelt inspired his fellow Americans not through great oratory but with his more homely "fireside chats". Both men were lucky to have able chiefs-of-staff, Marshall and Alanbrooke, to guide them. Hitler merely had the subservient Wilhelm Keitel.

For the Western Allies it was essential that the senior commanders were diplomats as well as soldiers. Dwight Eisenhower was the personification of this and it needed all his skills to damp down the friction that arose between his US and British subordinates. This was especially true between Montgomery and Patton, both of whom were fighting soldiers and prima donnas, but who instilled enormous confidence in their troops.

There were, too, the Bomber Barons – Spaatz, Eaker and Harris – who believed that their strategic air forces could win the war single-handed. Other supreme Allied commanders who proved to be good diplomats were Alexander in the Mediterranean and Mountbatten in South East Asia. In contrast, Douglas MacArthur, who commanded for so long in the south-west Pacific, was equally successful but drove his troops rather than led them. The Pacific was primarily a maritime war and US Admirals "Bull" Halsey and Chester Nimitz commanded their fleets with dash and verve, as did the British Admiral Cunningham in the Mediterranean.

The British and Americans considered Gerd von Rundstedt, known as the Last Prussian, to be the ablest German commander, but he grew old, and his peer was undoubtedly Erich von Manstein, who fought largely on the Eastern Front. The Panzer generals, especially Heinz Guderian and Erwin Rommel, believed in leading from the front and certainly gained the most spectacular successes. They had their Russian counterparts, particularly Georgi Zhukov and Ivan Koniev. Tomoyuki Yamashita, conqueror of Malaya and Singapore, was another of this breed, while Admiral Isoroku Yamamoto, who masterminded the Pearl Harbor strike, was one of the foremost tacticians of the war.

(Top) Rommel (left) in North Africa where, known as the "Desert Fox", he outwitted the British for almost two years.

(Above) Guderian was nicknamed "Schnell (Fast) Heinz": a name he more than lived up to.

(Right) Hermann Goering was head of the Luftwaffe and, for much of the war, Deputy Führer. He increasingly and unfairly blamed his pilots for the air force's failures.

(Left) From left to right: Bradley, Ramsay, Tedder, Eisenhower, Montgomery, Leigh-Mallory, Bedell-Smith. This team planned and executed the Normandy landings.

(Below) Nimitz briefs Leahy, Roosevelt and MacArthur on the situation in the Pacific. Nimitz and MacArthur commanded the two Pacific thrusts directed on Japan.

(Left) Zhukov, then commanding the Far Eastern army, talking with soldiers after his victory over the Japanese on the Manchurian border in August 1939. For the first part of the war he was Stalin's troubleshooter.

(Left) Isoroku Yamamoto was the ablest of the Japanese commanders. He was opposed to going to war with the USA, but his attack on Pearl Harbor was devastating. He later made the Americans fight hard for Guadalcanal. A Magic intercept enabled US fighters to shoot down his aircraft in April 1943.

JUNGLE FIGHTING

War in the jungle was as much a battle against the jungle itself as against the enemy. To become a successful jungle fighter, a soldier had to overcome the feeling of isolation, especially when enemy infiltration was only too easy, as well as learn practicalities. Jungle navigation was a special art in an environment where smoke, even from cigarettes, could be detected at a distance and jungle noises by night could mask the approach of an enemy. There was also the discomfort of the monsoon and the threat of disease. Casualties from malaria during the early part of the campaigns in Burma and the Far East far exceeded those from battle.

US Marines in the jungle of New Britain in the Bismarck Archipelago, January 1944. This gives a good idea of the problems the jungle undergrowth presented for stealthy movement. On the other hand, it provided the perfect medium for laying ambushes. Often the only way to ensure resupply was by air.

the first years of the war. Much of the Allied failure can be attributed to the low regard in which the Japanese fighting man and his equipment was held. This, however, was to forget that the Japanese army entered the Second World War considerably hardened and combat-experienced from its war against China and brushes with the Red Army on the Russo-Manchurian border. The Japanese army also held a considerable advantage over Western armies in that its soldiers were hardier and used to subsisting on a mere fraction of the logistic support required by their counterparts. The ability to advance unencumbered by an elaborate supply-system played no small part in their speedy overrunning of Malaya, Singapore, Burma and the Philippines. Their military code, which laid down that death for the Emperor in battle was the highest reward and that surrender was dishonourable, also meant that they pursued attacks more relentlessly and defended more bitterly.

Another key to the early Japanese successes on land was their ability quickly to feel their way round the enemy's flanks. This was especially noticeable during the advance down the Malayan peninsula (January 1941–February 1942). The British assumed that the Japanese would keep as much as possible to the roads and laid out their defences accordingly. They also had an aversion for operating in the jungle

being outflanked, always a problem in the desert, made him withdraw back into Tripolitania.

CASUALTIES British – 18,000 men; Axis – 34,000 men.

RESULT The British recaptured Cyrenaica, but were driven back to Gazala (January 1942) and el Alamein (May–June 1942).

FALL OF MALAYA AND SINGAPORE

DATE 8 December 1941–15 February 1942

CAMPAIGN Malaya

OBJECT To overrun Malaya and Singapore.

NUMBERS 50,000 Japanese and 80,000 British and Dominion troops.

DESCRIPTION The Japanese under Yamashita planned to strike across the Thai border, simultaneously landing troops by sea at Kota Bharu on the north-east Malayan coast. The landing here took place just after midnight, but RAF aircraft did cripple three transports and resistance on the beach was stiff. A beachhead was, however, secured. In the meantime British troops had crossed the border into Thailand to forestall the Japanese, but were too late and quickly forced to pull back. On 10 December Japanese aircraft sank the *Prince of Wales* and *Repulse*, pride of the Royal Navy in the Far East, and attacks on RAF airfields brought about the with-themselves. The Japanese coming up against these defences would melt into the jungle and then reappear deep in the rear of the defenders. Consequently, try as they might, the British were unable to anchor their defences and the hasty withdrawals became more frequent and longer. The Japanese could also use the same tactic in defence and demonstrated this during the disastrous British Arakan offensive in Burma at the end of 1942.

The Japanese victories created a belief among the Allied soldiers that the Japanese were superior in the jungle and before they could be overcome on the battlefield this had to be overcome. It was done so through jungle warfare schools, which taught soldiers not only how to fight effectively but also how to confidently live in the jungle. A key to defensive warfare in the jungle was not to withdraw when attacked. The Americans in the Guadalcanal beachhead and the British during the 1943 and early 1944 Japanese offensives in Burma stood and fought, even though surrounded. What, however, proved essential for this was having air superiority so that resupply by air could be undertaken. While many of the battles on the Pacific islands allowed little scope for generalship, being reduced to little more than concentrating all available firepower to blast the Japanese from each strongpoint, the final campaign in Burma in 1945 did incorporate deception and fast-moving advances, in which armour played a not insignificant part in providing intimate support for the infantry.

Most dramatic was the brief Soviet offensive against the Japanese armies in

Continued on page 210

A rare successful brush against the Japanese in Malaya, December 1941. This Australian two-pounder anti-tank gun crew has just destroyed three Japanese light tanks at a makeshift road-block. The Australians will now be outflanked through the jungle and forced to withdraw.

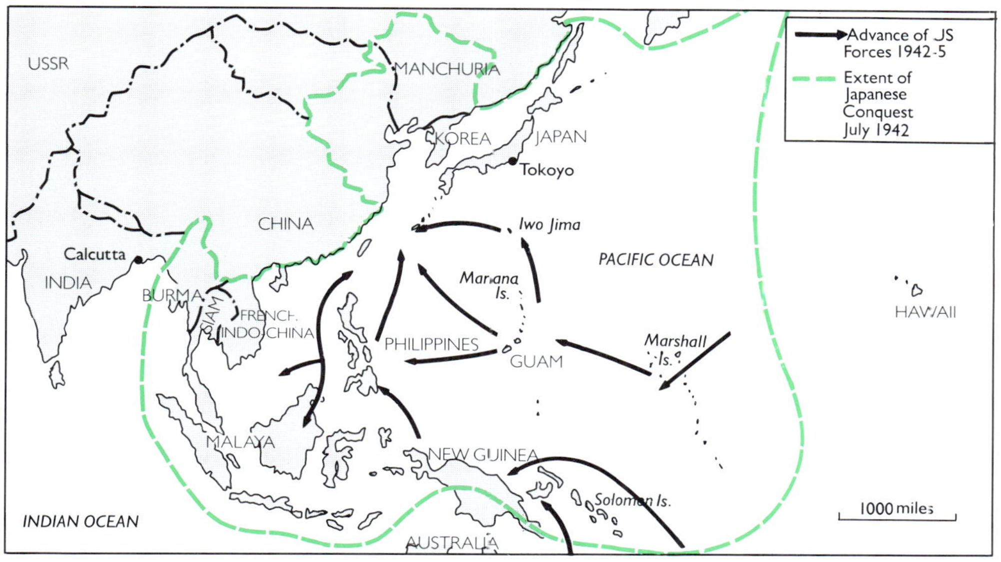

The limits of the Japanese Greater East Asia Co-Prosperity Sphere. This gave Japan the vital raw materials that she needed, but the US naval victories at the Coral Sea and Midway in spring 1942 and the landings on Guadalcanal in August saw the tide begin to turn in favour of the Allies.

1942

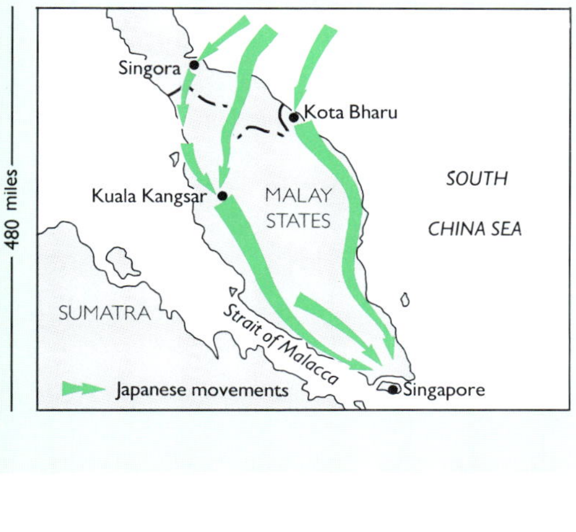

drawal of all aircraft to Singapore. The British forces began to withdraw from northern Malaya and attempted to halt the Japanese on a series of river lines, but Yamashita was too quick for them. Poor communications and inexperience among the defenders did not help and frequently led to unauthorized withdrawals triggered by no more than rumours. These were aggravated by the Japanese use of the jungle to outflank defensive positions. They also carried out a further series of amphibious landings on the west coast which helped to precipitate the British withdrawal. On 11 January the Japanese entered Kuala Lumpur, which had been the main British supply base, and a week later the British began to withdraw across the Causeway to Singapore Island, now under increasing air attack. By 31 January the evacuation of Malaya was complete and Churchill was exhorting the defenders of Singapore to hold on. On 8 February the Japanese landed on Singapore and a week ▸

SPECIAL FORCES

ONE OF THE SIGNIFICANT features of the Second World War was the use of special forces for intelligence gathering and offensive operations.

The Germans led the way with their Construction Battalion 800. This was raised by the Abwehr just before the outbreak of war and consisted of plain clothes men whose role was to seize or demolish key points. As such they were used in Poland and Scandinavia and were later known as the *Brandenburgers*. The Germans, too, carried out the first airborne operations of the war when paratroops dropped into Holland and glider-borne engineers knocked out the Belgian fortress or Eben Emael on 10 May 1940. It was Winston Churchill who, immediately after Dunkirk, instigated the creation of British special forces in the form of the Commandos and airborne forces.

The Commandos were initially created as a means of striking back at the Germans in occupied Europe, but later, together with their US counterparts the Rangers, came to be used as an amphibious spearhead for the major Allied landing operations. This also spawned a number of other special units ranging from beach reconnaissance to the US Navy Construction battalions, the Seabees, whose task was to clear obstacles from beaches, harbours and airfields. The Middle East was perhaps the most fertile theatre for special forces. Indeed, a wide range of "private armies" was raised, each with a different specialist role, including the Special Air Service (SAS), whose original role in the Second World War was the destruction of enemy aircraft on airfields.

The Special Operations Executive (SOE) and US Office of Strategic Services (OSS) represented another form of special forces. Their role was to support the resistance movements created in every country in occupied Europe. The Resistance itself provided valuable intelligence, as well as carrying out sabotage and other offensive missions in support of conventional Allied operations. In eastern Europe bands of partisans operating from the hinterland fulfilled a similar function.

(Above) British Commandos training with fighting knives, which became their symbol.

(Below) British Commandos in the highly successful amphibious raid on Vaagso in Norway, December 1941.

(Left) Somewhere in occupied Europe German troops round up partisans. Many Frenchmen fled to the Maquis region of south-west France to avoid deportation to Germany for forced labour. They proved a serious thorn in the side of the Germans.

(Right) The end for a resistance fighter.

OTTO SKORZENY

The German, Otto Skorzeny was a colourful special forces leader although he did not become involved in the field until 1943.

In April 1943 he was given charge of a special commando, and gained fame for the spectacular glider operation mounted to rescue Mussolini from captivity in the Abruzzi Mountains in September 1943. In truth, Skorzeny took part in the operation, but did not command it.

In October 1944, in another spectacular coup, he kidnapped the Hungarian Regent, Admiral Horthy, who was about to negotiate an armistice with the Russians. During the Ardennes counter-offensive of December 1944 Skorzeny commanded 150 Panzer Brigade. His task was to infiltrate men in Allied uniforms through the lines in order to cause chaos. They succeeded in making Eisenhower a virtual prisoner in his own headquarters for a few days, but most were quickly rounded up.

On release from post-war captivity Skorzeny settled in Spain and helped ex-SS men to escape from Germany.

(Left) Members of Skorzeny's commando before the Gran Sasso operation to rescue Mussolini.

(Below) Some of those who took part in Mussolini's rescue wave farewell as he takes off for Vienna. Following this operation, Skorzeny was promoted to major general.

(Right) Hitler with some who took part in the Eben Emael attack, 10 May 1940.

(Below) German paratroops in action. The capture of Crete in May 1941 was their largest operation, but heavy aircraft losses precluded any further major airborne attacks.

An Atlantic convoy. There were two types of convoy: slow (7.5-9 knots) and fast (9-15 knots). Ships steaming at 15 knots or above relied on their speed to outwit the U-boats. The convoy itself was commanded by a commodore, usually a retired senior naval officer, who sailed in one of the merchant vessels. The escort commander was, however, responsible for the safety of the convoyed ships and overrode the commodore in this respect. Too few escorts during the first part of the war were a major reason for the U-boat successes.

Manchuria in August 1945. This reflected the synthesis of the Red Army's four years' fighting on the Eastern Front and was marked by a high degree of deception (*maskirovka*) and surprise, two factors which the Russians now regarded as inseparable from one another, and impressive penetrations by mobile groups, as well as vast numerical superiority.

In sum, the main lessons to come out of the war on land during 1939–45 were not so much new as confirmation of the old. The degree of success of operations was dependent on the ability of the logistic system to sustain them, no one arm was paramount and victory went to the commander who best conducted the all-arms orchestra. Petrol-driven warfare and radio placed even more emphasis on the need to act quicker than one's opponent, and what had been realized by the end of 1918, that air superiority over the battlefield could be decisive, became of prime importance.

THE WAR AT SEA

The navies of the Second World War pursued traditional objectives, of which the two foremost were maritime supremacy and destruction of trade. In both cases what

1942

later General Percival surrendered, mindful that to resist further would aggravate the sufferings of the one million civilians on the island.

CASUALTIES Japanese – 9,000 men lost; British and Dominion – 140,000 (including 130,000 made prisoner).

RESULT The British had long been led to believe that Singapore, with its massive coastal guns, was impregnable. The Japanese, unfortunately, chose to attack from the other direction and Britain's jewels in the Far East were lost. The enormity of the defeat lowered British standing in the eyes of the indigenous population, with long-term consequences at the end of the war. In the meantime, those taken prisoner paid the penalty for pre-war neglect and underestimation of the enemy.

MIDWAY

DATE 3–6 June 1942

OBJECT Japan wished to capture the Midway Islands.

NUMBERS 4 Japanese and 3 US carriers.

DESCRIPTION Midway was perhaps the most significant turning point in the war in the Pacific, as well as being a prime example of carrier warfare. The Japanese target was the US base on Midway in the central Pacific Ocean, which they described as

differed from previous wars was the role played by naval air power, although by 1918 its potential had been recognized. This was reflected in the building of aircraft carriers, of which the first were in service before the end of the First World War. The size of the navies themselves generally reflected the proportions agreed by the 1922 Washington Treaties: the US and Royal Navies were the largest, followed by those of France and Italy and Japan. The Japanese Navy was supposed to be equal to the two last-named but, resentful of being not allowed parity with the US navy, it had embarked on an ambitious ship-building programme in the 1920s and by 1939 was the third largest in the world. The German navy was much smaller, but modern. In 1937 Hitler had laid down Plan Z, which was drawn up on the assumption that war with Britain was inevitable. This, however, would not come to fruition until 1943–8, and hence the outbreak of war came long before the navy was ready for it.

MARITIME SUPREMACY

Given the small size of her navy, there was no question in September 1939 of Germany risking, as she had during 1914–16, a major confrontation with the British fleet. Instead, her major surface vessels would concentrate on attacking British trade. Indeed, the only significant surface actions were during the opening days of the Norwegian campaign, and these largely involved destroyers.

Once Italy entered the war in June 1940 the situation changed. Mussolini termed the Mediterranean *Mare Nostrum* (Our Sea), but the British had traditionally regarded themselves as the dominant naval power here, maintained through the powerful Mediterranean Fleet and the naval bases at Gibraltar and Malta. However, the British had enough respect for the Italian navy and for the fact that Italian air coverage from the mainland, Sicily and islands in the eastern Mediterranean extended over much of the sea. Accordingly, all but the most urgent convoys to the Middle East were rerouted around South Africa, the Cape route, and the main fleet anchorage at Malta was moved to Alexandria, Egypt. Malta, however, was to remain crucial to the British strategy, for if the Axis powers could seize it Alexandria would be isolated from Gibraltar and the Axis supply routes to North Africa would be impossible to interdict. Thus, much effort was made to keep the island resupplied in the face of Axis air attacks, which were unceasing until autumn 1942. During 1940–1 there were several brushes between the two fleets, of which the largest was that off Cape Matapan in March 1941 (see page 198). More significant though was the strike made by carrier-based aircraft on the port of Taranto on the night of 11–12 November 1940, which severely damaged three of Italy's six battleships. Yet, while the British had the best of these engagements they did not have things all their own way, especially once German air units had been sent to Sicily in early 1941. During this year they lost one

1942

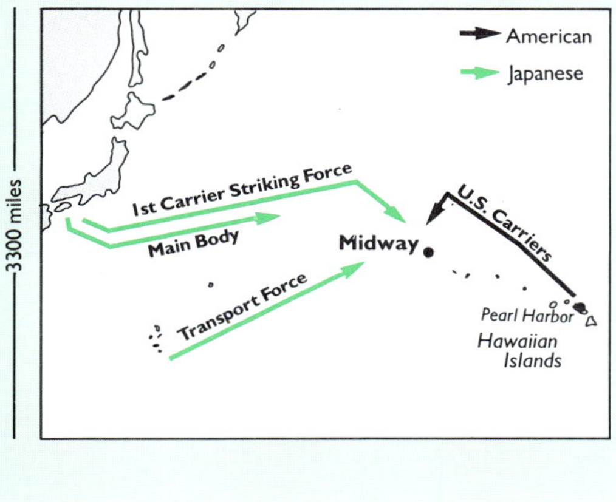

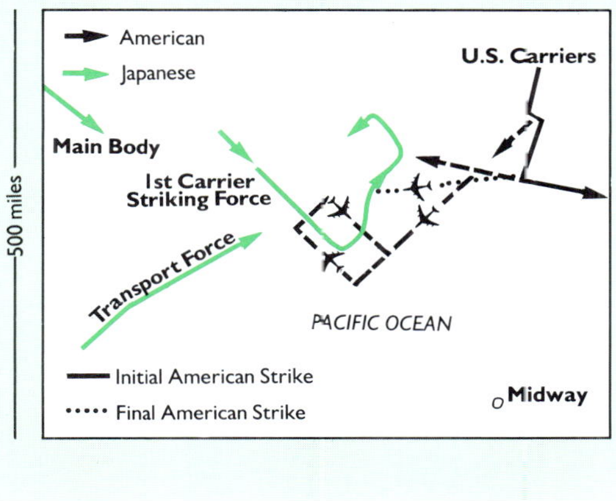

"Pearl Harbor's sentry". To deceive the Americans they also intended simultaneously to capture the Aleutians in the northern Pacific. US codebreakers (MAGIC – see p218) got wind of the plan and the US Pacific Fleet, still lacking battleships after the 7 December 1941 strike, sent two task forces, built around its three aircraft carriers, to Midway. The Japanese strike forces set sail on 27 May, and on 3 June the two US task forces met near Midway. Next day Japanese carrier aircraft ▸

Midway, 4 June 1942. Douglas Devastator torpedo-bombers being prepared for action on board USS Enterprise. *Their first attack on the Japanese carrier strike force would bring no success and only four of the Devastators would survive. A second attack launched later in the morning crippled three out of the four Japanese carriers.*

aircraft carrier to a U-boat and another was badly damaged by Sicily-based aircraft. Heavy losses were also suffered during the German airborne invasion of Crete in May (see page 200) and in December Italian frogmen crippled two battleships in Alexandria harbour. Yet, while the British carriers played a part, especially in reinforcing Malta with aircraft, given that the Mediterranean is virtually an enclosed sea it was land-based aircraft which were dominant. Until the Axis forces had been driven out of Libya at the beginning of 1943, they enjoyed the advantage in their ability to operate almost at will over the Mediterranean.

In the Pacific, where land bases were few and far between, the situation was different, although again air power quickly proved to be the dominant factor. The rationale behind the Japanese attack on the US Pacific Fleet base at Pearl Harbor on 7 December 1941 was the need to at least neutralize US maritime power in the Pacific while they secured their Pacific and south-east Asian empire which would give them the oil and other vital natural resources which they lacked at home. The inspiration behind the plan was the British success against the Italian fleet at Taranto. On the surface the attack was brilliantly successful. No less than six battleships were destroyed as well as most of the aircraft based in Hawaii. Yet, two vital targets had been missed, the oil storage tanks and the Pacific Fleet's two aircraft carriers, which were both at sea at the time. These, especially the latter, were to prove fatal.

During the next few months the Japanese overran almost all their objectives and among their successes was the sinking of the British ships *Prince of Wales* and *Repulse* off the Malayan coast, another demonstration of the vulnerability of capital ships to aircraft. Their Pacific onrush was finally halted by two naval actions, which marked the first carrier versus carrier battles. At the Coral Sea (7–8 May) a US task force, which included two carriers, engaged a similar Japanese force. One US carrier was sunk, as was one Japanese, and the other Japanese carrier disabled. Although it was the US task force which withdrew, it had frustrated a Japanese landing attempt at Port Moresby, Papua New Guinea. The following month came the more decisive Battle of Midway (see page 210), which forced the Japanese fleet on to the defensive.

There now began the long haul to recapture the territories seized by the Japanese and eventually to invade the Japanese mainland itself. This took the form of a series of amphibious landings, beginning with that on Guadalcanal in the Solomons in August 1942. For these to be successful it was essential that the landing forces had sufficient air and naval support, especially since the Japanese fiercely resisted every new thrust not just on land, but also in the sea and air. This inevitably meant further major naval actions, again dominated by carriers, and beginning with the Battle of the Eastern Solomons just after the Guadalcanal landings. This forced the Japanese to continue to reinforce Guadalcanal by night only, in what became known as the

1942

attacked Midway, but failed to neutralize the US land-based aircraft. Their aircraft immediately rearmed with torpedoes to attack the US task forces. They were then ordered to rearm with bombs in order to attack Midway again. But, after one abortive attempt, US carrier aircraft found the Midway strike force and damaged three of the four carriers in it while their aircraft were still being rearmed. The three sank during 5 June. On that afternoon, after air reconnaissance had spotted the Japanese force once more, a further US aircraft strike sank the remaining carrier, forcing a Japanese withdrawal. Their only successes came on 7 June when forces landed in the Aleutians and a submarine sank the US carrier *Yorktown*.

CASUALTIES Japanese – four carriers, one heavy cruiser, 322 aircraft; US – one carrier, one destroyer, 150 aircraft.

RESULT Midway forced the Japanese onto the defensive. Never again could they risk a major fleet-versus-fleet action.

DESTRUCTION OF CONVOY PQ 17

DATE 27 June–5 July 1942

CAMPAIGN Russian convoys

OBJECT To deliver war materials to Russia

NUMBERS 33 British merchant vessels and one tanker escorted by six destroyers, two anti-aircraft ships, four corvettes, three minesweepers, four trawlers, two submarines and supported by two battleships, one carrier, six cruisers, 17 destroyers.

Midway, 5 June 1942. US sailors struggle to limit the damage caused to USS Yorktown *by a Japanese air strike from the carrier* Hiryu *the previous day. Later she would be torpedoed by a Japanese submarine and her crew forced to abandon ship. The* Hiryu *herself, the last surviving Japanese carrier, was sunk on the same day.*

1942

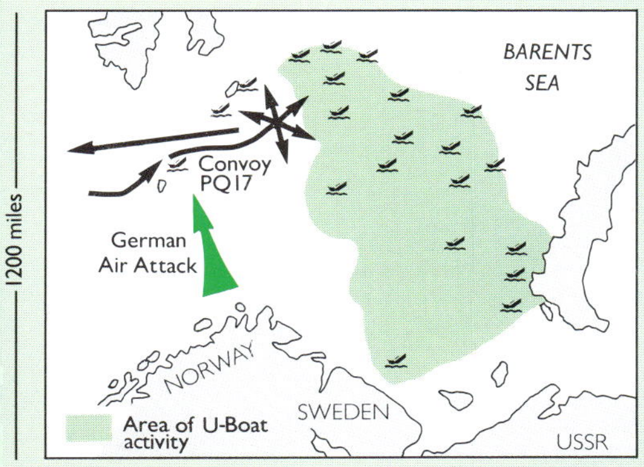

Germans had 202 aircraft and a naval squadron built around a pocket battleship, *Tirpitz*, and two heavy cruisers.

DESCRIPTION The British had been sending war supplies to the Russian ports of Murmansk and Archangel since September 1941. At the beginning of 1942 the Germans deployed *Tirpitz* and other naval units to northern Norway and also began to attack the convoys with U-boats and Norwegian-based aircraft. With the coming of the Arctic summer with its perpetual daylight, shipping losses increased. PQ 17 left Iceland on 27 June and was located by U-boats four days later. On 4 July it came within aircraft range and lost two vessels. At the same time it was learnt that *Tirpitz*, *Sheer* and *Hipper* intended to intercept the convoy. Because the supporting ships would not reach PQ 17 in time to prevent this, the convoy was ordered to scatter. During the next three days the Luftwaffe attacked the scattered ships and only ten merchant vessels eventually ▶

(Right) US naval task force under Japanese air attack during the Battle of Santa Cruz, 24–26 October 1942. This was one of the many naval actions surrounding the battle for Guadalcanal. Two Japanese carriers were damaged and the US carrier Hornet *was sunk.*

(Far right) US troops landing on Leyte in the Philippines, October 1944. The leading waves were now well inland, but it would take two months of hard fighting to clear the island of Japanese.

Tokyo Express. There were numerous clashes in The Slot, between Guadalcanal and Florida Island to its north, and often the Japanese performed better because of superior night-fighting techniques.

The last major fleet action in the Pacific was Leyte Gulf (October 1944), when the Japanese tried to destroy the US naval forces supporting the landings in the Philippines. The result was the loss of their remaining carriers and the death knell of the Japanese Navy. The battle also marked the debut of the *kamikaze* suicide aircraft, just about the last weapon left in the Japanese naval armoury and one which would cause the Allied fleets some discomfort, but no more.

What the Pacific demonstrated, more so than any other naval campaign, was that the carrier, with a strike range limited only by that of its aircraft, had now taken over from the battleship as the main surface unit. Furthermore, a prerequisite to achieving maritime supremacy was gaining maritime air superiority.

THE WAR AGAINST TRADE

Apart from the Allies' battle to throttle the Axis maritime communications across the Mediterranean to North Africa, there were two campaigns fought against sea

1942

reached port. *Tirpitz* and her consorts did sally out but returned to port after a Russian submarine nearly torpedoed the battleship.

CASUALTIES 23 merchant vessels lost.

RESULT The heavy losses caused a halt to Russian convoys until September. PQ 18 got through with a much strengthened escort, but for the loss of one destroyer and 13 merchantmen. There was then a further lull, before a proper resumption was made in December.

GUADALCANAL

DATE 7 August 1942–9 February 1943

CAMPAIGN South-West Pacific

OBJECT To secure Guadalcanal as a stepping stone for reducing the main Japanese south-west Pacific base at Rabaul.

NUMBERS 16,000 US Marines, supported by Admiral Frank J. Fletcher's three-carrier task force; 20,000 Japanese troops.

DESCRIPTION US forces landed on the island's north coast, close to an airstrip

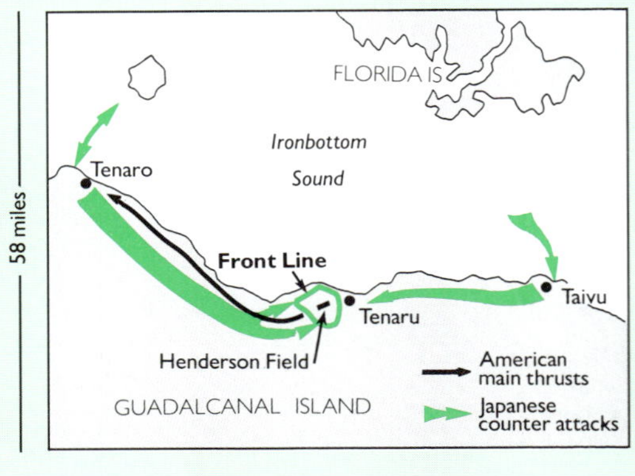

communications. The first was the German effort to sever Britain's maritime lifelines, described as the battle of the Atlantic, the longest campaign of the whole war. There was also the primarily US campaign to suffocate Japan by preventing her from importing the necessary raw materials needed to sustain her war effort. Both illustrate the dependence of island nations on the sea for survival, something which has not changed over the ages.

At the outbreak of war Germany possessed 57 U-boats, of which 17 were at sea, and the first shot of the Battle of the Atlantic was fired on 3 September, the day Britain declared war, when the liner SS *Athenia* was torpedoed and sunk. Britain immediately instituted convoying and declared a naval blockade of Germany. For the first nine months of the war, however, the U-boat would not be the main threat. Apart from the small number operational, convoying kept them at bay and their torpedoes proved unreliable. Even so, the British were conscious of their lack of suitable means to combat them and regretted their pre-war complacency, especially after U-47 penetrated the Home Fleet's anchorage at Scapa Flow in the Orkneys in October 1939, sinking the elderly battleship *Royal Oak*. The lack of suitable escorts, aggravated by the need to secure the cross-Channel supply lines needed to support

Continued on page 218

THE ATLANTIC BLACK GAP

It became apparent during the Battle of the Atlantic that the aircraft was the one means through which a truly aggressive defence against the U-boat could be conducted. To give total air coverage across the North Atlantic meant having sufficient very long range (VLR) aircraft. Until 1943 the Allied maritime air forces had to compete with the strategic bombing forces, who argued that they were taking direct offensive action against Germany while the Battle of the Atlantic was merely defensive. The bombing forces enjoyed priority in four-engined aircraft and airborne radar. Hence, as shown on the map, the Black Gap, that area which could not be covered by aircraft, was only closed by degrees. It was only after the need to win the Battle of the Atlantic was affirmed at the January 1943 Casablanca Conference that the situation changed.

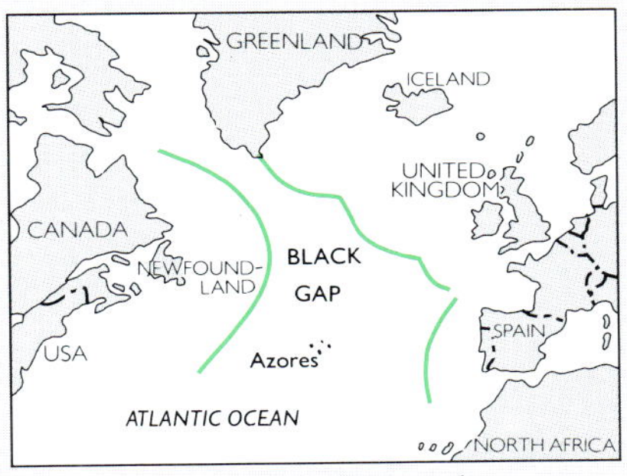

1942

which became known as Henderson Field. Simultaneous landings were made on islets off the south coast of Florida Island to the north. The airstrip was quickly secured and on 20 August US aircraft began operating from it. In the meantime the Japanese mounted numerous counter-attacks, reinforcing their garrison by sea through the Slot which ran between Guadalcanal and Florida Island. By 12 September, they were strong enough to launch an attack in divisional strength. The resulting battle of Bloody Ridge lasted for two days, the Japanese eventually withdrawing with heavy losses. Fighting continued over the ensuing months. The US Marines lacked the strength to move out of their perimeter around Henderson Field, but a number of naval actions were fought in the Slot, usually by night. In December the Marines were relieved by a force of three divisions which began to advance west through the jungle. The Japanese then began to withdraw and eventually, at the beginning of February, the Tokyo Express, their naval supply line, began to evacuate what remained of the garrison.

CASUALTIES US 6,000 men plus a further 12,000 disabled by disease. Japanese 24,000. Each side also lost numerous ships.

RESULT Guadalcanal marked the beginning of the long "island hopping" campaign which was eventually to bring the Allied forces to the threshold of Japan itself.

THE U-BOAT

THROUGHOUT THE WAR there were two basic types of U-boat: coastal (mainly Type VIIs) and ocean-going (Type IX). Both were primarily powered by diesel engines. The former had a surface range of some 5,000 nautical miles and the latter 11,000 miles.

Underwater propulsion was achieved through auxiliary electric engines, but speeds were no more than 4 knots, slower than any merchant vessel, and underwater range was limited to 80 nautical miles, because of the need to surface in order to recharge the batteries. This meant that the U-boat in the Atlantic had to spend most of its time on the surface and, as Allied detection methods and anti-submarine weapons improved, it became more vulnerable. This was especially so with regard to the threat from the air (aircraft accounted for half the U-boat losses during the war). The Germans therefore worked hard to improve underwater endurance and speed. The first solution was the *Schnorkel* tube, an idea which the Dutch navy had examined prior to the war, which enabled the main diesel engine to be operated under water. When on the surface it was clipped to the deck and then raised and attached to the conning tower before the U-boat dived. It was not wholly satisfactory. Underwater speeds of no more than 8 knots were achieved, navigation was very difficult, and in heavy seas water would slop down into the control room. Nevertheless, from 1943 onwards, a number of existing U-boats were converted. Two other solutions were, however, evolved during the latter half of the war. The first was the electro-boat. This, in the form of the Type XXI (ocean-going) and Type XXIII (coastal), used very powerful batteries and had a streamlined hull. The combination increased the submerged speed to 17 knots and submerged ranges to 200-300 nautical miles. The other concept was the Walter Boat. This used a revolutionary new turbine engine driven by steam and carbon dioxide, both created by breaking down sea water. The Walter boats could steam at 20 knots underwater for short periods, but their submerged range was somewhat less than the electro-boats'. Luckily for the Allies, these new types, like the V-weapons and jet aircraft, appeared too late to affect the course of the war significantly.

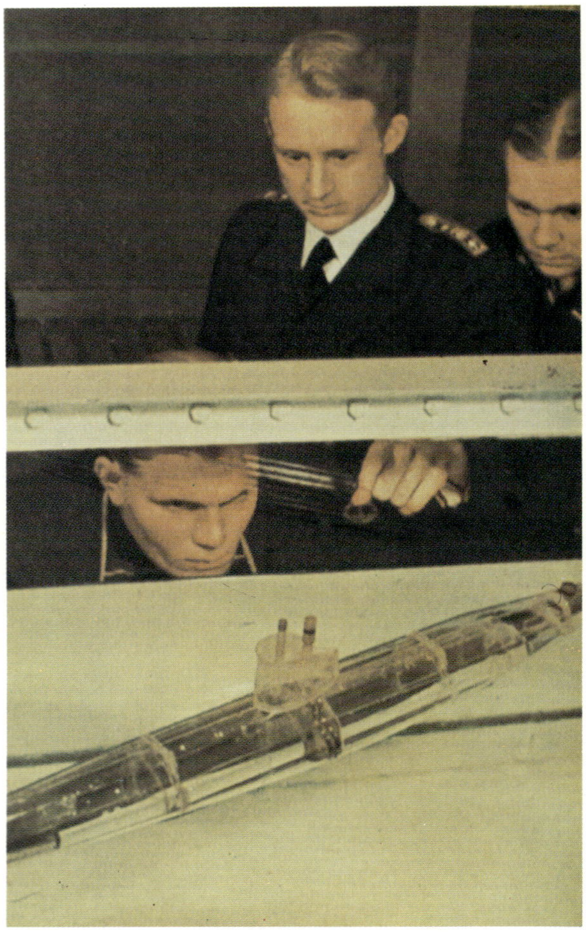

(Above) U-boat crews using a miniature U-boat in a transparent water tank to learn how to operate the boat under water. The quality of the crews declined as the war progressed.

(Below) A Type VIIC/42. She had a crew of 45 and had four bow and one stern torpedo tubes, with capacity for 16 torpedoes. The top surface speed was 18 knots and she had a surface range of 10,000 miles at 12 knots.

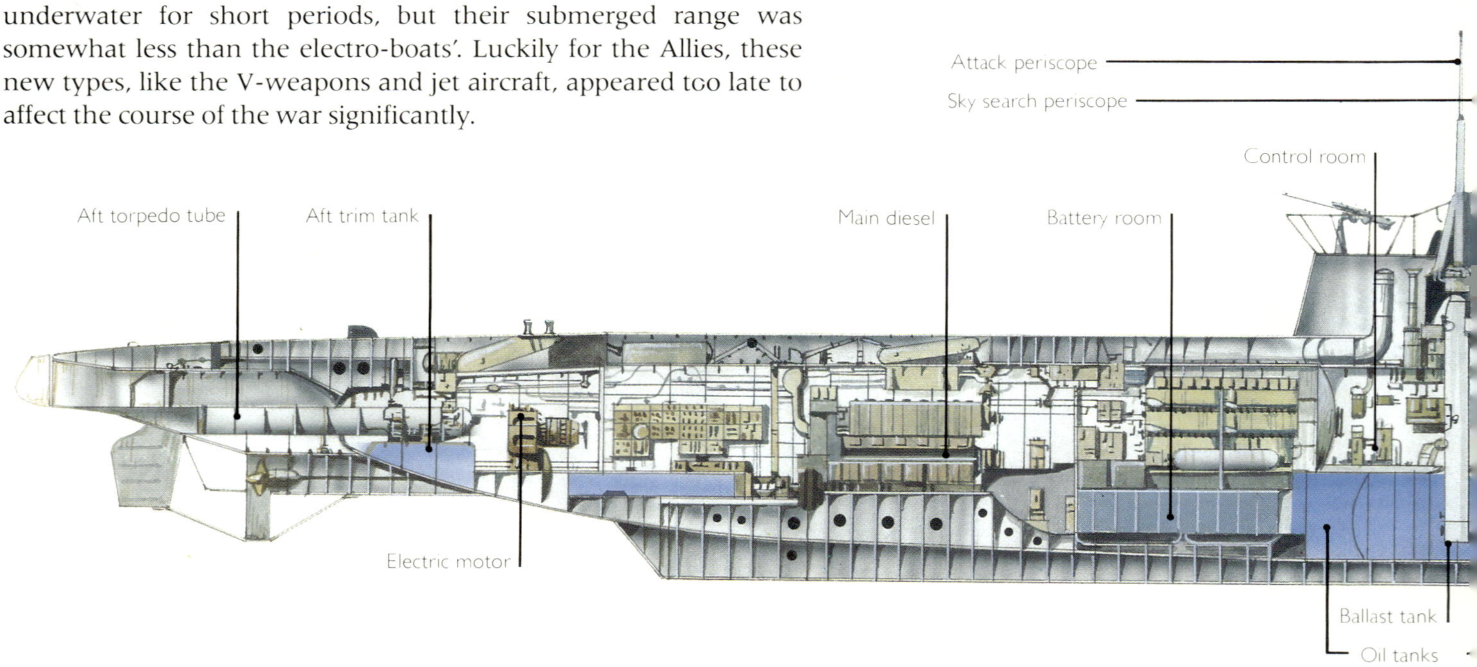

(Right) Admiral Karl Doenitz, centre, led the U-boat arm until early 1943, when he became Commander-in-Chief of the German navy.

(Far right) A blazing tanker off US eastern seaboard, spring 1942. It was at this time the Nazi submarine fleet first came close to severing the vital trans-Atlantic supply line.

(Above) Another U-boat victim. The confined on-board space meant that U-boats could not rescue the crews of sunk ships. They could only tell them where the nearest land was and perhaps supplement their food and water stocks.

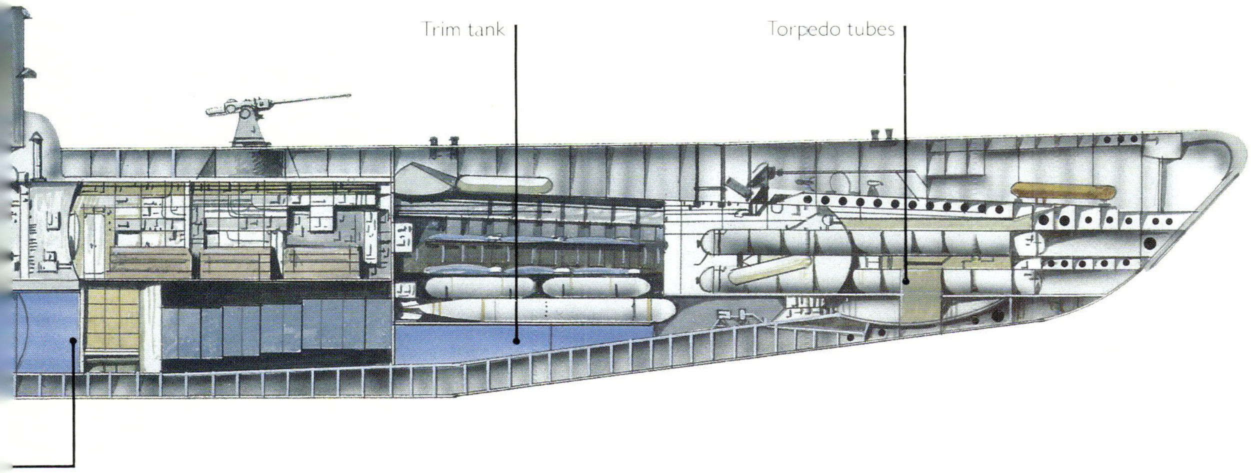

(Above) Type IX U-boat under air attack. Allied aircraft normally used depth charges, bombs and machine guns. Later in the war a very effective aerial homing torpedo, Fido, was introduced. Airborne radar also proved useful.

ULTRA/MAGIC

ULTRA and MAGIC were blanket codewords for the Allies' ability to decipher respectively the top-secret German and Japanese ciphers. In the case of ULTRA, it was the Poles, who had acquired Enigma cipher machines, available commercially before the war, who did the groundwork, which they brought west with them after the defeat of Poland. Teleprinter signals were picked up by radio eavesdroppers and then passed to the British decrypting centre at Bletchley Park. Modifications to the Enigma machine and the fact that the teleprinter was not the only means of communication meant that a complete picture of German plans and intentions could not usually be obtained. Often, too, the ideal counter might alert the Germans or was not possible to execute in time. Nevertheless, vital intelligence was obtained from this source. The same applied to MAGIC, an operation based in Washington DC, which was obtaining important intelligence even before Pearl Harbor. Neither the Germans nor the Japanese ever realized that their codes had been broken, a tribute to the tight security that surrounded both operations, and they made significant contributions to Allied victory.

the army in France, meant that convoys were protected for most of the trans-Atlantic passage by little more than a single armed merchant cruiser. Little thought had been given to hunting down U-boats. Indeed, during the first weeks task forces built round a carrier were used, but these were quickly abandoned after one carrier had suffered a near miss from a torpedo and another was sunk.

It was the surface threat which made the deepest impression on the British during the Phoney War. Two pocket battleships, *Deutschland* and *Graf Spee*, had set sail for the Atlantic in August 1939, but it was not until the end of September that they were let loose on the sea-lanes. While the *Deutschland* was forced to return to port early because of mechanical problems, *Graf Spee* soon began to leave a trail of havoc in the South Atlantic and Indian Ocean. No less than seven naval task forces were organized to hunt her down and it was eventually the southernmost, based on the Falkland Islands, which cornered her off the River Plate in December. In the meantime, two more capital ships had made brief forays into the Atlantic, triggering a sally by the Home Fleet, which failed to intercept them. Another early threat was the magnetic mine, laid by aircraft and submarine off British estuaries and ports. These caused a number of sinkings before the technical antidote, degaussing, was found.

The fall of France dramatically altered the situation. By now the Germans had overcome their torpedo difficulties and they were more reliable. More important was that they could now make use of the French Atlantic ports. This radically cut down the sailing time to the Atlantic and meant that more U-boats could now be on patrol. The result was the First Happy Time. From July 1940 shipping losses rose steeply, with the U-boat claiming the lion's share. The Luftwaffe, too, now joined in, with long-range Fockewulf Condors locating convoys and guiding the U-boats on to them, as well as sinking ships themselves. While the winter gales reduced U-boat activities, there was a resurgence of the surface threat. This culminated in May 1941 when the *Bismarck* sank the pride of the Royal Navy, the *Hood*, only to be slowed herself by carrier-based air attack and then sunk by the Home Fleet. This effectively marked the end of the surface raider in the Atlantic, although the threat remained.

In the meantime, the British managed to increase the number of escorts, initially thanks to 50 elderly US destroyers exchanged for Caribbean bases, and at the end of May the first trans-Atlantic convoy sailed with continuous escort, ending the First Happy Time. The basing of aircraft on Iceland increased air coverage and decryption of the U-boat Enigma cipher meant that convoys could sometimes be steered around U-boat concentrations. Increasing US involvement also helped, but once the USA entered the war there was a Second Happy Time for the U-boats, who concentrated during the first half of 1942 on the vulnerable eastern seaboard, which lacked the necessary anti-submarine defences until the late summer.

1942

SECOND EL ALAMEIN

DATE 23 October–4 November 1942
CAMPAIGN North Africa
OBJECT To destroy the Axis forces in Egypt.
NUMBERS British – 195,000 men, 1,100 tanks, 900 guns. Axis – 100,000 men, 500 tanks, 500 guns.
DESCRIPTION Rommel had been occupying his defensive positions since the beginning of July and they were strong, with numerous minefields. Montgomery's plan was to punch through the defences and then pass his armour through to trap the Axis forces. After a short but massive bombardment the British attacked in two places, clearing lanes through the minefields as they went. The fighting was bitter and after five days the British had still not broken through. Montgomery therefore changed his plan, aiming to tie down the bulk of the Axis forces in the coastal sector while he punched through to the south. This was put into effect on 2 November.

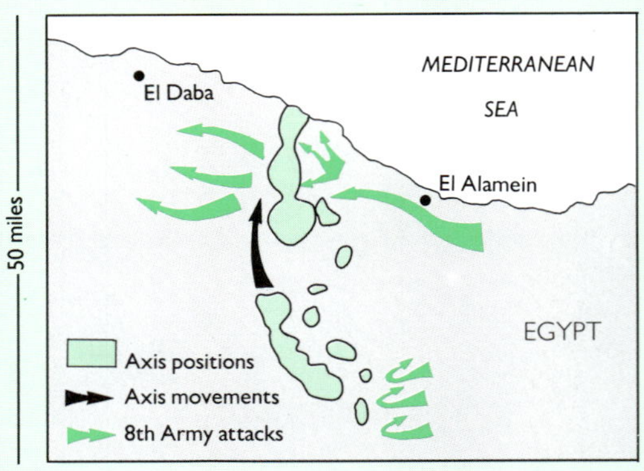

By now the battle of the Atlantic was becoming increasingly vital for the Allies to win in the context of re-entering the continent of Europe in order to defeat Germany, an agreed priority over Japan. Better escort drills, more escorts, including carriers, and improved technical aids for detecting and destroying U-boats helped, but the other side of the coin was that, in spite of efforts to slow it by bombing the U-boat industry, U-boat production was on the increase. New tactics, employing "wolf packs" which swept convoy routes line abreast and then concentrated to attack convoys, were also proving effective. The aircraft was playing an increasingly vital role, but the Battle could not be won until the Black Gap in the mid-Atlantic had been closed (see page 215). On the other side of the coin, German Norway-based aircraft and ships, including the *Tirpitz*, were creating grave problems for the Arctic convoys supplying Russia through her northern ports.

The climax came in spring 1943. After the "wolf packs" had worsted two convoys the pendulum suddenly swung the other way. In May 41 U-boats were sunk, forcing the Germans to temporarily withdraw them from the Atlantic and the merchant ship-building rate began to overtake that of losses. The U-boats soon returned to the Atlantic, but were not the force that they had been, in spite of improved torpedoes and the snorkel, which enabled the U-boat to spend a longer time submerged and hence reduce the air threat. Not until 1945 did the submerged long-range high-speed boats come into service, and then only a handful. Introduced earlier they might had had an effect, but by then it was too late. The Allies had won the technological and operational battle.

In contrast, the campaign against Japanese maritime trade had the opposite result. While the Japanese submarine fleet concentrated almost entirely on US warships, but with no great success, sinking only 149 ships of all types, the US submarines placed priority on merchant shipping, knowing that without it Japan would be starved of vital war supporting raw materials. By 1944 they were sinking 50 merchantmen a month, but then the success rate fell away simply because of the lack of targets. Failure to implement a proper convoy system and to develop effective anti-submarine weapons and detection aids were the reasons. By spring 1945 Japan's maritime communications had been virtually throttled, with over 1,000 ships sunk, and war production declined rapidly. The fatal flaw in the Japanese strategy had been to concentrate too much on destroying enemy surface sea power at the expense of protecting her ultimate lifeline.

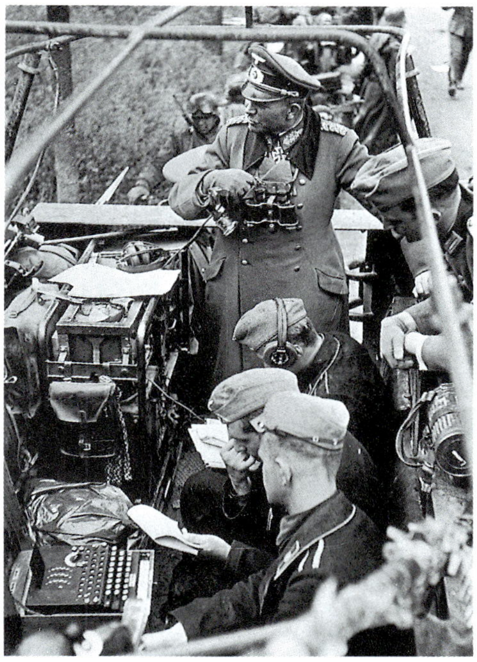

General Heinz Guderian, the armoured warfare expert, in his command vehicle. Note the Enigma cipher machine in the foreground. The operator keyed in the message, which was then automatically encoded by the machine through pre-set rotors. Much Allied mathematical and technical ingenuity enabled the codes to be broken.

THE WAR IN THE AIR

The previous two sections of this chapter have shown the important role that air power played in supporting the other two major dimensions of war. Indeed, one of its

1943

Rommel, now short of fuel and ammunition, began to withdraw, in spite of orders from Hitler to continue to stand and fight. On the 4th the British armour passed through, but failed to cut Rommel off and was then further delayed by rain. Rommel continued to withdraw through Libya, fighting skilful rearguard actions until crossing the border into Tunisia on 23 January.

CASUALTIES British – 13,500 men and 500 tanks. Axis – 22,000 men and 400 tanks.

RESULT This marked the beginning of the end of the campaign in North Africa, accelerated by the Allied landings in French North Africa on 8 November. El Alamein was also the last victory gained by British and Dominion forces alone.

THE DAMS RAID

DATE 16–17 May 1943

OBJECT To disrupt German war production.

NUMBERS 19 Lancaster bombers.

DESCRIPTION The idea of destroying the Ruhr dams in order to seriously affect German war production in the region had been postulated before the outbreak of war. It was not, however, until the designer Dr Barnes Wallis had developed a ►

AVRO LANCASTER

The Avro Lancaster was the outstanding heavy bomber of the war and became the backbone of the RAF strategic bombing offensive against Germany. It was derived from the Avro Manchester, which made its operational debut in February 1941, but soon proved unpopular because of the unreliability of its two engines. The four-engined Lancaster entered service at the beginning of 1942, its first operation being dropping mines off Brest on the night of 3–4 March 1942. By the end of the war no fewer than 7,377 had been built. Highly manoeuvrable and capable of withstanding heavy punishment, the Lancaster could carry 14,000 lb of bombs 1,660 miles, a performance only exceeded by the US B-29. Suitably modified, it also carried the heaviest bomb of the war, the 22,000 lb Grand Slam, which destroyed the Bielefeld viaduct in Germany in March 1945.

US B-17 Flying Fortresses, with the contrails of their escort fighters above them, en route for a target in Germany. Heavily armed, but carrying only half the bombload of the RAF Lancaster, they flew in a box-like formation. This was not sufficient to keep the Luftwaffe at bay without fighters escorting them all the way to the target.

1943

revolutionary bomb which, by skipping across the water, could attack the dams horizontally that it became more than an idea. To induce the bomb to skip meant flying at a very precise and very low height and a special RAF squadron (617), using modified Lancaster bombers, was formed in March 1943. The operation was mounted on the night of 16–17 May. The primary targets were the Möhne, Sorpe and Eder dams, with three others, the Ennepe, Lister and Diemel, as secondary

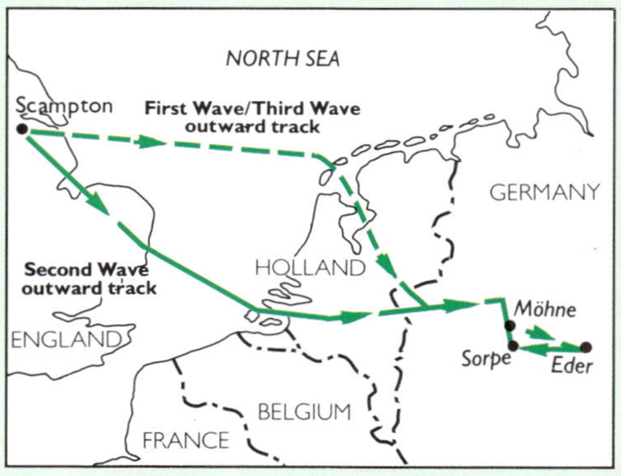

targets. The Möhne and Eder dams were successfully breached, causing widespread flooding and disruption of communications; the Sorpe was slightly damaged.
CASUALTIES 8 aircraft failed to return.
RESULT The effect on the Ruhr industries was not serious. Even so, the technical ingenuity involved and the cold-blooded courage of the crews provided a very welcome fillip to morale, not just for RAF Bomber Command, but also for the Western Allies as a whole.

(Left) The RAF purchased some B-17s, but found them unsatisfactory for night bombing. They were handed over to RAF Coastal Command, where they were useful as maritime patrol aircraft. Here an RAF crew has its final briefing before taking off for patrol over the Atlantic. The B-17 had a range of well over 3,000 miles.

(Above) Bombing up a Heinkel He-111 on the Eastern Front, June 1941. The Luftwaffe was a very effective tactical air force, but its lack of long-range strategic bombers proved fatal in Russia. Its aircraft had insufficient range to reach the Russian war industry east of the Ural Mountains and were unable to mount a sustained attack on Moscow.

two major roles was achieving either total (supremacy) or partial (superiority) command of the air space over land and maritime combat zones. Having achieved this it was possible for air forces to both give land and naval forces intimate or close air support within the battle area itself and also to attack the area immediately behind, through which the enemy had to pass the supplies and reinforcements needed to sustain his effort in the battle area. This was, and still is, termed "interdiction".

SUPREMACY AND INTERDICTION

During the *Blitzkrieg* campaigns, which relied on achieving shock and surprise from the outset, the aim of the German air force was to destroy its opponent on the ground, which meant attacking airfields, on the opening day. The Poles, in September 1939, prevented this by moving their aircraft to satellite airfields, but this

1943

KURSK

DATE July 1943
OBJECT A limited offensive by the Germans against the Russians.
NUMBERS Up to 5,500 tanks from both sides.
DESCRIPTION Kursk was the largest tank battle of the war. Hitler's intention was to conduct a limited offensive so as to blunt the Russian offensive capability and hence gain a breathing space in the aftermath of

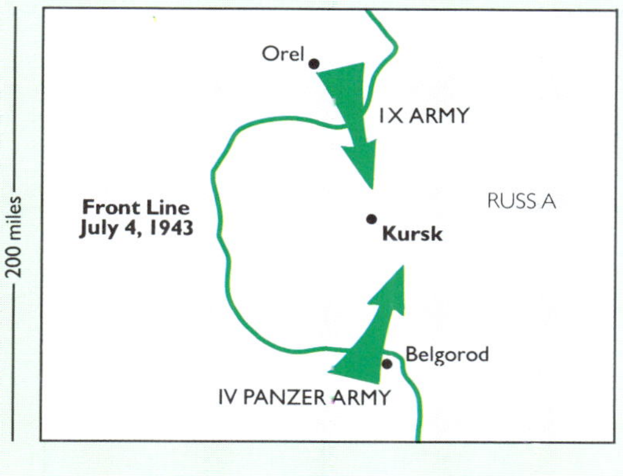

the Stalingrad débâcle. The removal of the most prominent salient on the Eastern Front, with Kursk at its base, was selected as the target. Simultaneous attacks from the north and south were to be conducted, both targeted on Kursk. The original intention was to mount the operation in mid-April, but deployment delays and Hitler's insistence on waiting for sufficient numbers of the new Panther and Tiger tanks to be delivered forced a postponement. The Russians soon became aware of what was ▸

Hawker Hurricanes taking off during the Battle of Britain. While not as fast as the Spitfire, and with a lower operational altitude, the Hurricane was highly manoeuvrable. One version, known as the Hurribomber, was equipped with bombs and rockets and used for close air support.

made little difference given their small numbers and obsolescence. It worked to a degree in May 1940 and was very effective against the ill-prepared Russians in June 1941. The Japanese, too, used the same technique during their initial offensives.

The one failure that the Germans had during the early years of the war was during late summer 1940. Air supremacy was an essential prerequisite for a successful invasion of Britain. The Battle of Britain (see page 197) began with the Luftwaffe trying to draw the British fighters into combat over the Channel, using attacks on convoys as the bait. This failed and hence, in August, the Germans turned to attacks on radar stations, airfields and the British aircraft industry in an attempt to destroy the infrastructure of RAF Fighter Command. Their fighters, however, were now operating at extreme range, having only 20 minutes' flying time over England, which put the RAF fighters at an advantage. Furthermore, they failed to concentrate sufficiently on each target to make it inoperative. Thus, while they put some radar stations and airfields out of action for a time, they also allowed them a breathing space for repairs. Finally, the switch to attacks on London at the beginning of September was an admission that they had failed to subdue the RAF.

By the time the Allies had begun to take to the offensive on all fronts, towards the end of 1942, they had adopted a more methodical approach. To take but one example, during the preparatory period before the Normandy landings in June 1944 the attacks by the Allied air forces on airfields and radars in northern France were very much more systematic than the Luftwaffe 1940 effort. Targets were attacked time and again until it was certain that they were destroyed. The result was that when the landings took place hardly a single German aircraft could be mustered over the invasion front.

It was realized from the outset that the best method of achieving this was to concentrate on communications and thus block the routes that the enemy was using to bring supplies and reserves. The abortive Allied efforts to destroy the Meuse bridges in May 1940 were an indicator of this and, having achieved early air supremacy, the Luftwaffe also concentrated on these targets. During the latter part of the war the Allies made interdiction a priority during the preparatory phase. Classic examples of this were the aptly named Operation *Strangle*, which was carried out prior to the successful May 1944 attacks on the Gustav Line in Italy and the sealing off of Normandy prior to D-Day through the destruction of road and rail bridges leading into it.

STRATEGIC BOMBING

So far the air roles discussed in this chapter have been largely in support of land and naval operations. The one mission that air forces could undertake totally inde-

1943

in the wind and began to construct three massive belts of defences and to bring up large quantities of armour. The German attacks opened on 5 July and, after some initial success, foundered amid the Red Army's defences. The climax came on 12 July when the Russians mounted massive counterstrokes against the rear of both attacking armies. That against the Fourth Panzer Army in the south witnessed the largest tank battle of the war. Some 3,000 tanks engaged, of which 800 were destroyed. These Russian blows forced the Germans to withdraw.

CASUALTIES "Citadel", as the attack was codenamed, cost the Germans insupportable armour losses.

RESULT The German army was forced strictly on to the defensive from then on. Kursk also showed the renewed confidence of the Red Army.

SCHWEINFURT-REGENSBURG

DATE 17 August 1943

OBJECT To disrupt German war production.

NUMBERS 376 B-17s, 276 P-47s, 180 Spitfires; 540 Fw190, Me109, Me110 sorties flown.

DESCRIPTION This was a twin daylight operation carried out by the US 8th Air Force against the ball-bearing industry at

pendently of the other armed services was strategic bombing, the means by which pre-war theorists believed that they could win wars single-handed. Given the technological state of the art at the time there was some justice in Stanley Baldwin's comment on the invincibility of the bomber. Ground detection devices, which were based on sound and visual means, had a very limited range and the relatively poor climb performance of the wooden biplane fighter meant that they could not intercept the bombers in time. The only alternative was standing patrols of fighters, a prohibitively expensive use of assets. The situation had changed dramatically by the late 1930s, however, thanks to the introduction of the all-metal monoplane fighter and radar. The effect of these was well illustrated by the Battle of Britain.

Yet, in September 1939 the rival air forces did not undertake the "knock-out" blow which at least civilian populations expected. Governments bound themselves by the 1923 Hague Draft Rules of Air Warfare, which, although never ratified, outlawed indiscriminate bombing and forbade attacks on other than strictly military targets. The bombing of Warsaw in September 1939 and Rotterdam in May 1940 were the first cracks in these ground rules. However, Warsaw had become a military target by virtue of its refusal to surrender, although Rotterdam was a more marginal case. But, in spite of these, a small degree of indiscriminate bombing was being carried out, albeit unintentionally.

The problem was that the bomber of 1939 could not bomb accurately. Navigation was reliant on dead reckoning and astro fixes, both of which were very prone to error. Indeed, that is why most bombing during the early months of the war was done by day. By early 1940, because of high aircraft casualties, the British were forced to switch to night, which increased navigational inaccuracy. Even if the target was correctly identified, the bombsights of the time, which had not been significantly improved since 1918, were not very accurate. The Germans were the first to improve navigation with their *Knickebein* (Crooked Leg) system, which was based on radio signals intersecting over the target, but this could be countered by jamming or transmitting "spoof" signals.

The "area bombing" or "city busting", which was to dominate the strategic bombing offensives against England, Germany and Japan, really began by accident when a German bomber dropped bombs on London in error in late August 1940. The British retaliated by attacking Berlin and then began the long drawn-out Blitz on London and other British cities during winter 1940–1. The Blitz showed, however, that the pre-war belief that civilians would quickly cave in under bombing attacks was mistaken. If anything it strengthened their resolve to resist and hit back. It also revealed a serious shortfall in the Luftwaffe's order of battle: the lack of a true strategic bomber, with long range and large bombload. The reason was that the Luftwaffe was

Royal Marine Commandos coming ashore on Sword Beach, Normandy, 6 June 1944. On the beach itself can be seen various types of specialized armoured vehicle. Known affectionately as "funnies", they included swimming tanks, bridging vehicles, vehicles equipped with devices for clearing lanes through minefields, and for destroying concrete strongpoints.

1943

Schweinfurt and Luftwaffe fighter plants at Regensburg deep in southern Germany. 376 bombers took off, escorted by P-47 Thunderbolts and Spitfires. The Schweinfurt group was to return to its East Anglian bases after the attack, while that attacking Regensburg was to fly on to North Africa. Shortage of fuel forced the escort fighters to turn back just short of the German border, but even before they did so German fighters were beginning to hack down bombers. The attacks grew in intensity the ▸

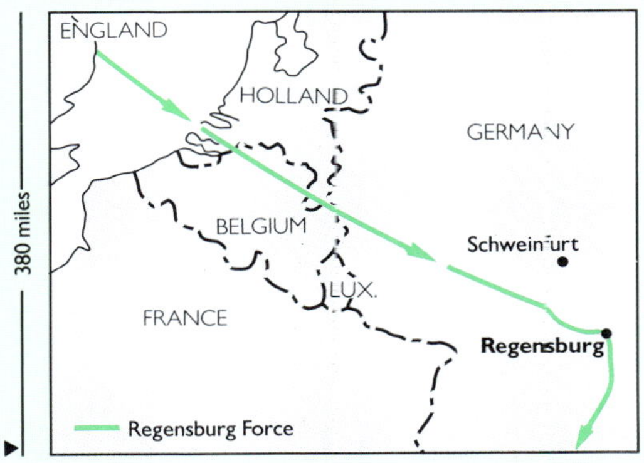

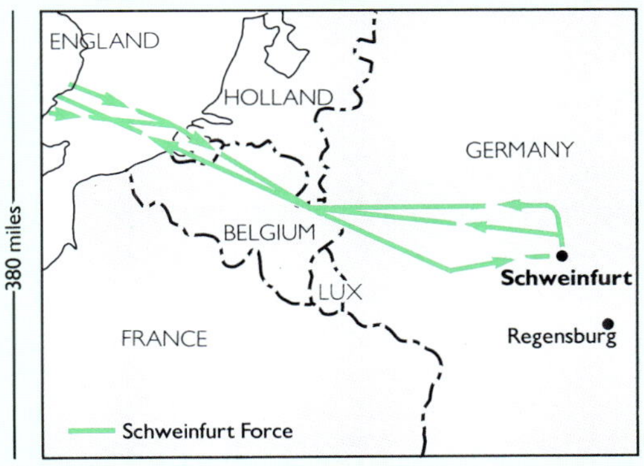

Londoners emerge from a garden shelter after a V-1 flying bomb strike, summer 1944. Hitler designated this, and the very much larger V-2 rocket, "revenge weapons" – and believed that they could alter the course of the war, but they were deployed too late. The first V-1 struck England on 13 June, a week after the Normandy landings, and the first V-2 on 8 September. They caused some 33,000 civilian casualties and much damage in southern England and also later in Belgium before the attacks ended in March 1945.

seen by Hitler when he created it as a *Risikoflotte* (Risk Fleet) designed to impress Germany's neighbours by its size rather than its quality. The production rate for two-engined aircraft was much greater than that for four-engined and the Luftwaffe needed to grow quickly. The RAF fell into the same trap in the mid-1930s when it tried to match the Luftwaffe in numbers, although by 1937 specifications had been drawn up for heavy bombers, which began to come into service at the beginning of 1941. The Luftwaffe's lack of a strategic bomber was really revealed during the war against Russia. Not only was it unable to mount a sustained air offensive against Moscow, but it also lacked the range to attack the Russian war industry behind the Urals.

It was not until 1942 that the British bombing offensive against Germany really got underway. Before then bomber numbers had been too few to make much of an impression. New technical aids, increasing numbers of heavy bombers and a dynamic new commander, Arthur Harris, began to make the bombing bite. No technical aid was invulnerable to a counter and while bombing accuracy improved to an extent it was still not precise enough, although there were exceptions, such as the Dams Raid (see page 219). Thus, RAF Bomber Command was drawn increasingly to area bombing because it lacked the means to do anything else. The self-justification for it was that it was more effective in both lowering civilian morale and keeping munitions workers from their beds and hence reducing production. Spurred by the post-Casablanca Conference directive, which laid down the dislocation of the German military, economic and industrial systems and the fatal undermining of morale as the main aims of the strategic bombing offensive, RAF Bomber Command waged three consecutive campaigns, against the Ruhr, Hamburg and Berlin during 1943–4. That against the Ruhr was made more difficult by the industrial haze that covered the region, but did help to drive the German industry into the countryside, where, during 1944, its production would peak. Hamburg was the closest that Harris got to fatally undermining morale when the heart of the city was torn out through firestorms, but Berlin proved too tough to overcome. Bomber casualties mounted in the face of an ever more technically sophisticated air-defence system and it was as well that the decision to switch the strategic bombing forces to support of the Normandy landing preparation halted it at the end of March 1944.

The US strategic bombing "barons" entered the war with a different view. While they agreed that bombing could be decisive, they argued that daylight attacks gave better accuracy and hence were more effective. By giving their bombers the maximum defensive armament they believed that they could ward off the enemy fighters. It was not until spring 1943 that they were able to take a full part in the offensive and began to concentrate on industrial targets by day, while the RAF

1943

deeper into Germany they penetrated. Even so, the Regensburg attack was remarkably accurate and caused some extensive damage. This group, by turning south over the Alps, was able to surprise the air defences in the area and quickly shook off its attackers. The bombing of Schweinfurt, in contrast, was scattered and the bombers had to endure the same punishment during the homeward trip as they had on the outward.

CASUALTIES The combined attack cost 60 US bombers compared with 27 German fighters shot down.

RESULT It forced the Eighth Air Force to withdraw to short-range targets for a time. A second raid on Schweinfurt on 14 October, accompanied part of the way by longer-range P-38 Lightning escorts, suffered even greater casualties and finally convinced the Americans that deep-penetration daylight operations were too costly without a fighter which could escort all the way to the target.

THE NORMANDY LANDINGS

DATE 6 June 1944

OBJECT Invasion of France by Allied forces.

NUMBERS 8 Allied divisions (including 3rd airborne) against 1 Panzer and 4 infantry divisions.

DESCRIPTION The planning of Operation "Overlord", which took place on 6 June 1944, began in earnest in April 1943. The planners knew that the Germans expected

attacked cities by night, a strategy which was known as "round the clock bombing". Their belief in the invincibility of the B-17 Flying Fortress and other bombers was cruelly shattered during operations in the late summer and autumn of 1943 when the loss rate in bombers was as high as 30 per cent. The bomber could not get through modern air defences on its own by day, and they seriously thought of switching to night attacks. Salvation, however, came in the shape of the long-range escort fighter, the P-51 Mustang, and confidence was restored during the last year of the war in Europe.

The temporary placing of the strategic air forces under Eisenhower's command during the spring and summer of 1944 did not please the bomber commanders, who believed that this would give Germany a valuable breathing space. Yet they played a significant part in the interdiction operations and were also used in direct support of the ground forces, although their "carpet-bombing" techniques more than once caused casualties to their own side and created added mobility problems. When they returned to concentrating their attacks on Germany in mid-September 1944, the German transportation system was quickly brought to a virtual halt. When the Allies eventually overran Germany in spring 1945 it was a totally devastated country.

There is no doubt that strategic bombing did contribute to victory against Germany. It was, too, for so long the only means of striking directly at the German heartland. Yet, it was not in itself decisive and the belief that Germany could be reduced to such a state that the land forces would be left with a mere police action on their hands did not come to pass. Too much faith was placed on morale attacks, which continued until the end of the war, with the attack against Dresden in February 1945 being the most controversial. As the Blitz did not break British morale, so the Germans stood up against a much longer and heavier campaign. True, the Allied policy of unconditional surrender probably contributed to this in that German propaganda was able to instil in people a belief that there was nothing to be gained by early surrender, but even so the pre-war theorists had been disproved.

The strategic bombing offensive against Japan took very much longer to be mounted for the simple reason that the Japanese mainland remained out of reach of the bombers for so long. Indeed the only US air attack on Japan before 1944 was in April 1942 when carrier-launched B-25s dropped a few bombs on Japanese cities and then crash-landed in China, but this was as much to boost Allied morale at an especially dark time as to achieve any larger purpose. It was not until the B-29 Superfortress came into service that the US Air Force had an aircraft capable of reaching Japan from land bases with a useful payload. They began by operating from bases in South China in June 1944, but the results were disappointing. A Japanese offensive then forced them to evacuate.

One of the war's most dramatic air operations was on 18 April 1942. Sixteen B-25 Mitchell bombers led by Colonel James H. Doolittle took off from the carrier Hornet *750 miles east of Tokyo. They bombed a number of Japanese cities and then flew to China, where, out of fuel, all crash-landed. Many of the crews, including Doolittle, (who was awarded the Congressional Medal of Honor) were rescued by the Chinese. It was not until June 1944 that bombers, B-29s operating from China, again attacked Japan.*

1944

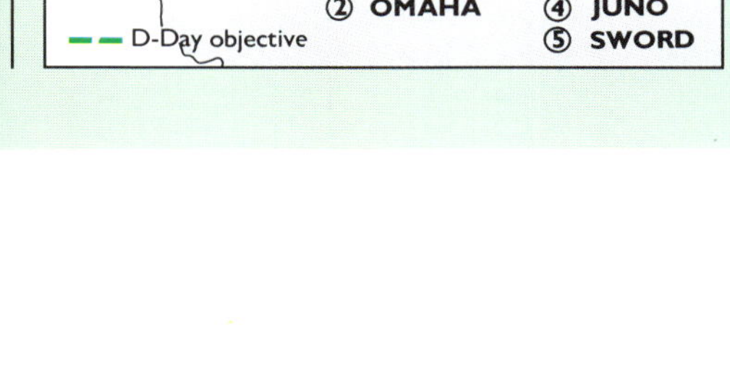

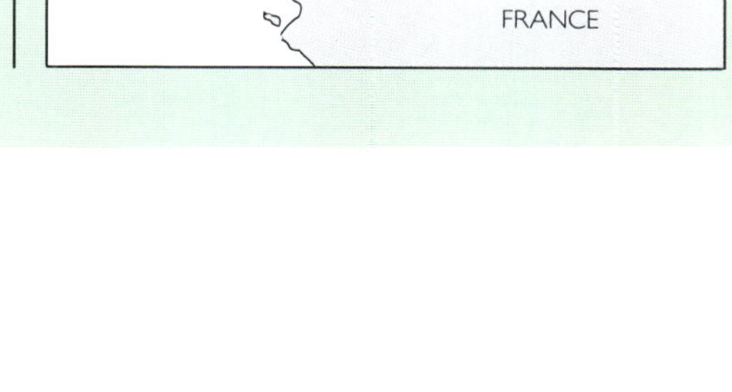

a landing and that the most likely place was the Pas de Calais, where the English Channel is at its narrowest. Therefore, in order to try and achieve some surprise, they looked for another suitable area. This could not be too far from the south coast of England from where it would be mounted, and the landing beaches had to be suitable. Much detailed topographical intelligence had to be acquired before the decision to opt for Normandy was taken. In order to prevent the Germans from finding out ▶

Tokyo in August 1945. The damage had mainly been caused by a series of attacks by B-29s based in the Marianas in the Pacific. Their bombloads included a high percentage of incendiaries which destroyed the city's largely wooden houses by fire. This level of destruction took some months, but that caused by the atomic bombs on Hiroshima and Nagasaki took merely minutes. The other difference was that the atomic bomb caused radiation sickness, which often did not manifest itself in its victims until some time later.

The securing of Saipan and Tinian in the Marianas by the beginning of August 1944 had, however, at last given the Americans a Pacific base close enough to Japan and the B-29s were moved here. They began operations in November, relying on high-altitude bombing by day. The results were again disappointing, with haze especially interfering with accuracy. Accordingly the decision was made to employ lower-level attacks by night using a high proportion of incendiary bombs. The new offensive opened in March and brought devastating results to the largely wooden structures of the Japanese cities. In the space of a week four cities, including Tokyo, suffered heavy destruction, but then the Americans ran out of incendiary bombs and had to pause to restock. By early April further US conquests had brought P-51 escort fighters within range of Japan and the B-29s were able to resume attacks by day. The effects, combined with those which had been caused by US submarine operations, were calamitous for Japanese war production but, as with Germany, they did not induce surrender or much thought of it. Indeed, as the fighting on Iwo Jima and Okinawa showed, Japanese resistance was as fierce as ever and the prospect of invading the islands of mainland Japan was daunting. Again, conventional strategic bombing had made a significant but not decisive contribution to final victory.

1944

about this, elaborate deception plans under the codename *Bodyguard*, were drawn up. The necessary landing craft for such a huge undertaking had to be gathered and specialized equipment developed from scratch to ensure its success. The invasion fleet had to be secured against the air, surface and sub-surface threats. Since no port lay within the landing area, artificial "Mulberry" harbours and PLUTO (Pipeline under the Ocean) were created so that the forces in the beachhead could be supplied and reinforced across the beaches. The tides had to be right, which imposed limitations on the choice of date, and the weather fair, the cause of a 24-hour postponement. All elements taking part had to be thoroughly rehearsed over British beaches similar to those in Normandy. Air and French Resistance operations during the preparatory phase had to be closely co-ordinated. These were just some of the planning factors that had to be considered and the success of 6 June 1944 was as much that of the planners as of those who actively participated. In short, successful major amphibious operations could not be mounted without very careful preparation.

CASUALTIES Allies – approximately 15,000; Germans – approximately 10,000.

RESULT Consolidation of the beachhead marked the beginning of the end for German forces in the West; once the Allies broke out of Normandy it was only a matter of time before they reached the German border.

AMPHIBIOUS WARFARE

Between the two world wars no nation paid much attention to amphibious warfare. The British experience in the Dardanelles in 1915 had convinced most people that major landings on hostile shores were too risky to be a viable operation of war. Yet nine months after the outbreak of the war the Germans were confronted with the possible necessity of having to carry out this very operation.

Operation *Sealion*, the invasion of Britain, was not a contingency that they had thought of before the end of the campaign in France, let alone earlier. Even though they tried to convince themselves that it would be no more than a large-scale river crossing, and Poland and the recent campaign in the west had given them plenty of opportunity to perfect these, they were wholly unequipped to cross the English Channel. Indeed, Hitler himself recognized this to the extent of refusing to order more than preparations for it. He recognized that an essential prerequisite was air supremacy over both the Channel and landing area and was not prepared to execute the operation until this had been achieved. While Goering set out to achieve this, the German naval commander-in-chief, Erich Raeder, increasingly expressed his doubts over his ability to protect the invasion armada from the ravages of the Royal Navy. Von Rundstedt, on the other hand, who was to command the landing forces, showed cynical lack of interest in the whole concept, never believing that it would happen. As it was, the task of gathering together suitable craft from the waterways of Europe was

US Marines during the bloody fighting on Tarawa in the Gilbert Islands, November 1943. This and the landing on its sister island of Makin marked the first of a series of operations in the central Pacific, which culminated in the landings on Okinawa in April 1945. The Tarawa garrison of 5,000 men fought to the last, inflicting 3,500 US casualties.

1944

THE ARDENNES COUNTER-OFFENSIVE

DATE 16 December 1944–January 1945
CAMPAIGN North-West Europe
OBJECT To split the Americans from the British and seize the port of Antwerp.
NUMBERS German – 210,000; US – 83,000.
DESCRIPTION Hitler ordered planning of this in the strictest secrecy as early as September 1944. In October troops began to be concentrated for it, although not until

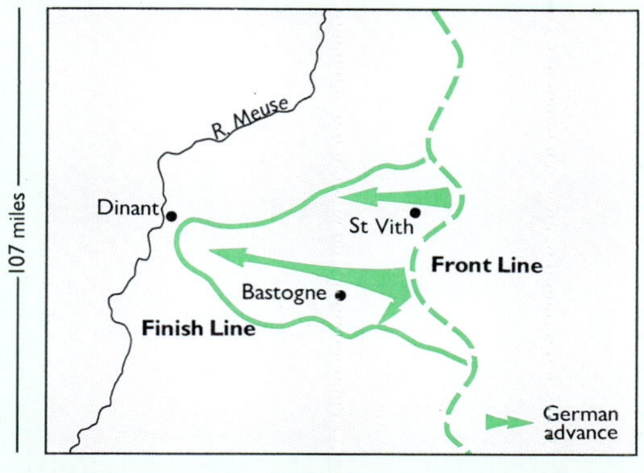

just before the attack did they know of it. The Germans planned to strike through the wooded Ardennes, a quiet sector occupied by US divisions, some recovering from the heavy fighting to the north, others as yet unblooded. The main blow would be struck by Dietrich's Sixth Panzer Army, consisting largely of Waffen-SS divisions, with von Manteuffel's Fifth Panzer Army to its south advancing in step. Their first objective was the bridges over the River Meuse. The attack took the US troops by ▸

The shore line at Dieppe after the abortive Allied cross-Channel raid of 19 August 1942. This operation remains clouded in controversy, but it did provide valuable lessons in amphibious operations, especially in the planning of the Normandy landings. Not least of these was that landings stood a better chance on open beaches than against a defended port.

immense, especially given the time available, and few were really suitable. Its indefinite postponement, after the Luftwaffe had failed to best the RAF, was therefore generally greeted with relief and the Germans never would carry out a major amphibious operation. The Japanese, on the other hand, had planned for amphibious landings during the 1941–2 offensive. While they did not possess the specialist equipment on which the Western Allies came to rely, they were successful during the early months of the war in the Pacific because they often achieved surprise and enjoyed naval and air supremacy.

The Western Allies formally recognized at the first of their major wartime conferences, in December 1941, that total victory in Europe and the Far East could not be achieved without landing forces from the sea. Indeed, the British had already been carrying them out, albeit on a very small scale, with their Commando raids and had set up the Directorate of Combined Operations, the title reflecting the tri-service nature of this operation of war. With regard to Europe, the Americans wanted to carry out cross-Channel landings in France as soon as possible, but their ally preferred to secure the Mediterranean periphery first, in spite of Stalin's demands for the instant creation of the Second Front. The disastrous Dieppe Raid of August 1942 showed that the Allies were not ready to make a successful invasion of France, but the lessons learnt from it proved invaluable. Further experience was gained from the successful *Torch* landings in French North Africa (November 1942) and the Sicilian (July 1943) and Italian (September 1943) landings and the culmination in Europe came with the Normandy landings (see page 224).

The first major US landing in the Pacific, on Guadalcanal in August 1942 (see page 214), was planned in a hurry and with few resources. Indeed it became called *"Operation Shoestring"*. Consequently, although the troops successfully got ashore, it was to be weeks before the initial beachhead could be expanded and it took six months to secure the island. The main lesson learnt was that the launching base must not be too distant if the build-up of force and sustainability necessary to exploit the landings inland was to be achieved. This, and the desirability of land-based aircraft able to cover the landings, influenced what became known as the "island-hopping" strategy practised by MacArthur in the south-west Pacific and, with more difficulty, Nimitz in the central Pacific.

So great a role did amphibious operations come to play in Allied strategy that the rate of production of the specialized equipment needed for them could not keep up with demand and inevitably some very feasible schemes, which might have shortened campaigns, had to be rejected. As US chief-of-staff George C. Marshall is reputed to have said: "Prior to the present war I never heard of any landing craft except a rubber boat. Now I think about little else."

1944

surprise and poor weather prevented Allied airpower from playing a part. Dietrich's tanks, however, found the hilly terrain hard going; only one Panzer force was able to penetrate to any depth but it was eventually thwarted by US engineers blowing bridges in its path. Von Manteuffel was more successful, but the important communications centre of Bastogne held out against him. Patton's Third US Army to the south was ordered to wheel north and relieved Bastogne on the 26th, while Montgomery, who took control of the northern half of the salient, sent troops to guard the Meuse bridges. Improving weather enabled Allied aircraft to join the battle and by early January the Germans had been halted and were forced to withdraw.

CASUALTIES Allied 76,900; German 67,500.

RESULT The German offensive delayed the Allied advance to the Rhine by some six weeks, but at this stage they could ill afford their losses in men and material.

HIROSHIMA

DATE 6 August 1945

OBJECT The first occasion on which the newly-developed atom bomb was used in warfare, the aim being to force the unconditional surrender of Japan and so avoid the need of a costly Allied ground invasion of the Japanese home islands.

DESCRIPTION The attack was launched by a single B-29 SuperFortress, the "Enola Gay", which flew from its base at Tinian on

LEGACY OF THE SECOND WORLD WAR

The Second World War did not produce any startlingly new principles of war. Rather, it served to reaffirm the tried and trusted principles that have been observed throughout the history of warfare. Likewise, the age-old problems of coalition warfare, especially that of trying to reconcile national interests with the good of the alliance as a whole, did not change. Where it did differ from its predecessors was in its totality and complexity.

Technological advances both during the pre-war years, and accelerated during the war itself, especially in the fields of communications and propulsion, generally meant that it was conducted at a much faster pace than hitherto. Commanders therefore had to think and react much more quickly. At the same time, the increase in information sources and the factors that they had to consider, largely brought about by the much wider range of resources available with which to conduct war, made decision making a much more difficult business. While total victory was still represented by the man with his rifle and bayonet standing in the enemy's seat of government, the means to get him there had grown more complex. At the highest strategic level the problem was compounded by the fact that it was very much more of a global war than its predecessor, with many more parts of the world being actively fought over. Indeed, it became almost two separate wars, one against the Axis powers in Europe, the other the conflict with Japan. The increased technological character of war also meant that the "tail to teeth" ratio, the numbers supporting each individual directly engaged with the enemy, had dramatically increased, at least in Western armies.

While 1939–45 was by no means the first total war – indeed, there are numerous instances of these throughout history – it directly affected people in many more parts of the world than ever before. National resources and populations were, to use Giulio Douhet's expression, "sucked into the maw of war" to a greatly increased extent. Conscription of the civil population for war work was widespread. Strategic bombing placed the civilian increasingly in the firing line. Women became more directly involved, whether in the Resistance movements of Axis-occupied Europe, tracking enemy aircraft by radar, or, in the Russian case, actually fighting. With increased totality came increased ruthlessness in the way in which the war was waged. The Holocaust and the Japanese treatment of prisoners of war are but two examples.

The development, too, of increasingly destructive weapons added to this totality, and none was more so than the atomic bomb. While it finally brought the Second World War to an end, it opened the door to an ever more awesome concept of future war. Even though Hiroshima and Nagasaki might have finally proved the pre-war air prophets right, they would have taken little comfort from it.

THE RACE TO CREATE THE ATOMIC BOMB

By 1939 investigations into the make-up of the atom and the realization that when uranium isotopes were bombarded with neutrons proportionately vast amounts of energy were released, convinced nuclear scientists this energy could be used to create a bomb of enormous power. Its power would come through nuclear chain reaction, but this needed heavy water to slow the neutrons down. The only plant producing this was at Vermork, Norway. This fell into German hands in April 1940, but not before the French had seized the existing stocks and brought them to England. By July 1941 the British became convinced that an atomic bomb could be built, but lacked the resources to do it. In June 1942 Churchill agreed to pooling resources with the USA, who now took the Allied lead, under the umbrella of the Manhattan Project. Efforts were made to slow German development of the bomb by sabotaging Vermork. By early 1944 this had been achieved, but it was not until 16 July 1945 that the first atomic bomb was successfully tested. The Western Allies had decided to use it against Japan if she refused surrender. No clear-cut acceptance was received. Two bombs were dropped on Hiroshima (6 August) and Nagasaki (9 August).

1945

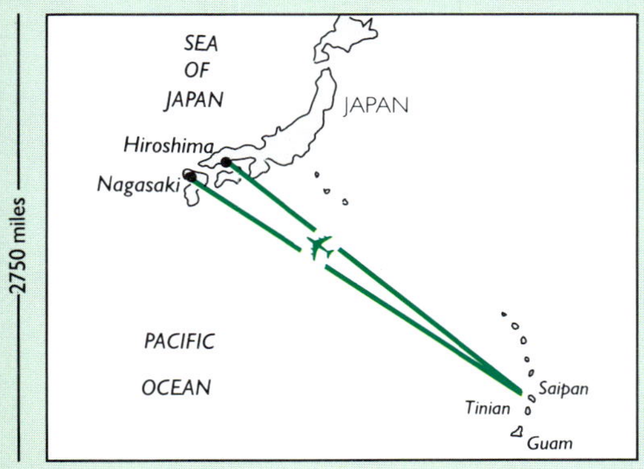

the Mariana Islands to drop its bomb, nicknamed "Little Boy" at 8.15 am on 6 August. Precisely one minute later, Hiroshima to all intents and purposes ceased to exist. Of the 320,000 soldiers and civilians in the city that morning, around 78,000 died instantly, many thousands more later perishing or being seriously affected by radiation sickness; out of 90,000 buildings, nearly 62,000 were flattened by the explosion.

RESULT The impact of Hiroshima – and that of a second bomb, dropped on Nagasaki three days later, killing 39,000 people – was immediate. The Japanese peace party, which had already been gaining strength, was now joined by the Emperor and unconditional surrender swiftly followed. The long-term consequences were even more momentous. Hiroshima inaugurated a totally new age in warfare, in which a single bombing raid could produce total destruction on a scale that was hitherto undreamed of.

12

WARFARE TODAY AND TOMORROW

Supplies for West Berlin are loaded aboard a US Air Force C-54 transport plane at Wiesbaden Air Base, West Germany, in March 1949. The Soviet Union's imposition of a land blockade of the part of the city administered by France, Britain and the US crystallized the post-war hostility between the superpowers and stimulated the formation of NATO.

CONFLICT IN THE POST-WAR WORLD has been waged in the shadow of the mushroom clouds that blossomed over Hiroshima and Nagasaki in August 1945. The possession of nuclear weapons conferred the status of "superpower" on the nations that were able to develop them. And the assumption that such weapons were available as a last resort, initially to the USA, subsequently to the USSR, UK, France and China, and more recently to South Africa, India, Pakistan and others, has had profound consequences for the relationships between those states and their neighbours.

One consequence of the power that was demonstrated in the nuclear attacks on Japan was that the distrust between the wartime Allies crystallized into the climate of fear, loathing and distrust that became known as the Cold War. In the immediate aftermath of the war it became apparent that the Soviet Union was unwilling to treat the states of eastern Europe as anything but satellites. At the same time, the USA began to exert its own influence on a global basis. The result was what the wartime British prime minister, Winston Churchill, described in 1946 as an Iron Curtain dividing Europe into East and West.

NATO AND THE WARSAW PACT

The groupings that polarized around the United States on the one side and the Soviet Union on the other were formalized in two alliances that dominated European defence strategy until the break-up of the USSR in the early 1990s. On 4 April 1969, spurred by the Soviet land blockade of West Berlin, the USA and Canada combined with Belgium, Denmark, France, Iceland, Italy, Luxembourg, the Netherlands, Norway, Portugal and the United Kingdom to form the North Atlantic Treaty Organization, or NATO. Greece, Turkey, West Germany and Spain joined subsequently, while France withdrew from the organization's integrated military structure to pursue an independent defence policy in 1966.

On the other side of the Iron Curtain a similar alliance was forged. On 14 May

1945

CHRONOLOGY OF POST-WAR CONFLICT

1945 CHINESE CIVIL WAR War between Mao Tse-tung's Red Army and Nationalists under Chiang Kai-shek resumed after Japanese surrender; Nationalist resistance ended December 1949.

1945–9 INDONESIAN WAR OF INDEPENDENCE Indonesian People's Army's resistance to restoration of Dutch colonial rule; independence achieved December 1949.

1946–9 GREEK CIVIL WAR Communist guerillas of the Democratic Army of Greece opposed to restoration of monarchy defeated October 1949 by US-backed Greek government forces.

1946–54 INDO-CHINA WAR Return of French colonial rule to Indo-China resisted by Viet-Minh; French withdrew and North and South Vietnam created, plus independence of Laos and Cambodia recognized July 1954 after French defeat.

1946–8 ISRAELI WAR OF INDEPENDENCE Jewish guerilla campaign against British forces administering Palestine under 1920 League of Nations Mandate; state of Israel proclaimed March 1948.

1946–4 PHILIPPINES HUK REBELLION Revolt by People's Anti-Japanese Army following independence in July 1946.

1947–9 INDIA–PAKISTAN WAR Kashmir acceded to India in October 1947 after Muslim rebellion; Indian and Pakistani troops involved in fighting until January 1949 ceasefire mediated by UN.

1955, three days after West Germany was admitted to NATO, and a year after a Soviet application to join was rejected, the leaders of Albania, Bulgaria, Czechoslovakia, East Germany, Hungary, Poland, Romania and the Soviet Union met in Warsaw to sign a treaty of mutual defence and economic co-operation, commonly known as the Warsaw Pact. Ostensibly similar to that of NATO, the Warsaw Pact's military structure differed in that it was completely dominated by the Soviet Union.

Soviet tanks deployed on the streets of Budapest in November 1956 to suppress the Hungarian uprising underlined the Soviet Union's determination to maintain its authority over the East European states which had joined the Warsaw Pact the previous year. Such scenes were repeated in Prague in August 1968.

THE PEOPLE'S REPUBLIC OF CHINA

The third claimant to superpower status during the Cold War was China. The Chinese civil war ended in 1949 with the proclamation by victorious communist leader Mao Tse-tung of the People's Republic of China. Originally aligned with the USSR, China broke off relations in 1959. Five years later China exploded its first atomic bomb.

Although China has undergone an economic and technological transformation in recent years, the country's military capabilities are nowhere near as strong as the United States. Its huge army of around 2.8 million is poorly trained and equipped; its 8,500 tanks are slow, small and out-of-date and, apart from two squadrons of Russian Su-27 fighter planes, its airforce is old. However, China's 400 nuclear warheads, allied to its huge population and the certainty of continued technological development, make it a major player on the world military stage.

THE NUCLEAR ARSENALS

In order to maintain its new-found superpower status, the USA pursued the development of atomic weapons with great vigour. The three weapons used for the July 1945 test at Almogordo, New Mexico, and the subsequent attacks on Japanese cities were the only ones built before the end of the war, but within five years annual production of atomic bombs was exceeding 100. A stark measure of the power of nuclear weapons is the terminology used to describe their yield, or explosive force. This is measured in kilotons and megatons, or the approximate equivalent in thousands or millions of tons of conventional TNT.

New delivery systems and new forms of atomic weapons were also investigated. In 1952 the US army deployed a 280mm gun with nuclear shells. By 1955 it had added the Corporal and Honest John surface-to-surface missiles as well as nuclear landmines. Meanwhile, the Soviet Union had tested its first plutonium bomb in 1949 and by 1953 both the USA and the USSR had developed hydrogen bombs. So-called H-bombs use fusion rather than fission to release atomic energy, and they can have yields measured in tens of megatons rather than the few tens of kilotons to which the early bombs were limited.

Further advances were achieved with the development of intercontinental

Continued on page 234

1950

1948– BURMA CIVIL WAR **Struggle for autonomy by Karen National Liberation Army plus (until April 1989) insurgency by Communist Party of Burma following independence from UK in January 1948.**

1948 COSTA RICA CIVIL WAR **Rebel army formed March 1948 to enforce results of general election after attempt by incumbent government to annul it; regular army defeated and abolished.**

1948 COLOMBIA CIVIL WAR **Insurgency by Revolutionary Armed Forces of Colombia plus, subsequently, guerilla movements.**

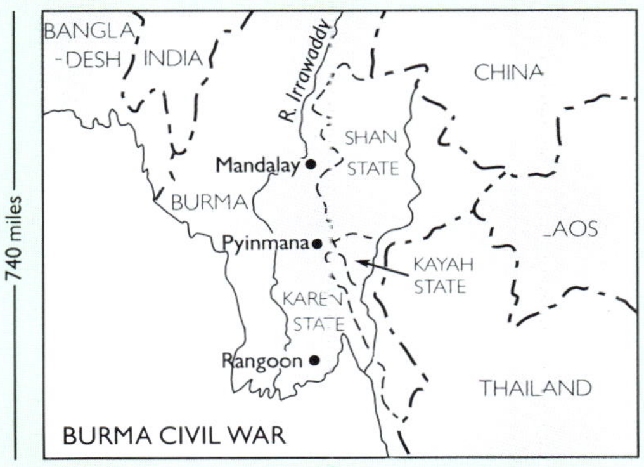

1948–9 ARAB–ISRAELI WAR **Egypt, Iraq, Jordan, Lebanon and Syria invaded Israel when British mandate ended in May 1948; final armistice recognized Israeli victory.**

1948–60 MALAYAN EMERGENCY **Emergency declared by Britain in June 1948; Malayan Communist Party insurrection contained by Malaysian independence in August 1957 and emergency lifted July 1960.**

1950–53 KOREAN WAR **Initial success of June 1950 invasion of South Korea by North ▸**

DISMANTLING THE COLD WAR ARSENALS

THE DRAMATIC COLLAPSE of Soviet hegemony in eastern Europe in 1989 was prefigured by Soviet moves to reduce the numbers of troops deployed in non-Soviet Warsaw Pact countries. And even before the conclusion of the 1989-90 Vienna negotiations on conventional forces in Europe (CFE), unilateral force reductions on both sides of the NATO-Warsaw Pact divide had made it clear that the peak of the post-war arms build-up had been passed.

The aim of the CFE talks was to agree ceilings on the numbers of weapon systems in various categories deployed in NATO and Warsaw Pact European countries. Before that could happen there was the difficulty of establishing accurate totals for the numbers of systems actually deployed. To some extent, differences in each side's estimates of the other's holdings were academic. However, they were important as negotiating points and to enable each side to be able to verify the other's reductions.

The table below shows the figures produced by the two sides, including the Warsaw Pact's first public statement of its own holdings. They include weapons in store, and they vary substantially

(Above) The disparity between NATO and Warsaw Pact forces deployed in Europe has been particularly great in the case of tanks, which are the principal weapon of modern land armies.

(Below) Electronic warfare capabilities have mushroomed in recent years. The US Air Force's EF-111A is designed to protect friendly aircraft by jamming air-defence radar.

(Left) Air-launched cruise missiles, first deployed aboard US Air Force B-52 strategic bombers in the mid-1980s, added flexibility to the US strategic deterrent force by enabling manned bombers to launch attacks from stand-off ranges.

(Below) An early US Department of Defense depiction of the mobile launcher for the SS-20 long-range nuclear missile, one of the weapons whose deployment was ended by the 1987 treaty eliminating US and Soviet intermediate nuclear forces.

CONVENTIONAL WEAPONS IN EUROPE*

	NATO	Warsaw Pact
Main battle tanks (NATO figures)	22,224	57,300+
(WP figures)	30,690	59,470
Armoured combat vehicles (NATO)	47,639	101,535+
(WP)	46,900	70,330
Artillery weapons (NATO)	17,328	46,270+
(WP)	57,060	71,560
Combat aircraft (NATO)	4,507	8,780+
(WP)	7,130	7,876
Helicopters (NATO)	2,599	3,880+
(WP)	5,270	2,785
Ground troops (NATO)	2,213,593	3,090,000
(WP)	3,660,200	3,573,100

*Figures from *Conventional Forces in Europe: the Facts* (NATO, March 1988) and *Correlation of the Numbers of Troops and Armaments of WTO and NATO in Europe and Adjoining Seas* (Warsaw Pact, January 1989)

(Below) One Soviet response to NATO's nuclear defence was the development of conventional forces combining large numbers of tracked vehicles with armed and troop-carrying helicopters capable of mounting rapid offensive operations on a vast scale.

at least in part because of the difficulty of counting such massive inventories, but more importantly because of the differences in definitions applied.

Perhaps most interesting is the light the published figures shed on the sheer scale of the arsenals that were created during 45 years of Cold War between East and West. Even after the substantial reductions called for by a CFE treaty, each side was allowed to retain 20,000 tanks. Yet in 1940 the German army embarked on a campaign that was to defeat most of western Europe with barely one-eighth that number, deploying 2,574 tanks against the 3,609 mustered by France and Britain between them.

The revelation of the scale of chemical weapon stockpiles in Europe, and the difficulties involved in disposing of them, was one of the most disturbing aspects of the arms reduction process. NATO's strategy to dispose of its chemical weapons stocks involved transporting 100.000 artillery shells containing some 7,000 tons of nerve agent to Johnston Atoll in the Pacific, where they were burnt in special incinerators.

The agreements on chemical and conventional weapons were prefigured by the December 1987 treaty committing the United States and the Soviet Union to eliminate all nuclear missiles with ranges of between 500km and 5,500km. The resulting declarations of stocks revealed that the US had deployed 309 Tomahawk ground-launched cruise and 120 Pershing II ballistic missiles. At the same time, Soviet short-range (500-1,000km) missile deployments amounted to 220 SS-12 and 167 SS-23; in addition, there were 405 SS-20 and 65 SS-4 long-range missiles deployed at operational sites.

(Below) The US Multiple Launch Rocket System (MLRS) is one of the principal weapons developed to help NATO forces deal with the threat of a potentially overwhelming Soviet armoured offensive in central Europe.

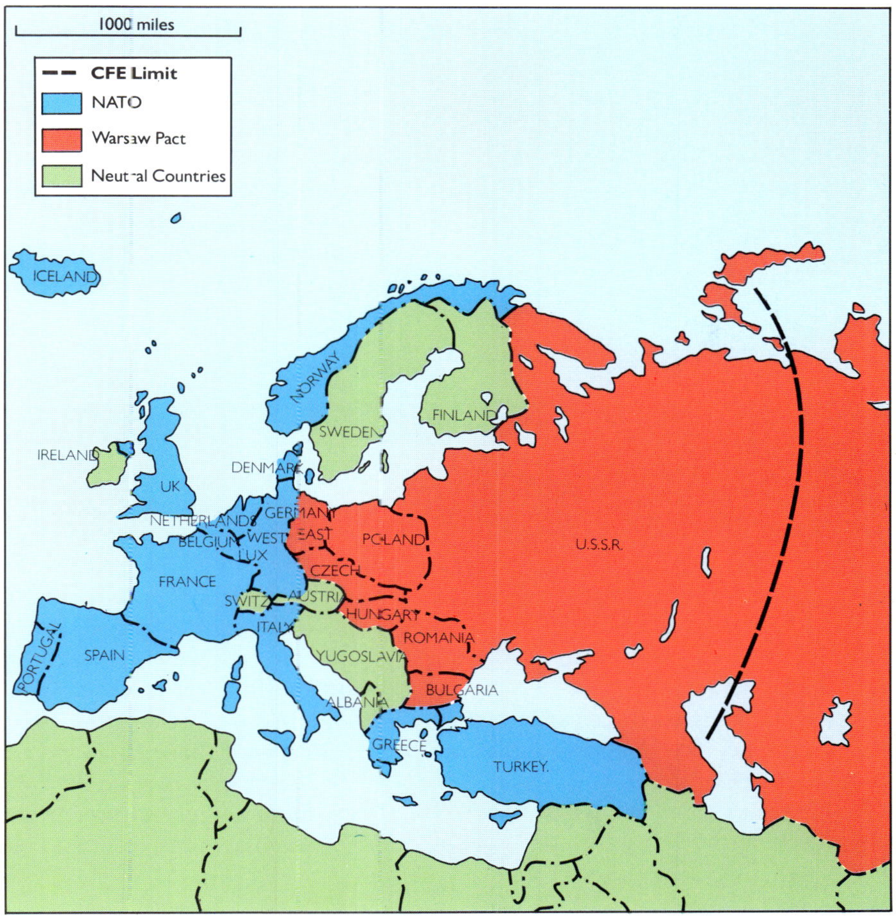

American troops in South Korea prepare to launch an "Honest John", one of the first post-war US missiles to become operational, in February 1968. The rapid development of tactical nuclear delivery systems alongside the strategic weapons that posed the threat of mass destruction on an unprecedented scale helped fuel the paranoia of the Cold War.

ballistic missiles (ICBMs) and submarine-launched ballistic missiles (SLBMs), some of which in turn were equipped with multiple warheads. Later the warheads themselves were made independently targetable, and accuracy was increased to the point where half the warheads launched would be expected to land within a few hundred yards of a designated target at ranges of anything up to 5,000 miles. Even more accurate were air-launched cruise missiles, though these need to be launched much nearer their targets than ICBMs.

DETERRENT STRATEGY

Initially the USA aimed for simple superiority in nuclear forces. By the mid-1950s the goal had been reduced to sufficiency, but the strategy was still one of massive retaliation in the event of an attack. The early 1960s saw the development of the strategy of flexible response, in which both conventional and nuclear weapons would be used and the goal was the "assured destruction" of enemy armed forces, not civilian populations. There was also a move to develop anti-ballistic missiles to limit the damage that an enemy attack could inflict on the USA itself.

By the end of the 1980s the purpose of US nuclear forces was defined as being to deter aggression, particularly nuclear attacks, against the United States and its allies. To do so they had to be effective, flexible, survivable and enduring. Effectiveness was achieved by accuracy both of weapons systems and target information, so strategic reconnaisance systems – satellites, aircraft and electronic systems – were deployed in substantial numbers. Flexibility was provided by manned bombers, particularly the B-1 and B-2, while ICBMs in hardened silos and missile-armed submarines patrolling in distant oceans contributed to survivability. The Soviet Union had a similar range of weapons by the end of the 1980s, though it had more ICBMs, some of them mobile, and had a more comprehensive air-defence system against bombers.

Meanwhile, in the post Cold War era, the UK and France have insisted on retaining independent nuclear capabilities as deterrents to aggression.

LIMITING THE ARMS RACE

One purpose of the strategy of mutual assured destruction was to make instability so dangerous to both sides that it would inhibit the development of new capabilities that could disturb the strategic balance. Accordingly, the deployment of nuclear forces was accompanied by efforts to agree limits on their size and capabilities.

One development which threatened to upset the strategic balance was the deployment of missiles designed to intercept and destroy ballistic missile warheads. Both the USA and the USSR deployed such systems in the early 1970s, the American Safeguard system involving Sprint and Spartan interceptors being based in North

1950

Korea was followed by a successful UN counter-offensive in September; UN forces pushed back by Chinese involvement from October; then prolonged war of attrition before ceasefire and new border with demilitarized zone along existing front line agreed July 1953.

1950 CHINESE INVASION OF TIBET Lhasa occupied September 1951 after invasion started in October 1950.

1952–60 KENYAN EMERGENCY State of emergency declared by Britain 1952 in response to Mau Mau terrorism; revolt contained by 1956, emergency lifted 1960.

1954–75 LAOS CIVIL WAR Pathet Lao resistance movement supported by North Vietnam defeated US-backed Royal Laotian Army in civil war following July 1954 independence from French colonial rule.

1954 GUATEMALA COUP AND GUERRILLA WAR Overthrow of Guatemalan government by US-backed exiles in June 1954 followed by continuing counter-insurgent war against the Guerilla Army of the Poor (EGP),

Dakota to protect ICBM silos while the Soviet Galosh missiles were installed around Moscow. After detailed negotiations the 1972 Anti-Ballistic Missile Treaty limited each side to only 100 ABMs at a maximum of two sites; the US system was dismantled, though the Soviet system was maintained and upgraded.

Along with the ABM Treaty, Stage I of the Strategic Arms Limitation Talks (SALT) resulted in an agreement to freeze the number of ICBMs and SLBMs on each side at their existing levels for five years. In 1979 SALT II concluded with an agreement to limit the total number of delivery systems on each side to 2,400 initially and 2,250 by the end of 1981, with sub-limits on the numbers of ballistic missiles carrying multiple independently targettable warheads. The two Strategic Arms Reduction Treaties (START I and START II) both seek to reduce the number of warheads and delivery systems available to the US and Russia. START I was originally signed in July 1991, but after the break-up of the USSR, Belarus, Kazakhstan and Ukraine also became signatories. By 2001, the strategic arsenals of the US and Russia had been reduced by 30-40%, and Belarus, Kazakhstan and Ukraine had eliminated the nuclear arsenals left over from the USSR. Building on this START II aims to eliminate heavy ICBMs and all other multiple-warhead (MIRVed) ICBMs, as well as reducing the total number of nuclear weapons deployed by both countries by two-thirds below pre-START levels.

CONVENTIONAL WARS AND LOW-INTENSITY CONFLICT

In some countries the Second World War never really stopped. In many others the new order of the post war world represented an opportunity to pursue dreams of liberation. The result was an astonishing variety of wars in the Cold War period, with superpower involvement ranging from full-scale military intervention to behind-the-scenes support for one side or the other.

Many of the conflicts during the Cold War were the result of straightforward territorial or economic disputes. But there were other factors at work. One was the enlistment of Third World nations in the geopolitical strategies of the two superpowers. Another was the sheer quantity of surplus military equipment that had been produced in World War II. A third was the often arbitrary new national boundaries that the tides of conflict had left in their wake. Yet another was the example set by the movement that was soon to win control of the most populous nation on earth.

The Chinese revolution, along with independence for India, resulted in the emergence of new regional superpowers in Asia. In the Middle East the creation of the state of Israel provided a focus for hostilities reaching back thousands of years. In Africa the end of colonialism was by no means always a peaceful affair. And Central America became a battleground for rival ideologies in an area where the cocaine trade introduced new economic distortions.

1956

Revolutionary Armed Forces (FAR) and Revolutionary Army of People in Arms (ORPA) guerilla groups.

1954–62 ALGERIAN WAR OF INDEPENDENCE **Algerian National Liberation Front started terrorist attacks November 1954; revolution largely suppressed 1957-8 and independence granted in 1962 after violent opposition by French colonists.**

1955–59 CYPRUS EMERGENCY **Britain proclaim state of emergency November 1955 in response to National Organization of**

Cypriot Fighters (EOKA) bombings; emergency ended in December 1959 and Cyprus became independent in August 1960.

1955–72 SUDAN CIVIL WAR **Conflict between northern Arab Muslim government forces and Anya Nya guerilla army of southern black minority population following January 1956 independence.**

1956 HUNGARIAN UPRISING **Soviet troops withdrew in response to October uprising, but returned and crushed opposition 3–14 ▸**

THE BLUE HELMETS

In June 1948 the United Nations (UN) established a Truce Supervision Organization (UNTSO) to oversee the truce in Palestine. Since then UNTSO has also supervised the 1949 General Armistice and the ceasefire following the 1967 Arab-Israeli War, while the UN has mounted peacekeeping operations around the world.

A UN Emergency Force (UNEF I) was formed in November 1956 to supervise the withdrawal of British, French and Israeli forces from Egypt. UNEF II was set up in October 1973 to supervise the ceasefire after that month's war between Israel and Egypt, and in June 1974 a Disengagement Observer Force (UNDOF) was established to monitor the ceasefire between Israel and Syria.

The Military Observer Group in India and Pakistan (UNMOGIP) was formed in January 1949 to supervise the ceasefire between the two countries in the disputed north Indian states of Jammu and Kashmir. The UN mounted a major operation in the Congo (ONUC), and since March 1964 the Peace keeping Force in Cyprus (UNFICYP) has tried to keep Greek and Turkish forces on the island apart. In recent times, UN forces have been deployed to monitor the Gulf War cease-fire, the Soviet pull-out from Afghanistan, to supervise Namibia's transition to independence, and to keep peace in the former Yuogoslavia.

THE CHINESE REVOLUTION

The success of the communist revolution in China constituted both an inspiration to would-be revolutionaries around the world and a practical model for the organization and execution of their revolutions. By the time the war ended it had already passed through what have become recognized as the first and second phases of classic revolutionary warfare; the way was clear for the final phase.

The Japanese surrender in 1945 left the US-backed Kuomintang forces under Chiang Kai-shek as the only opposition to the Red Army of the Communist Party of China. The Red Army expanded and reorganized, drawing on the support built up over decades of political and military activity, and prepared for the transition from guerilla warfare to full-scale civil war. In July 1946 Mao announced the formation of the People's Liberation Army (PLA), and although Chiang controlled the major towns and cities at this stage, the PLA occupied the countryside between them.

By the summer of 1947 the PLA had expanded to the point where it was gaining the upper hand. During 1948 the Fourth Field Army picked off the cities of Manchuria one by one; by October the Kuomintang was faced by a total of five PLA field armies; and within the next 12 months Chiang's forces were routed.

At the Battle of Xuzhou (Suchow) in November 1948 the best-equipped Kuomintang formations were defeated by combined PLA forces. The remaining pocket of resistance in the north, centred on Beijing (Peking) and Tianjin (Tientsin), was eradicated in January 1949. In April the PLA crossed the Chang Jiang (Yangtze) river in the course of its southward advance. Nanjing (Nanking) and Shanghai were taken. Finally, Chiang and the remnants of his forces fled to Taiwan, leaving Mao to proclaim the People's Republic of China on 1 October 1949.

WAR IN KOREA

Victory in the civil war did not leave the PLA idle. Attempts to pursue Chiang to Taiwan were soon abandoned, but in 1950 seven PLA divisions occupied Tibet, and soon afterwards a force of 300,000 volunteers crossed the Yalu river into Korea.

Previously occupied by Japan, Korea had been divided along the 38th parallel at the end of the war, with Soviet troops occupying the north and US forces in the south. The North Korean president, Kim Il Sung, claimed the whole of the country, but elections in the south produced a government which was friendly to the United States, and by 1949 both Soviet and US troops had been withdrawn. In June 1950, however, the North Korean People's Army (KPA) invaded the south.

Within weeks the KPA had occupied all of South Korea except for a small area round Pusan in the southeast, where the USA had assembled a predominantly American multinational force under the banner of the United Nations (UN).

1956

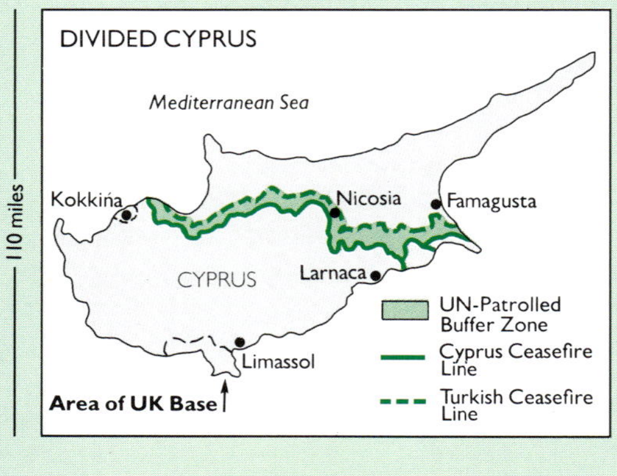

November after Hungary abrogated Warsaw Pact and declared neutrality.

1956 SUEZ INVASION British and French paratroops landed in Suez Canal Zone 5 November after October invasion by Israel; ceasefire announced 7 November followed by Israeli withdrawal concluded March 1957.

1956–9 CUBAN REVOLUTION Guerilla movement started by Fidel Castro in Cuba in November 1956; overthrew government of Fulgencio Batista 1 January 1959.

1958 LEBANESE CIVIL WAR Fighting between Syrian-backed Muslim and Maronite Christian militias from May ended in September after US intervention in July.

1958 NICARAGUAN CIVIL WAR Sandinista guerilla movement founded in 1958 finally succeeded in overthrowing government of Anastasio Somoza in July 1979; Sandinista government subsequently opposed by US-backed contra rebels until defeated by opposition parties in 1990 election.

However, on 25 September the UN commander-in-chief, General Douglas MacArthur, mounted an amphibious landing at Inchon, high up the west coast of South Korea, which combined with a successful breakout from Pusan to drive the remnants of the KPA back into the North and bring the UN forces within striking distance of the Yalu. Then, on 26 November, the Chinese mounted their counter-attack, driving the UN troops back across the 38th parallel as quickly as they had advanced into the North.

The PLA intervention was not a success. It suffered heavy losses before being forced back to the pre-war border by UN counter-attacks in the spring of 1951. MacArthur, too keen to expand the war to involve China itself, was dismissed by US President Truman, and the war settled down into two years of attrition. By mid-1953, with the South Korean army strong enough to defend the country itself and the North's supporters tired of what had become an unwinnable struggle, the two sides were ready for an armistice which came into effect on 27 July.

INDIA AND PAKISTAN

In 1945 India was still a part of the British Empire, but a decades-old independence movement could not be resisted much longer. However, the problem of a society divided between 250 million Hindus and 90 million Muslims was not wholly resolved by partitioning the subcontinent into Hindu India and Muslim East and West Pakistan, and within weeks of the two countries becoming independent on 15 August 1947 they were at war.

The northern state of Kashmir had a Muslim majority population but a Hindu Maharaja who attempted to remain independent of both sides. However, a Muslim uprising in October 1947 forced his hand, and he accepted union with India. The ensuing fighting between the armies of India and Pakistan ended in a UN-negotiated ceasefire on 31 December 1948 with the former in control of the south and Pakistan occupying the northern mountains.

Subsequently India became involved in skirmishes with China over disputed border areas in the far northern Ladakh district and the North-east Frontier Agency (now Arunachal Pradesh), where Indian border posts were overrun in October 1962 before the Chinese called a halt to the fighting in November and withdrew. India's reaction was a concerted drive to expand and modernize its armed forces, with results that would be apparent within 10 years.

India has been troubled by other border insurrections, but Pakistan has remained its main opponent. In 1965 there was renewed conflict in Kashmir and in the Rann of Kutch, on the border between India and West Pakistan, with sporadic clashes erupting into undeclared war in September. A new UN ceasefire was imposed after

MAO'S PRINCIPLES OF WARFARE

Mao Tse-tung defined his principles of revolutionary warfare in a theory of "people's war". In the first phase of Mao's revolution, he established base areas among the peasants.

The second phase was what is now recognized as classic guerilla warfare. Opportunistic attacks were mounted against the government forces, but with no attempt to engage them in battle. Afterwards, the guerillas would melt into the countryside. Only when the guerillas were strong enough would they form conventional armies and begin open warfare.

The main advantage of the insurgent is the ability to avoid combat with superior forces. As the North Vietnamese showed in the 1968 Tet offensive, a premature escalation of guerilla into conventional warfare is likely to be counter-productive; on the other hand, as the Tamil Tigers in Sri Lanka demonstrated, conventional armed forces using conventional tactics can do little against opponents they cannot find.

1961

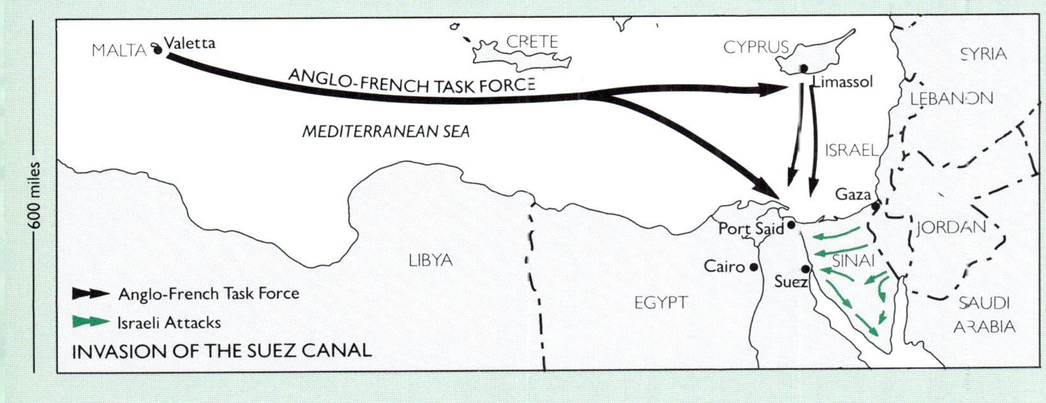

1960–5 CONGO CIVIL WAR Civil unrest, army mutiny and attempted secession by Katanga from former Belgian Congo (now Zaïre) following independence in June 1960 and involving Belgian forces plus foreign mercenaries and the biggest ever UN peacekeeping operation; situation stabilized November 1965 after second coup by army commander Joseph Mobutu.

1961–75 VIETNAM WAR US involvement in South Vietnam expanded from small-scale aid to full-scale campaign involving more ▸

A Mujaheddin guerrilla in Afghanistan poses for cameramen with one of the US Stinger anti-aircraft missiles supplied to the Afghan resistance following the ultimately unsuccessful Soviet invasion of a country which had proved equally resistant to earlier British attempts to pacify its perpetually warring factions.

22 days, but not before the biggest tank battle since the Second World War had taken place in the area around Sialkot.

The major war that had been threatening to break out between India and Pakistan ever since independence came finally in 1971, after East Pakistan had declared itself the independent state of Bangladesh. West Pakistan attempted to suppress the independence movement, and the ensuing civil strife cost hundreds of thousands of lives. Up to 10 million Bengalis took refuge in India, where initial support for guerilla operations soon gave way to preparations for full-scale military intervention with the assistance of the Soviet Union.

On 3 December, Pakistan attempted to forestall the impending Indian invasion of Bangladesh by launching a pre-emptive invasion of Kashmir and the Punjab. The Indian Air Force survived attacks on its airfields, and the next day the Indian invasion in the east began. Within 13 days the Pakistani commander in Bangladesh had surrendered with 85,000 men, while in the west the Indian army halted the Pakistani advance. By 17 December it was all over – Pakistan had lost Bangladesh.

In 1998, the two nations were involved in a tense nuclear stand-off. Following a Pakistani test of a nuclear missile in April, India detonated five nuclear bombs underground in May. Pakistan responded with five underground tests of its own later that same month. Despite US pressure, neither country has signed the Non-Proliferation Treaty or the Comprehensive Test Ban Treaty.

AFGHANISTAN

The Soviet invasion of neighbouring Afghanistan in the December following the September 1979 coup against Nur Muhammad Taraki's government resulted in Pakistan becoming a reluctant host to refugees from the fighting and a major conduit of arms destined for the *mujaheddin* resistance groups.

Although the *mujaheddin* succeeded in forcing the Soviets to increase their originally modest invasion force and to adopt new tactics to counter the threat of US Stinger surface-to-air missiles, they never managed to unite in their opposition to the new government installed in Kabul and its Soviet backers. At the same time, the Soviet forces could not quell the resistance, and after eight years of war the Soviet withdrawal was announced in March 1988. After years of fighting, a group called the Taliban finally took control of the country in 1996, following their capture of Kabul. They were ousted from power by a US-led coalition following 11 September 2001.

SRI LANKA

India's direct involvement in Sri Lanka began in July 1987, when an Indian Peacekeeping Force (IPKF) was sent to the island in response to a request from

1961

than 500,000 troops by 1969; subsequent reduction of direct involvement and ultimate US withdrawal in 1973 followed by North Vietnamese victory in April 1975.

1961– ERITREA WAR Ethiopian annexation of Eritrea in 1961 opposed by Eritrean (later Eritrean People's) Liberation Front and Tigrean People's Liberation Front.

1962 SINO–INDIAN CONFLICT Chinese offensives across the Himalayan borders of India's Ladakh district and Northeast Frontier Agency (NEFA) terrritory

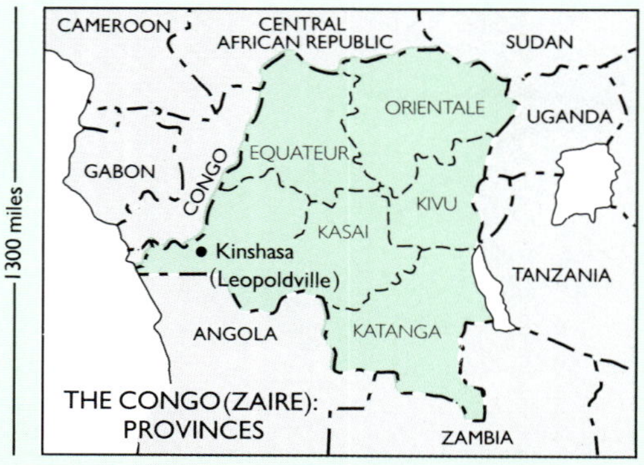

(Arunachel Pradesh) in October 1962 followed by November ceasefire and subsequent partial Chinese withdrawal.

1962–6 BORNEO CONFRONTATION December 1962 rebellion by Kalimantan Liberation Army in Brunei followed by Indonesian incursions into British colonies (Malaysian states from September 1963) of Sarawak, Sabah and Brunei from Kalimantan on Borneo; opposed by British forces; peace agreed August 1966.

1962– INDONESIAN CIVIL WAR Continuing

President Jayawardene, whose army, largely drawn from the Sinhalese Buddhist majority population, had found it impossible to contain the Hindu Tamil separatists' guerrilla campaign for a separate Tamil state in the north-east of the island. Since the former British colony of Ceylon had become independent in 1948, there had been repeated outbreaks of inter-communal violence, and in the event the arrival of Indian troops only precipitated more.

While the Indians tried with as little success as the Sri Lankans themselves to disarm the Tamil Tiger guerillas, the Sri Lankan government found itself facing a new insurgency in the south, where the left-wing Sinhalese JVP organization began a violent campaign against the Indian presence. In the end, the Indians withdrew their last troops from the island in March 1990. The withdrawal has however failed to halt further outbreaks of violence on the island.

Tamil separatist. The continuing civil war in Sri Lanka, where even India's armed forces proved incapable of ending the Tamil Tigers' armed insurrection against the island's government, revolves around the Tamil population's demands for autonomy. By mid-1990 the war was in full swing again after prolonged negotiations had failed to resolve the dispute.

SOUTH-EAST ASIA

Most of the pre-war British, French, Dutch and US colonies in south-east Asia had been overrun by the Japanese during the Second World War, and the defeat of the colonial powers had given new hope for the budding independence movements in the region. In the wake of the Japanese surrender Vietnam, Laos, Cambodia and Indonesia were declared independent by nationalist leaders, and by 1949 the Dutch had been forced by guerilla resistance and US and United Nations pressure to accept the inevitability of independence for Indonesia, which duly became a federal republic in the following year. Its subsequent history has included local uprisings and a confrontation with the British over northern Borneo in the early 1960s, while its annexation of West Irian (now Irian Jaya) in 1963 and of the former Portuguese colony of East Timor in 1976 have provided further opportunites for conflict with separatist insurgents.

In Vietnam the communist Viet Minh, under the political leadership of Ho Chi Minh and his military commander, Vo Nguyen Giap, were ready to resist the return of the French. The reoccupation of Hanoi in 1946 was to prove a misleading prologue to an eight-year war in which a classic guerilla campaign under Giap's leadership saw the Viet Minh first consolidate their support in rural areas and then, with the support of the newly victorious Chinese communists from 1949, prepare to go on the offensive. Giap's first attempt to do so, in 1951, ended disastrously with three major defeats, but in 1953 the French decided to establish a base in the northern highlands at Dien Bien Phu. The result was a five-month siege which ended in the surrender of 10,000 French troops in May 1954 and an agreement by France to leave Vietnam, Cambodia and Laos, though Vietnam itself was to be divided, with the Republic of Vietnam in the south run by a non-communist government.

1964

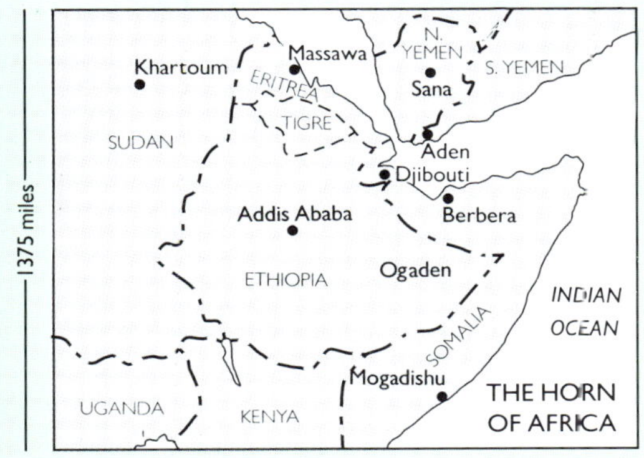

insurgency in Java and, since 1963 uprising, in West Irian (formerly Netherlands New Guinea).

1962–9 NORTH YEMEN CIVIL WAR Fighting between Egyptian-backed Republican Army and Royalist forces before Yemen Arab Republic established 1970.

1963–4 CYPRUS CIVIL WAR Intercommunal fighting between Greeks and Turks erupted in December 1963; deployment of UN peace keeping force in April 1964 but outbreaks of violence continued.

1964–7 SOUTH YEMEN WAR OF INDEPENDENCE Guerilla war in the British colony of Aden and South Arabian Federation develops into civil war between rival groups; British withdrawal in November 1967 followed by formation of People's Republic (Democratic Republic 1970) of Yemen.

1964–75 MOZAMBIQUE WAR OF INDEPENDENCE Frelimo guerrilla war against Portuguese colonial authorities; independence attained July 1975.

1964–80 ZIMBABWE CIVIL WAR British colony ▸

The door gunner of a US army helicopter fires his M60 machine gun at an unseen target on the ground in Vietnam. The search-and-destroy tactics developed by the Americans in Vietnam, with troops landed by helicopter at remote locations for sweeps through the countryside in search of their elusive opponents, proved ineffective despite the massive scale of the US military involvement in the country. US combat operations had ended by January 1973, and South Vietnam finally fell in April 1975.

THE VIETNAM WAR

Ho Chi Minh and the North Vietnamese did not rest on their laurels after ousting the French, and their infiltration of the South, along with continuing Communist insurgency in Laos and Cambodia, saw US support for South Vietnam's new president, Ngo Dinh Diem, grow steadily more military in nature. In the late 1950s it progressed from training the new republic's army to deploying military advisers in the country, and by 1962 the arrangement had been formalized with the establishment of the Military Assistance Command. Within three years the number of US advisers had grown to 27,000, and in March 1965 President Johnson's decision to commit combat troops to the war was symbolized by the landing of US Marines on the beaches at Da Nang.

The ensuing 10 years of war saw the US forces' frustration grow in line with their size. Operating largely by helicopter from fortified bases, but also mounting massive bombing raids involving a whole panoply of new aircraft and weapons, the Americans rarely found targets to match their massive firepower. An exception was provided by the all-out Tet (New Year) offensive mounted by the North Vietnamese Army in February 1968, but although this proved an expensive failure for the North, its unprecedented scale also served to undermine US claims that it was making progress in the war.

By the beginning of 1969 there were more than half a million US military

1964

of Southern Rhodesia declared independent as Rhodesia 1965; Rhodesian security forces opposed by guerilla armies of Zimbabwe African National Union (ZANU) and African People's Union (ZAPU) until 1980 ceasefire and independence under ZANU leader Robert Mugabe.

1965 DOMINICA CIVIL WAR Civil war following military coup to restore ousted President Juan Bosch ended by US military intervention in May 1965.

1965 INDIA–PAKISTAN WAR Renewed fighting in Kashmir and in the Rann of Kutch 1–23 September ended by UN intervention.

1965–75 DHOFAR REBELLION South Yemen-backed Dhofar Liberation Front opposed by Sultan of Oman's armed forces with British and (after 1970 coup in Oman) Iranian assistance; large-scale Iranian operations from December 1973 and war declared over in December 1975.

1966–89 NAMIBIA WAR OF INDEPENDENCE People's Liberation Army of Namibia (PLAN), military wing of South West African People's Organization (SWAPO), opposed by South African forces from July 1966 until Namibian independence in April 1989.

1967–70 NIGERIAN CIVIL WAR Attempted secession of Biafra in May 1967 defeated by federal government of General Gowon.

1967 ARAB – ISRAELI WAR In six days from 3 June Israel responded to Arab states' aggression by destroying the Egyptian air force on the ground and occupying Sinai; occupying Jordanian territory on the west

Casualties of Tet. Wounded US Marines are treated by a medic in the provincial capital of Hue during the North Vietnamese Tet offensive of February 1968. Although the operation was a military failure for the North, the size of the conventional forces it was able to unleash surprised its opponents and undermined US commander General Westmoreland's claims that the war was being won. The following year saw Richard Nixon replace Lyndon Johnson as US president and the start of the process of Vietnamization in pursuit of "peace with honour".

personnel in the country, but public support for the war had begun to erode: President Johnson had declined to stand for re-election, and his successor, Richard Nixon, had committed himself to "Vietnamization" of the war and "peace with honour" for the United States. In effect, this meant a steady reduction in the number of US personnel in South Vietnam, the transfer of military hardware to the South Vietnamese Army of the Republic of Vietnam (ARVN) and an increased reliance on bombing, first to extend the war into Cambodia and Laos and later to repel a new North Vietnamese offensive in the spring of 1972.

The 1972 US bombing campaigns, Linebacker I and II, were ended in December, and in January 1973 peace talks in Paris finally produced a ceasefire agreement. By this stage the US army had ceased combat operations in the country and, during the next two years, the North Vietnamese army increased the number of troops deployed in the south in support of the Viet Cong guerillas. In March 1975 the North Vietnamese began a new full-scale offensive, and on 30 April Saigon fell, finally ending a war that had lasted 20 years.

APOCALYPSE AND AFTER: VIETNAM AND CAMBODIA

The Communist victory in Vietnam was paralleled by the Khmer Rouge takeover in Cambodia in April and the accession to power of the Pathet Lao in Laos later in the year. Pol Pot's regime in Cambodia renamed the country Kampuchea, emptied the

1969

bank of the River Jordan; and defeating Syrian forces in the Golan heights.

1968 SOVIET INVASION OF CZECHOSLOVAKIA Occupation by Soviet troops on 21 August 1968 to reverse liberalization instituted by Czech President Alexander Dubcek's April "Prague spring" reforms.

1968–88 CHAD CIVIL WAR Government of former French Equatorial Africa opposed by Frolinat guerillas; subsequent intervention by France and Libya before 1987 ceasefire left Libya with Aouzou Strip and

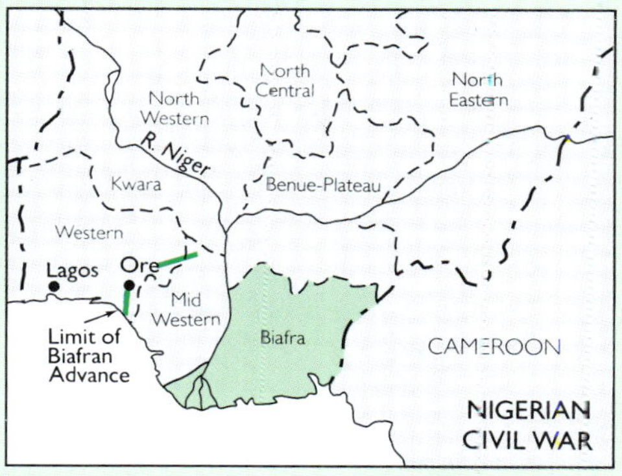

French forces deployed in the south.

1969 HONDURAS–EL SALVADOR WAR Invasion of Honduras by El Salvadorean troops on 14 July after riots following a World Cup football match; ended by withdrawal of invading forces on 30 July.

1969– NORTHERN IRELAND British troops deployed in UK province of Northern Ireland to counter Irish Republic Army (IRA) terrorism since first deployment in Londonderry and Belfast August 1969.

1969– PHILIPPINES INSURGENCY Marcos and ▶

An Israeli tank commander surveys the desert landscape during the Israeli armed forces' 1956 campaign in the Sinai, where Moshe Dayan's typically swift and tactically brilliant conquest of Egyptian territory east of the Suez canal paved the way for the abortive joint invasion by Britain and France of the Suez Canal Zone.

capital of its inhabitants and set up a "re-education" programme that involved wholesale slaughter of the population. The resulting flood of refugees into Vietnam, coupled with Khmer incursions across the border, provoked Vietnam to invade Kampuchea in 1978, driving Pol Pot back into the jungle and installing a new government in Phnom Penh.

Under the administration of the UN in 1993, Cambodia held elections, which led to the establishment of a new constitution and the reinstatement of Norodom Sihanouk as king. The Khmer Rouge refused to take part in the elections, rejected peace talks and were finally outlawed by the Cambodian government in 1994. Following Pol Pot's death in 1998, the UN pulled out of trials of other top-level Khmer Rouge leaders because of doubts that the tribunals were independent. Today, Cambodia is ruled by Hun Sen's Cambodian People's Party.

ISRAEL AND ITS NEIGHBOURS

Wars in the Middle East between Israel and its neighbours have not matched events further east in terms of the size and numbers of countries involved, the numbers of casualties or the sheer scale of conflict. However, the Israeli armed forces have established a reputation as one of the most effective military organizations ever seen with their repeated victories over the armies of much bigger Arab states across the country's borders.

Israel's Declaration of Independence in 1948 effectively constituted a declaration of war, and the new state's armed forces were confronted immediately by the armies of Transjordan, Syria, Lebanon, Iraq and Egypt. United Nations intervention helped secure a series of temporary truces which reinforced Israeli military success and by July 1949 all five Arab countries had conceded defeat.

However, none had conceded Israel's right to exist, and the region has seen a series of subsequent wars. In 1956 Israel joined Britain and France in invading Egypt, demolishing Egyptian resistance in the Sinai before withdrawing from the conquered territory. In June 1967 the Israeli armed forces defeated those of Egypt, Syria and Jordan in the space of six days, and in 1973 they took barely three times as long to repel attacks by Egypt and Syria.

Subsequently Israel became involved in the Lebanon, where Palestinian guerillas had begun operations after being expelled from Jordan in 1970 and where conflict between the Christian and Muslim populations erupted into civil war in 1975.

Israel invaded southern Lebanon in 1978 and mounted a full-scale invasion in 1982, forcing the Palestinian Liberation Organization to quit the country but finding itself entangled as a result. Israel finally withdrew its forces in 1985, though it has

1969

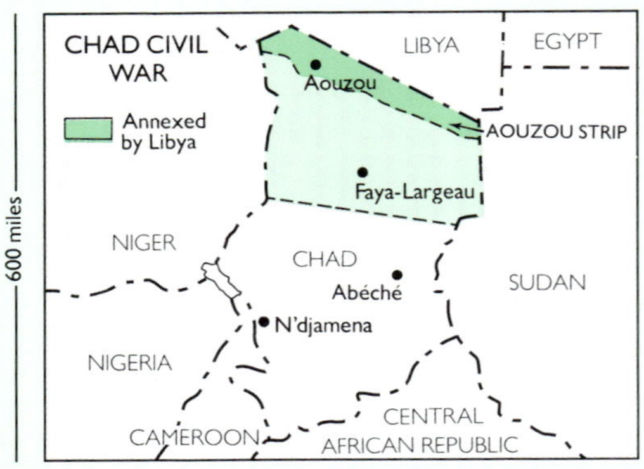

subsequent governments opposed by communist New People's Army in most provinces, Muslim separatist Moro National Liberation Front on Mindanao.

1970 JORDANIAN CIVIL WAR Clashes between Palestinian guerillas and Jordanian government forces in February and June, followed by large-scale fighting in September; ceasefire 24 September.

1971–1993 CAMBODIA CIVIL WAR North Vietnamese-backed Khmer Rouge victory in 1975 followed by genocide and invasion by Vietnamese forces in 1978; Vietnamese withdrawal (1989) left Cambodian government facing continued guerilla operations by Khmer Rouge and other factions; peace and elections in 1993.

1971 SRI LANKA REVOLT April 1971 rebellion by People's Liberation Front (JVP) suppressed by early May.

1971 INDIA–PAKISTAN WAR India defeated West Pakistan in Bangladesh (formerly East Pakistan) and on India's western borders, 3–17 December.

continued occasional military intervention, and since December 1987 it has had to cope with civil insurrection in the territories on the West Bank of the Jordan and the Gaza Strip. The peace process established in the 1990s has stalled in recent years.

One remarkable feature of Iran's military effort during the eight-year Gulf War precipitated by Iraq's September 1980 invasion was the creation of a miniature battlefield near Tehran, where demonstrations of the Iranian revolutionary armed forces' achievements were staged for the benefit of non-participants.

IRAN-IRAQ WAR

In contrast to the short-lived Arab-Israeli wars, the war that began in September 1980 when President Saddam Hussein of Iraq began an invasion of the new Islamic republic of Iran was to drag on for nearly eight years. By the time it ended in July 1988 it had cost a million lives and an estimated thousand billion dollars.

Militarily inconclusive, the war involved some worrying new developments. It fostered a growth in new sources of modern weapons, as the arms industries of developing countries helped to fulfil the appetite for guns, artillery rockets and ammunition that the traditional suppliers of munitions officially declined to meet. It also saw the use of chemical weapons and the development of capabilities for the manufacture of ballistic missiles in both countries, as each sought means to strike at the other's cities, and highlighted the spread of such missiles to large areas of the Third World. In addition, attacks on third-party oil tankers drew Western naval forces into the Persian Gulf, and the Iranian threat led Saudi Arabia to acquire intermediate-range ballistic missiles from China.

THE END OF EMPIRE IN AFRICA

In 1945 much of Africa was administered by the old colonial powers of Europe. The ensuing decades have seen their administrations replaced by independent national governments, frequently after wars of independence and seldom without subsequent conflicts ranging from low-level insurgency to full-blown civil war.

Probably the biggest conflict on the continent in recent years was the war fought in Congo, which raged between 1998 and 2002. Dubbed by some as "Africa's World War", the conflict involved the armies of six nations, split the vast country into rebel- and government-held regions, and killed an estimated two-and-a-half-million people, largely through disease and starvation. Rwanda and Uganda joined Congolese rebels in their fight against Congo's leader, Laurent Kabila, because they accused him of backing groups, particularly the Hutu militia, which threatened their security. In response to this, the surrounding countries of Zimbabwe, Namibia and Angola joined forces with Kabila. A peace treaty was signed in 2002, following a pledge by Congo to disarm and arrest Rwandan Hutu militia in return for the withdrawal of Rwandan troops. The following year agreement was reached between the warring factions within Congo to end hostilities. Under the agreement, Joseph Kabila (Laurent's son) will remain President until 2005-2006, after which Congo will hold democratic elections.

Continued on page 246

1975

1971 BANGLADESH GUERILLA WAR New government's attempt to evict tribal peoples from Chiltagong hills resisted by Buddhist Jana Sanghati Samity and Chakma Shanti Bahini movements.

1973 ARAB–ISRAELI WAR Egyptian and Syrian attacks launched 6 October succeeded initially but were repelled; by 24 October ceasefire Israel had occupied additional territory; Sinai ultimately returned to Egypt by April 1982.

1974 TURKISH INVASION OF CYPRUS Coup by (Greek) National Guard on 15 July followed by landing of Turkish troops on 20 July; 16 August ceasefire left eastern third of island in Turkish hands.

1975–1990 LEBANESE CIVIL WAR Renewed fighting in April 1975 between Christian and Muslim factions ended October 1976 by Syrian invasion, but sporadic fighting continued involving Druze and Shi'ite Muslim militias, Christian militias and Syrian, Lebanese and Israeli armed forces. March 1978 Israeli invasion of southern Lebanon ▸

PRECISION GUIDANCE

(Above) Threat warning and target information are vital if guided weapons are to be used effectively. The E-3 airborne warning and command system (AWACS) aircraft operated by the US Air Force and several of its allies can monitor a large volume of sky and transmit target coordinates to friendly forces.

THE MOST DRAMATIC advance in military technology of the last half-century has been the application of precision guidance techniques to virtually every class of weapon. The earliest form of missile guidance to be used operationally, in the shape of the German Fritz X and Hs 293 air-to-surface missiles of 1943, was command guidance, which uses a wire or radio link to transmit the operator's steering commands to the missile.

Early manual command-guided missiles were steered by the operator using a joystick, but the process is automated in modern semi-automatic systems such as the US TOW wire-guided anti-tank missile and Patriot long-range SAM. However, in both cases the system must track both target and missile – visually in the case of TOW or by means of radar in the case of Patriot's aircraft and missile targets – in order to generate the appropriate steering commands. Many missiles dispense with this complication by providing the missile itself with a means of tracking and homing on the target.

Homing guidance relies on the ability of a seeker carried by the missile to detect radiation emitted by or reflected from its target. It is classified as active, semiactive or passive, according to whether the missile generates the radiation itself, detects the reflections of a signal from another source, or homes on the target's own emissions.

To guide the missile effectively, the seeker needs to be able to distinguish the target from background radiation, so aircraft against the neutral background of the sky are a principal target for radar-homing missiles. Active radar guidance is used by the US Phoenix long-range AAM and advanced medium-range AMRAAM, both of which carry their own radar transmitters to illuminate the target. Other medium-range AAMs, such as the US Sparrow and its British Skyflash and Italian Aspide derivatives, rely on the launch aircraft's radar to provide the target illumination.

(Above) The US Army's Apache uses a sophisticated nose-mounted sensor system to detect and track targets for the Hellfire laser-guided anti-tank missiles mounted on its wings.

Some Soviet missiles were reported to have seekers capable of homing on hostile aircraft radar emissions, but the main Western application of passive radar homing is in weapons like the US Harm and British Alarm, which are designed to locate and attack hostile ground-based radar transmitters.

Aircraft are also good targets for passive infra-red homing missiles, which seek out the heat radiated by engine exhausts or hot areas of the airframe. Both short-range AAMs such as Sidewinder and low-level SAMs such as Stinger use infra-red seekers to guide them to their targets. Laser homing, using the coherent light beams emitted by lasers, is used to illuminate targets for many types of guided weapon, from the Copperhead artillery round to the Hellfire anti-tank missile that arms the US Army's AH-64 Apache helicopter.

Long-range weapons such as cruise and intercontinental ballistic missiles are guided by navigational rather than homing systems. The most common is inertial navigation, which uses accelerometers and gyros to measure the rate and direction of the vehicle's acceleration and calculate its range and bearing from the launch point.

(Above and left) The US Copperhead guided projectile is fired from a conventional 155mm howitzer, shown left. Like the Paveway laser-guided bomb, the Copperhead is unpowered but can be steered in the terminal stages of its flight, using its laser seeker and control system, to hit a designated target (above).

(Below) The eight stages of an attack on a submarine by an air-dropped Sting Ray torpedo. Once under water, the torpedo is on its own.

(Right) Ballistic missile submarines need extremely precise navigation systems to enable them to target their weapons accurately.

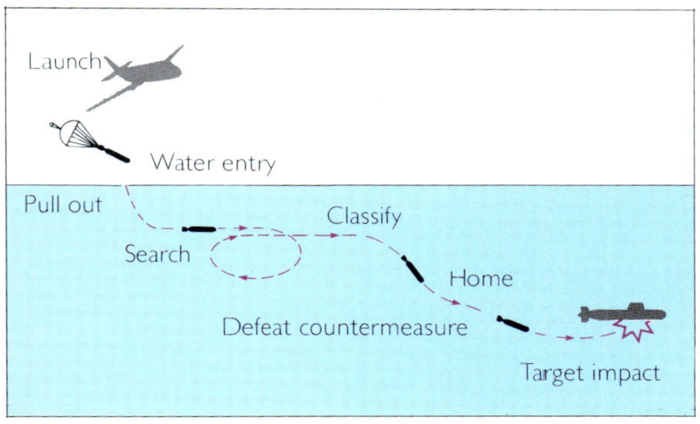

(Left) This sequence shows the terminal stages of a submarine-launched Tomahawk cruise missile trial. At the end of a 400-mile flight, inertial guidance plus a terrain contour matching system enable it to hit the target building.

Related to the war in Congo, the slaughter of around 800,000 people belonging to the Tutsi tribe in 1994 will go down as one of the bloodiest epsisodes in African history. Carried out by soldiers, policemen and ordinary members of the public, the Hutu population's 100-day genocide was sparked by the death of Hutu President Juvenal Habyarimama, whose plane was shot down over Kigali airport on 6 April 1994, but had its roots in 80 years of resentment and inequality between the two tribes.

CONFLICT IN LATIN AMERICA

The Central American states of Guatemala, Honduras, El Salvador, Nicaragua, Costa Rica and Panama appear to exist in a perpetual condition of actual or incipient insurgency. The endemic lack of stability in the region was highlighted by the 1969 war that erupted between Honduras and El Salvador, ostensibly over the riots that accompanied a World Cup football match between the two countries in San Salvador but actually reflecting Hondurans' resentment at the numbers of Salvadorean immigrants in their country. In the eighties and early nineties general economic inequality, frequently sustained by military rule and the widespread use of terror as an instrument of government, ensured no shortage of recruits to the various guerilla movements, and counter-insurgency campaigns against them had liitle effect.

Further south, the trade in cocaine grown in Bolivia and Peru and processed in Colombia for shipment to the USA and Europe was coming to be seen at the start of the 1990s as a potential military problem. Sendero Luminoso guerillas were active throughout Peru and particularly in the coca-growing area of the Upper Huallaga Valley, where their protection for the coca-growers and -shippers was causing concern both locally and in Washington that alliances between the enormously wealthy cocaine cartels and guerillas with long experience of jungle warfare could add a new dimension to the insurgents' activities.

The military coups that have been a feature of South America's modern history have usually involved more violence against their own inhabitants than external aggression, though the military government that came to power in Argentina in 1976 managed to become involved in a war with Britain over the sovereignty of the Falkland (or Malvinas) islands in the South Atlantic. Ultimately the task force despatched by Britain was able to recapture the islands from the Argentine forces that occupied them in April 1982.

THE HIGH-TECH BATTLEFIELD

In the immediate post-war years atomic weapons were the main area of military research and development. But there were other advances that would increase the range, power and effectiveness of conventional weapons. In the course of the

1975

followed by withdrawal of troops in June after UN intervention.

1975–1990 ANGOLAN CIVIL WAR Since Angola's independence from Portugal in 1975 UNITA, backed by South Africa and the US, fought the Soviet-backed MPLA government and its Cuban troops in a civil war that started in 1960 as a war of independence; a peace deal was agreed in 1990.

1975–1999 EAST TIMOR RESISTANCE WAR Opposition to November 1975 Indonesian annexation of former Portuguese colony by Fretilin independence movement guerillas. UN administration took over in 1999; East Timor became fully independent in 2002.

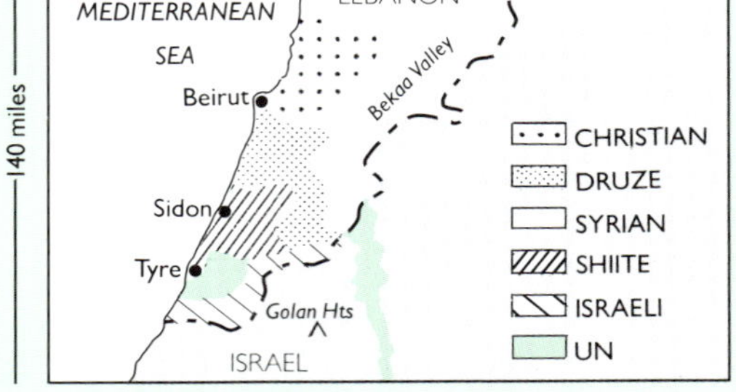

1975–1991 MOROCCO-POLISARIO WAR February 1976 declaration by Algerian-backed Popular Front for the Liberation of Saguia al-Jamra and Rio del Oro (Polisario) of independent Sahrawi Arab Democratic Republic in Western Sahara opposed by Morocco and Mauritania; Morocco's subsequent attempts to occupy the former Spanish colony, including construction of

subsequent decades tanks, warships, submarines and aircraft have all exploited new methods of propulsion, taken on board new classes of weapons, and been equipped with new types of sensors plus the computers needed to control them.

The result is that aircraft now routinely achieve supersonic speeds, submarines remain submerged for weeks on end, many surface warships have been relieved of the need for frequent refuelling, and tanks have achieved new levels of speed and agility. Missiles have affected every area of warfare. And radar, infra-red and laser technology have provided unprecedented levels of accuracy in the detection and tracking of targets and the aiming and guidance of the weapons used to engage them.

JETS AND ROCKETS

The first jet aircraft were in service before the Second World War ended. They were already faster than their piston-engined counterparts, but the full potential of jet propulsion is even now a long way from realization. The US F-86 Sabres and Soviet MiG-15s that fought the first jet combats over Korea were powered by heavy, thirsty engines that were capable of better than 600mph. By the end of the 1950s the addition of afterburners, which mix fuel with the jet exhaust and reignite it to boost the thrust, had enabled fighters to exceed twice the speed of sound, though only for brief periods because of the amount of fuel consumed.

Since then, engines have become steadily lighter, more powerful and more fuel-efficient. Vectored thrust has enabled aircraft to take off in a matter of a few tens of yards and land vertically. And techniques for deflecting the exhaust of a standard fighter have added new levels of manoeuvrability.

Of course, it was rocket propulsion that propelled the first manned aircraft through the sound barrier. But the main application of rocket technology has been in missiles, which are now deployed in all sizes from lightweight shoulder-launched anti-aircraft and anti-tank weapons to multi-stage ballistic missiles.

THE MISSILE THREAT

There have been times in the last 50 years when the lethality of missiles has seemed to be about to make whole classes of weapons redundant. Instead, the result has been new forms of anti-missile defence and, in turn, new methods of increasing missiles' effectiveness.

In 1967 the Israeli destroyer *Eilat* was sunk by a Soviet Styx missile fired by an Egyptian gunboat. The initial conclusion drawn from this encounter was that warships of any size were suddenly hopelessly vulnerable to attacks by the smallest missile-armed vessel. However, just as the analogous threat to the torpedo at the end of the nineteenth century was contained by appropriate defensive measures, so new

Joint training: with the exception of the December 1989 invasion of Panama, the US has largely avoided direct military involvement in Latin America, but various forms of military assistance are used to help combat insurgency and, more recently, the drugs trade. Here soldiers from the US and Ecuadorean armed forces take part in a combined exercise.

1979

1,000-mile Hassan Wall, frustrated by Polisario forces from Mauritania; a ceasefire and peace process was agreed in 1991.

1977–1992 MOZAMBIQUE CIVIL WAR Renamo resistance movement formed 1977 by Rhodesian intelligence officer to oppose Frelimo government; backed subsequently by South Africa, Portugal, Morocco, Saudi Arabia, Zaïre and US religious fundamentalists, Renamo's activities included massacring thousands of peasants and making hundred of thousands of people homeless; peace was agreed between the two sides in 1992.

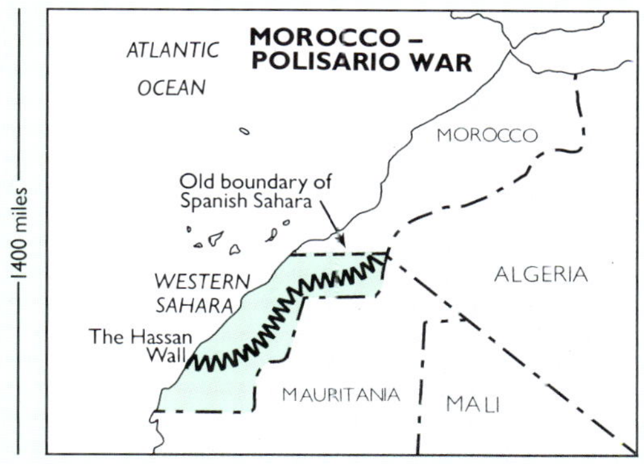

1977–88 OGADEN WAR Guerilla campaign by Western Somalia Liberation Front (WSLF) against Ethiopian army in Ogaden region of south-eastern Ethiopia, followed by open war involving Somali government forces from 1977 until negotiated settlement May 1988.

1979 CHINA–VIETNAM WAR Chinese invasion of Vietnam on 17 February 1979 in retaliation for deployment of Vietnamese troops ▶

Tomahawk launch: the 60 years since the end of the Second World War have seen the appearance of whole new classes of weapons. The Tomahawk sea-launched cruise missile shown here being launched from a US warship has a range of 1,500 miles against land targets or 300 miles against ships, and can carry nuclear as well as conventional warheads.

warships were equipped with rapid-fire guns and anti-missile missiles capable of reducing the threat to acceptable levels. The more recent sinking of HMS *Sheffield* in the South Atlantic in 1982 and the damage inflicted on USS *Stark* in the Persian Gulf in 1987 were made possible because the sensors that should have detected the approach of the Exocets were not functioning at the time.

Similarly, the early stages of the 1973 Arab-Israeli war saw many Israeli tanks and aircraft destroyed by the Egyptians' Soviet shoulder-launched missiles. Once again, some analysts were quick to conclude that the missile threat had made armour and air power too vulnerable to survive on the battlefield. Yet again, however, countermeasures in the shape of new forms of tank armour and air-launched infra-red decoys have sent the missile designers back to the drawing boards to work on multiple or top-attack warheads for anti-tank missiles and more discriminating surface-to-air missile-seekers able to distinguish real jet exhausts from decoys.

A similar cycle may be underway in the field of air-to-air combat. The first missiles designed to be launched by aircraft against other aircraft were unguided, so they were either fired in salvoes to increase the probability of a hit or carried nuclear warheads to increase their lethal range. More promising was the addition of infra-red homing warheads designed to locate and home in on hot jet exhausts. The first such heat-seeking missile was the US Sidewinder, advanced versions of which are still in service along with similar weapons produced in many other countries.

Infra-red homing missiles are limited to relatively short ranges, and radar seekers, such as those used on the US Sparrow and the more recent AMRAAM, promised to be able to engage hostile aircraft at much longer ranges. However, there are problems in distinguishing friendly aircraft from hostile ones at ranges beyond the visual, and Sparrow has achieved only limited success in combat. A new complication is the appearance of anti-radar missiles designed to home in on the radar signals of either the fighter or the missile itself, a development which some analysts have suggested could make current radar-guided air-to-air missiles obsolete at a stroke.

LAND COMBAT

The perceived threat to the tank in the early 1970s was very serious because the tank was and remains the principal battlefield weapon. Its combination of mobility and firepower makes it the most powerful and versatile weapon in the modern army and consequently the lynchpin of both offensive and defensive tactical operations.

The armies with the most sophisticated arsenals are Russia and members of NATO, particularly the United States. Designed primarily to fight and win a conventional war in central Europe, they were developed in accordance with contrasting strategies and operational concepts, though their weapons show many similarities in function

1979

in Cambodia followed by fierce fighting involving heavy casualties and destruction of several Vietnamese cities; Chinese withdrawal completed on 17 March.

1979–1996 AFGHANISTAN WAR Soviet invasion in December 1979 intended to quell popular Muslim uprising followed by unsuccessful 10-year fight against Mujaheddin guerillas; Soviet withdrawal complete February 1989, followed by war between government forces and Mujaheddin groups and then between the resistance groups themselves; war ended with victory for the Taliban.

1980–8 GULF WAR Iraqi attack on Iran in September 1980 followed by a war of attrition involving attacks on neutral shipping, ballistic missile bombardments of cities and the use by Iraq of chemical weapons as well as conventional warfare; ceasefire agreed August 1988.

1980–1992 EL SALVADOR CIVIL WAR Insurgency by Farabundo Marti National Liberation Front (FMLN) guerillas opposed by armed forces and death squads.

Tactical airpower: an early firepower demonstration by a British Royal Air Force Harrier STOVL (short take-off, vertical landing) close-support aircraft. Rotatable nozzles on the fuselage sides provide the vectored thrust that gave the early Harriers and the developed versions now in use by the US Marine Corps as well as the RAF the ability to take off from short forward airstrips and land vertically in small clearings. Such tactical flexibility is just one example of the enhanced capabilities provided by modern technology.

and capabilities. Soviet determination to avoid a repetition of the enormous casualties suffered during the Second World War gave rise to a strategy of offensive operations involving massive firepower and rapid manoeuvre. Soviet exercises showed that the basic tactics involved heavy concentrations of self-propelled artillery used to soften up the defences before rapid thrusts by tanks and mechanized infantry formations exploit any openings created, driving forward to seize strategic objectives such as cities so that tactical nuclear weapons used against them would end up destroying the very things they were supposed to protect.

NATO, with its ability to withdraw and counter-attack in the face of an offensive constrained by the need to avoid the territory it was designed to defend becoming a battlefield, tried to counter Soviet numerical superiority by the application of advanced technology. In the days when a Soviet offensive was a possibility, NATO's defences involved the use of everything from long-range artillery to short-range missiles and rockets, with tanks concentrating on their opposing counterparts supported by infantry and tactical air assets.

Air power has become an integral part of land warfare. The rapid deployment of troops and equipment is effected by helicopters, while armed gunships have been developed to engage armoured targets. Tactical fighter-bombers carrying out close air-support and battlefield-interdiction missions are part of any commander's ideal

1983

1980 PERUVIAN INSURGENCY Guerilla war against government forces by Sendero Luminoso (Shining Path) movement.

1982 FALKLANDS CONFLICT Occupation of Falkland islands by Argentine forces in April 1982 ended by British invasion and Argentine surrender on 14 June.

1982 ISRAELI INVASION OF LEBANON Full-scale Israeli invasion in June 1982; Syrian and Palestine Liberation Organization (PLO) forces defeated and PLO made to evacuate Beirut before 1985 withdrawal of Israeli forces to south Lebanon buffer zone.

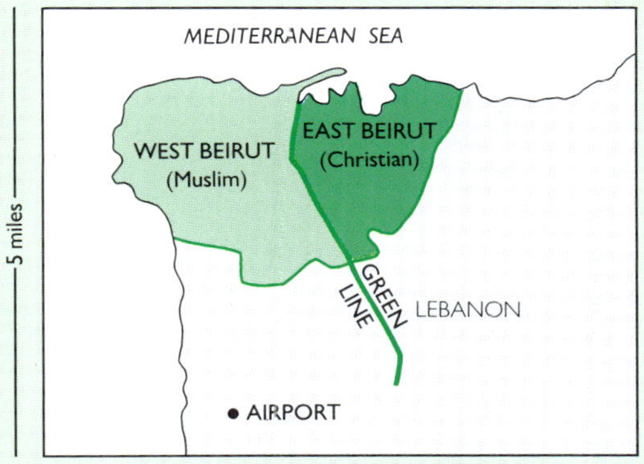

1983 US INVASION OF GRENADA US forces invade 25 October 1983 after assassination of Grenadan leader Maurice Bishop.

1983– SRI LANKA CIVIL WAR Rebellion by ethnic separatist Tamil groups against Sinhalese government leads to army reprisals and emergence of Liberation Tigers of Tamil Eelam (Tamil Tigers) as dominant resistance group; July 1987 Indo-Lankan Peace Accord and deployment of Indian ▸

CONFLICTS IN THE MIDDLE EAST

Since the beginning of the 1990s, the Middle East has been the arena for several significant conflicts.

The six-week war that ended Iraq's occupation of Kuwait in January-February 1991 was most notable for demonstrating the effectiveness of the latest generation of military technology, as Saddam Hussein's ostensibly powerful armed forces were overwhelmed by a sustained campaign of aerial bombardment and an overwhelming armoured ground offensive.

The war in Afghanistan in late 2001 was precipitated by the September 11th attacks in New York and Washington of the same year. With Afghanistan's Taliban régime protecting the Al-Qaeda terrorist group responsible for the attacks, it was always likely to be a target of the West. On October 7th, 2001, British and American forces launched their aerial bombing campaign. With the help of Afghan forces opposed to the Taliban, the coalition was able to drive Mullah Omar's regime from all their strongholds by early December. However, despite the continued presence of special forces in the area, neither Mullah Omar nor Osama Bin Laden have been traced.

Arguably the most contentious and controversial conflict since Vietnam, the Iraq War of 2003 pitted the military might of the US-led coalition against the remnants of Saddam Hussein's armed forces. Justified largely on the basis of Saddam's ownership of weapons of mass destruction (WMDs) and his alleged links to terrorist organizations, the war was declared all but over by George W. Bush just 34 days after the start of hostilities. However, with no WMDs found and with growing insurgency and terrorist attacks within Iraq, it is fair to say that the coalition is finding it harder to win the peace.

tactical repertoire, airborne sensors provide much of the information on which decisions must be based, and air-combat fighters to provide battlefield air superiority are essential if friendly air-power is to be exploited effectively and hostile interference from the air avoided.

NAVAL WARFARE

Like other examples of modern military technology, warships have become vastly more capable since 1945. Only the US navy has managed to sustain the enormous expense of nuclear-powered aircraft carriers operating a comprehensive range of fighters, bombers and anti-submarine aircraft. But the Harrier, Sea Harrier and Harrier II STOVL (short takeoff/vertical landing) aircraft have enabled several smaller navies to operate compact but effective carriers, and both the Soviet and French navies were developing new large aircraft carriers at the beginning of the 1990s.

At the same time, even small frigates are capable of operating anti-submarine helicopters while mounting a medium-calibre gun along with varying mixes of anti-ship, anti-aircraft and anti-submarine missiles and the means of detecting and tracking targets for them. Electronic counter-measures, ranging from jammers able to interfere with the seekers of hostile missiles to launchers for radar decoys are a vital part of their armoury. And lightweight sonar systems provide the means for guarding against the ever-present menace of the submarine.

In fact, underwater warfare is an area where there is little scope for relaxation. Because ballistic missile-armed submarines are the last line of nuclear deterrence, there is ceaseless activity aimed at identifying their characteristics so that they can be tracked and attacked if necessary.

Conventional submarines also threaten the surface ships on which international trade depends and the navies that are the principal means of projecting national power overseas in defence of national interests. Accordingly, maritime patrol aircraft, surface ships and their helicopters, and hunter-killer submarines constantly practise the techniques of detecting, tracking and attacking hostile submarines against the day when they may need to do it for real.

THE COMPUTER REVOLUTION

The ability of modern military hardware to carry out its designated tasks rests to a large extent on computer technology. Everything from radios designed for counter-jamming by rapid changes in frequencies, to aircraft in terrain-following flight, depends on the ability of computers to sort and analyze data and command the appropriate response. The eventual aim is to use computers to analyze the whole tactical picture and to be able to suggest appropriate courses of action to the commander.

1983

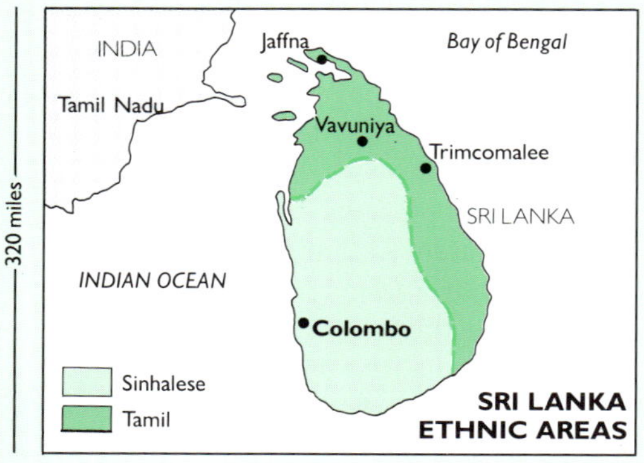

forces against Tigers results in Sinhalese leftist JVP rebellion, subsequently suppressed; Indian forces withdrawn in 1990 but fighting resumes; Ceasefire started in 2001, but no lasting peace deal as yet agreed.

1983– SUDAN CIVIL WAR **Sudan People's Liberation Army (SPLA) formed in southern Sudan 1983 to oppose northern government following imposition of Islamic law; war estimated to have caused over two million deaths.**

1987–1993 PALESTINIAN INTIFADA **Arab "shaking**

STEALTH AIRCRAFT

One of the most exotic of all modern military technologies is that of low observables, or stealth, which has found its most spectacular embodiment in the United States Air Force's F-117A ground-attack aircraft and B-2 bomber.

Designed to be all but undetectable by hostile radars and other sensors, the Lockheed F-117A and Northrop B-2 are as unconventional in appearance as they are radical in conception. The two aircraft represent first- and second-generation stealth technology, and their roles are clearly very different. However, their sheer expense indicates both the value placed on being able to survive in the face of current and future air-defence systems and the difficulty of designing an aircraft able to do so. Stealth technology first saw action in the Gulf in January 1991, when B-2 bombers spearheaded Allied attacks on Iraqi targets.

B-2 stealth bombers under construction at Northrop's Palmdale, California, factory in April 1990.

TERRORISM AND ROGUE STATES

Following the collapse of Communism in the Soviet Union and Eastern Europe in the early 1990s, which effectively ended the Cold War, many people declared that the world was a safer place. In many ways, this is true. With the end of the Soviet Union, the dynamic of two ideologically-opposed military superpowers competing for dominance, which had prevailed since the end of the Second World War, was ended, and the world emerged from the shadow of potential nuclear apocalypse. However, with the end of this dynamic has come uncertainty and instability.

Most analysts in the West tend to agree that the greatest threat facing the world in the 21st century is the coming together of terrorist organizations, certain "rogue states" and weapons of mass destruction (WMDs). The terrorist threat is particularly difficult to combat, because, unlike a nation, a terrorist organisation is not bounded by national borders and territory. As a result of this, Western strategy consists of a combination of intelligence gathering, military force against states suspected of fostering and supporting terrorism (as in the case of Afghanistan and Iraq) and diplomacy aimed at bringing certain "rogue states" in from the cold (as in the case of Libya). It is hoped that this three-pronged approach will stop WMDs from falling into terrorist hands.

2004

free" campaign involving stone-throwing, strikes, economic boycotts and other non-military methods of resistance against Israeli occupation of West Bank started in December 1987.

1989 INVASION OF PANAMA US forces crush Panamanian resistance after 16 days, following President Noriega's declaration of war.

1989–2003 LIBERIA CIVIL WAR 14 years of fighting ended in 2003 with introduction of power-sharing government.

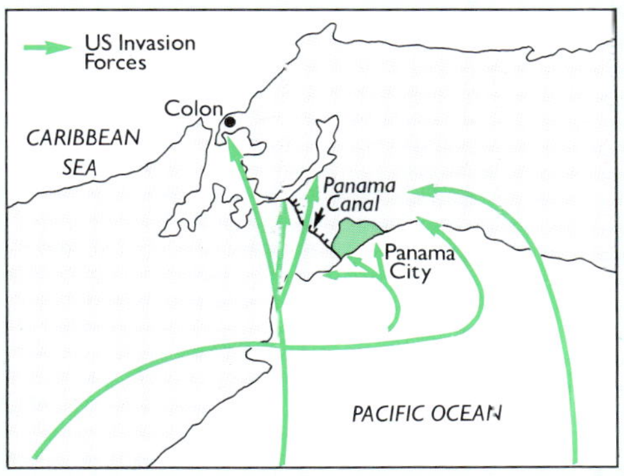

1990–1991 GULF WAR US-led coalition defeats Saddam Hussein's forces following the Iraqi invasion of Kuwait in August 1990.

1992–1999 YUGOSLAVIA CIVIL WAR Series of conflicts between the various ethnic groups.

2001 AFGHANISTAN WAR US-led coalition, including Afghan tribes, defeats Taliban régime following the Al-Qaeda attacks on September 11th, 2001.

2003 IRAQ WAR US-led coalition deposes the Saddam Hussein régime as part of the 'War on Terror'.

INDEX

Page numbers in *italic* refer to illustrations and captions.

L

M

N

O

P

Q

R

ACKNOWLEDGEMENTS

Quarto would like to thank the following for their help with this publication and for permission to reproduce copyright material.

Key: t = top, b = bottom, r = right, l = left, m = middle

9 E T Archive; **10** C M Dixon; **11** C M Dixon; **12** C M Dixon; **13** C M Dixon; **16** C M Dixon; **17** C M Dixon; **18** E T Archive; **19** C M Dixon; **20** C M Dixon; **21** Sonia Halliday; **22** C M Dixon; **23** E T Archive; **24** C M Dixon; **25** *l* Mansell Collection, *r* Hilly Cook; **26** Mansell Collection; **27** British Museum; **29** Mansell Collection; **32** Mansell Collection; **33** Mansell/Alinari; **35** Werner Forman Archive; **36** C M Dixon; **37** *tl* C M Dixon, *tr* Mansell Collection; **38** C M Dixon; **39** E T Archive; **40** C M Dixon; **41** Duncan Campbell; **42** Duncan Campbell; **44** C M Dixon; **45** Jamie Simson; **48** Edgar Knobloch/Barbara Heller; **49** Bibliothèque Nationale, Paris; **51** E T Archive; **52** *l* E T Archive, *r* Sonia Halliday; **53** *tr* Bildarchive Preussischer Kulturbesitz, *b* Roger Tomlin; **54** Roger Tomlin; **55** *l* C M Dixon, *r* Bibliothèque Publique et Universitaire, Geneva; **56–7** Bayerisches Staatsbibliothek; **59** *t* Magyar Nemzeti Muzeum; **60** C M Dixon; **61** C M Dixon; **62** C M Dixon; **63** Mansell Collection; **64** Werner Forman Archive; **65** *l* Werner Forman Archive, *b* E T Archive; **66** *t* E T Archive, *b* C M Dixon; **67** E T Archive; **68** MARS; **69** E T Archive; **72** C M Dixon; **72** C M Dixon; **72–3** Musée de la Tapisserie, Bayeux; **72–3** Musée de la Tapisserie, Bayeux; **72–3** Musée de la Tapisserie, Bayeux; **72–3** Musée de la Tapisserie, Bayeux; **74** E T Archive; **75** *t* E T Archive, *r* Faces Picture Library; **76** Sonia Halliday; **77** E T Archive; **78** Mansell Collection; **81** *t* C M Dixon, *b* Museum of St John; **84** E T Archive; **85** MARS; **86** E T Archive; **87** E T Archive; **88–89** MARS; **89** E T Archive; **90** E T Archive; **91** E T Archive; **94** MARS; **95** *r* MARS; **96** *r* University of Göttingen/E T Archive; **96–97** m and *b* Bodleian Library; **97** *t* and *b* Bodleian Library; **98** *l* MARS, *r* Offentliche Kunstsammlung Basel; **99** MARS; **100** *t* MARS, *b* National Maritime Museum; **101** London Library; **102** MARS; **103** MARS; **104** *t* MARS, *b* Whitaker, Duke of Marlborough; **105** *t* Kunsthalle, Hamburg, *b* National Portrait Gallery, London; **106** London Library; **107** Dr John Hobbert; **109** *tl, tr, ml* and *mr* Bodleian Library, *b* National Portrait Gallery, London; **112** Bridgeman Art Library; **113** National Maritime Museum, Greenwich; **115** National Army Museum; **116** National Portrait Gallery; **116–117** National Maritime Museum/Bridgeman Art Library; **117** Pepys Library; **120** Peter Newark's Military Pictures; **121** Peter Newark's Military Pictures; **124** *t, m* and *b* Peter Newark's Military Pictures; **125** *t* MARS, *b* National Army Museum; **126** Peter Newark's Military Pictures; **127** MARS; **129** MARS; **131** Science Museum; **132** ECPA; **133** ECPA; **134** MARS; **136** Philip Haythornthwaite; **137** National Maritime Museum, Greenwich; **139** MARS; **140** *t* National Army Museum, *b* MARS; **141** Bayerische Verwaltung der Staatl. Schlösser; **143** MARS; **146** MARS; **147** MARS; **151** MARS; **152** *t* Bodleian Library; **152–153** National Army Museum; **153** *t* MARS, *b* National Army Museum; **154** MARS; **155** MARS; **156** National Army Museum; **158** National Army Museum; **161** MARS; **162** Bildarchiv Preussischer Kulturbesitz; **164** MARS; **165** MARS; **166** US Navy; **167** *b* Quarrie; **168** Peter Newark's Military Pictures; **169** *t* Peter Newark's Military Pictures, *b* MARS; **171** IWM; **172** MARS; **173** MARS; **174** IWM; **175** MARS; **176** *t* National Army Museum, London, *m* MARS; **177** *t* IWM, *m* MARS, *b* ECPA; **178** Robert Hunt Library; **179** IWM; **180** Robert Hunt Library; **182** *t* IWM; **183** *b* MARS; **184** *t* IWM, *b* MARS; **185** *t, l* IWM, *t, r* MARS; **186** MARS; **187** IWM; **190** IWM; **192** MARS; **193** IWM; **195** ECPA; **196** *t* and *b* MARS; **197** *t* and *b* MARS; **198** IWM; **199** MARS; **200** *tl* and *tr* MARS; **201** *t* and *b* MARS; **202** MARS; **203** US Navy; **204** *t* MARS, *m* Robert Hunt Library; **204–205** MARS; **205** *t* IWM, *m* Robert Hunt Library, *r* and *b* US Navy; **206** US Department of Defense; **207** IWM; **208** *t* and *m* PRO London, *b* MARS; **208–209** MARS; **209** *tl* and *m* MARS; **209** *br* Bundesarchiv Koblenz, *bl* Robert Hunt Library; **210** US Navy; **212** US Navy; **213** US Navy; **214** US Navy; **215** US Navy; **216** MARS; **217** *tl* and *tr* MARS; **217** *bl* Bundesarchiv Koblenz/E T Archive, *br* US Navy; **219** Bundesarchiv Koblenz/Robert Hunt Library; **220** *t* IWM, *b* Boeing Airplane Company; **221** *t* IWM, *b* MARS; **222** RAF Museum, Hendon; **224** IWM; **225** US Navy; **226** US Air Force; **227** US Department of Defense; **228** MARS; **230** US Air Force; **231** Camera Press; **232** *t* MARS, *m* Boeing Aerospace, *b* US Department of Defense; **232–233** Grumman Aerospace; **233** *b* LTV Corporation, *t* US Department of Defense; **234** US Army; **238** US Department of Defense; **239** Rex Features; **240** US Army; **241** US Marine Corps; **242** Camera Press; **243** Frank Spooner Pictures; **244** *t* Boeing Aerospace Company, *m* Martin Marietta Corporation, *b* General Dynamics Corporation; **245** *tl* and *tr* Martin Marietta Corporation, *m* US Navy, *bl* and *br* General Dynamics Corporation; **247** D A V A; **249** British Aerospace; **251** Northrop Corporation.

IWM = Imperial War Museum, London; MARS = Military Archive and Research Services

Every effort has been made to trace and acknowledge all copyright holders. Quarto would like to apologise if any omissions have been made.